THE SEVEN DEADLY SINS

nakaba suzuki presents

36

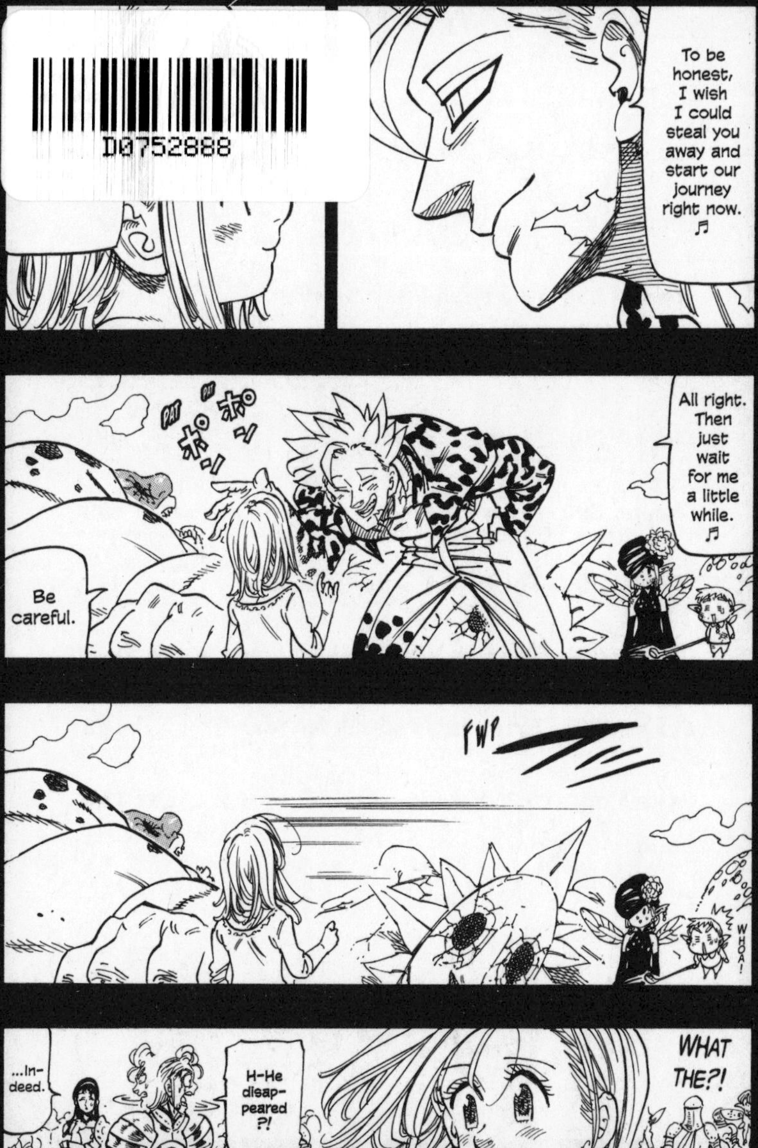
To be honest, I wish I could steal you away and start our journey right now. ♬
All right. Then just wait for me a little while. ♬
PAT
PAT
Be careful.
FWP
WHOA!
WHAT THE?!
H-He disappeared?!
...Indeed.

CONTENTS

BOAR HAT

The Seven Deadly Sins

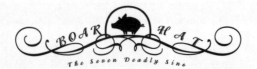

Chapter 294 - Hope, Conflict, and Despair

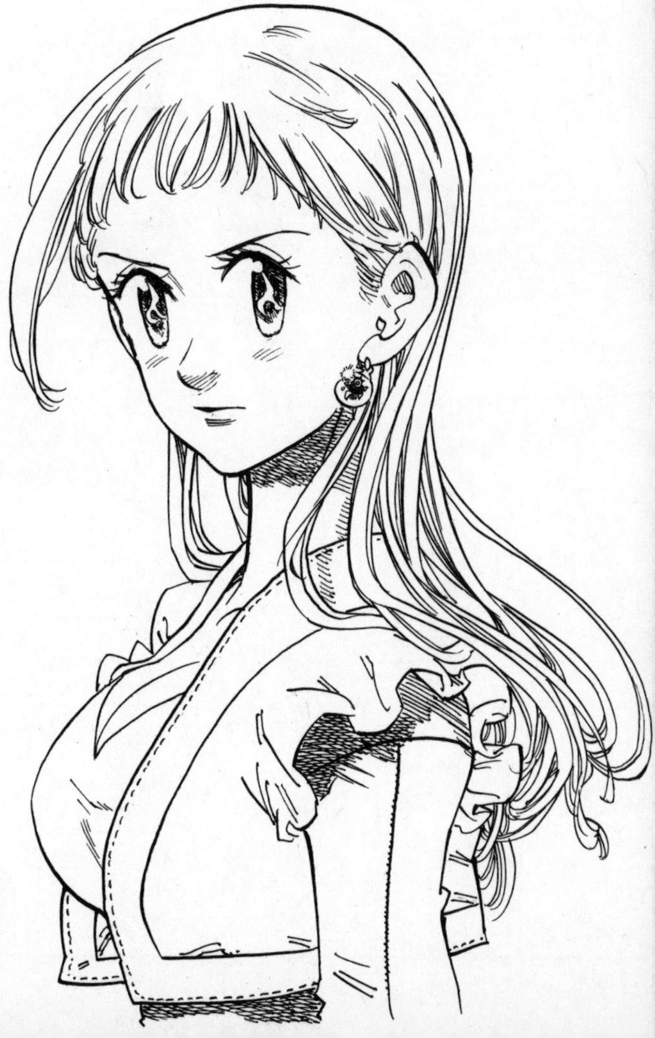

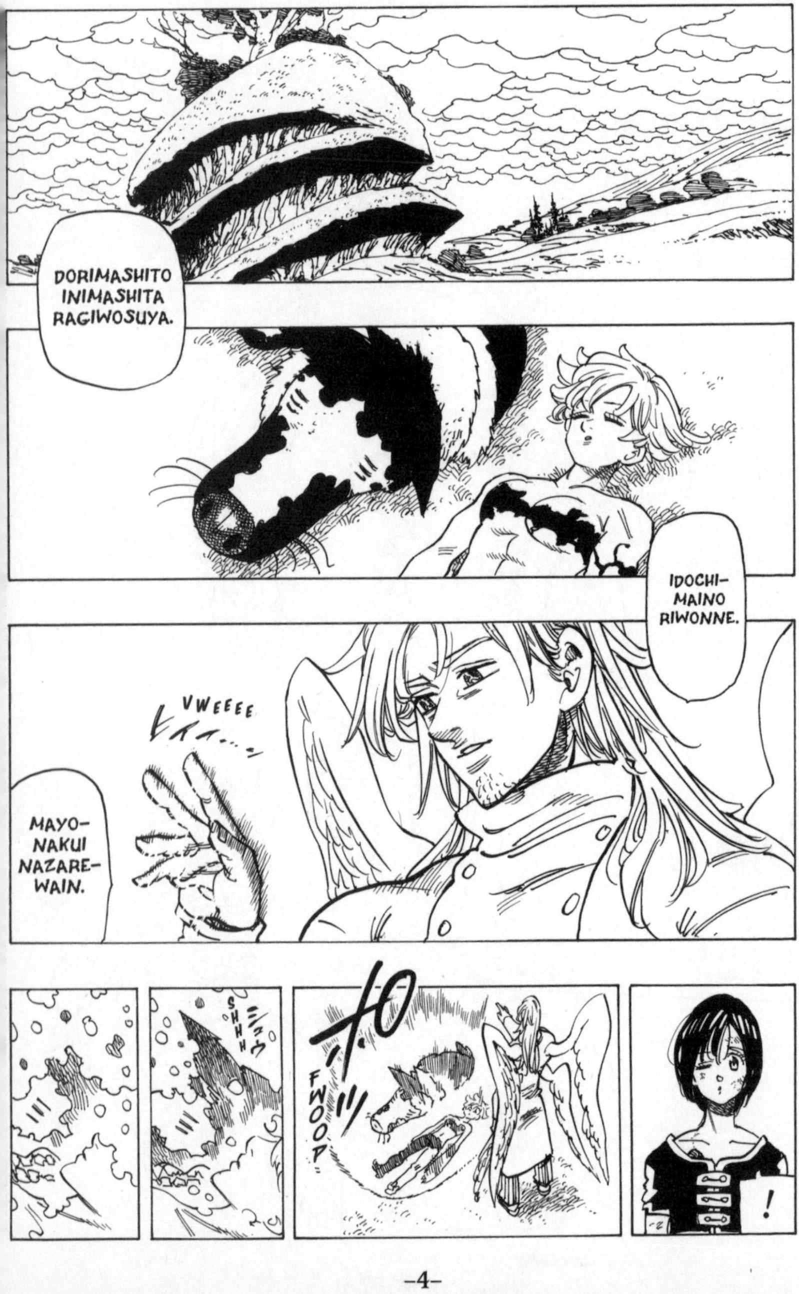
DORIMASHITO INIMASHITA RAGIWOSUYA.
IDOCHI-MAINO RIWONNE.
VWEEEE
MAYO-NAKUI NAZARE-WAIN.
!
FWOOP
SHHH

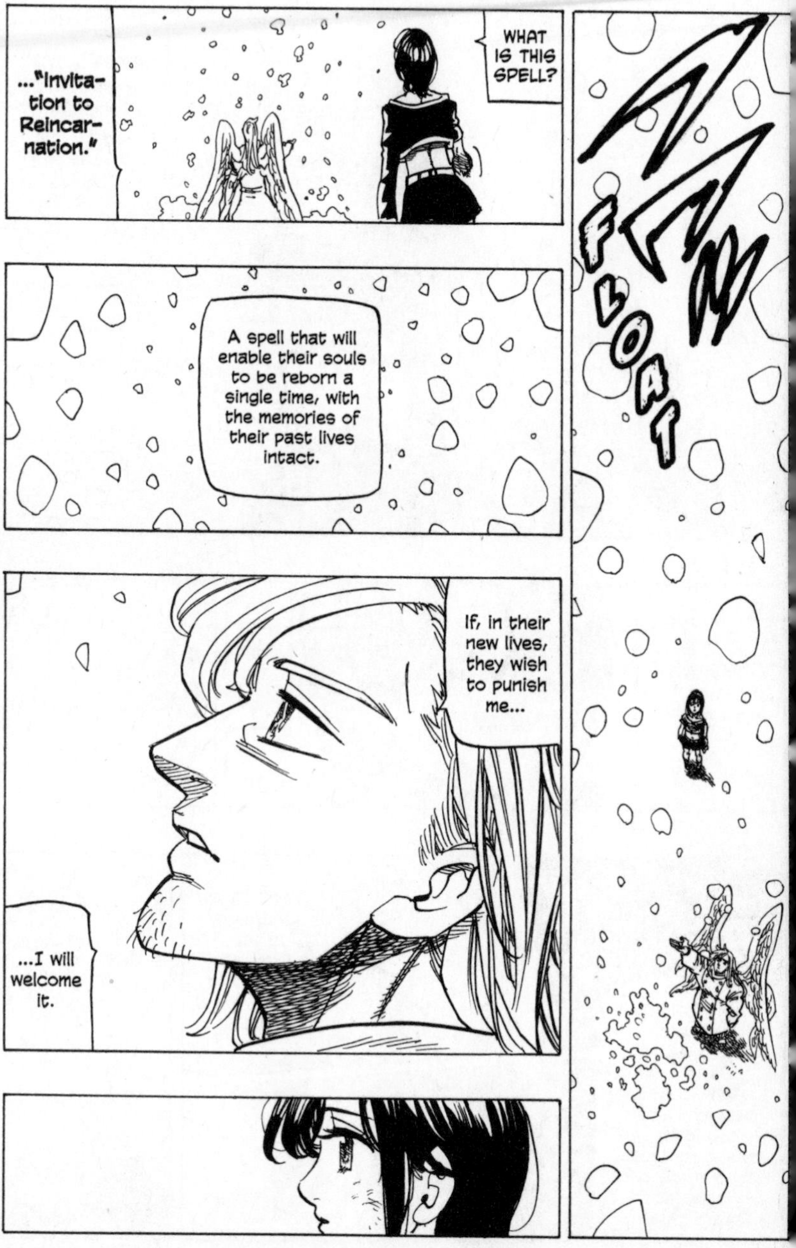
FLOAT
WHAT IS THIS SPELL?
..."Invitation to Reincarnation."
A spell that will enable their souls to be reborn a single time, with the memories of their past lives intact.
If, in their new lives, they wish to punish me...
...I will welcome it.

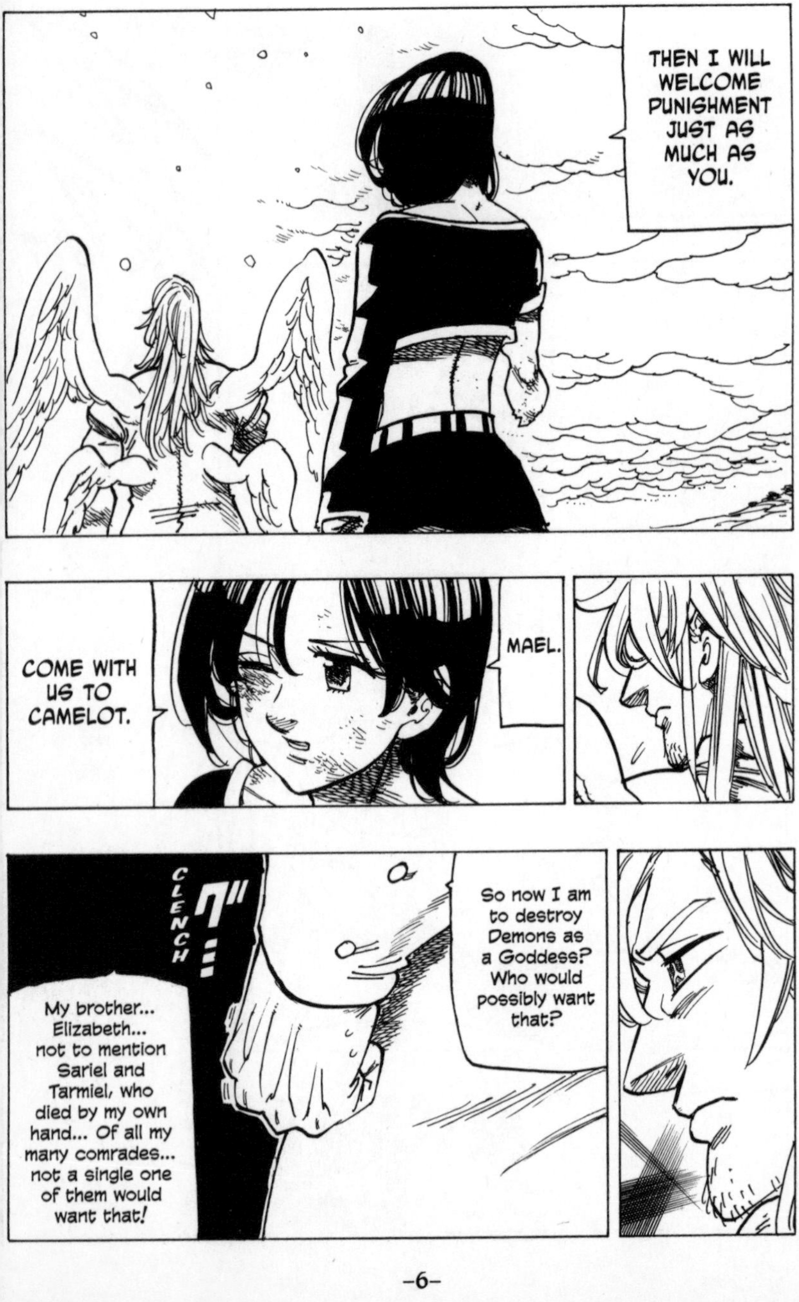
THEN I WILL WELCOME PUNISHMENT JUST AS MUCH AS YOU.
MAEL.
COME WITH US TO CAMELOT.
So now I am to destroy Demons as a Goddess? Who would possibly want that?
CLENCH
My brother... Elizabeth... not to mention Sariel and Tarmiel, who died by my own hand... Of all my many comrades... not a single one of them would want that!

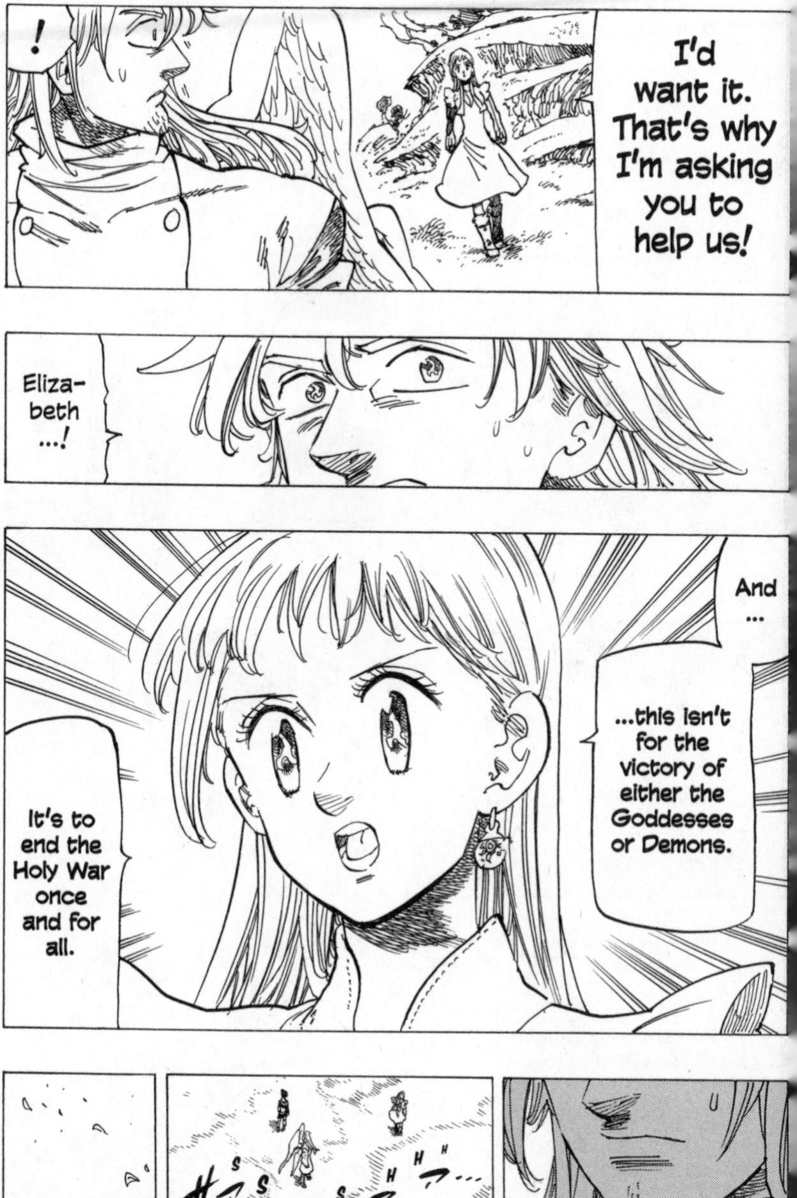
I'd want it. That's why I'm asking you to help us!
!
Eliza-beth ...!
And ...
...this isn't for the victory of either the Goddesses or Demons.
It's to end the Holy War once and for all.

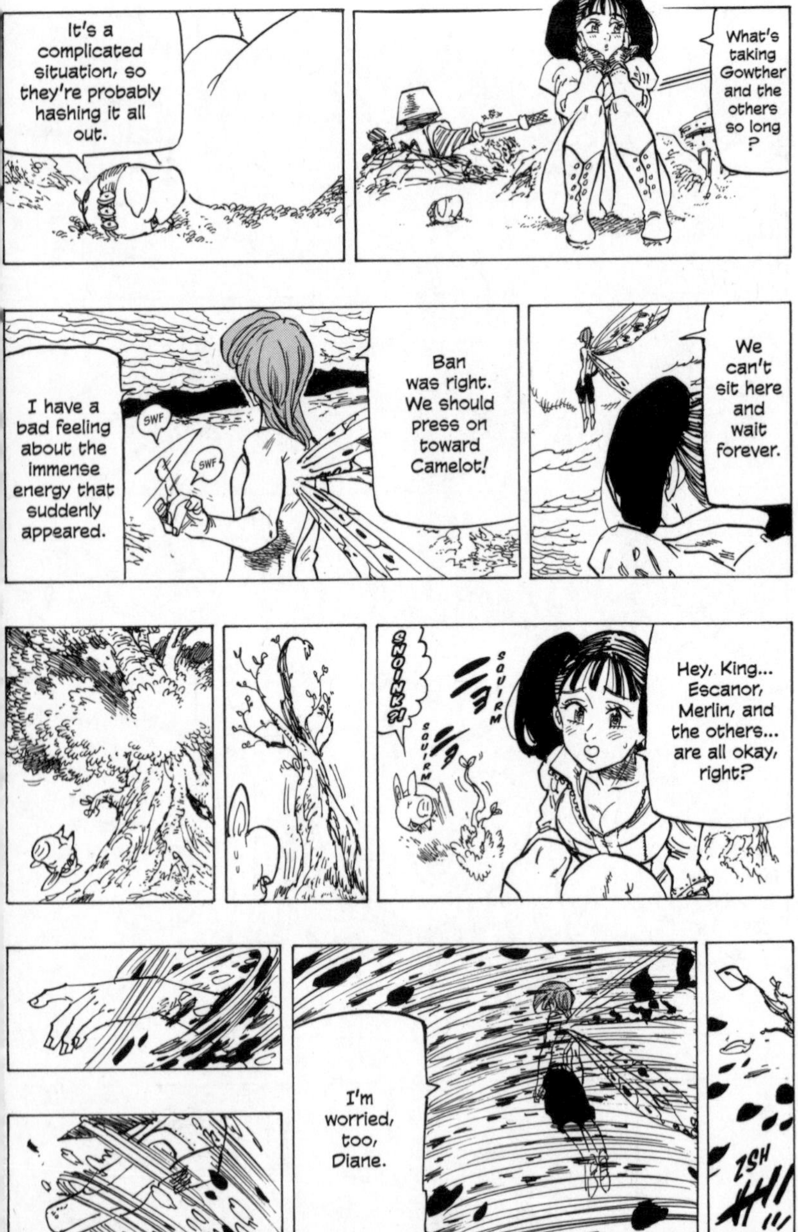
What's taking Gowther and the others so long?
It's a complicated situation, so they're probably hashing it all out.
We can't sit here and wait forever.
Ban was right. We should press on toward Camelot!
SWF
SWF
I have a bad feeling about the immense energy that suddenly appeared.
Hey, King... Escanor, Merlin, and the others... are all okay, right?
SQUIRM
SQUIRM
SNOINK?!
ZSH
I'm worried, too, Diane.

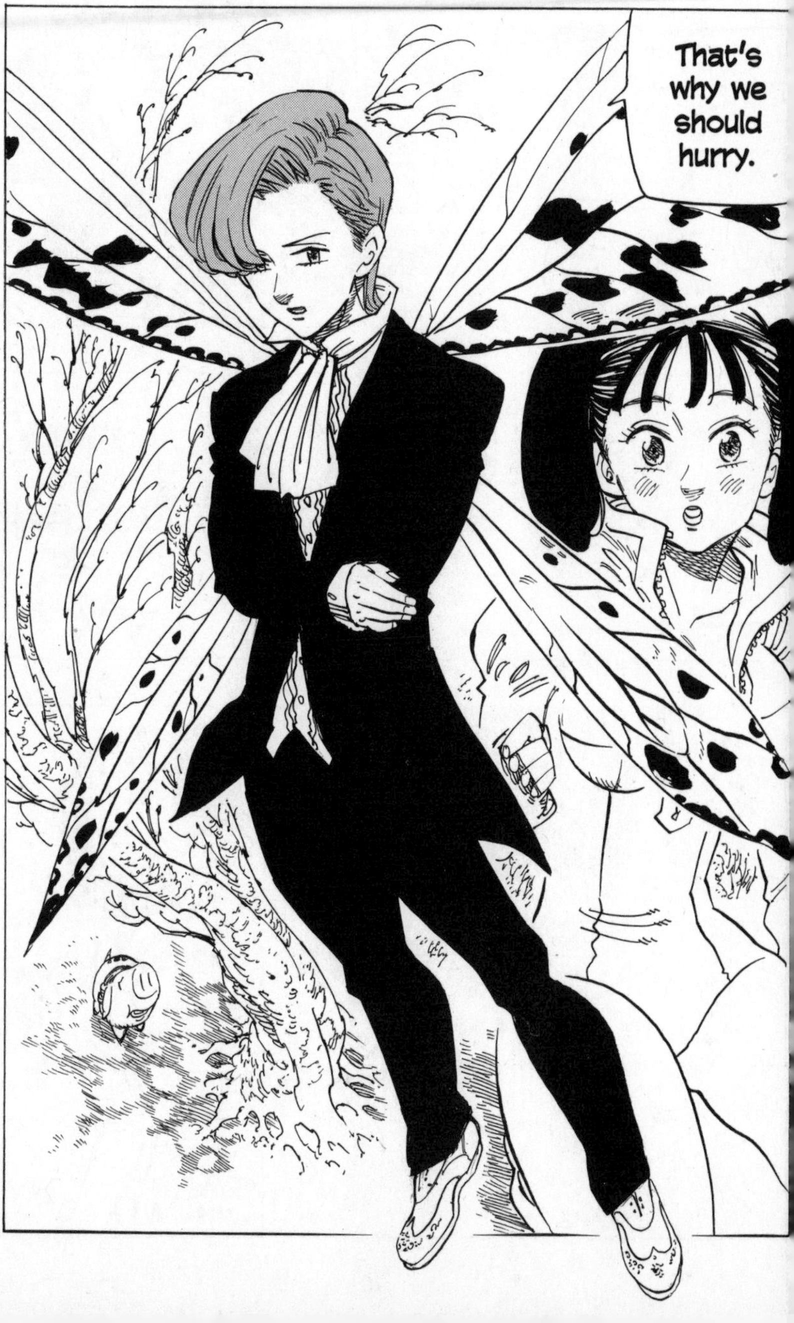
That's why we should hurry.

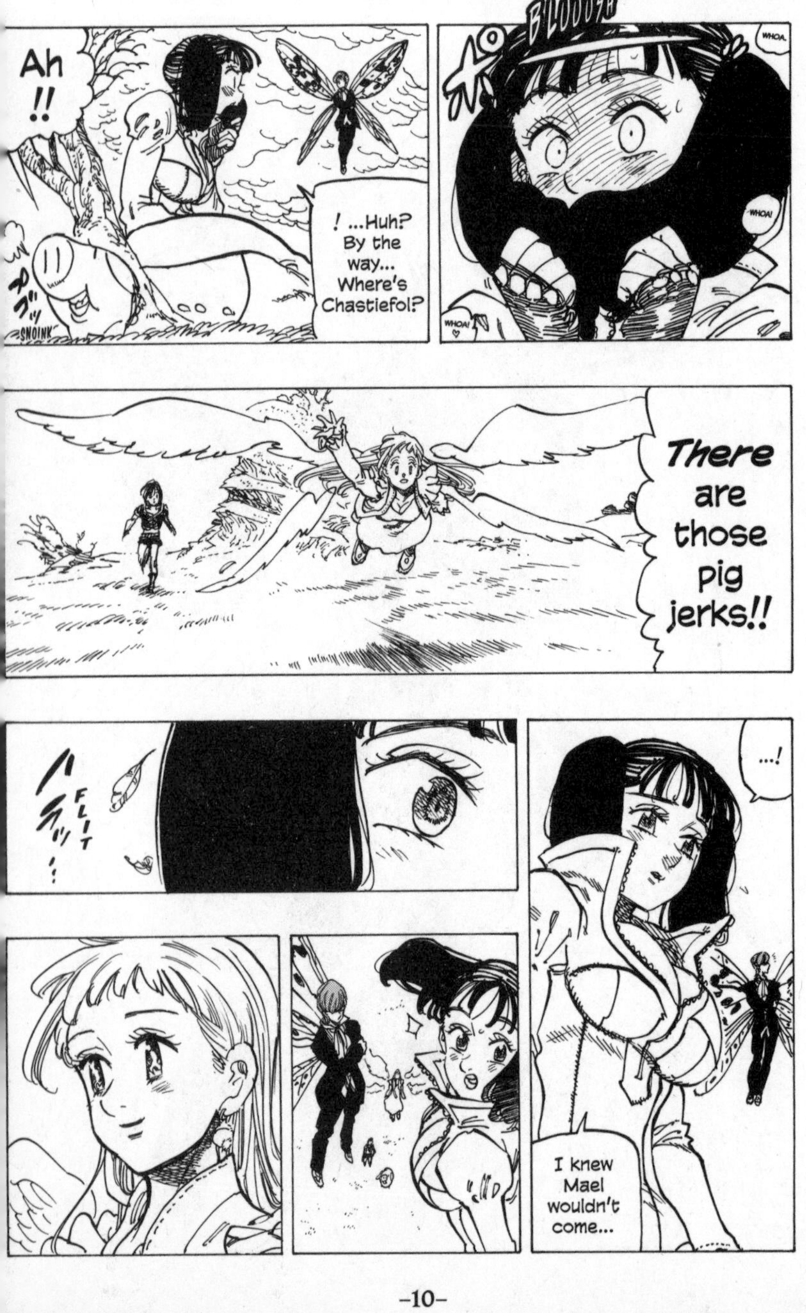
BLOUUSH
WHOA.
WHOA!
WHOA! ♡
! ...Huh? By the way... Where's Chastiefol?
Ah!!
SNOINK
There are those pig jerks!!
...!
I knew Mael wouldn't come...
FLIT

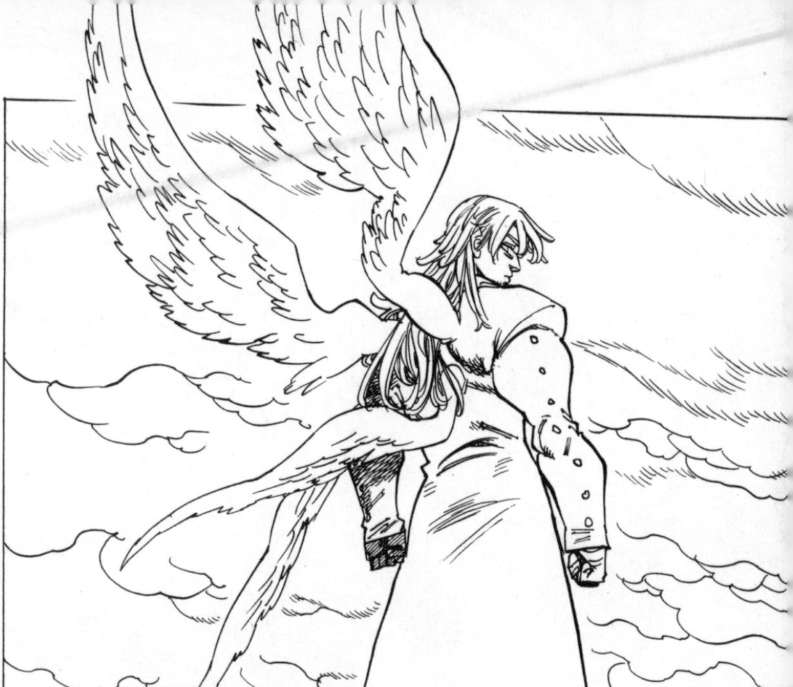

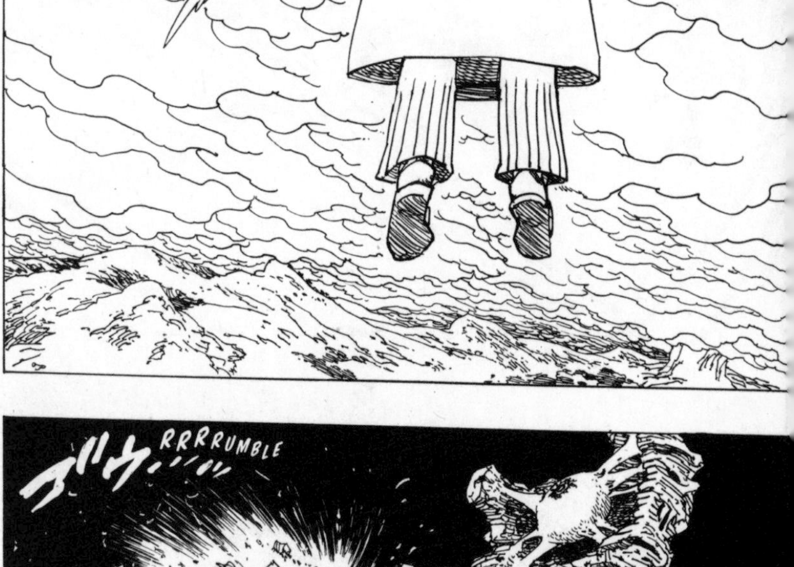
RRRRUMBLE

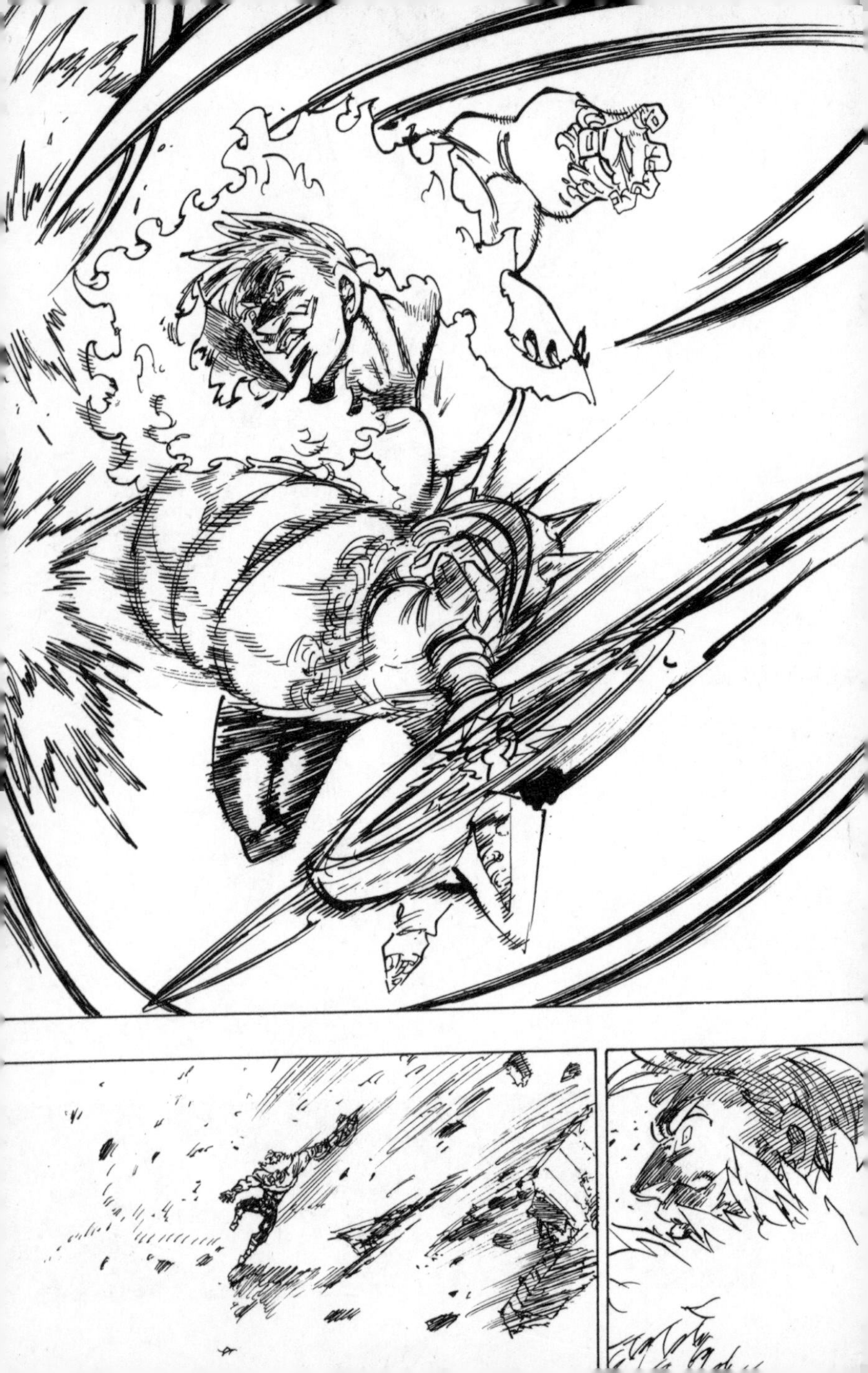

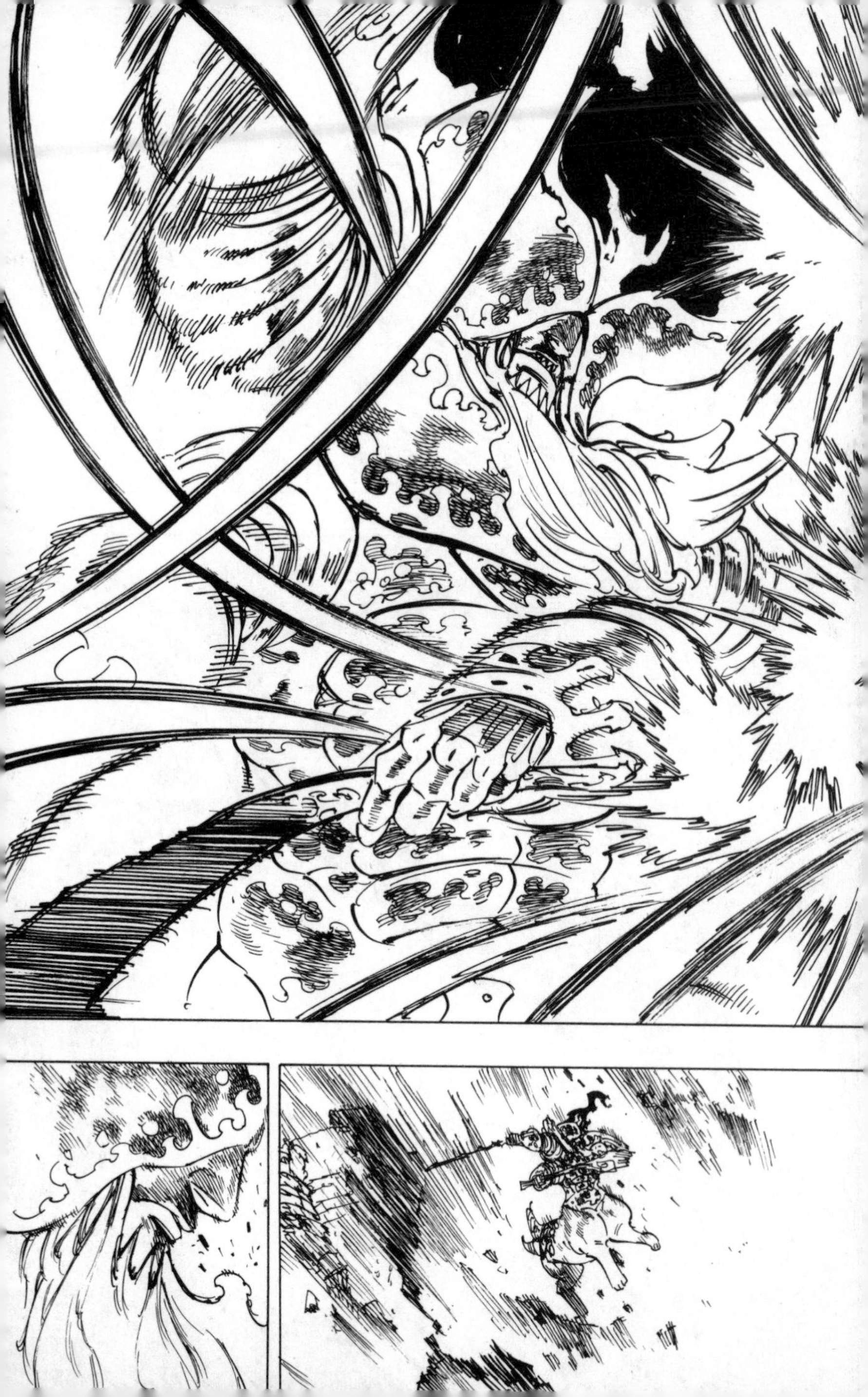

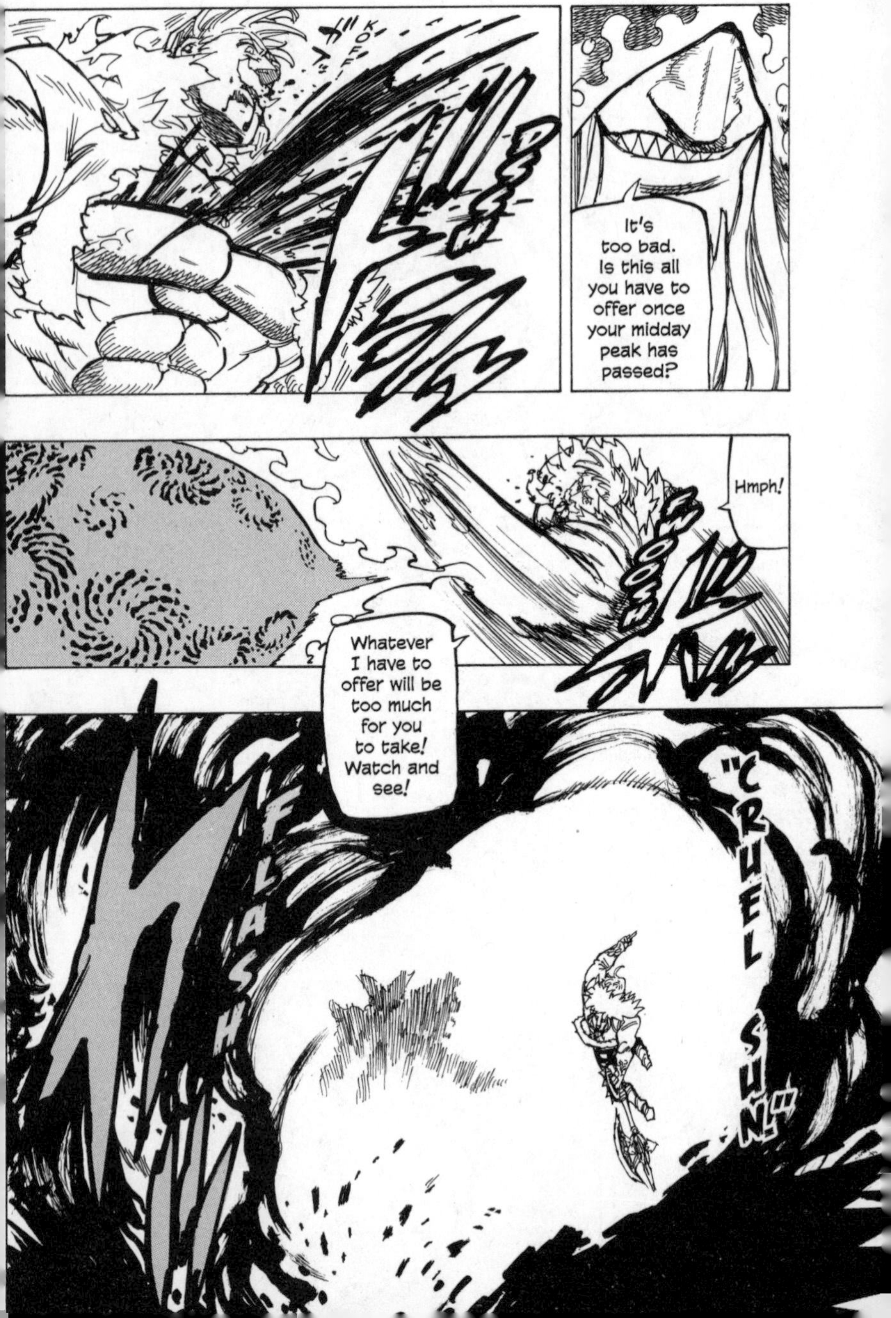
It's too bad. Is this all you have to offer once your midday peak has passed?
KOFF
Hmph!
WHOOSH
Whatever I have to offer will be too much for you to take! Watch and see!
"CRUEL SUN!"
FLASH

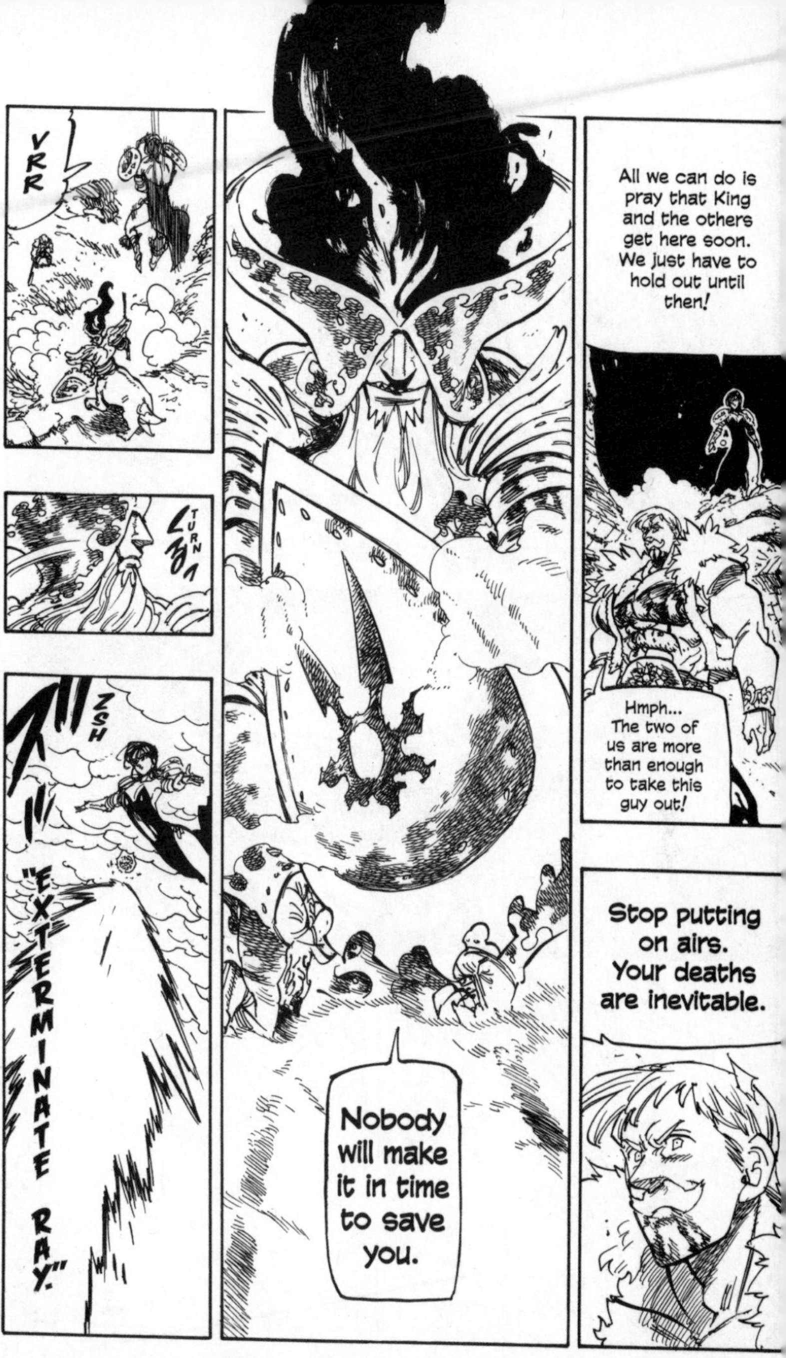
All we can do is pray that King and the others get here soon. We just have to hold out until then!
Hmph... The two of us are more than enough to take this guy out!
Stop putting on airs. Your deaths are inevitable.
Nobody will make it in time to save you.
VRR
TURN
ZSH
"EXTERMINATE RAY."

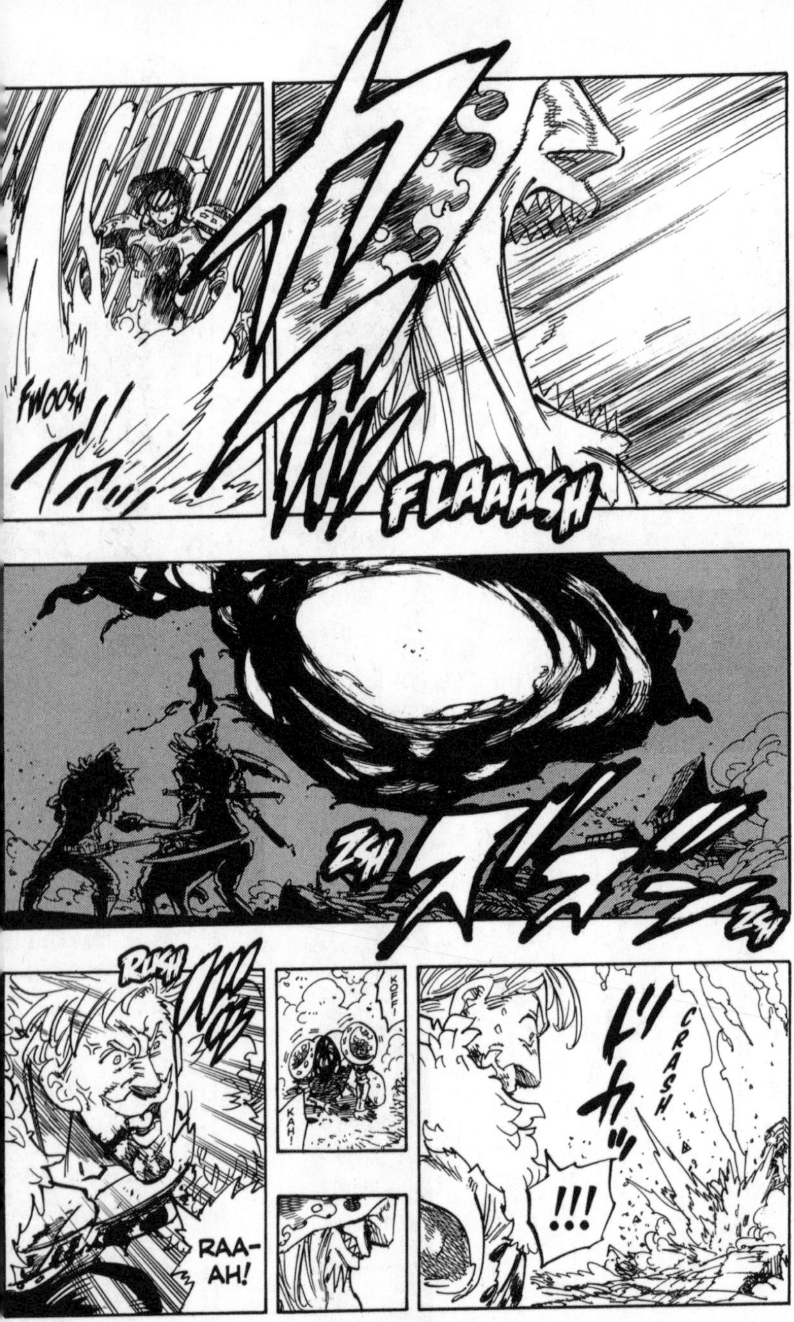
FLAAASH
FWOOSH
ZSH
ZSH
CRASH
!!!
KOFF
KAH!
RUSH
RAA-
AH!

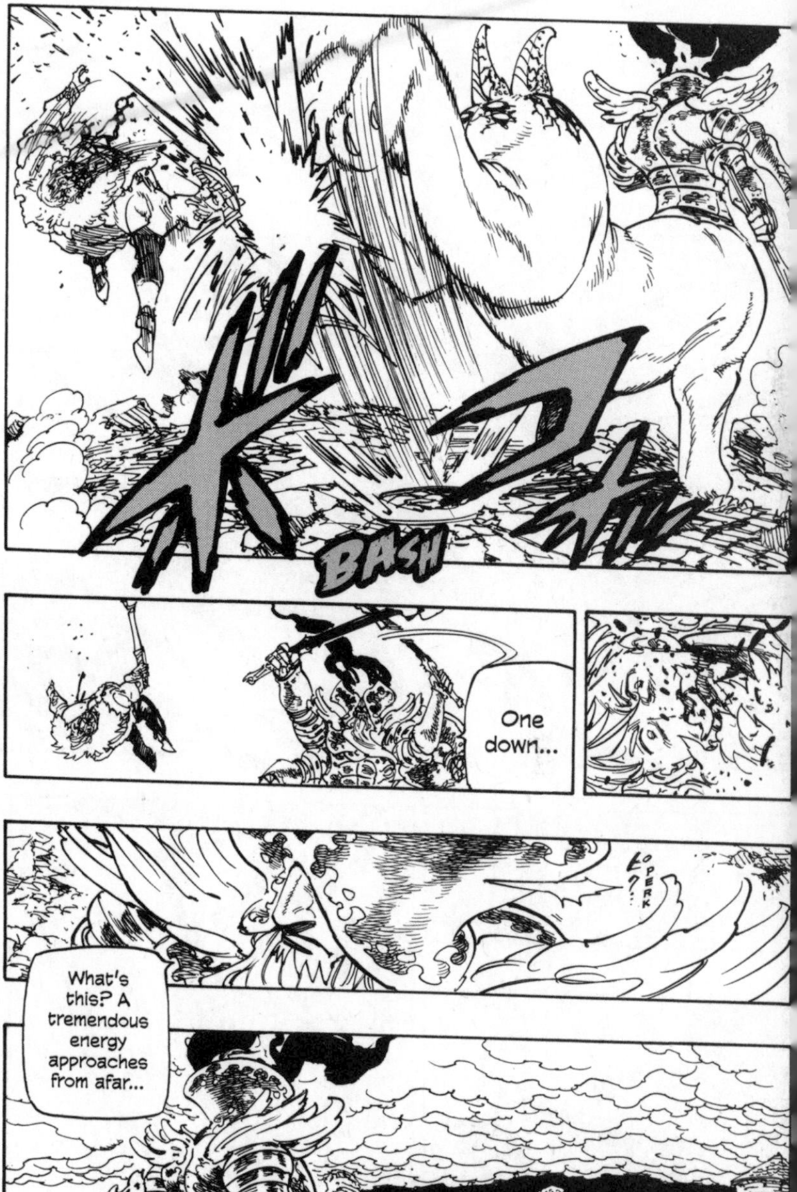
BASH
One down...
PERK
What's this? A tremendous energy approaches from afar...

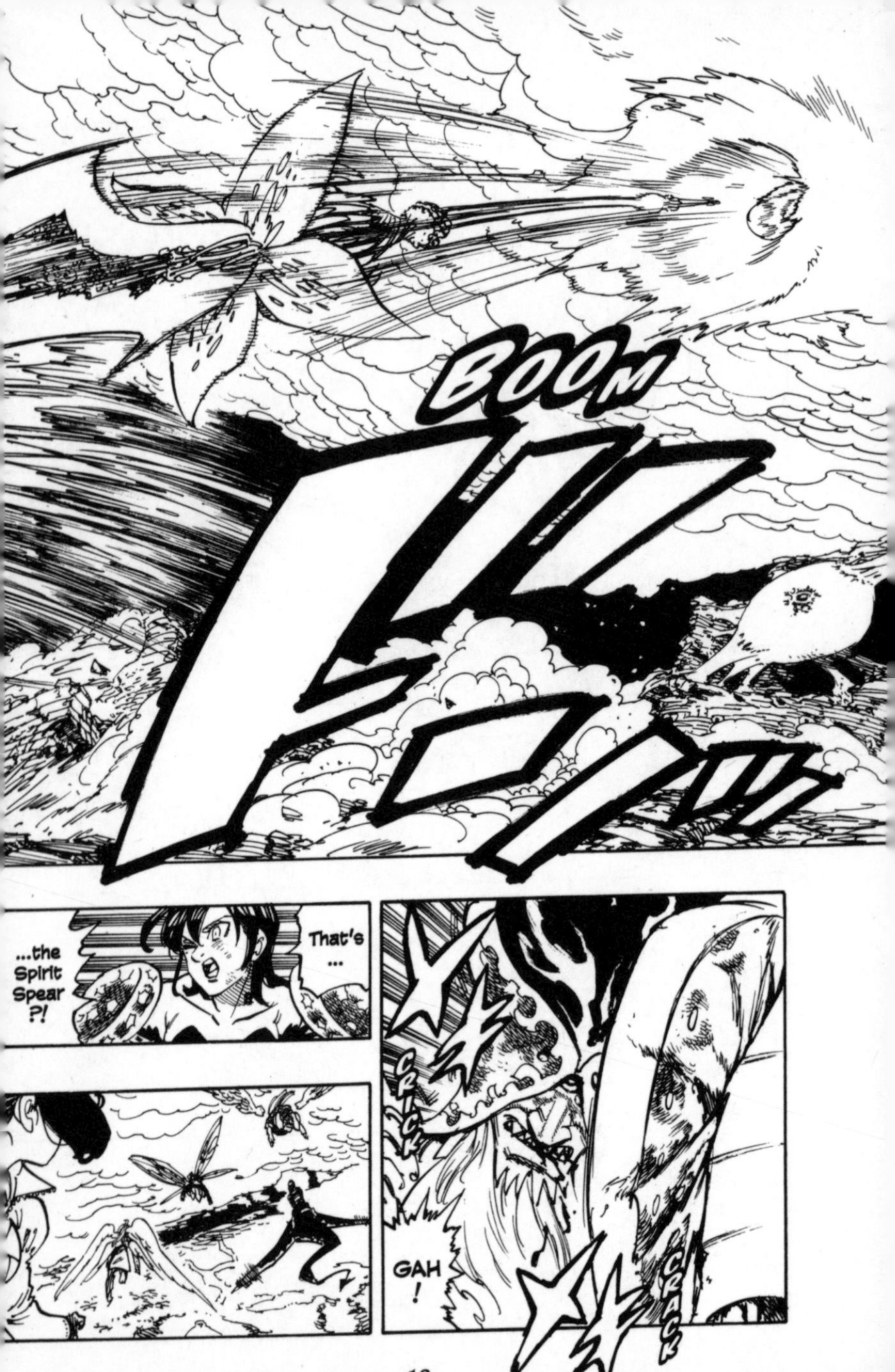
BOOM
CRICK
GAH!
CRACK
That's ...
...the Spirit Spear?!

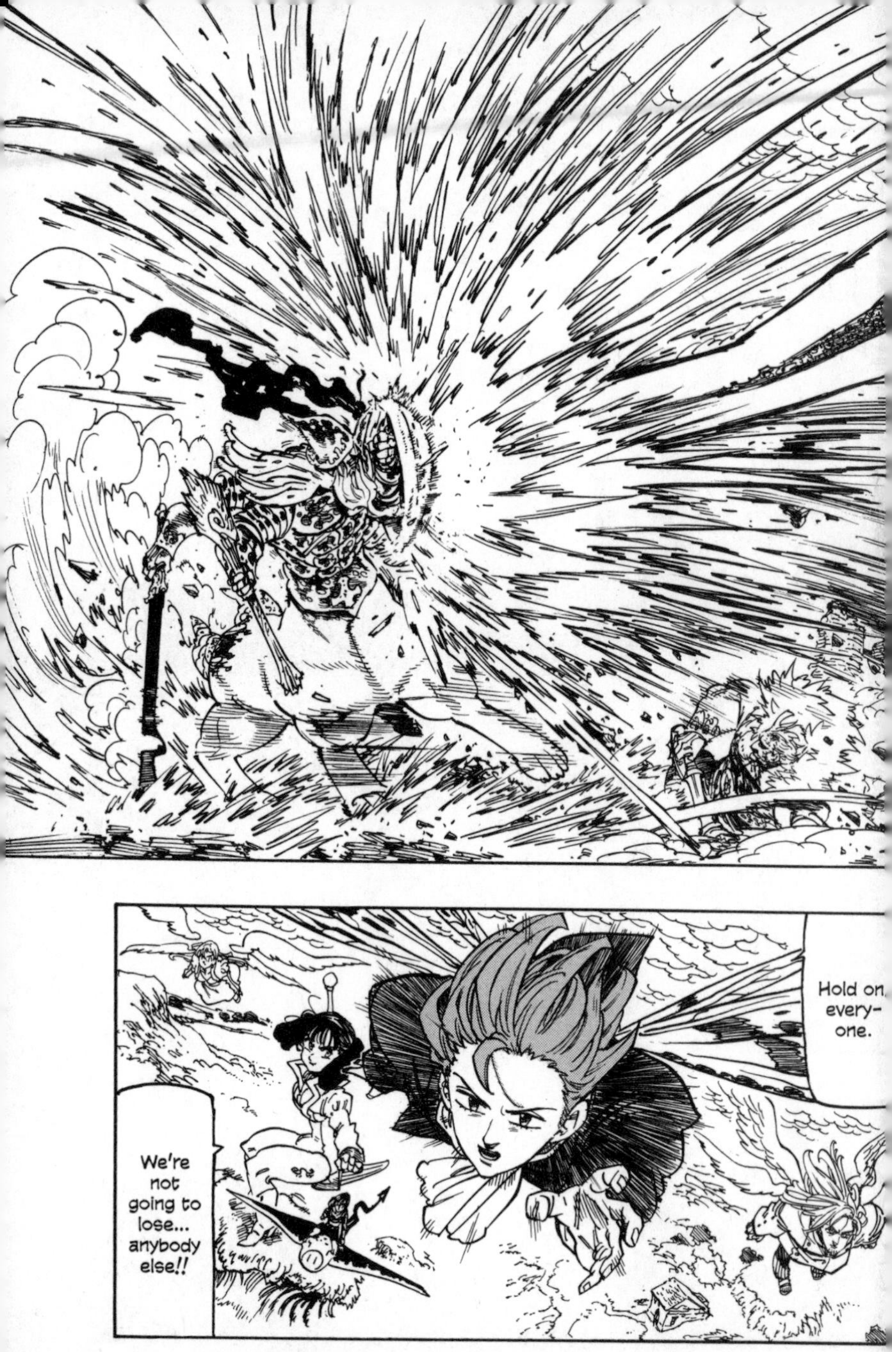
Hold on, everyone.
We're not going to lose... anybody else!!

"The Seven Deadly Sins" Q&A Corner

"Chatting Knighthood"

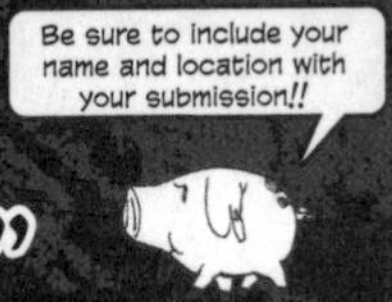
Be sure to include your name and location with your submission!!

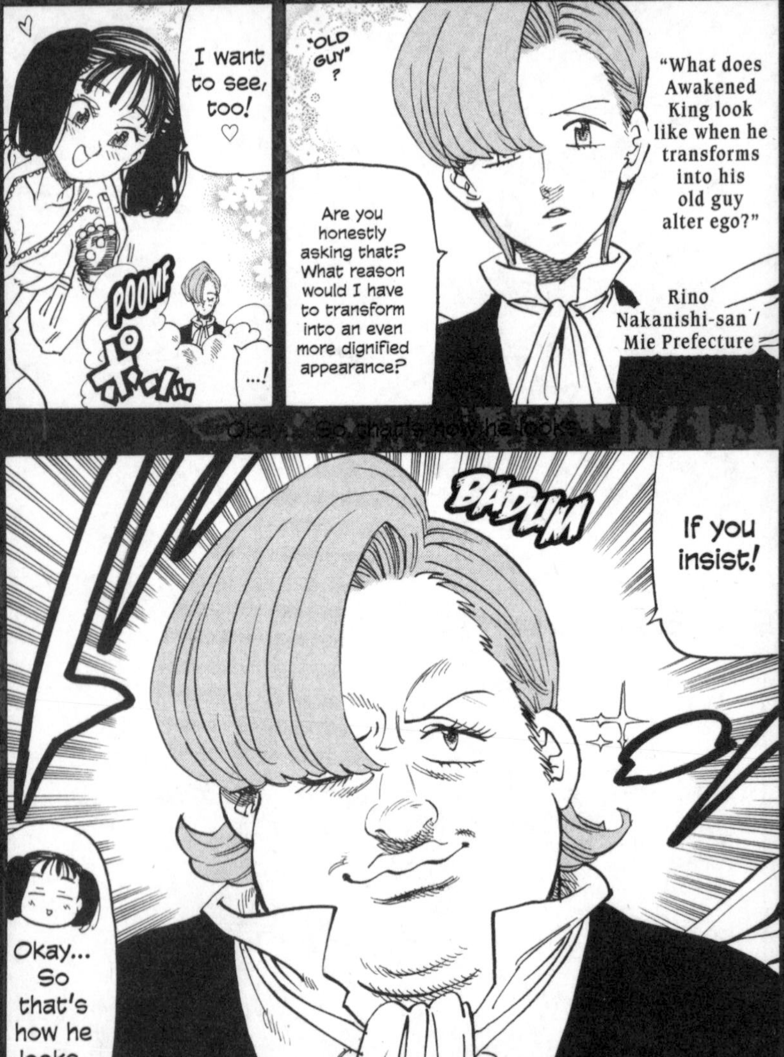
"What does Awakened King look like when he transforms into his old guy alter ego?"
Rino Nakanishi-san / Mie Prefecture
"OLD GUY"?
Are you honestly asking that? What reason would I have to transform into an even more dignified appearance?
I want to see, too! ♡
POOMF
...!
BADUM
If you insist!
Okay... So that's how he looks.

← To Be Continued on Page 122

Chapter 295 - That Which Gather

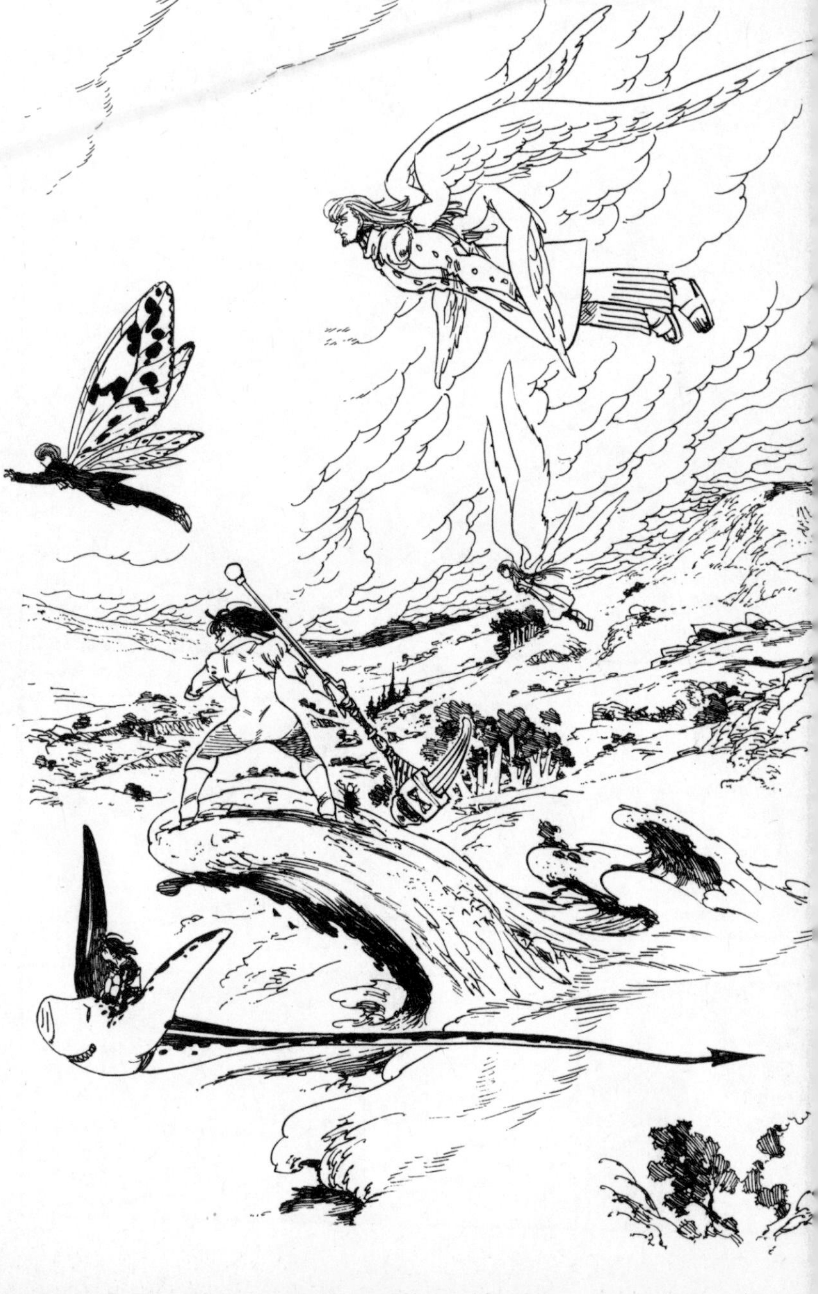

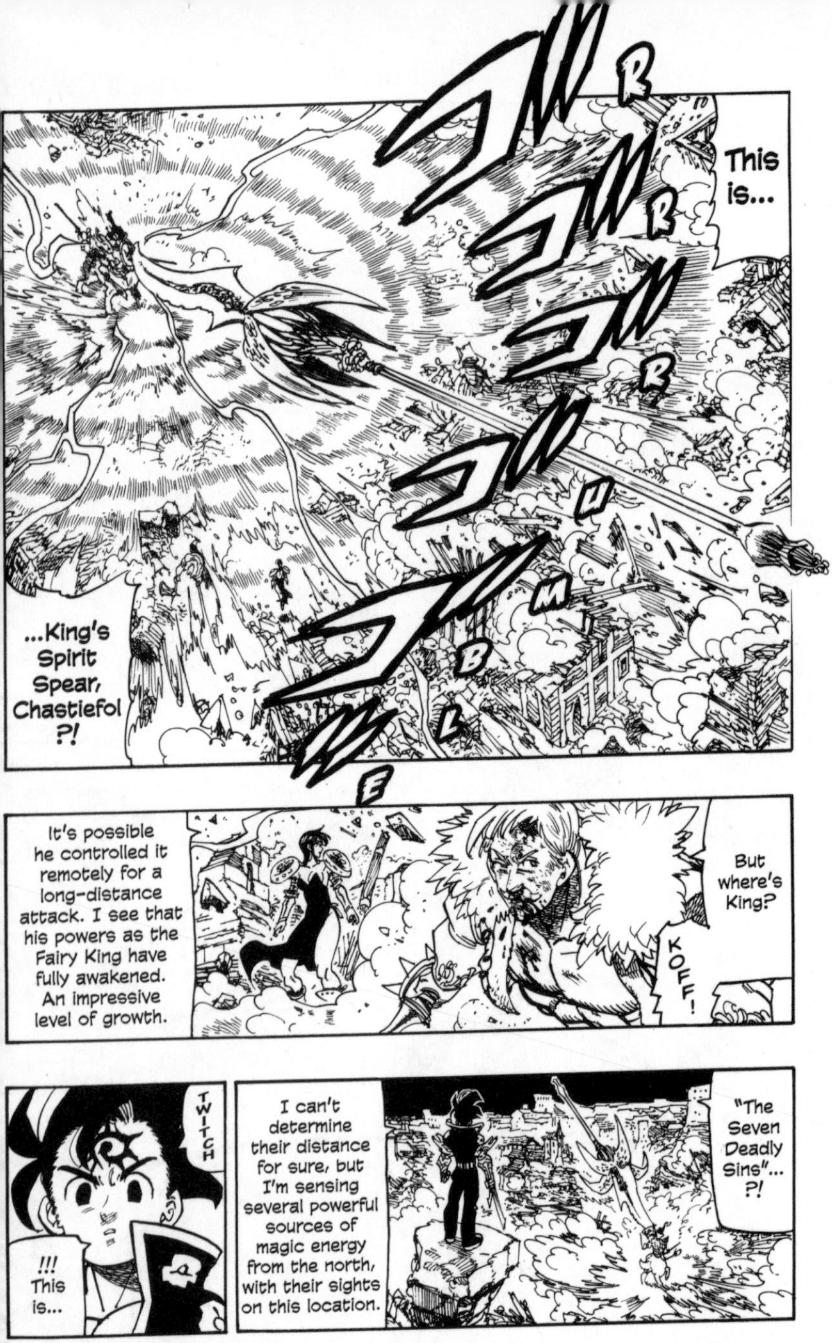
This is...
RRRUMBLE
...King's Spirit Spear, Chastiefol ?!
But where's King?
KOFF!
It's possible he controlled it remotely for a long-distance attack. I see that his powers as the Fairy King have fully awakened. An impressive level of growth.
"The Seven Deadly Sins"... ?!
I can't determine their distance for sure, but I'm sensing several powerful sources of magic energy from the north, with their sights on this location.
TWITCH
!!! This is...

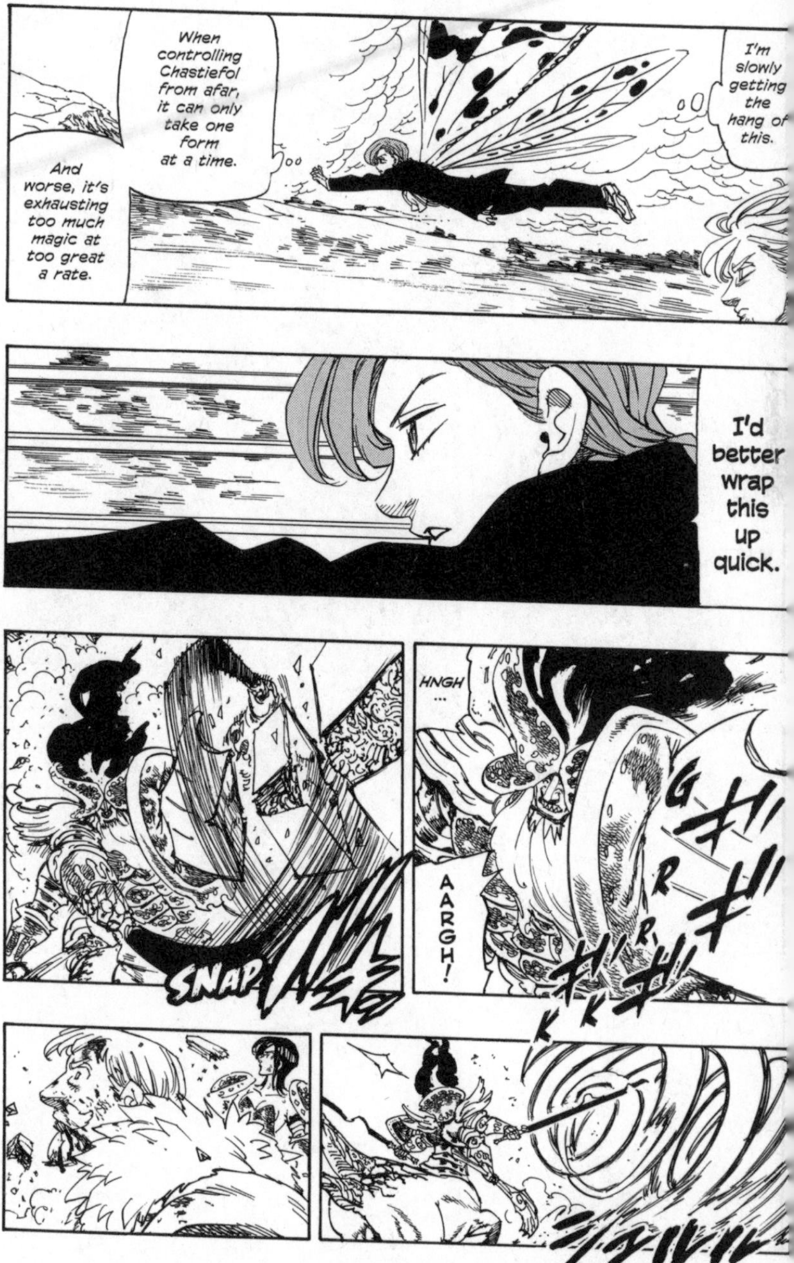
I'm slowly getting the hang of this.
When controlling Chastiefol from afar, it can only take one form at a time.
And worse, it's exhausting too much magic at too great a rate.
I'd better wrap this up quick.
HNGH...
AARGH!
GRRKKK
SNAP
SHWF SHWF SHWF

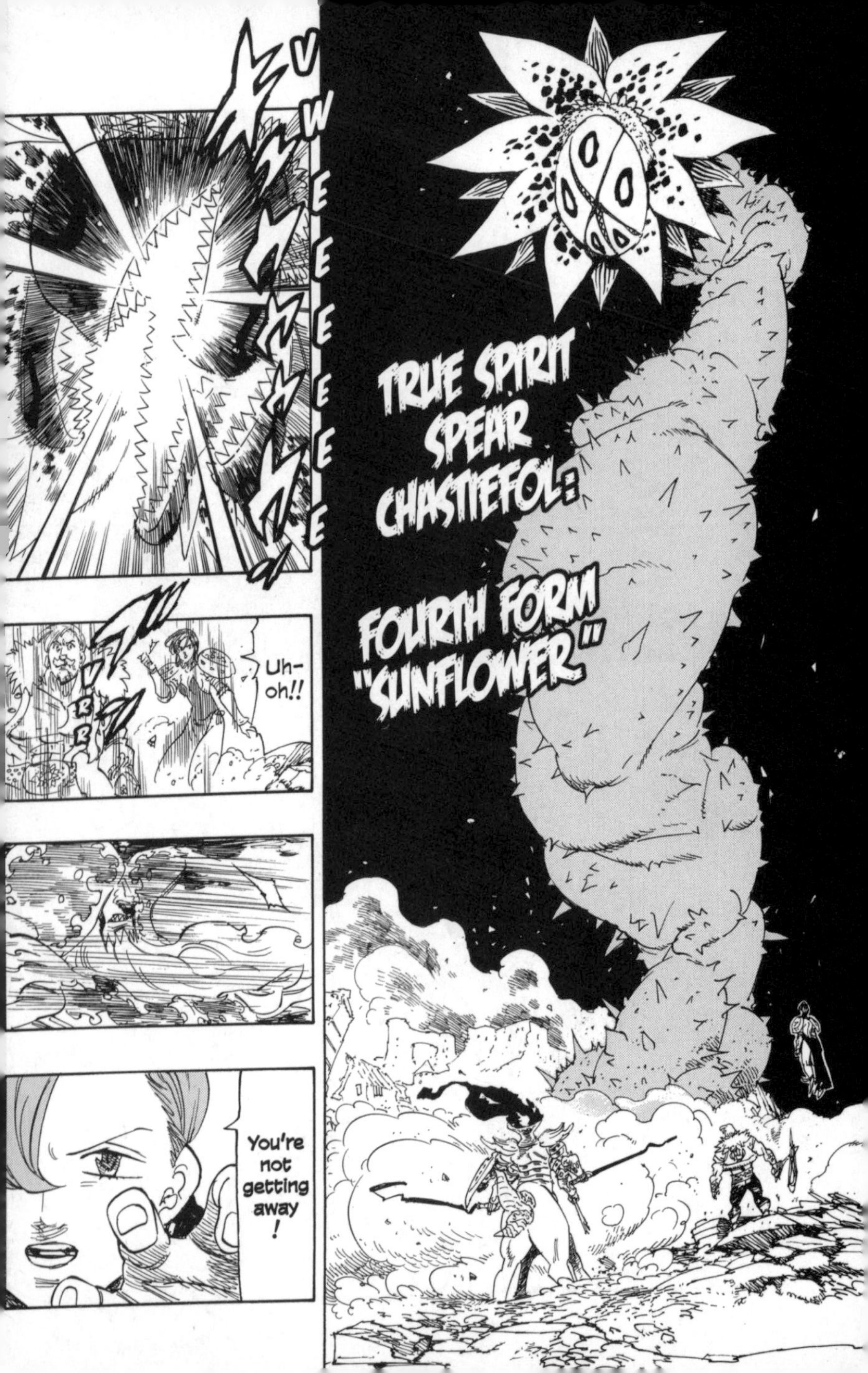
TRUE SPIRIT SPEAR CHASTIEFOL:
FOURTH FORM "SUNFLOWER"
VWEEEEEE
VRR
Uh-oh!!
You're not getting away!

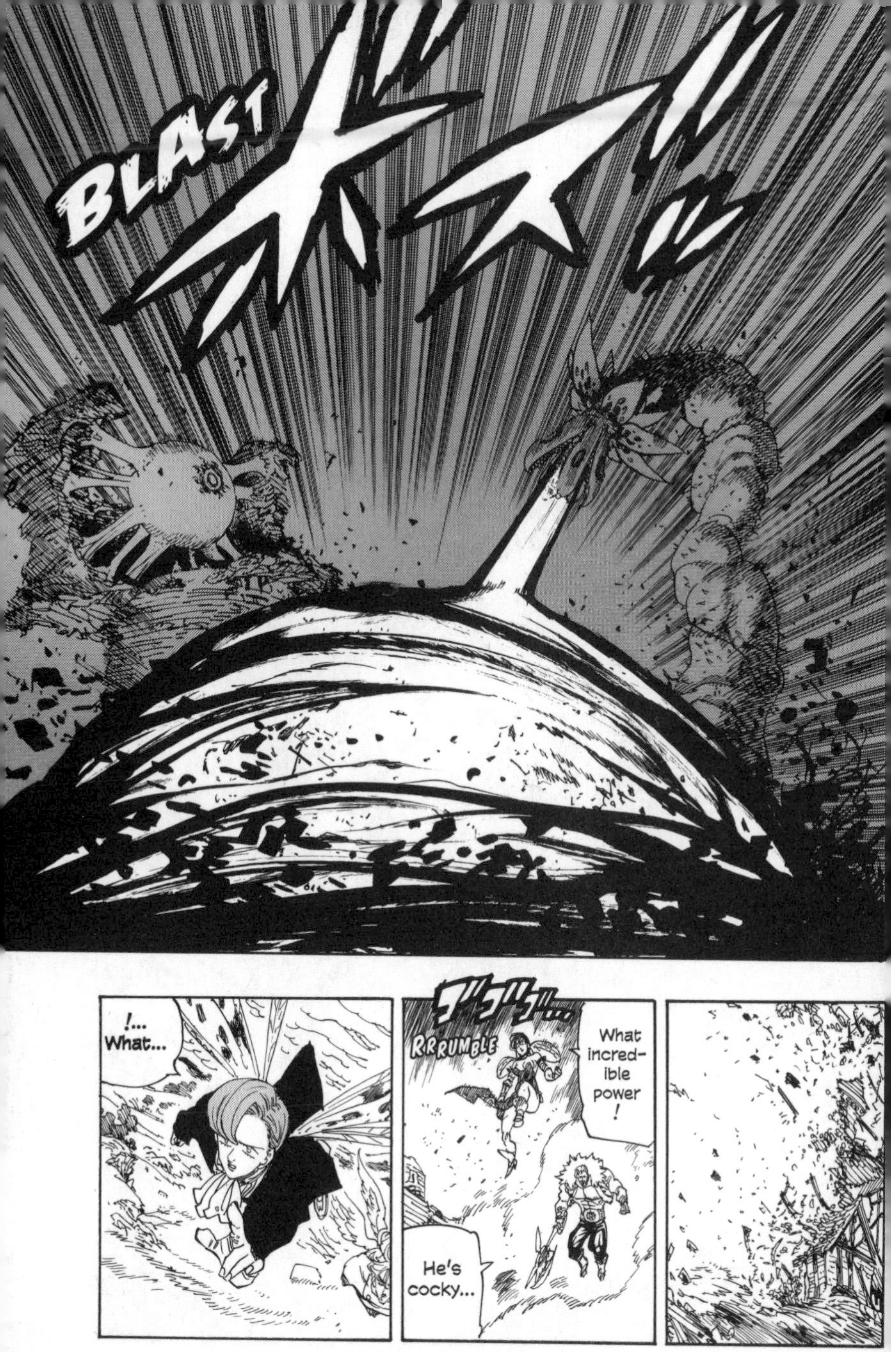
BLAST
RRRUMBLE
What incred-ible power!
He's cocky...
!... What...

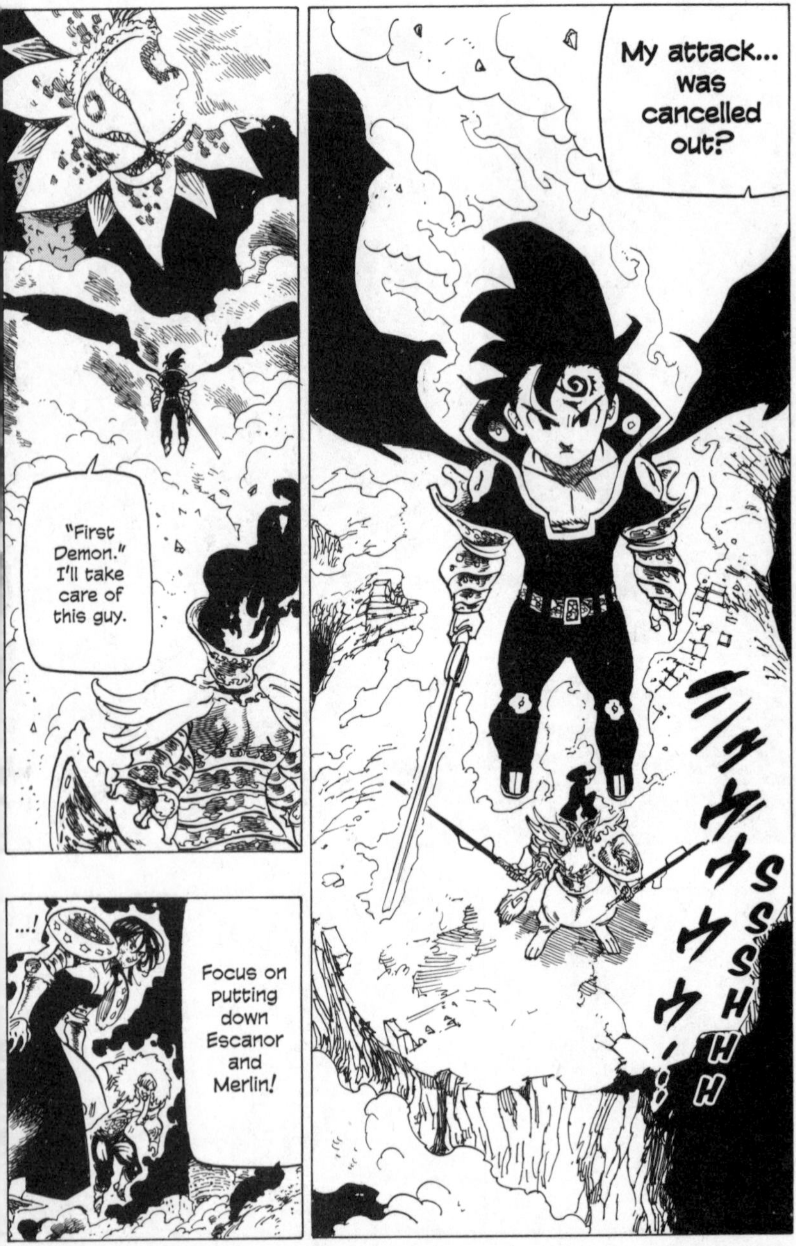
My attack... was cancelled out?
SSSHHH
"First Demon." I'll take care of this guy.
...!
Focus on putting down Escanor and Merlin!

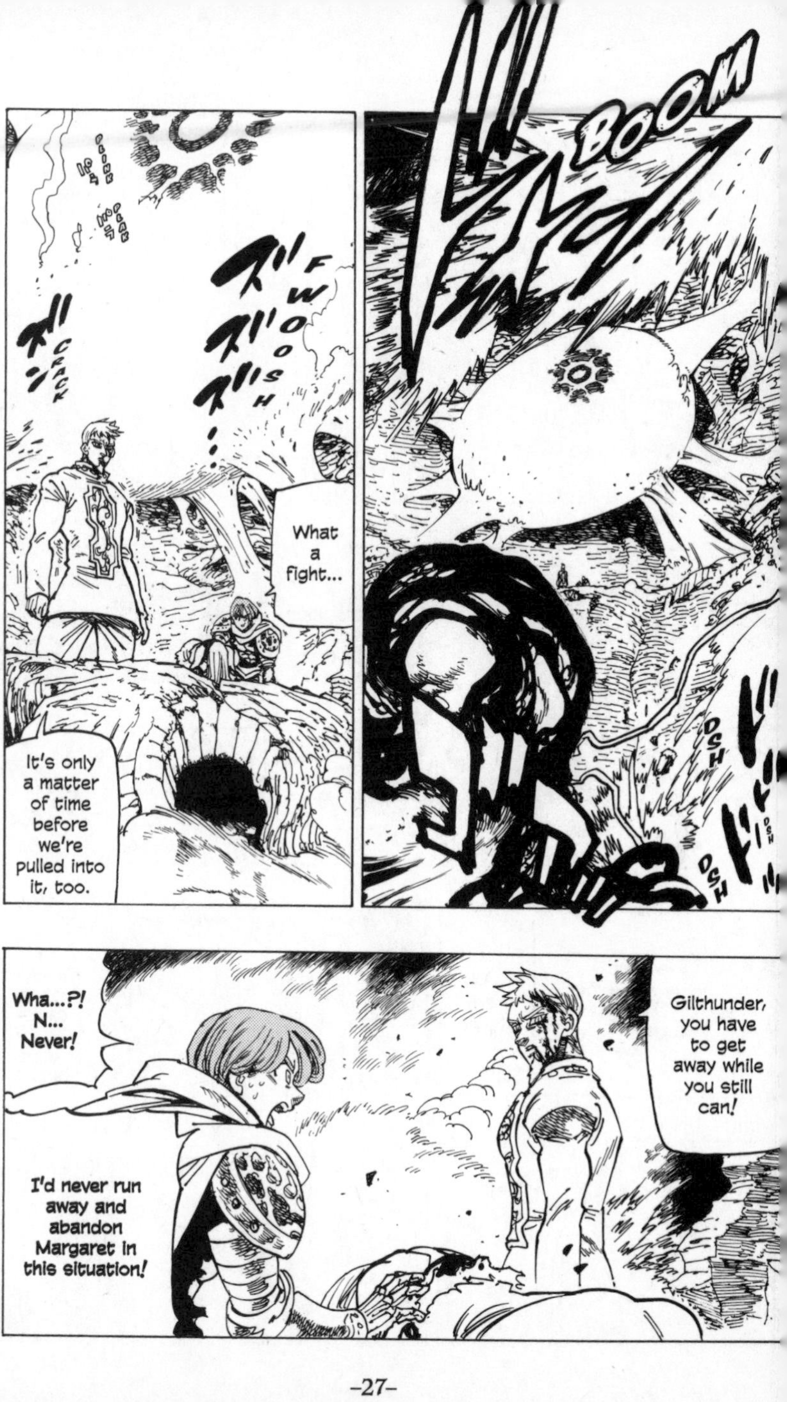
BOOM
DSH
DSH
DSH
CRACK
FWOOOSH
PLINK
PLAK
What a fight...
It's only a matter of time before we're pulled into it, too.
Gilthunder, you have to get away while you still can!
Wha...?! N... Never!
I'd never run away and abandon Margaret in this situation!

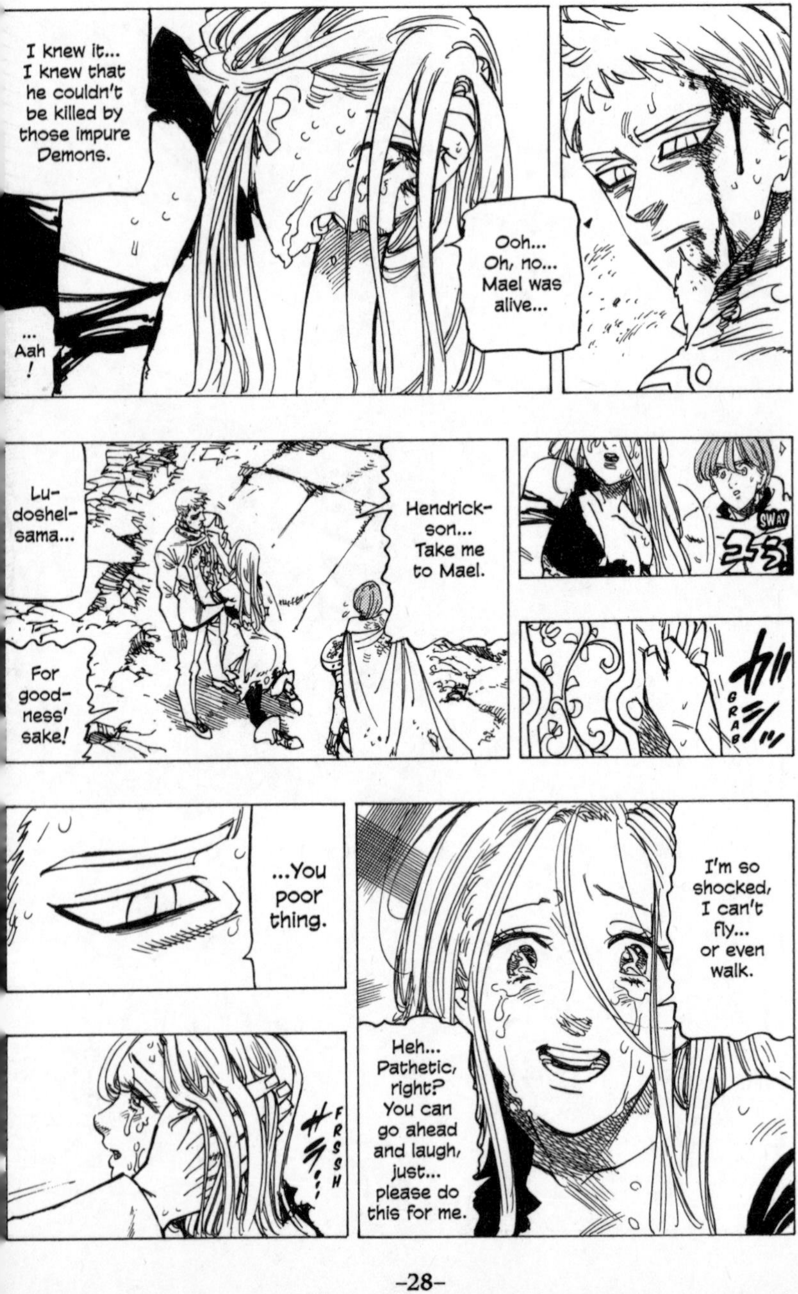
Ooh... Oh, no... Mael was alive...
I knew it... I knew that he couldn't be killed by those impure Demons.
...Aah!
SWAY
GRAB
Hendrick-son... Take me to Mael.
Lu-doshel-sama...
For good-ness' sake!
I'm so shocked, I can't fly... or even walk.
Heh... Pathetic, right? You can go ahead and laugh, just... please do this for me.
...You poor thing.
FRSSH

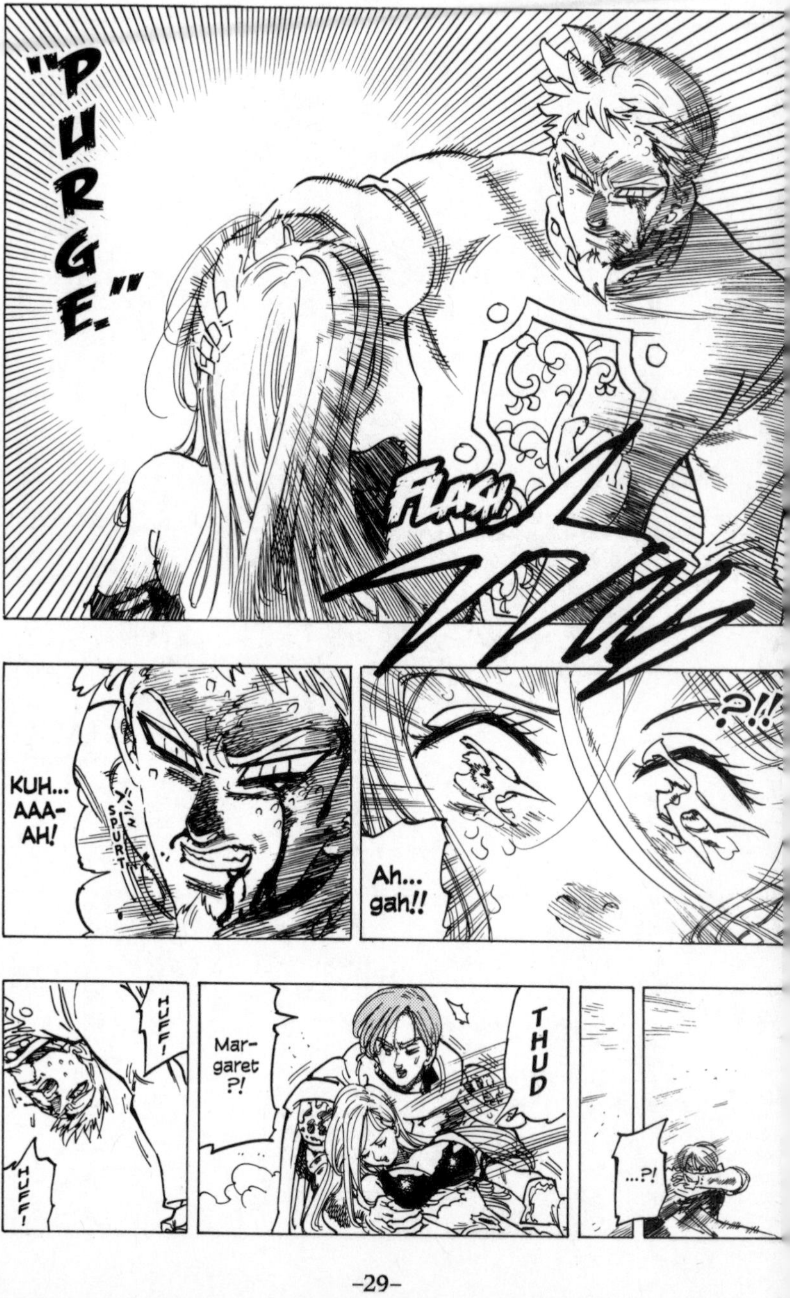
"PURGE."
FLASH
?!!
Ah... gah!!
KUH... AAA-AH!
SPURT
...?!
THUD
Mar-garet?!
HUFF!
HUFF!

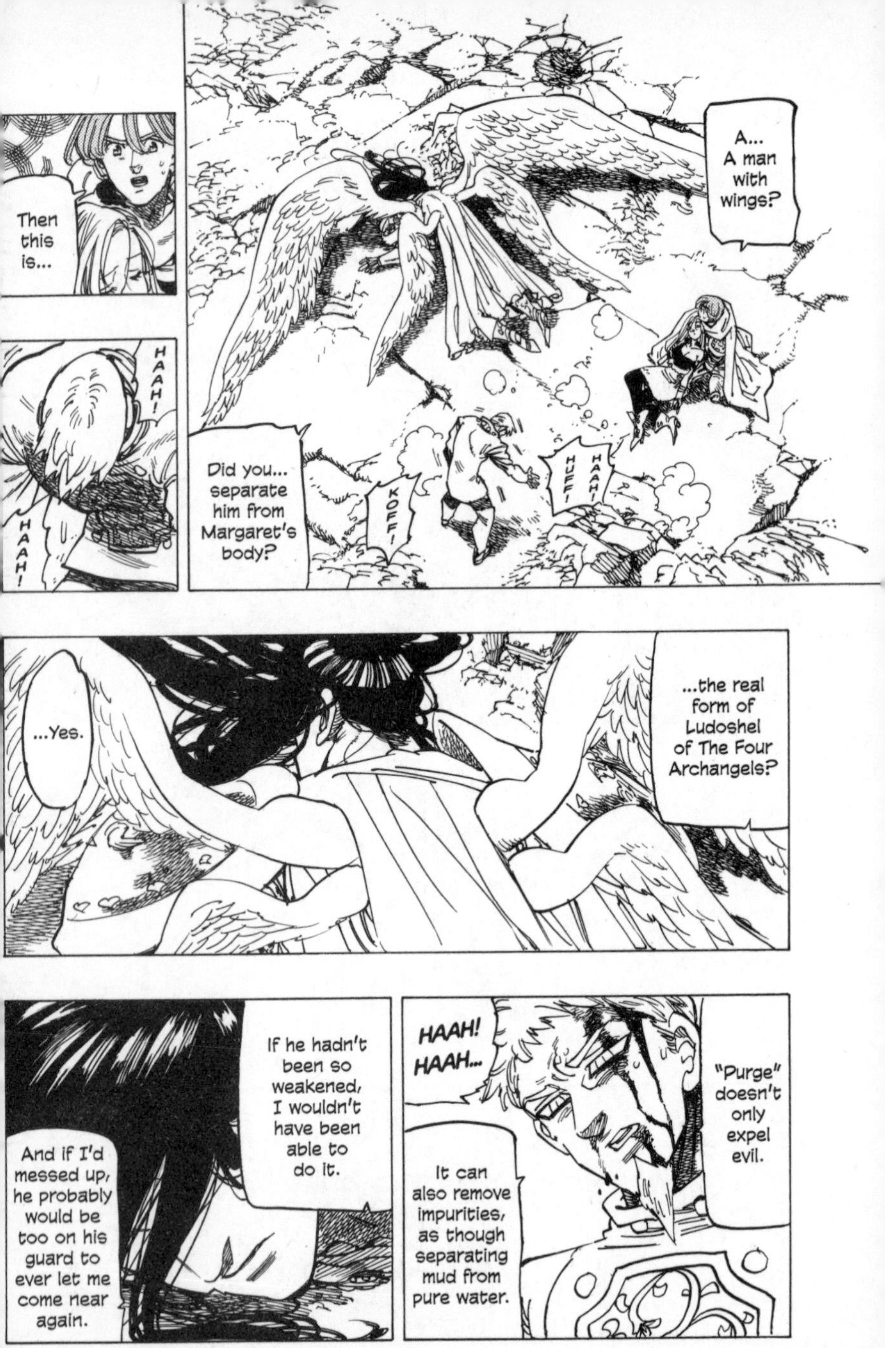
A... A man with wings?
HAAH! HUFF!
KOFF!
Did you... separate him from Margaret's body?
Then this is...
HAAH! HAAH!
...the real form of Ludoshel of The Four Archangels?
...Yes.
HAAH! HAAH...
"Purge" doesn't only expel evil.
It can also remove impurities, as though separating mud from pure water.
If he hadn't been so weakened, I wouldn't have been able to do it.
And if I'd messed up, he probably would be too on his guard to ever let me come near again.

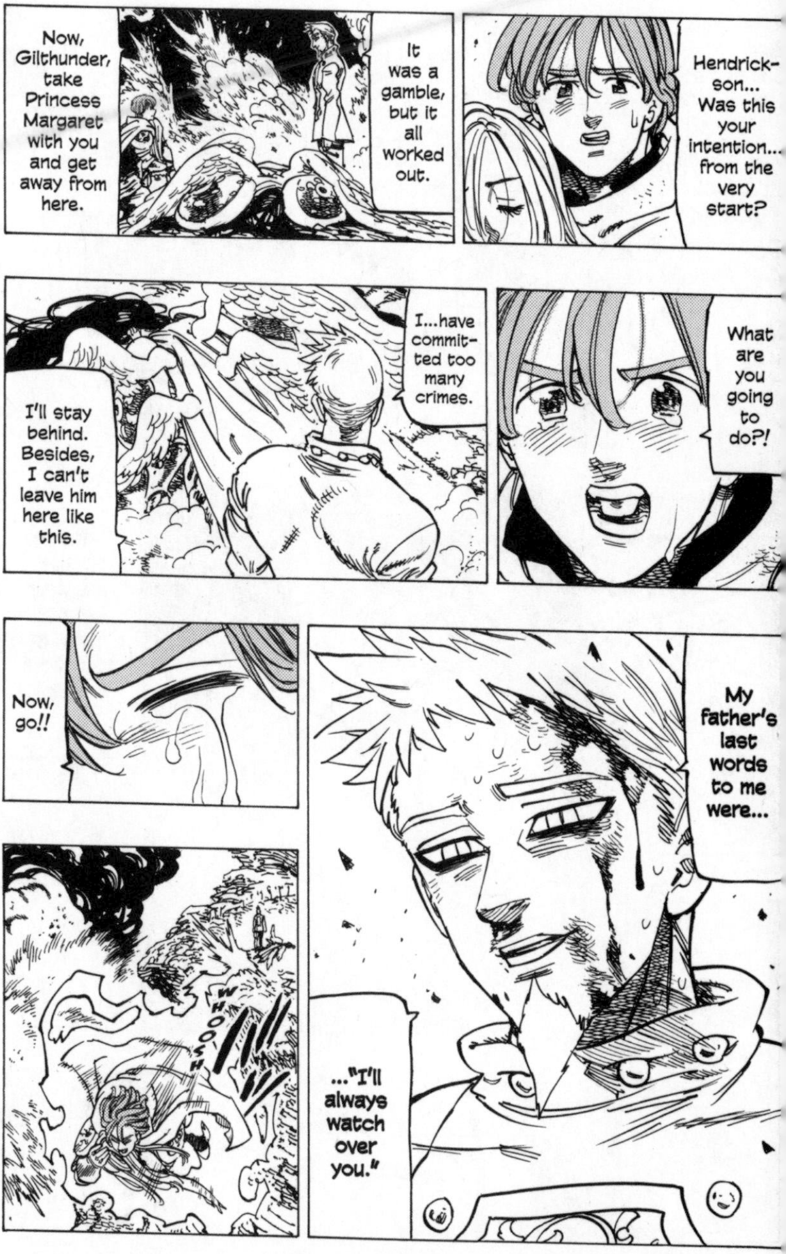
Hendrickson... Was this your intention... from the very start?
It was a gamble, but it all worked out.
Now, Gilthunder, take Princess Margaret with you and get away from here.
What are you going to do?!
I...have committed too many crimes.
I'll stay behind. Besides, I can't leave him here like this.
My father's last words to me were...
..."I'll always watch over you."
Now, go!!
WHOOOSH

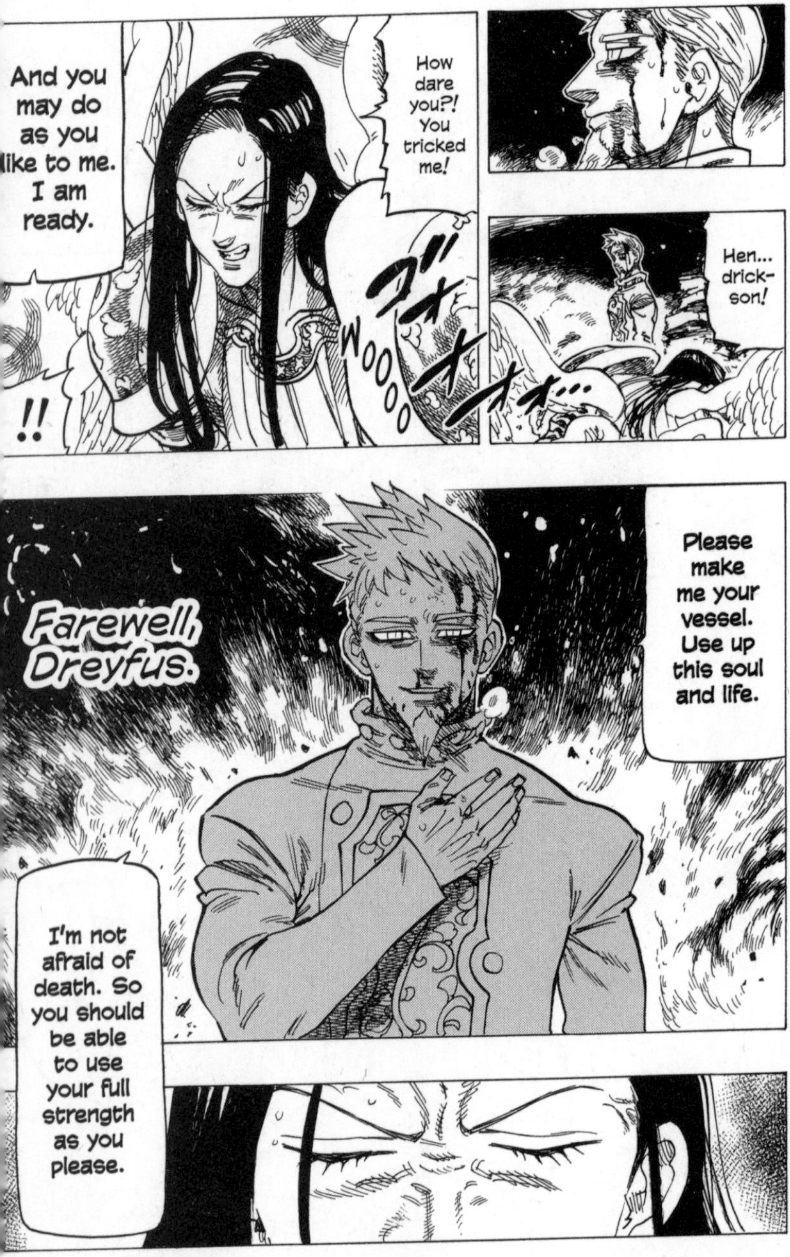
Hen... drick- son!
How dare you?! You tricked me!
And you may do as you like to me. I am ready.
!!
WOOOOO
Please make me your vessel. Use up this soul and life.
Farewell, Dreyfus.
I'm not afraid of death. So you should be able to use your full strength as you please.

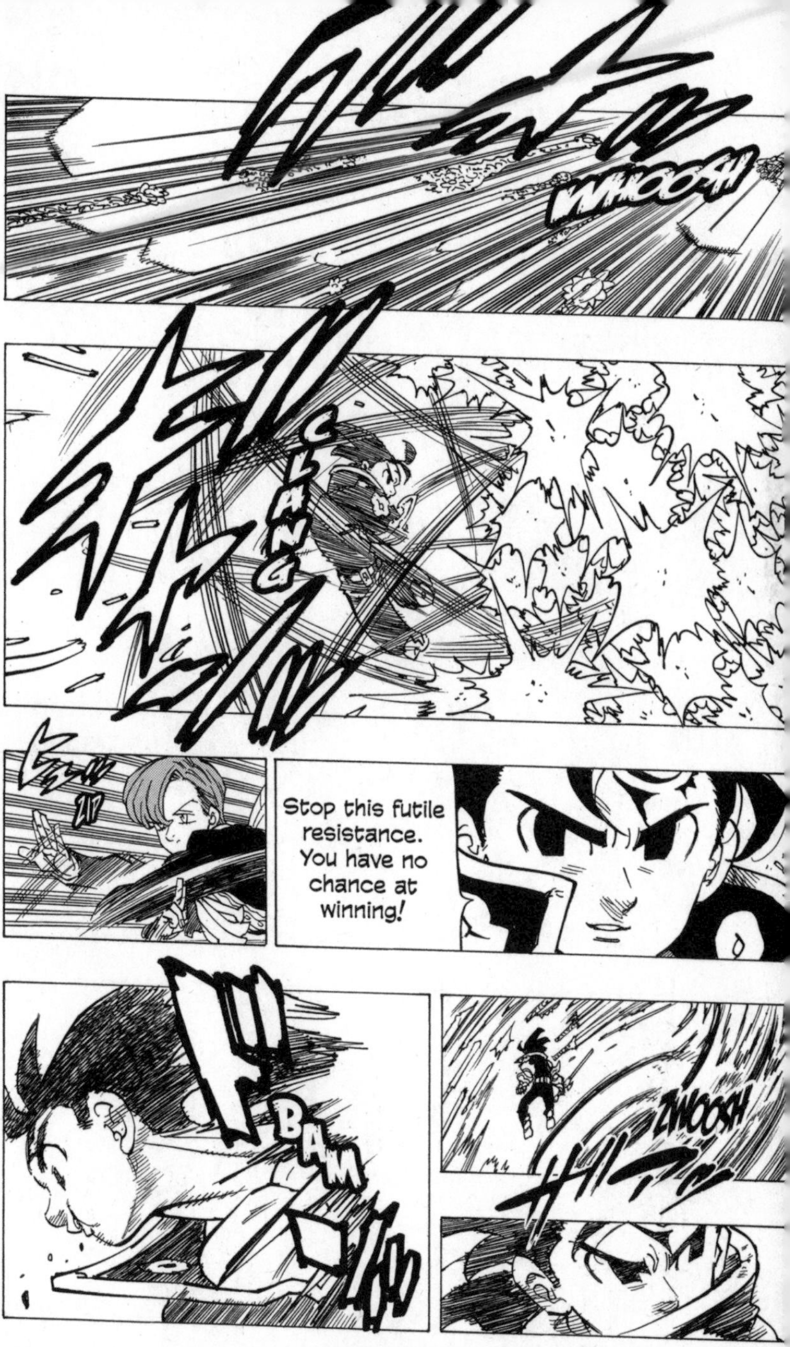
WHOOSH
CLANG
Stop this futile resistance. You have no chance at winning!
ZWOOSH
BAM

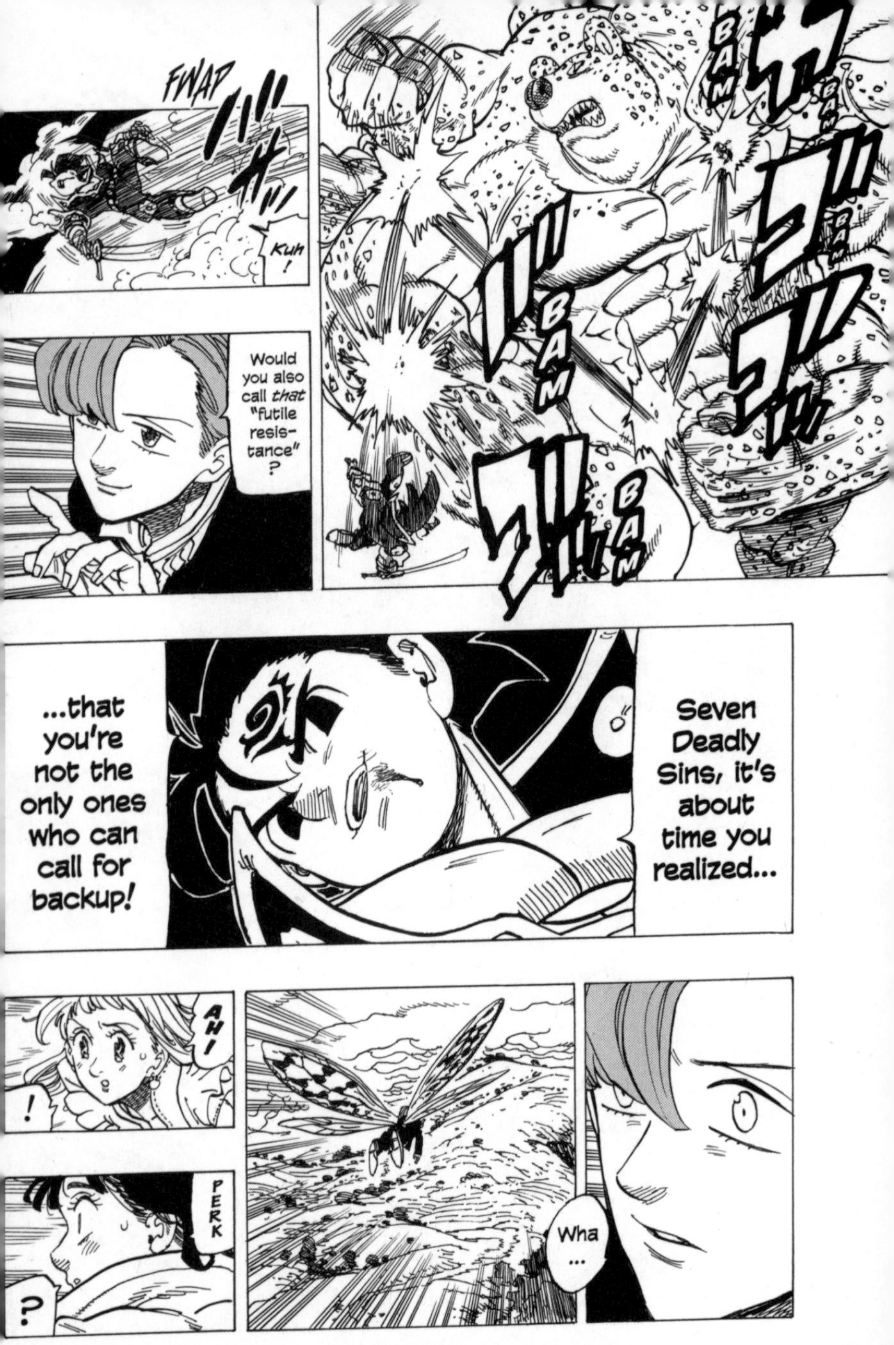

BAM
BAM
BAM
BAM
BAM
FWAP
Kuh!
Would you also call *that* "futile resistance"?
Seven Deadly Sins, it's about time you realized...
...that you're not the only ones who can call for backup!
Wha...
AH!
!
PERK
?

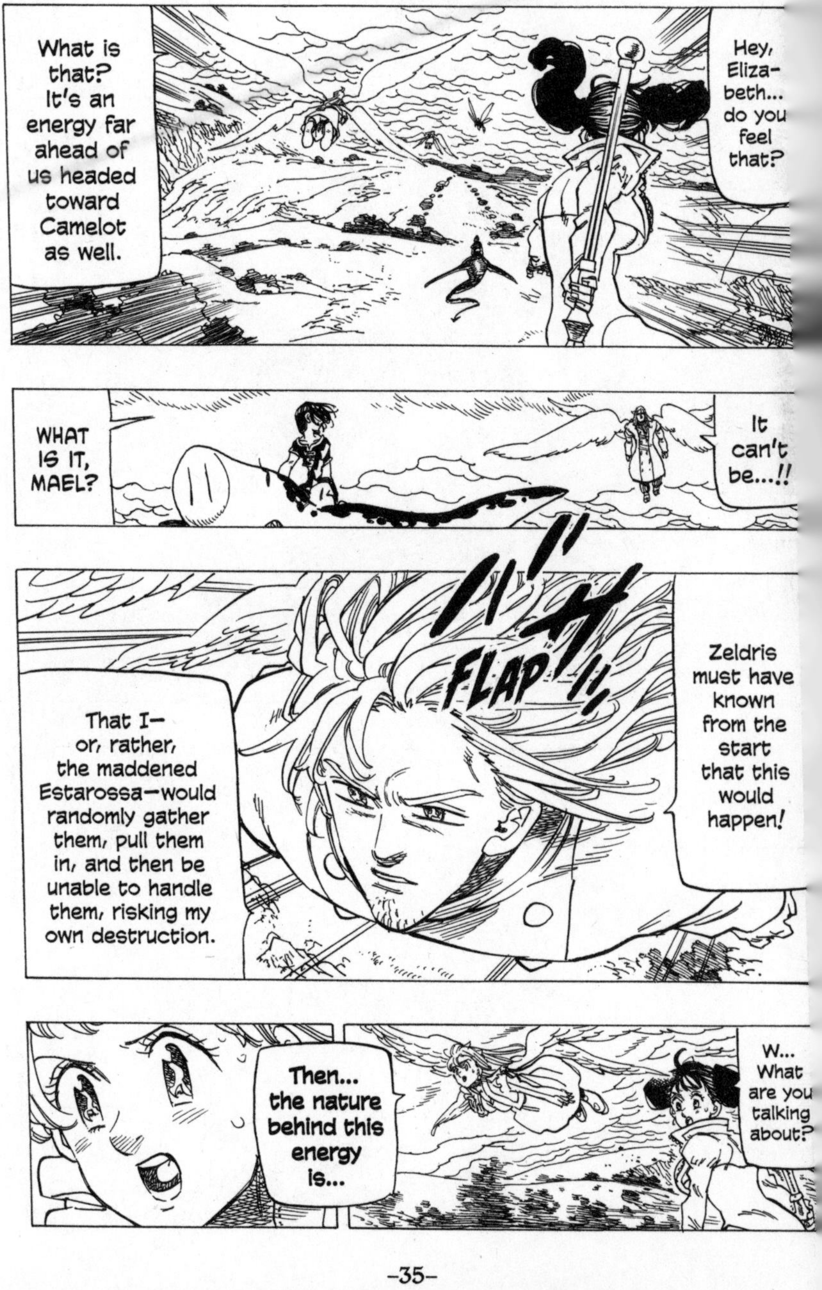
Hey, Elizabeth... do you feel that?
What is that? It's an energy far ahead of us headed toward Camelot as well.
It can't be...!!
WHAT IS IT, MAEL?
Zeldris must have known from the start that this would happen!
FLAP
That I—or, rather, the maddened Estarossa—would randomly gather them, pull them in, and then be unable to handle them, risking my own destruction.
W... What are you talking about?
Then... the nature behind this energy is...

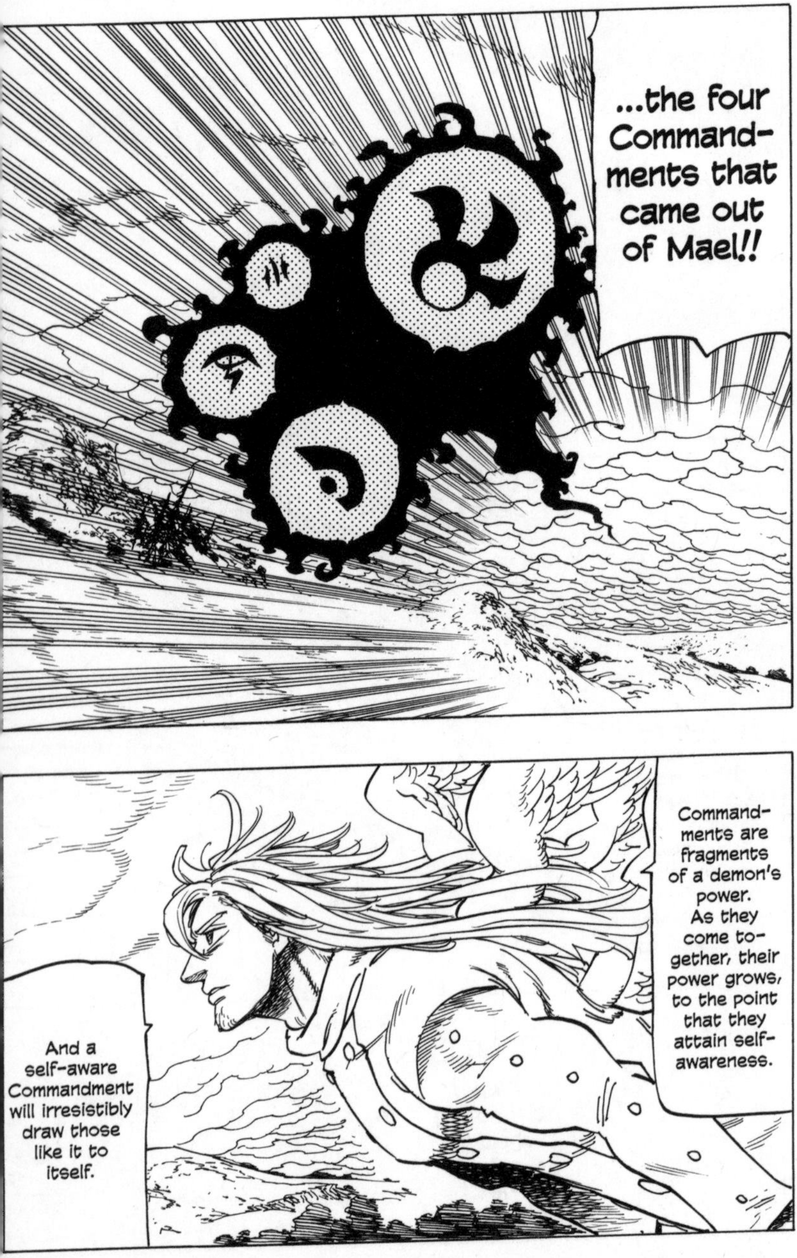
...the four Commandments that came out of Mael!!
Commandments are fragments of a demon's power. As they come together, their power grows, to the point that they attain self-awareness.
And a self-aware Commandment will irresistibly draw those like it to itself.

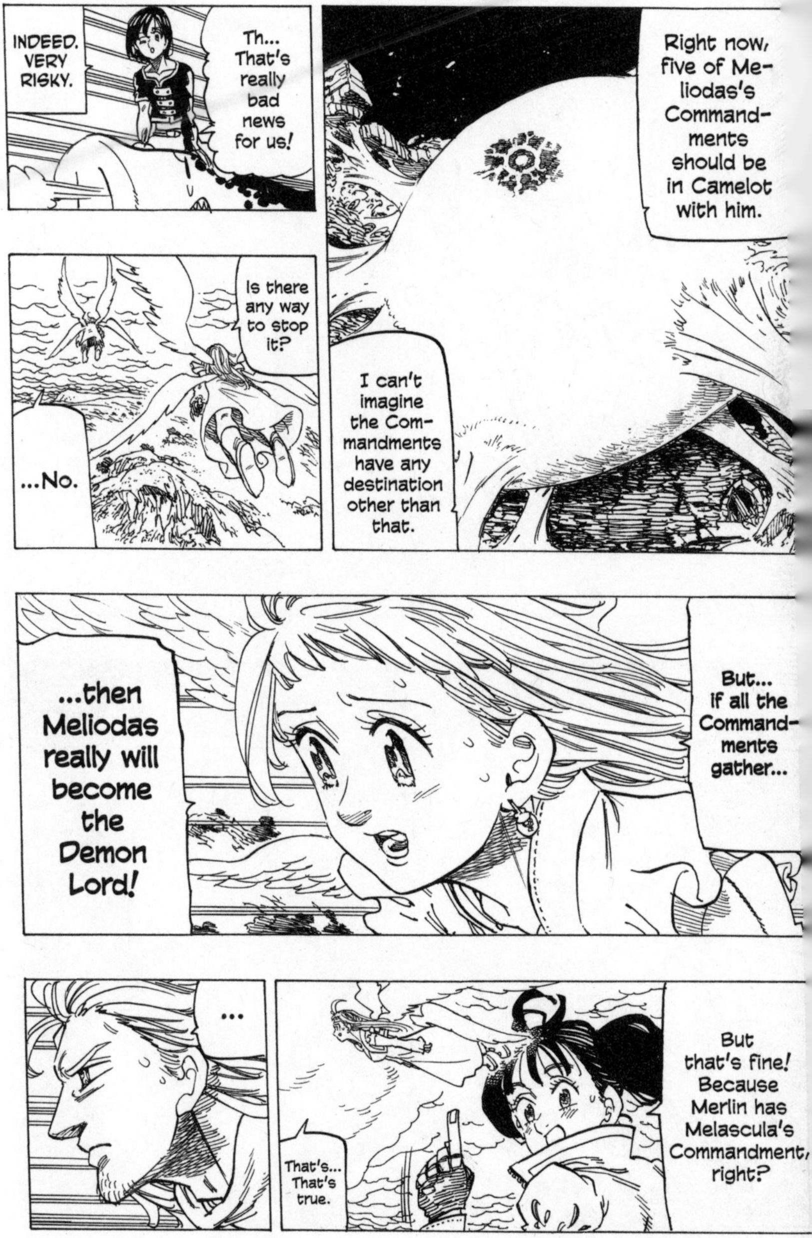

Right now, five of Meliodas's Commandments should be in Camelot with him.
I can't imagine the Commandments have any destination other than that.
Th... That's really bad news for us!
INDEED. VERY RISKY.
Is there any way to stop it?
...No.
But... if all the Commandments gather...
...then Meliodas really will become the Demon Lord!
But that's fine! Because Merlin has Melascula's Commandment, right?
That's... That's true.
...

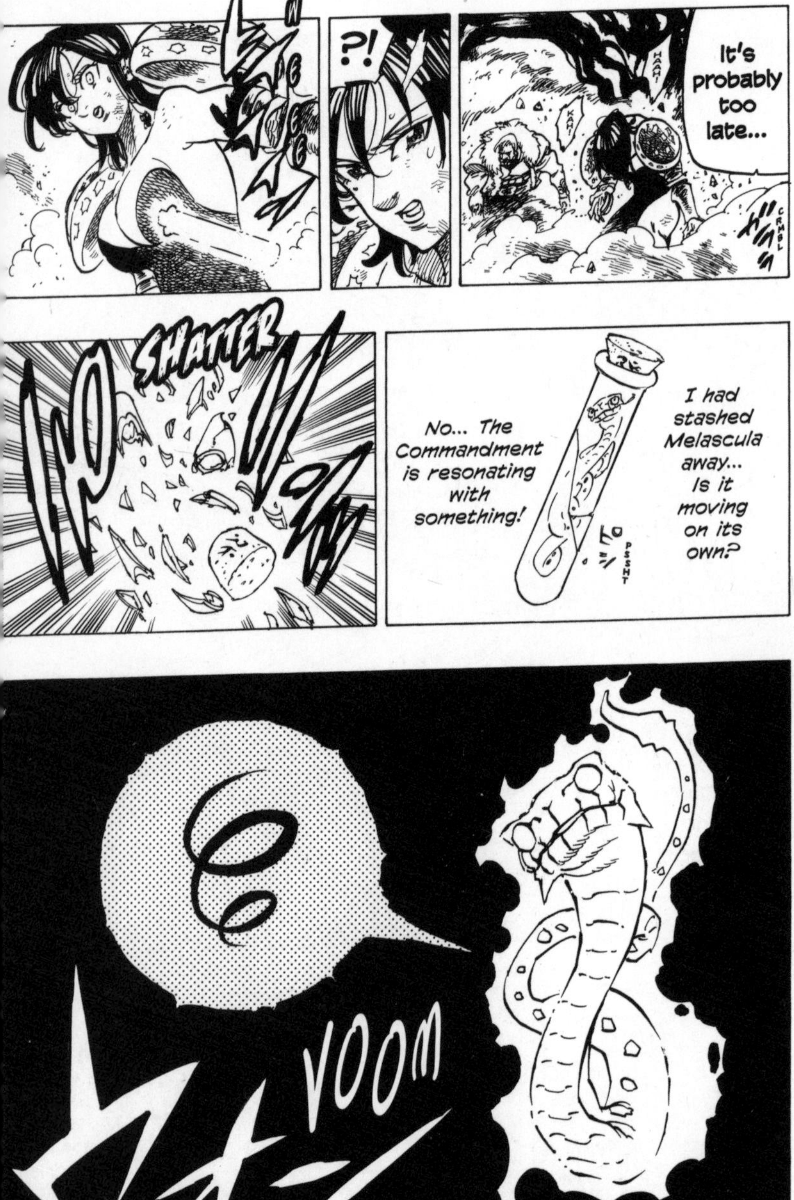
HAAH!
KAH!
It's probably too late...
CRMBL
?!
VWEEEE
No... The Commandment is resonating with something!
I had stashed Melascula away... Is it moving on its own?
PSSHT
SHATTER
VOOM

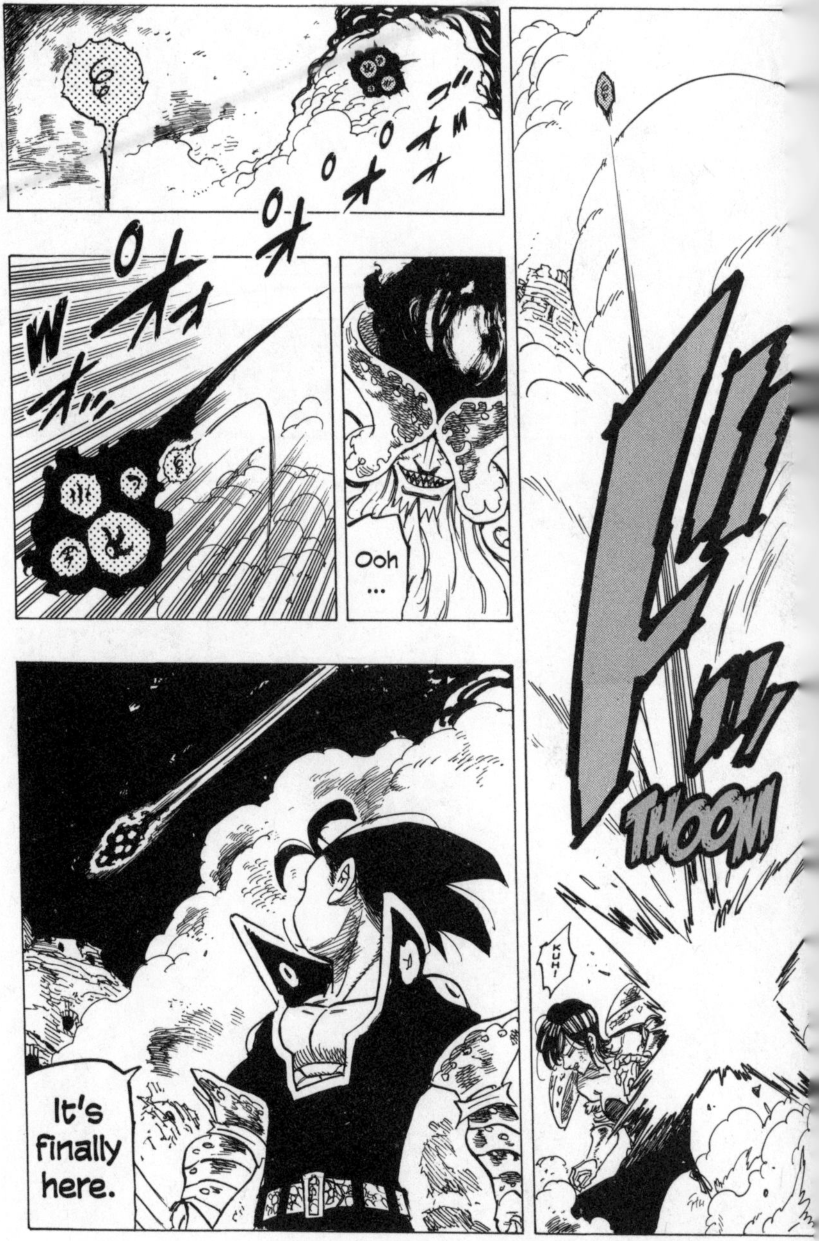
THOOM
KUH!
Ooh ...
It's finally here.

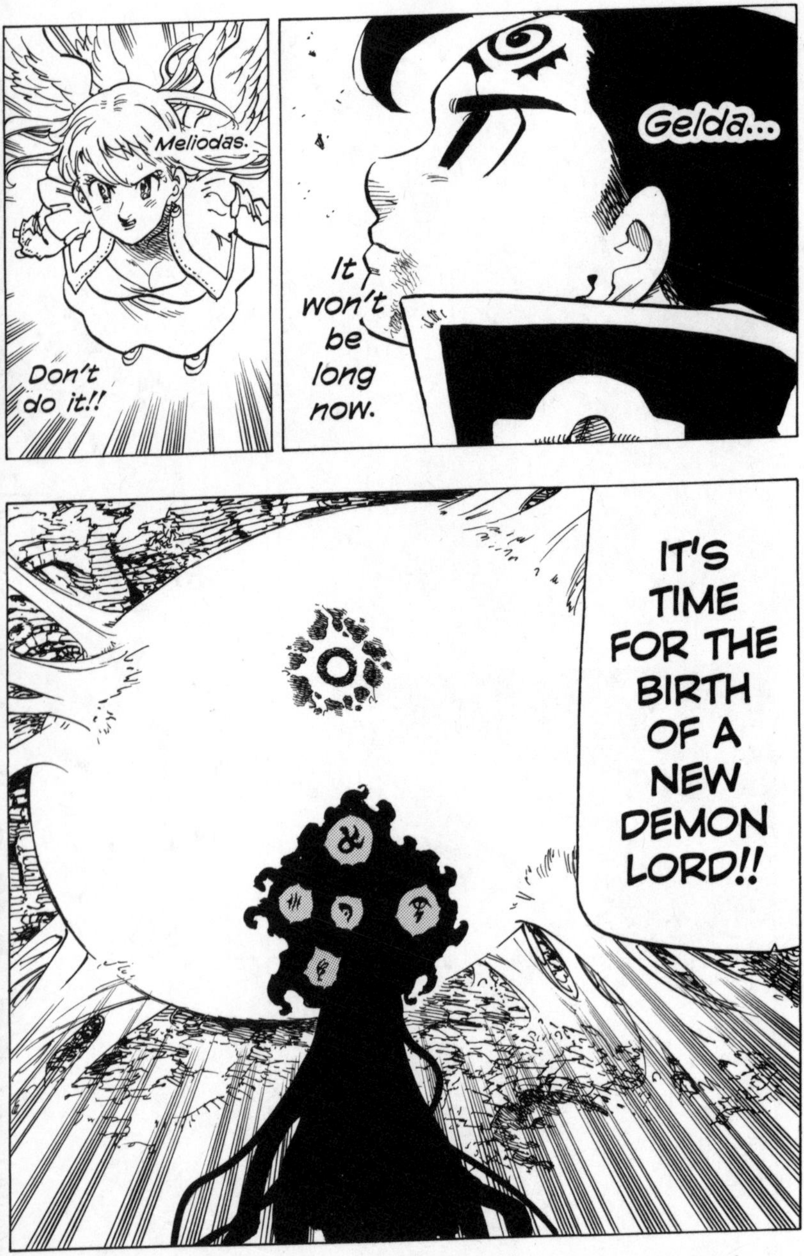
Gelda...
It won't be long now.
Meliodas.
Don't do it!!
IT'S TIME FOR THE BIRTH OF A NEW DEMON LORD!!

Chapter 296 - As a Friend, As a Brother

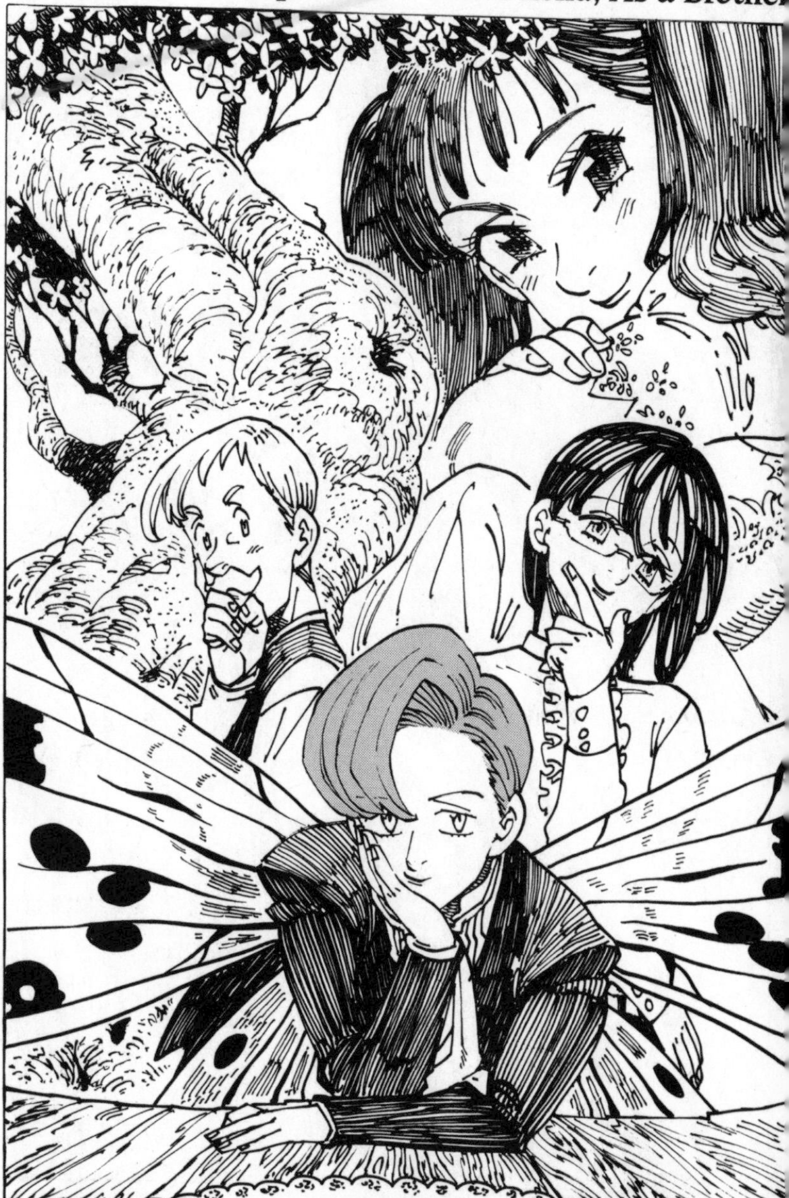

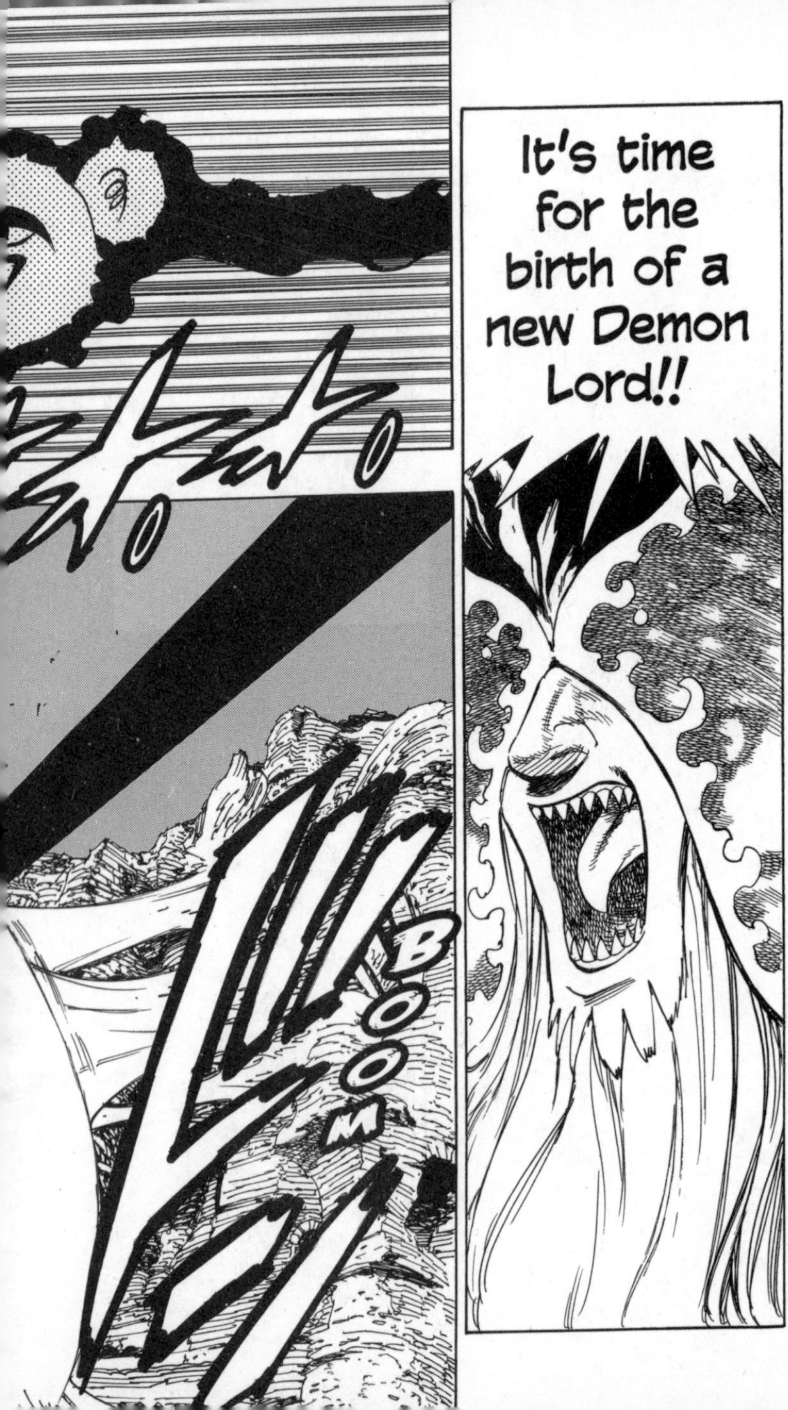
It's time for the birth of a new Demon Lord!!
BOOOM

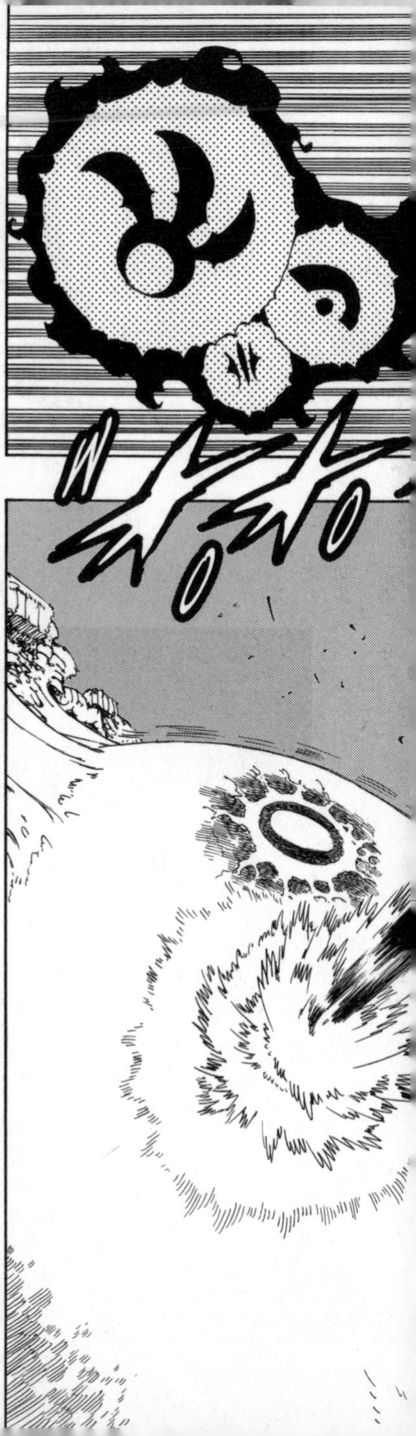

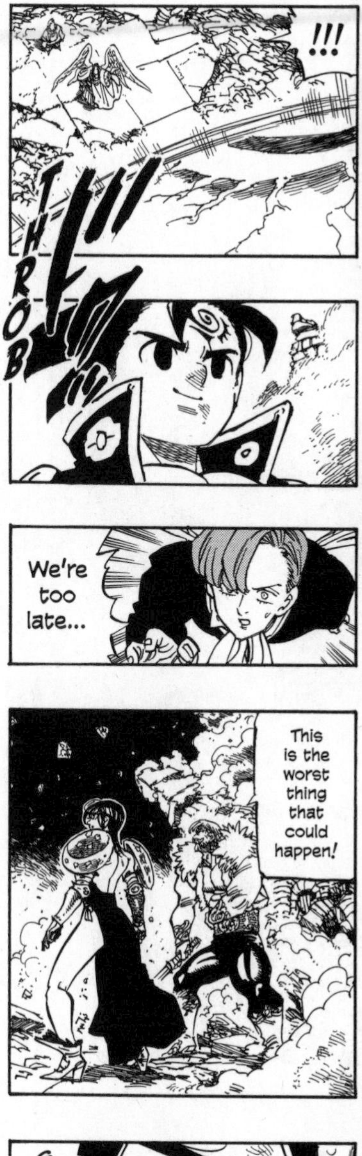
!!!
THROB
We're too late...
This is the worst thing that could happen!
GRIT

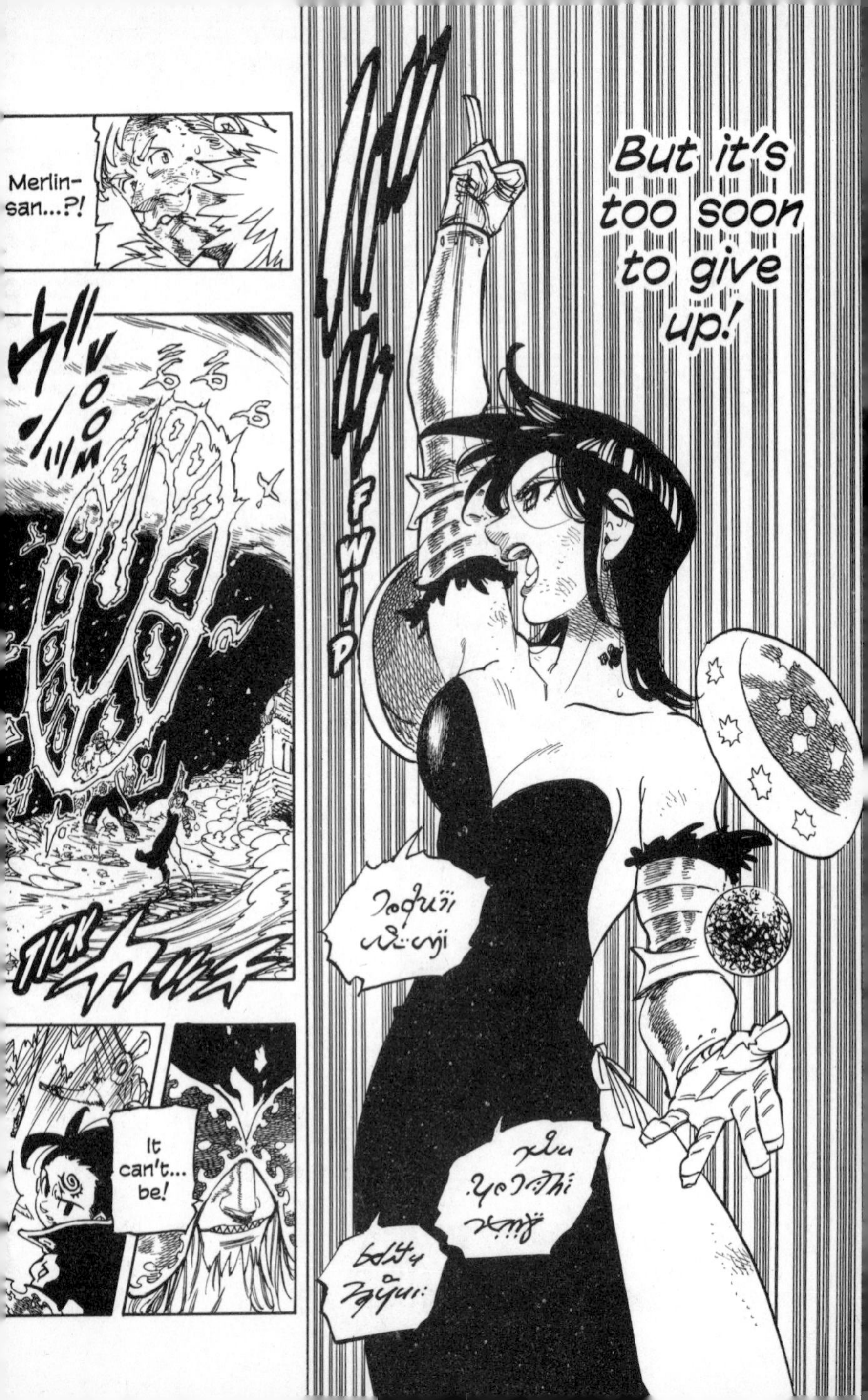
But it's too soon to give up!
FWIP
Merlin-san...?!
VOOOM
TICK
It can't... be!

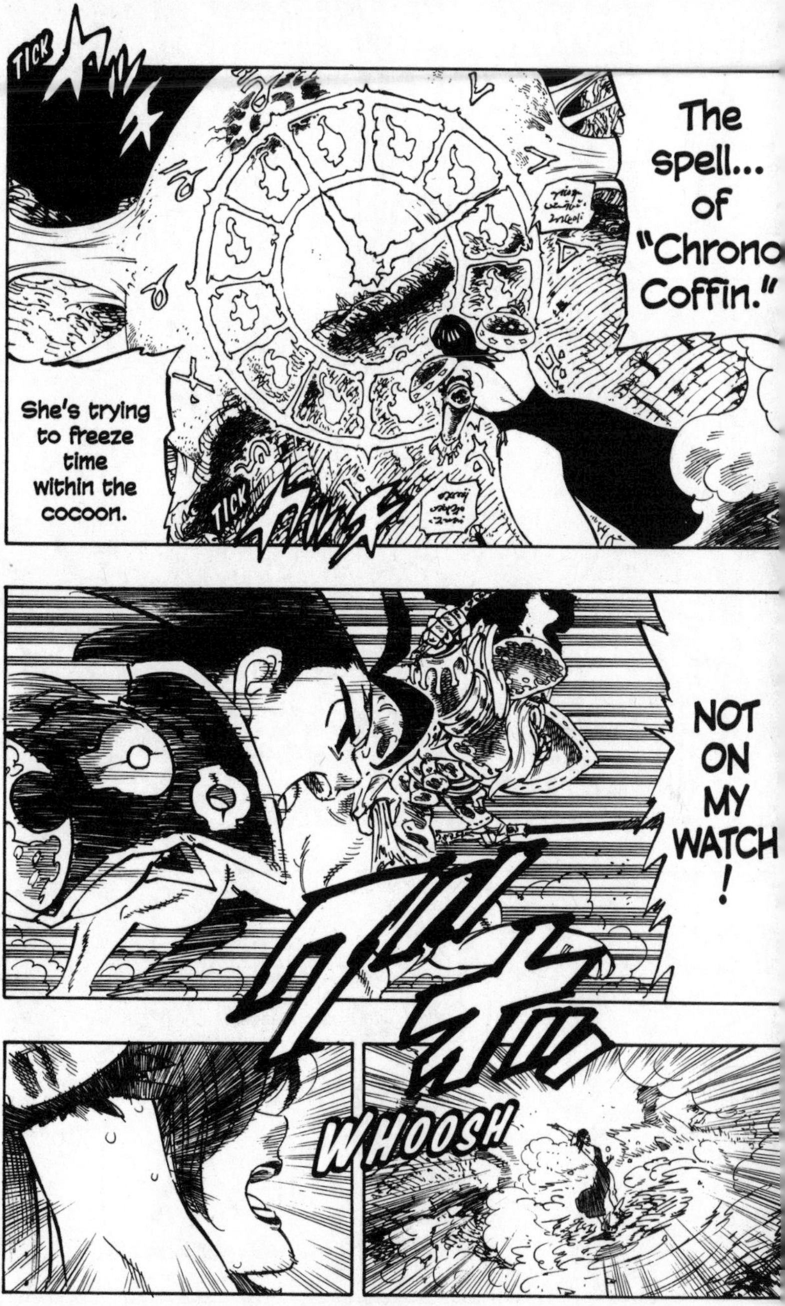
TICK
The spell... of "Chrono Coffin."
She's trying to freeze time within the cocoon.
TICK
NOT ON MY WATCH!
WHOOSH

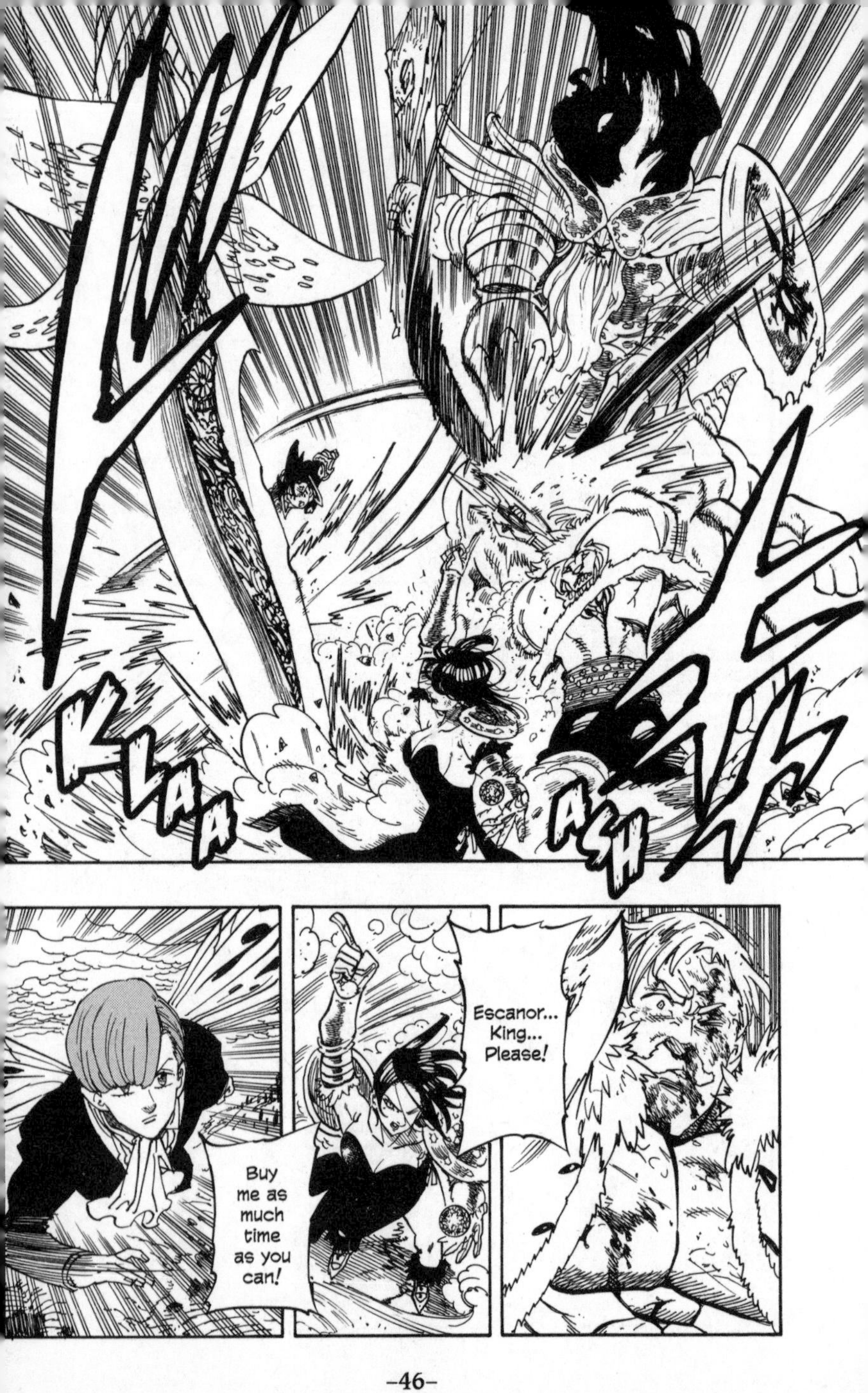
KLAAASH
Escanor... King... Please!
Buy me as much time as you can!

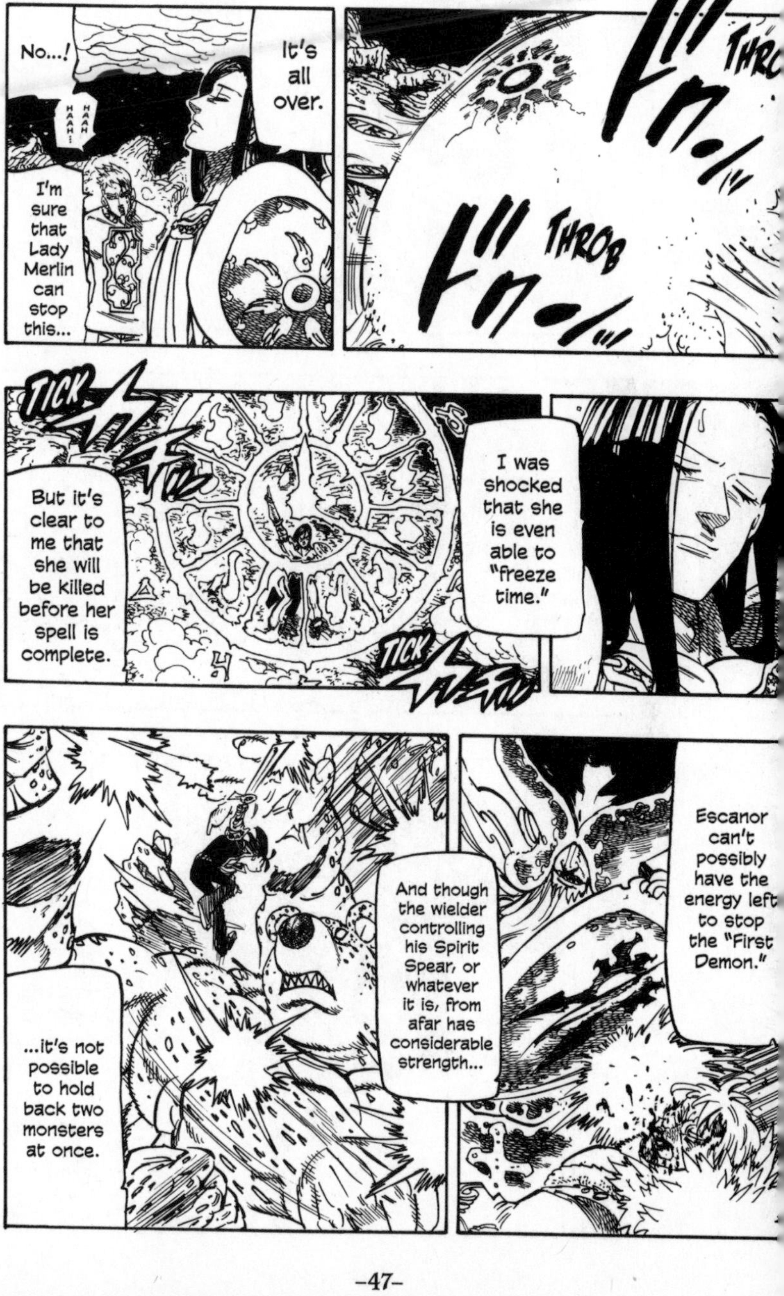
THROB
It's all over.
No...!
HAAH HAAH
I'm sure that Lady Merlin can stop this...
I was shocked that she is even able to "freeze time."
TICK
But it's clear to me that she will be killed before her spell is complete.
TICK
Escanor can't possibly have the energy left to stop the "First Demon."
And though the wielder controlling his Spirit Spear, or whatever it is, from afar has considerable strength...
...it's not possible to hold back two monsters at once.

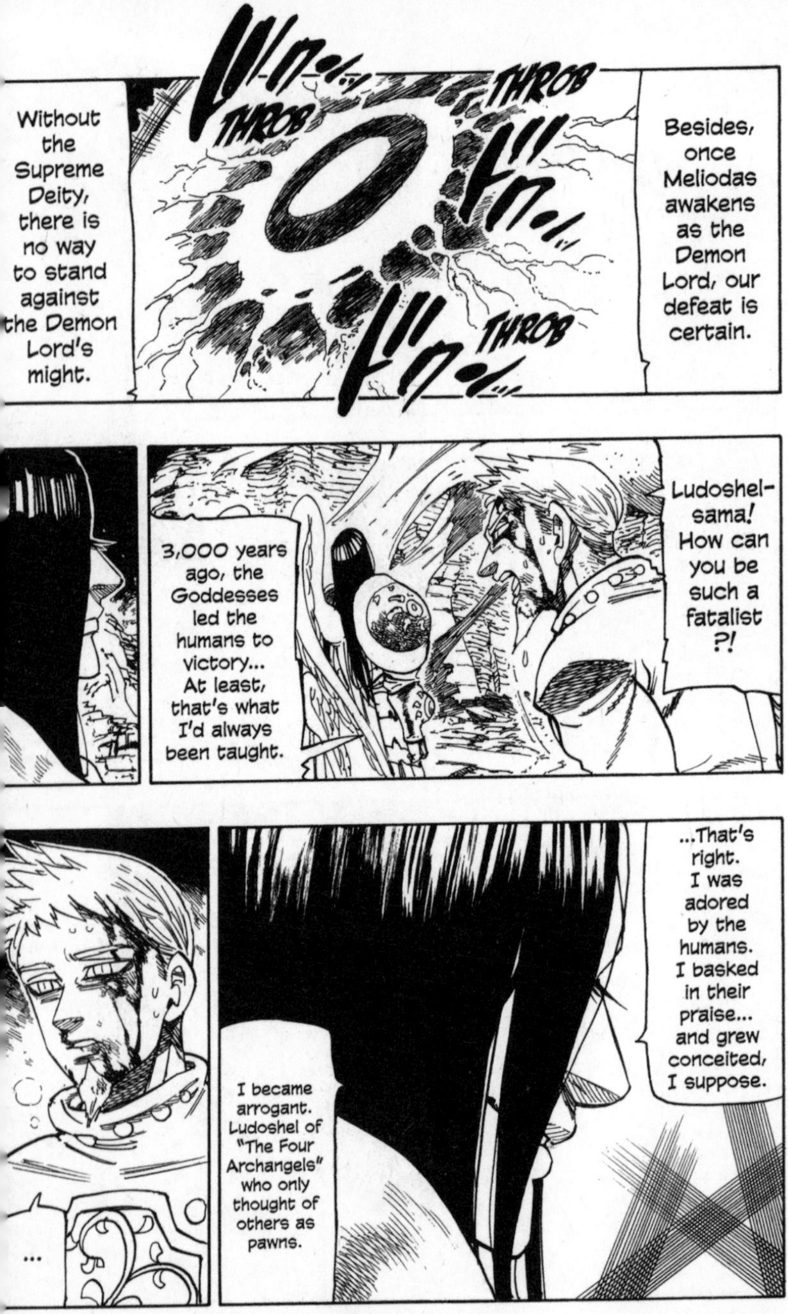
Besides, once Meliodas awakens as the Demon Lord, our defeat is certain.
THROB
THROB
THROB
Without the Supreme Deity, there is no way to stand against the Demon Lord's might.
Ludoshel-sama! How can you be such a fatalist ?!
3,000 years ago, the Goddesses led the humans to victory... At least, that's what I'd always been taught.
...That's right. I was adored by the humans. I basked in their praise... and grew conceited, I suppose.
I became arrogant. Ludoshel of "The Four Archangels" who only thought of others as pawns.
...

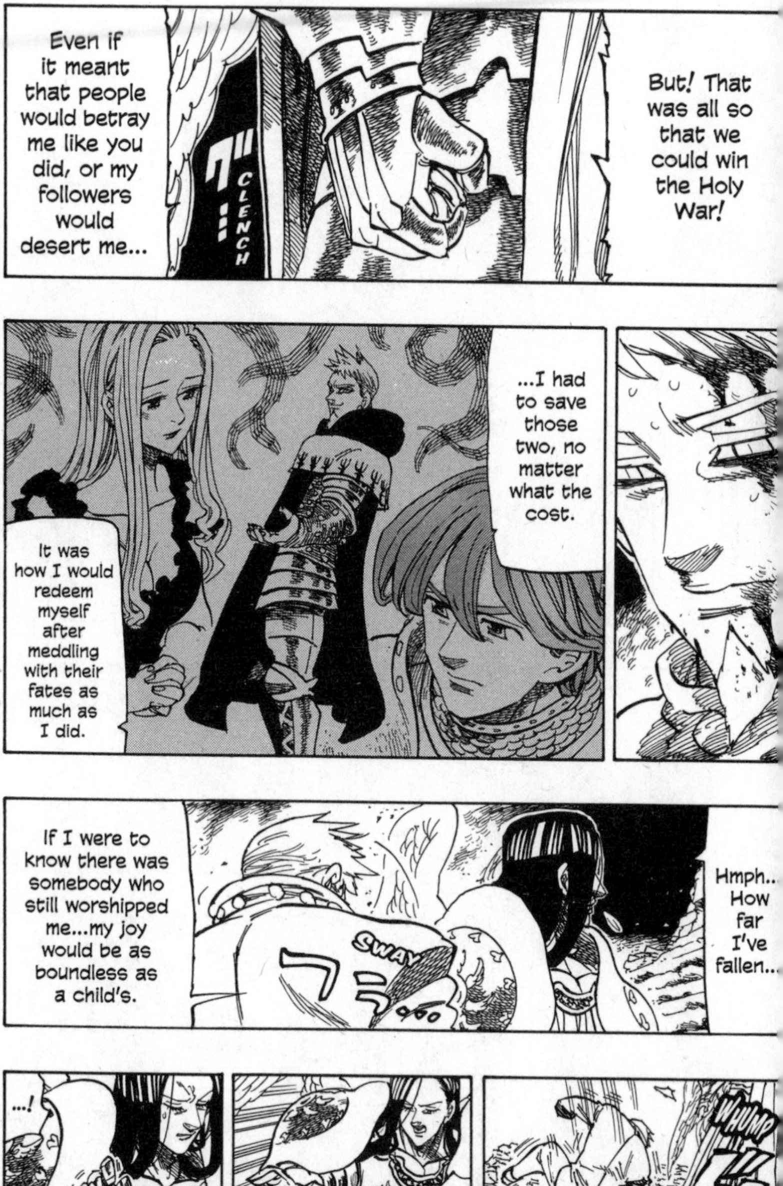
But! That was all so that we could win the Holy War!
Even if it meant that people would betray me like you did, or my followers would desert me...
CLENCH
...I had to save those two, no matter what the cost.
It was how I would redeem myself after meddling with their fates as much as I did.
Hmph... How far I've fallen...
If I were to know there was somebody who still worshipped me...my joy would be as boundless as a child's.
SWAY
WHUMP
!!
...!

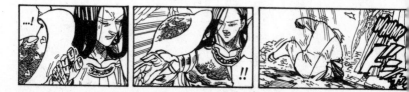

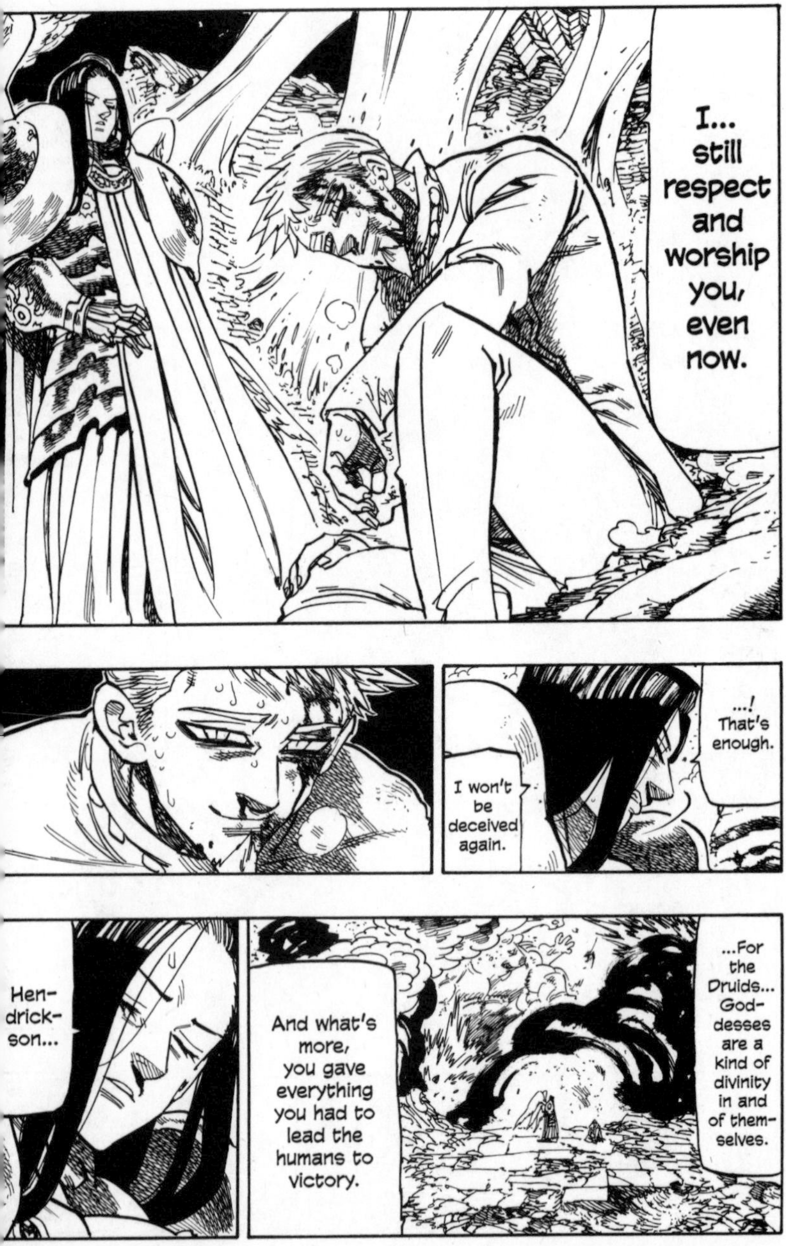
I... still respect and worship you, even now.
...! That's enough.
I won't be deceived again.
...For the Druids... God-desses are a kind of divinity in and of them-selves.
And what's more, you gave everything you had to lead the humans to victory.
Hen-drick-son...

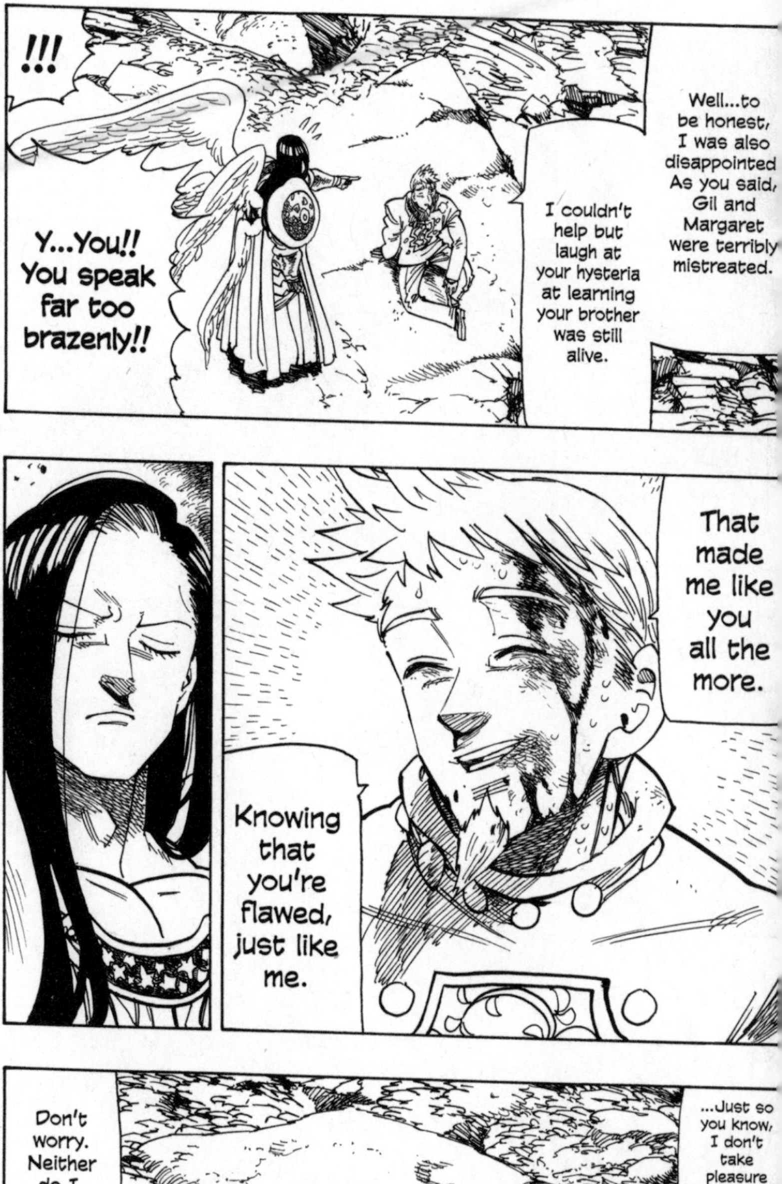

Well...to be honest, I was also disappointed As you said, Gil and Margaret were terribly mistreated.
I couldn't help but laugh at your hysteria at learning your brother was still alive.
!!!
Y...You!! You speak far too brazenly!!
That made me like you all the more.
Knowing that you're flawed, just like me.
...Just so you know, I don't take pleasure in the company of men.
Don't worry. Neither do I.

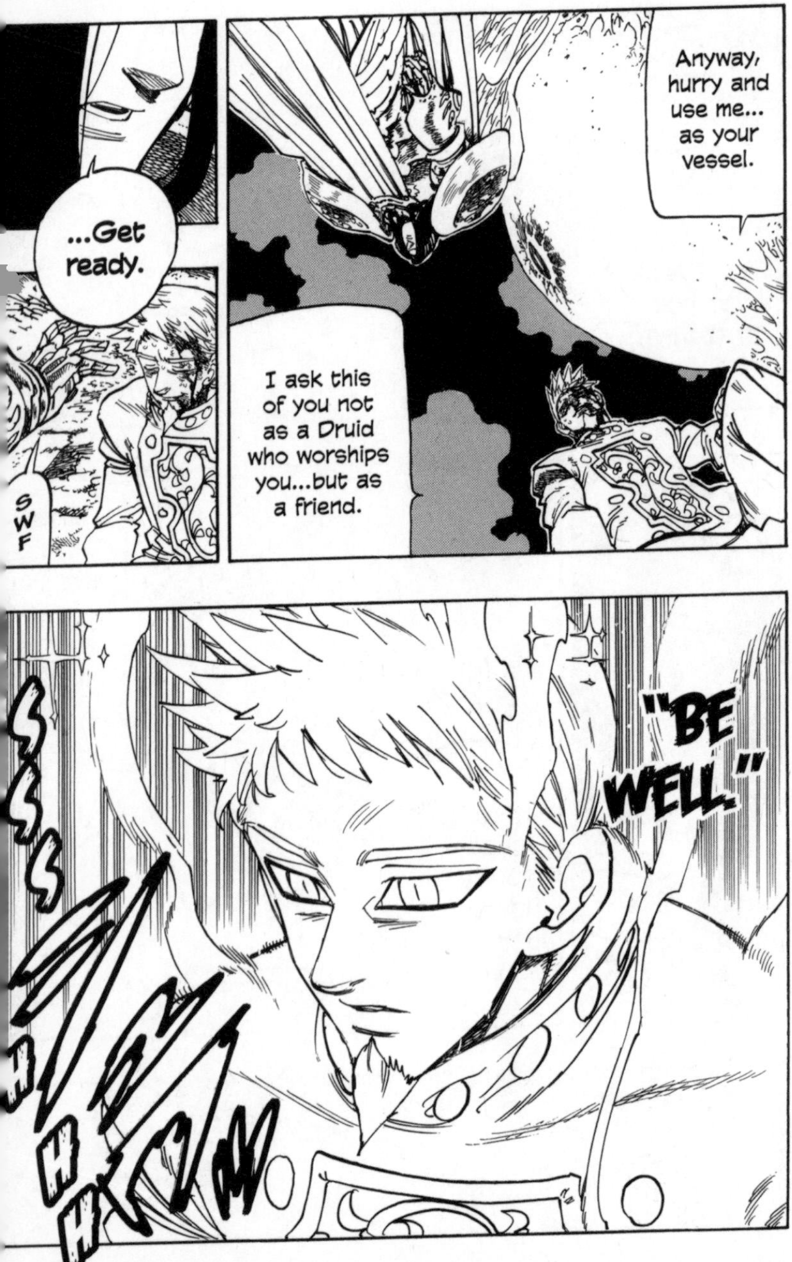
Anyway, hurry and use me... as your vessel.
I ask this of you not as a Druid who worships you...but as a friend.
...Get ready.
SWF
"BE WELL"

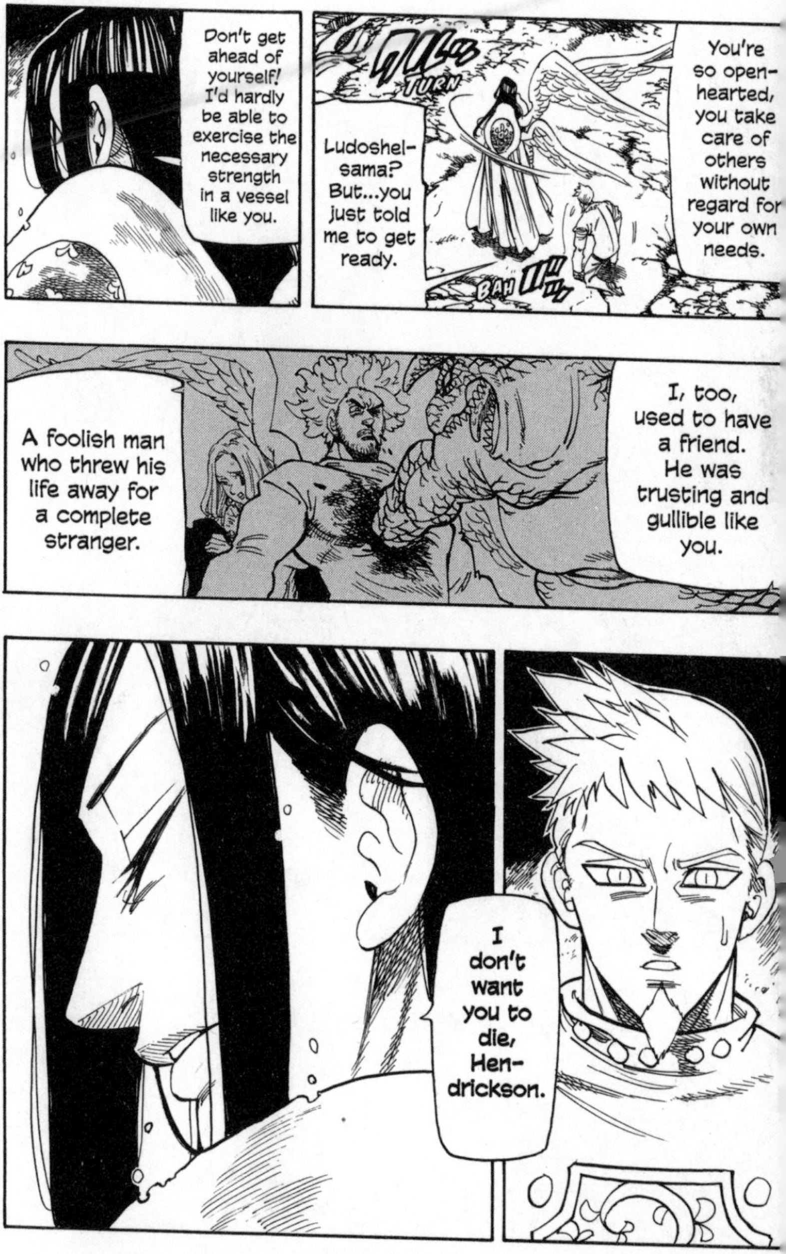
You're so open-hearted, you take care of others without regard for your own needs.
TURN
Ludoshel-sama? But...you just told me to get ready.
BAH
Don't get ahead of yourself! I'd hardly be able to exercise the necessary strength in a vessel like you.
I, too, used to have a friend. He was trusting and gullible like you.
A foolish man who threw his life away for a complete stranger.
I don't want you to die, Hendrickson.

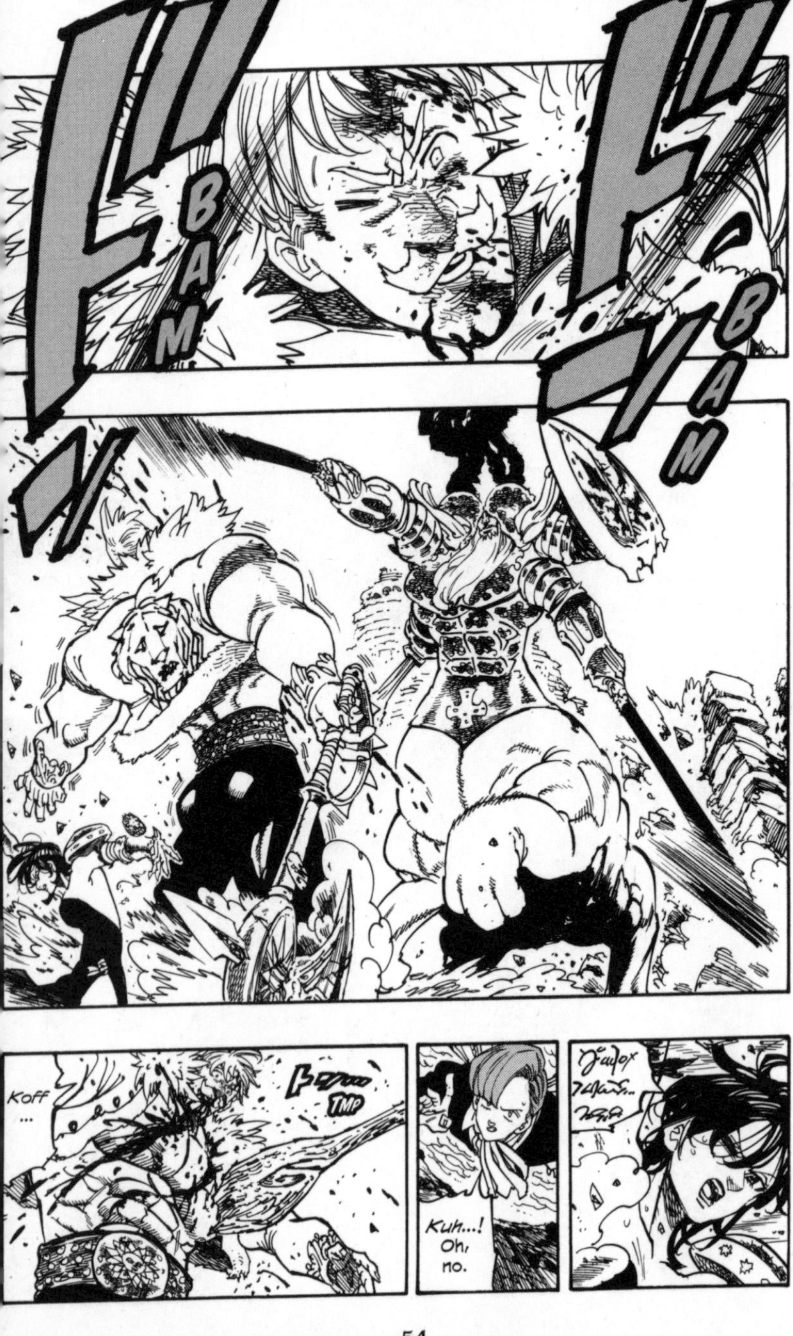
BAM
BAM
Kuh...!
Oh, no.
TMP
Koff ...

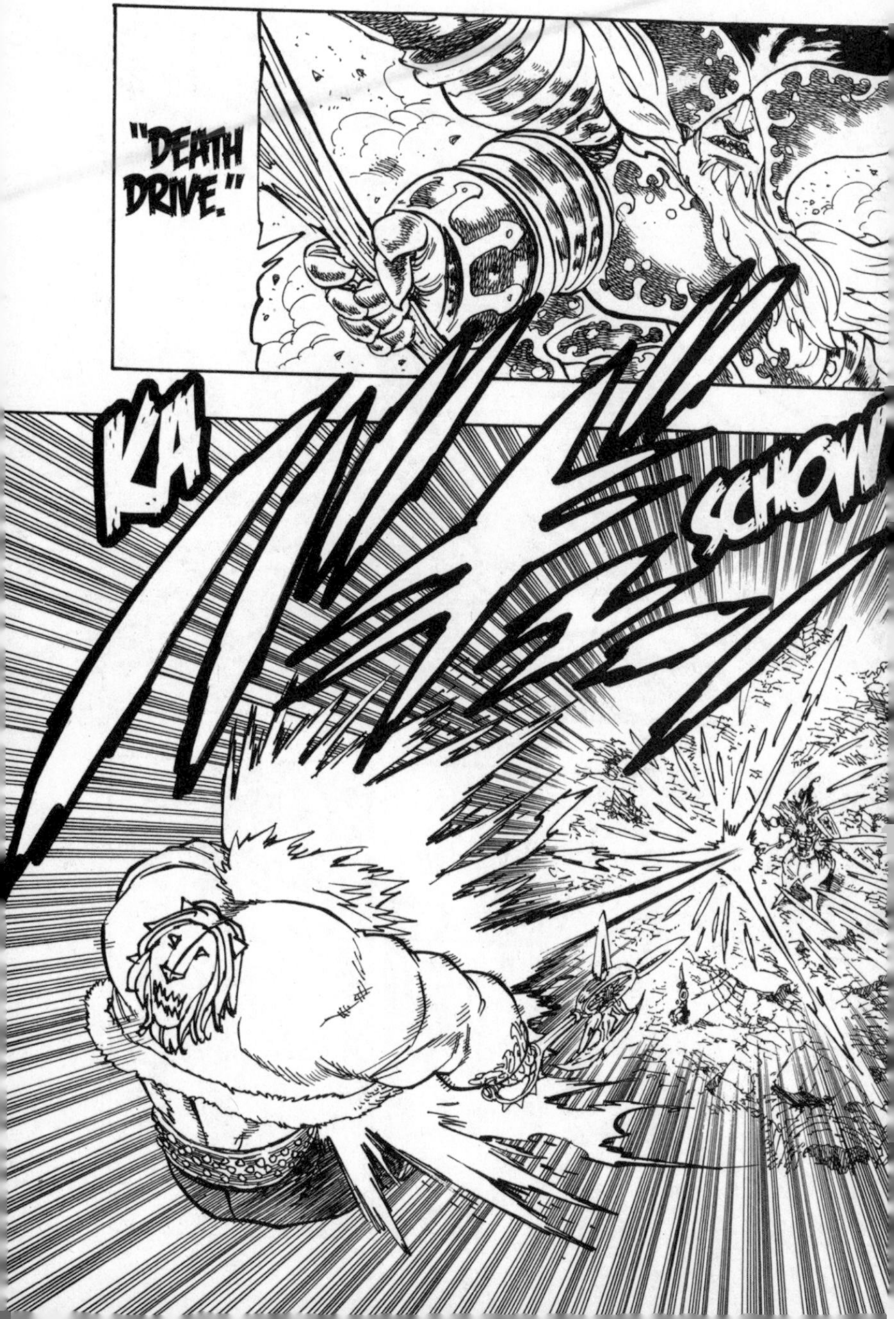
"DEATH DRIVE."
KA
SCHOW

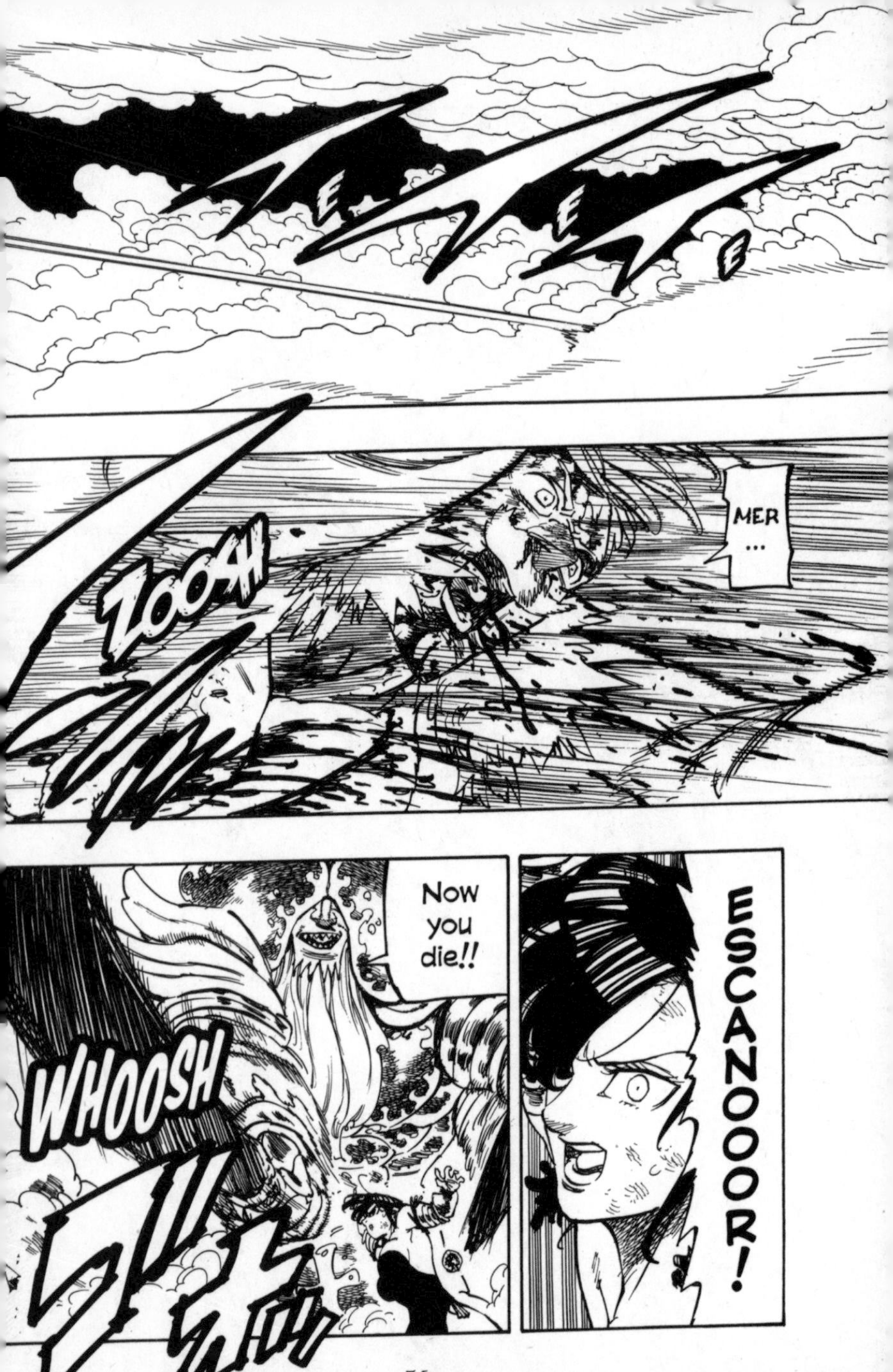
ZOOSH
MER...
ESCANOOOOR!
Now you die!!
WHOOSH

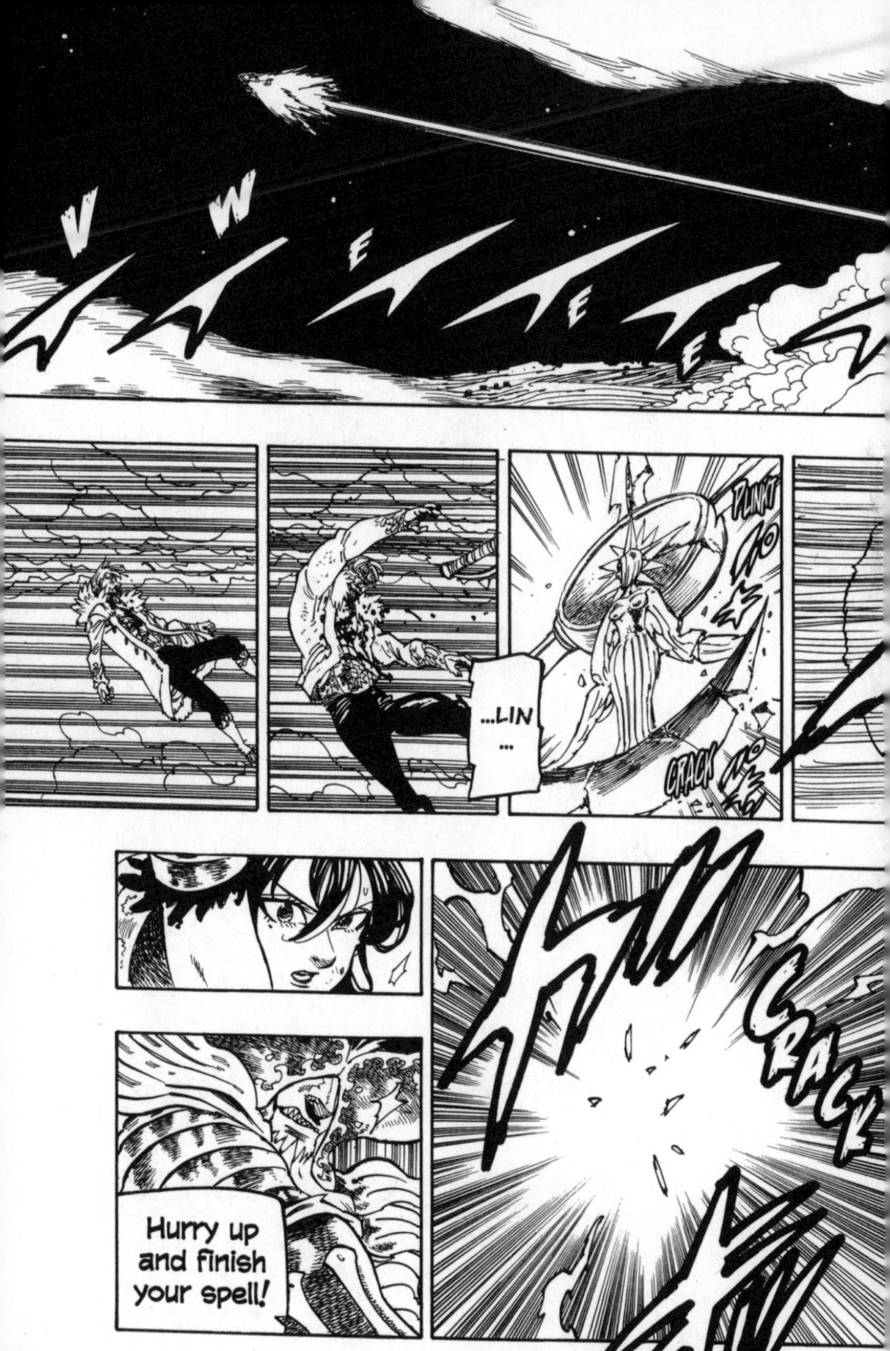
VWEEEE
PLINK
CRACK
...LIN
...
CRACK
Hurry up and finish your spell!

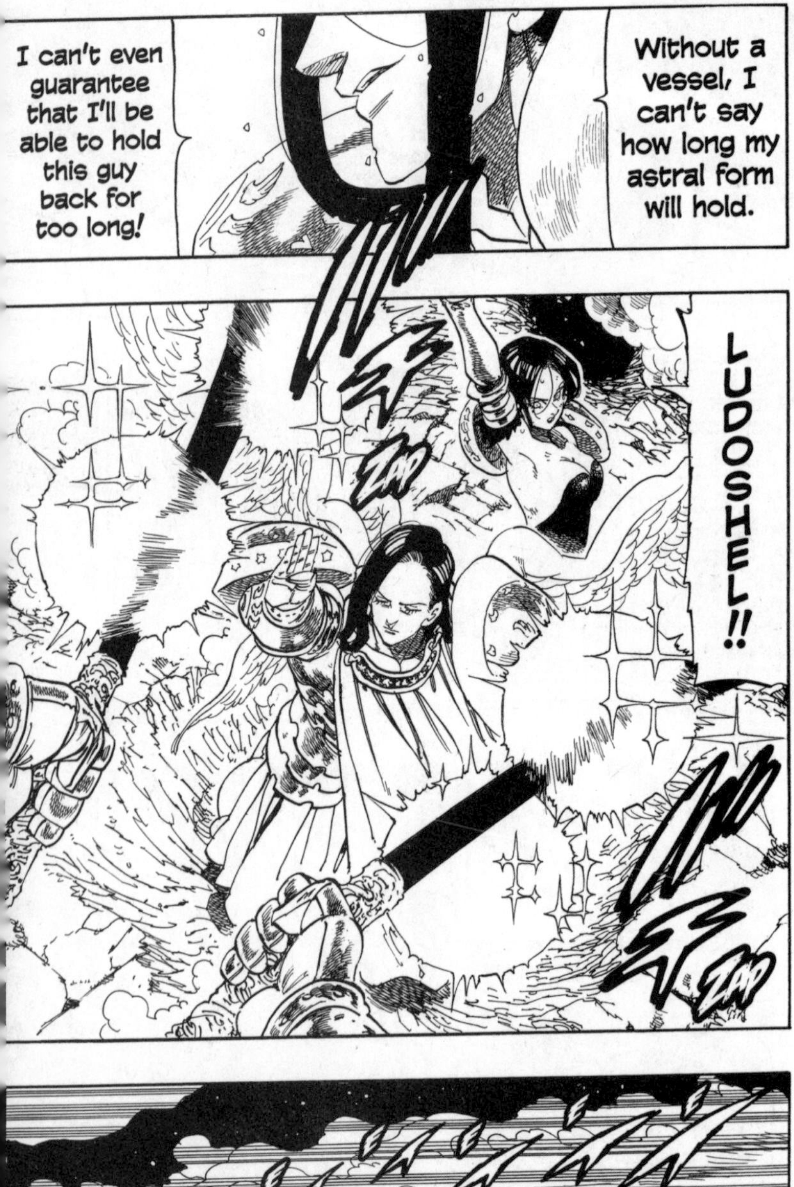
Without a vessel, I can't say how long my astral form will hold.
I can't even guarantee that I'll be able to hold this guy back for too long!
LUDOSHEL!!
ZAP
ZAP

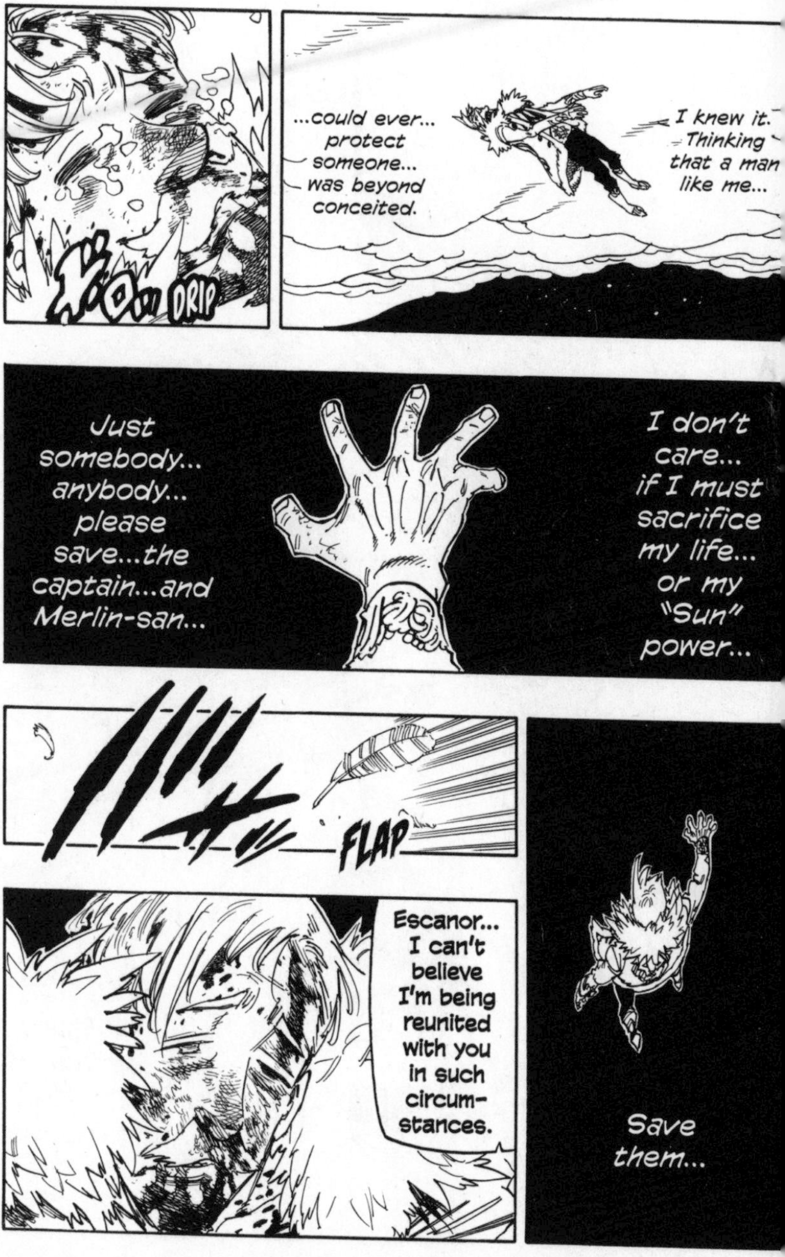
I knew it. Thinking that a man like me...
...could ever... protect someone... was beyond conceited.
DRIP
I don't care... if I must sacrifice my life... or my "Sun" power...
Just somebody... anybody... please save...the captain...and Merlin-san...
Save them...
FLAP
Escanor... I can't believe I'm being reunited with you in such circum-stances.

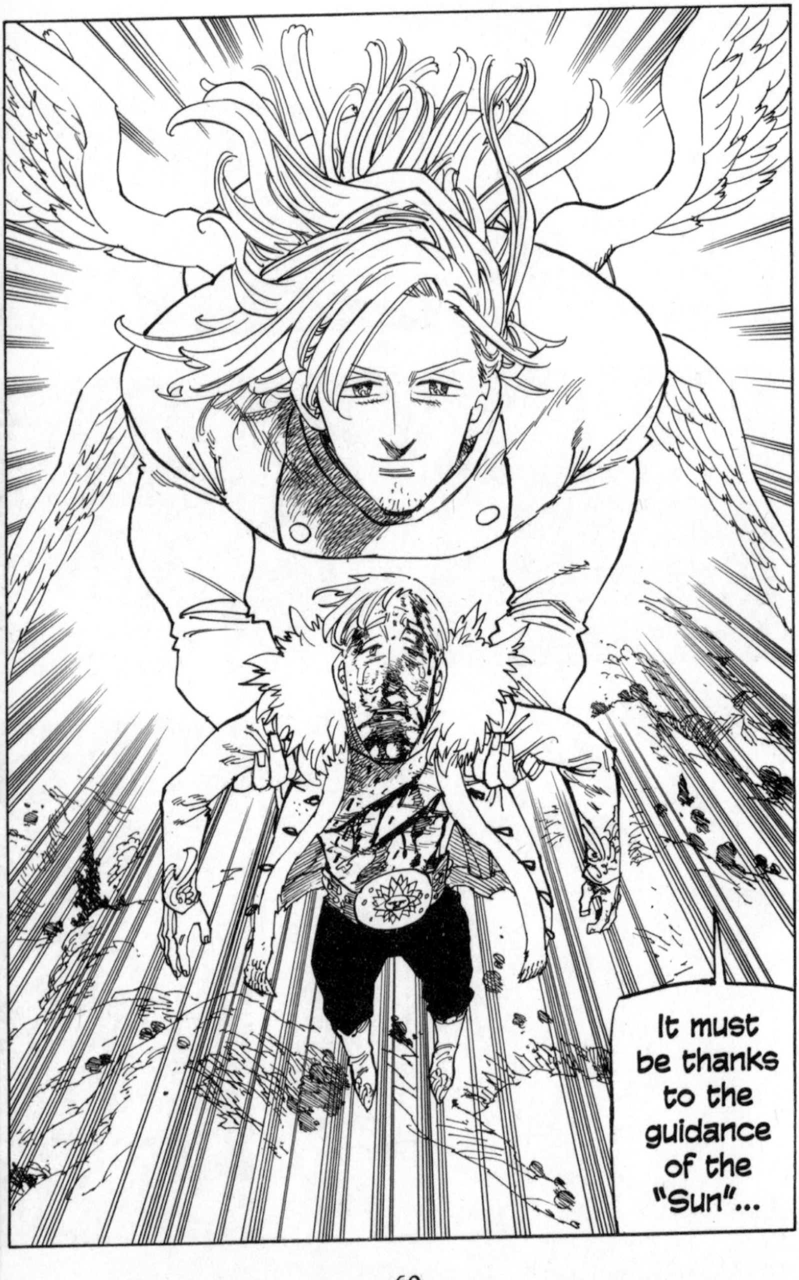
It must be thanks to the guidance of the "Sun"...

Chapter 297 - The Salvation of the Sun

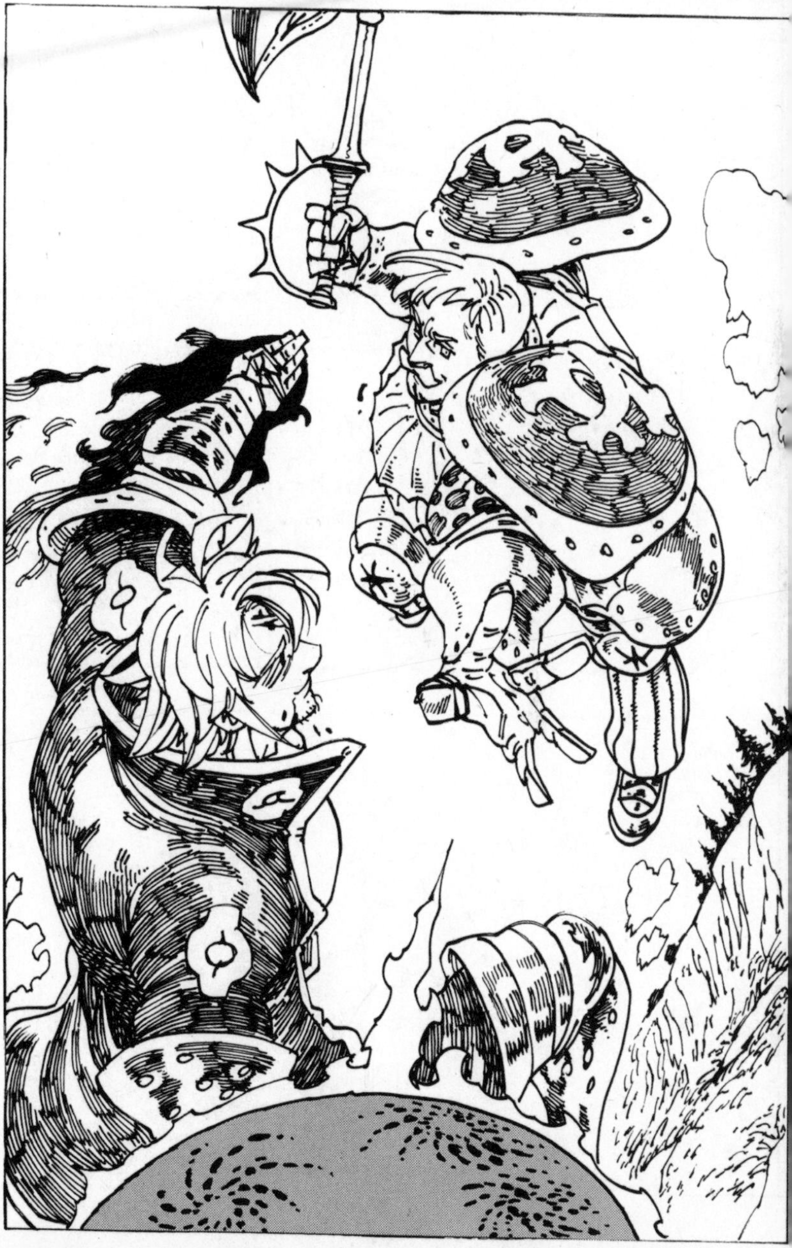

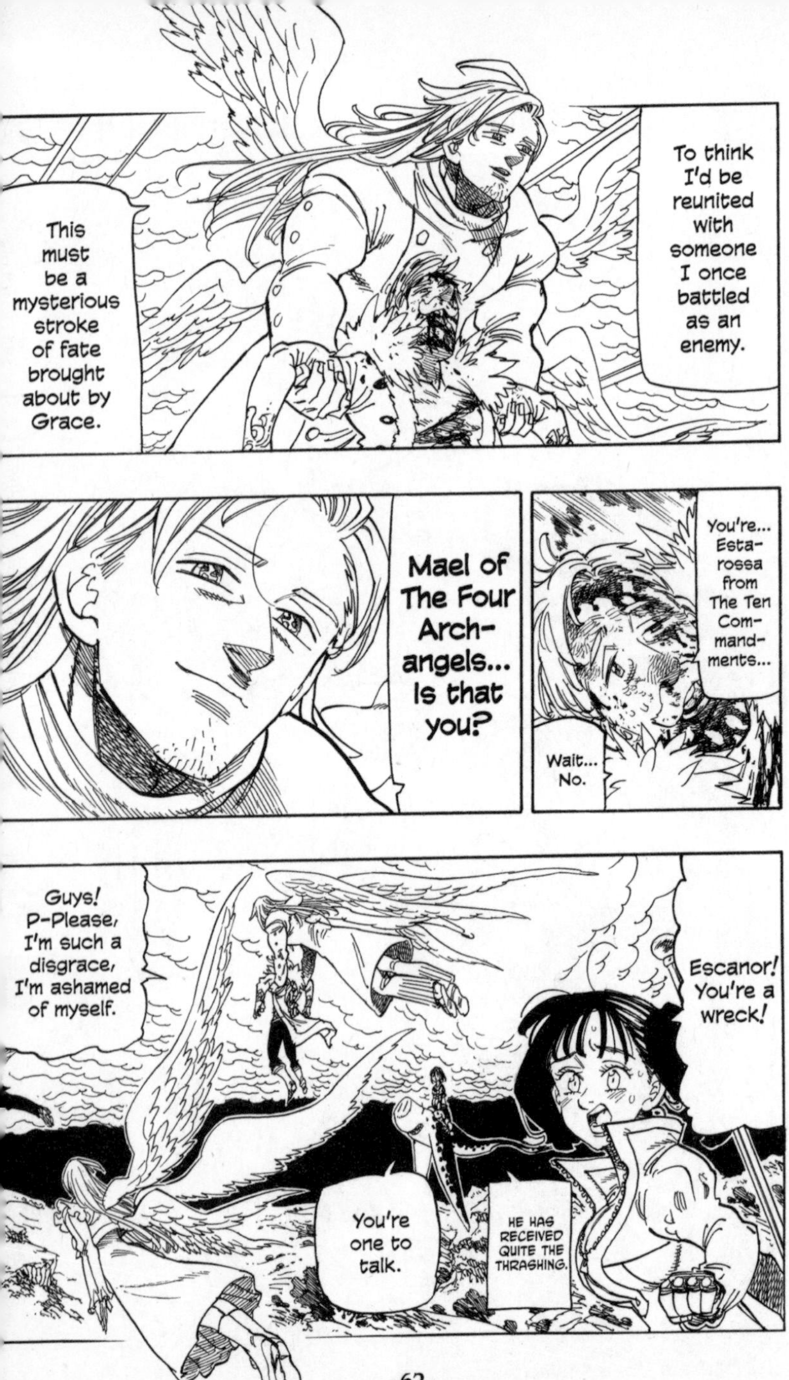
To think I'd be reunited with someone I once battled as an enemy.
This must be a mysterious stroke of fate brought about by Grace.
You're... Estarossa from The Ten Commandments...
Wait... No.
Mael of The Four Archangels... Is that you?
Escanor! You're a wreck!
Guys! P-Please, I'm such a disgrace, I'm ashamed of myself.
HE HAS RECEIVED QUITE THE THRASHING.
You're one to talk.

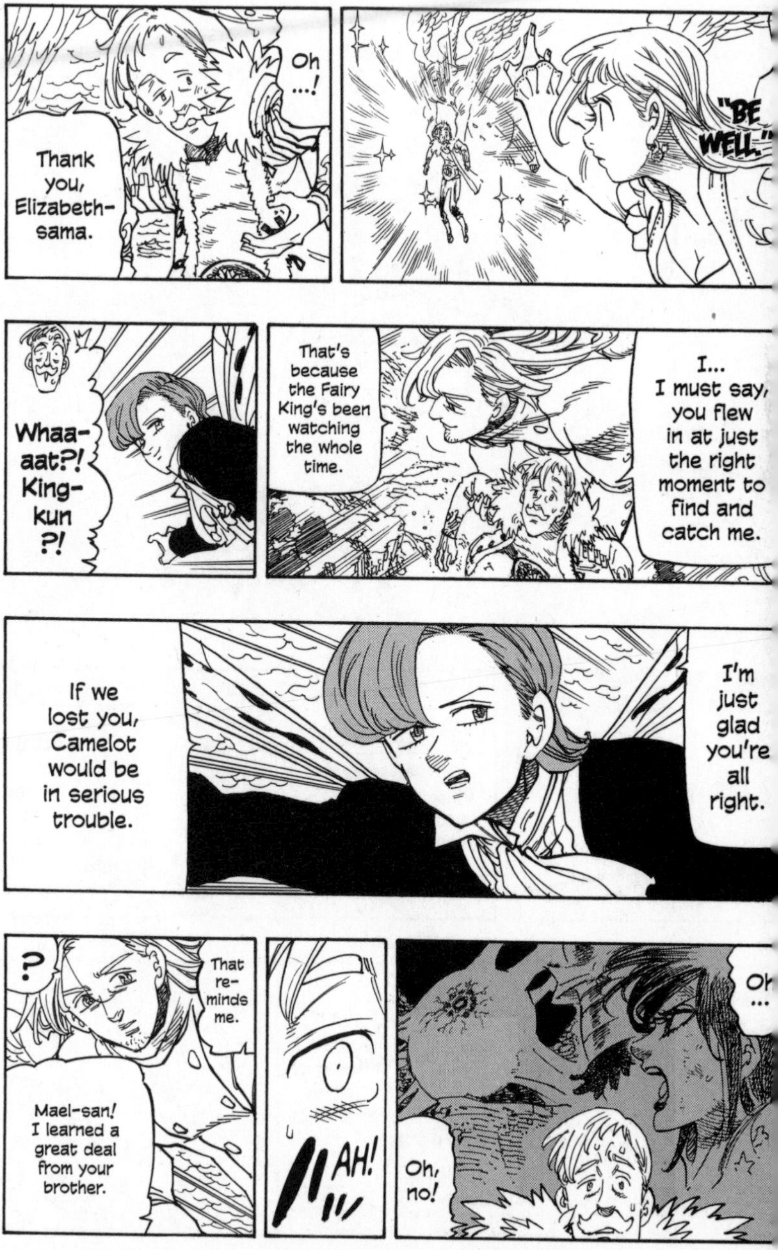
"BE WELL."
Oh ...!
Thank you, Elizabeth-sama.
I... I must say, you flew in at just the right moment to find and catch me.
That's because the Fairy King's been watching the whole time.
Whaaa-aat?! King-kun ?!
I'm just glad you're all right.
If we lost you, Camelot would be in serious trouble.
Oh ...
Oh, no!
AH!
?
That re-minds me.
Mael-san! I learned a great deal from your brother.

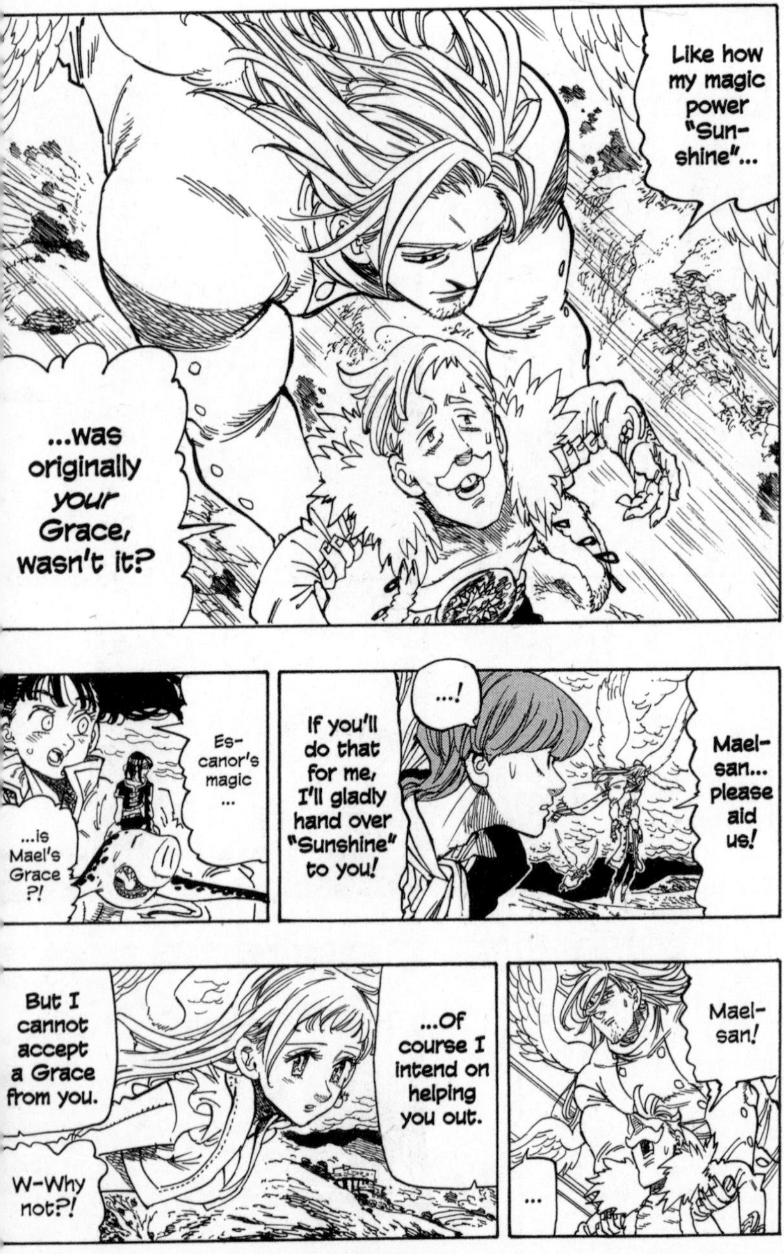
Like how my magic power "Sun-shine"...
...was originally *your* Grace, wasn't it?
Mael-san... please aid us!
...!
If you'll do that for me, I'll gladly hand over "Sunshine" to you!
Es-canor's magic ...
...is Mael's Grace ?!
Mael-san!
...
...Of course I intend on helping you out.
But I cannot accept a Grace from you.
W-Why not?!

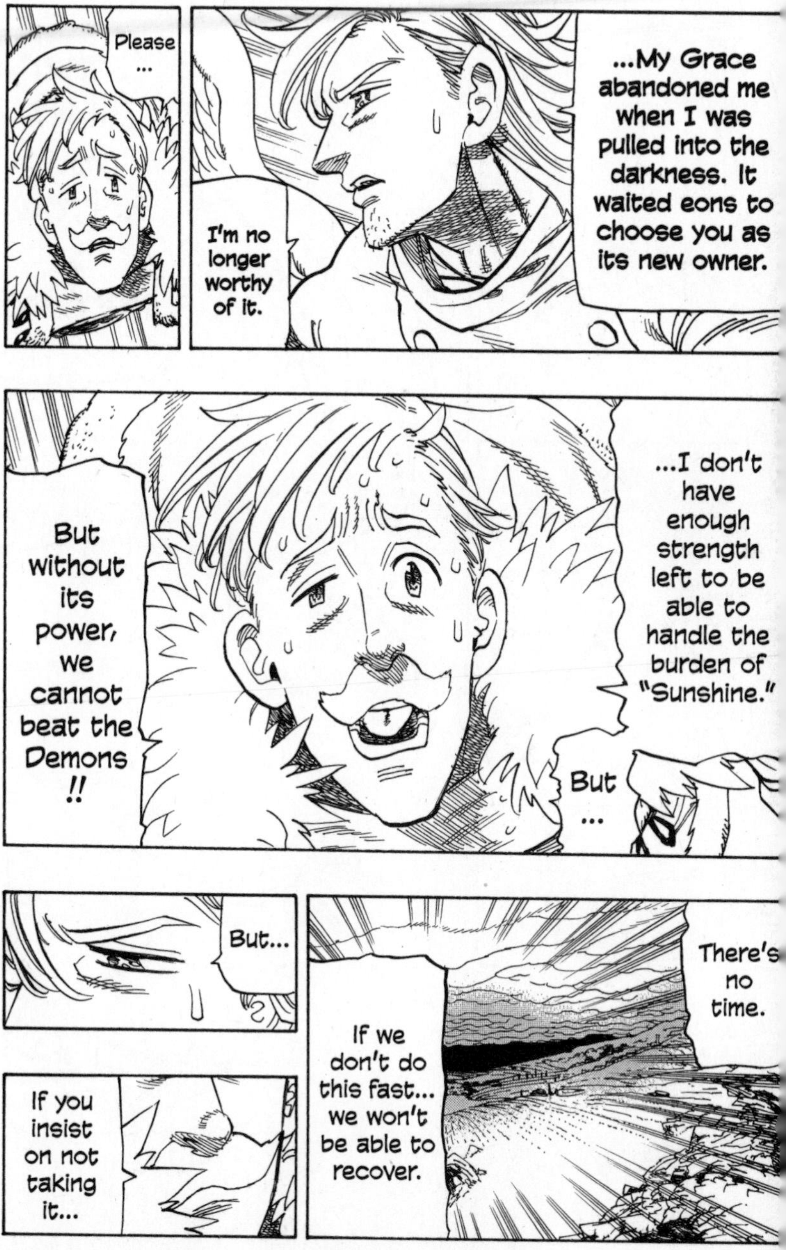
...My Grace abandoned me when I was pulled into the darkness. It waited eons to choose you as its new owner.
I'm no longer worthy of it.
Please ...
...I don't have enough strength left to be able to handle the burden of "Sunshine."
But ...
But without its power, we cannot beat the Demons !!
There's no time.
If we don't do this fast... we won't be able to recover.
But...
If you insist on not taking it...

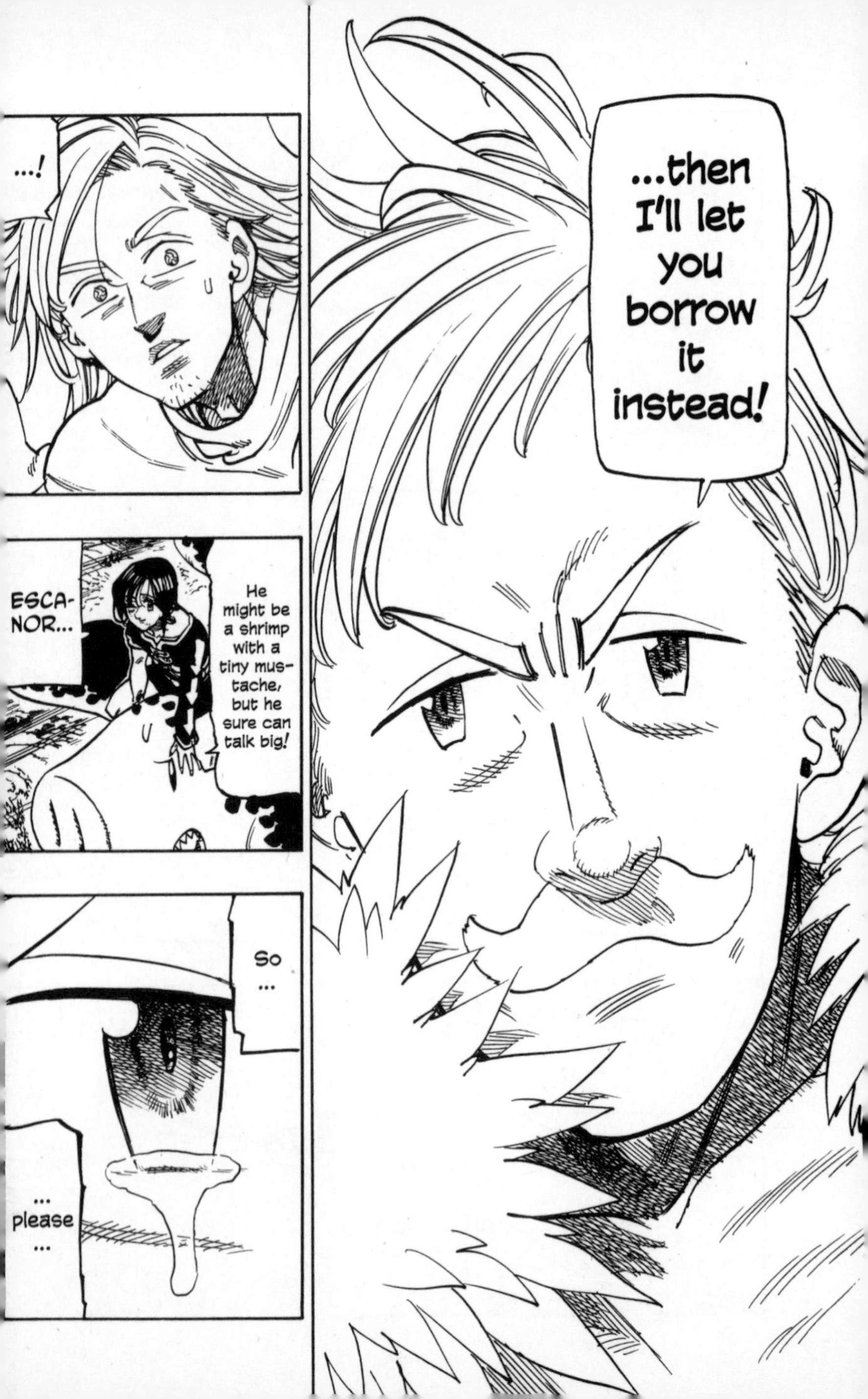
...then I'll let you borrow it instead!
...!
He might be a shrimp with a tiny mus-tache, but he sure can talk big!
ESCA-NOR...
So ...
... please ...

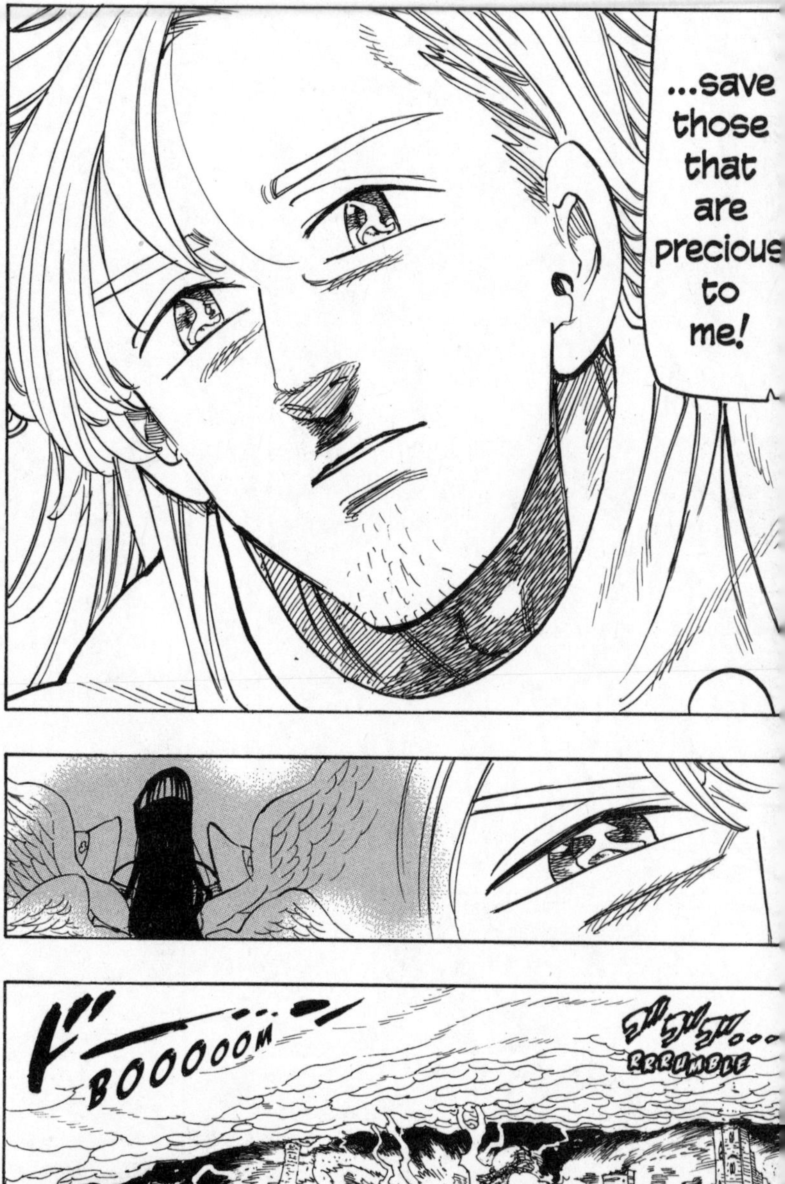
...save those that are precious to me!
BOOOOOM
RRRUMBLE

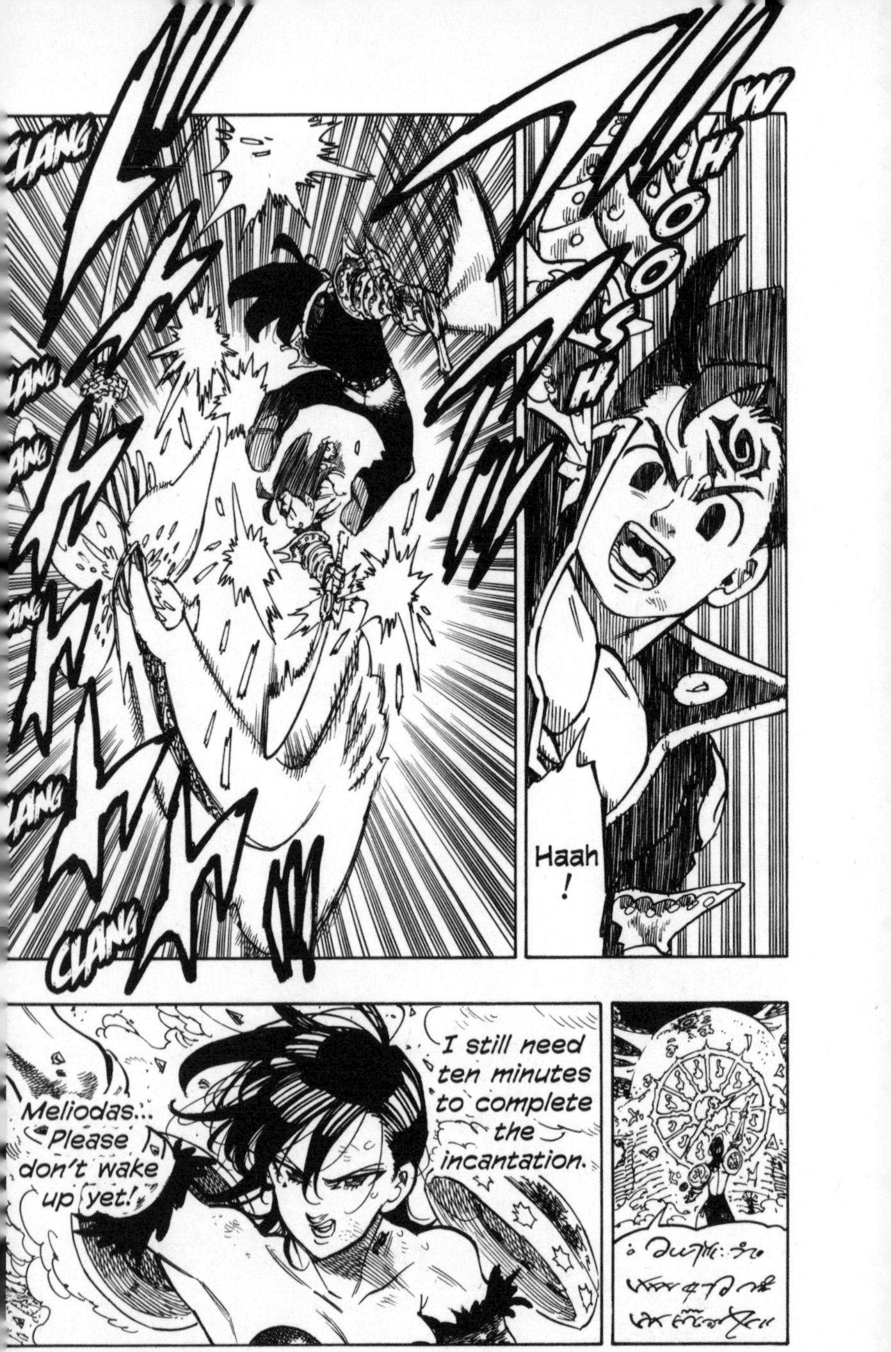
Haah!
CLANG
I still need ten minutes to complete the incantation.
Meliodas... Please don't wake up yet!

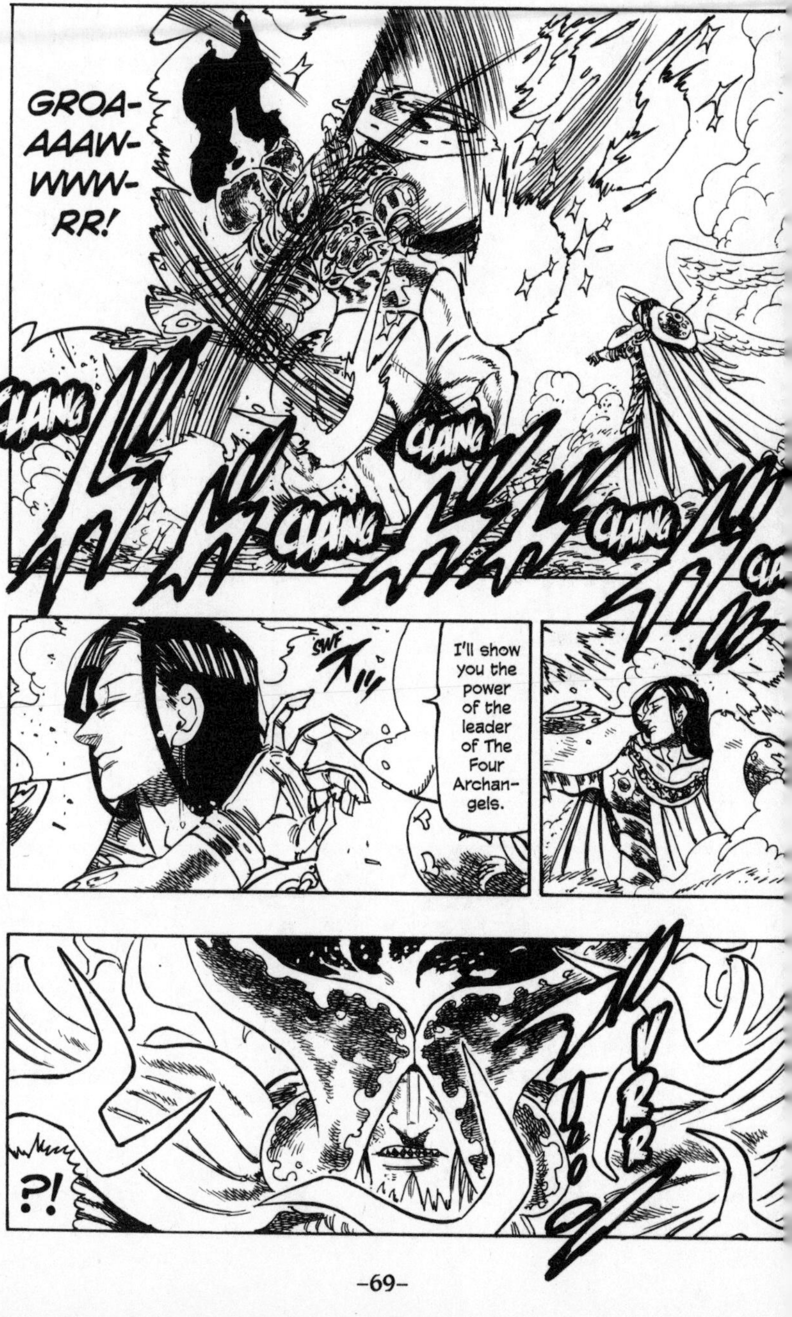
GROA-AAAW-WWW-RR!
CLANG
CLANG
CLANG
CLANG
CLANG
SWF
I'll show you the power of the leader of The Four Archan-gels.
?!

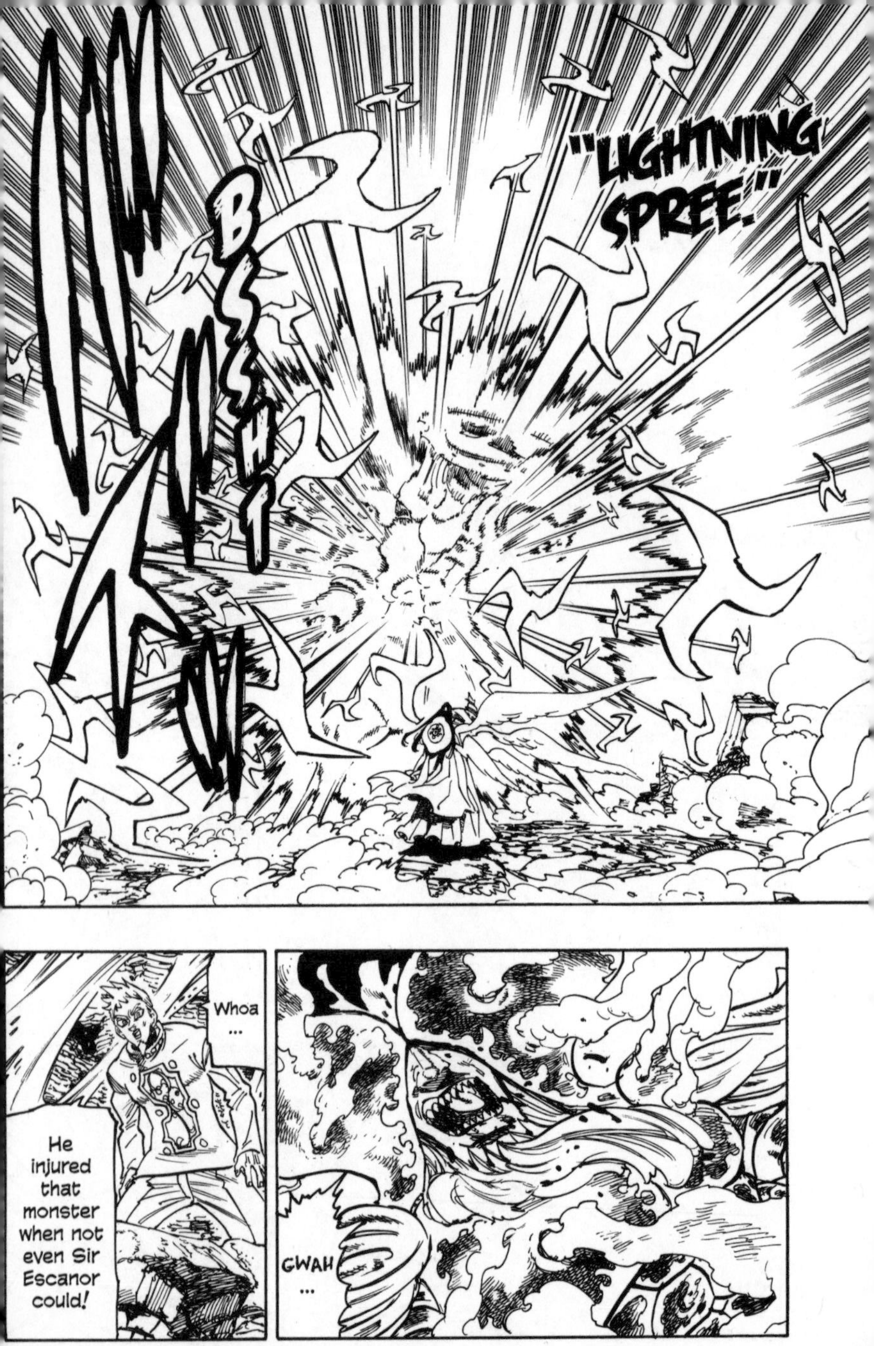
"LIGHTNING SPREE."
GWAH ...
Whoa ...
He injured that monster when not even Sir Escanor could!

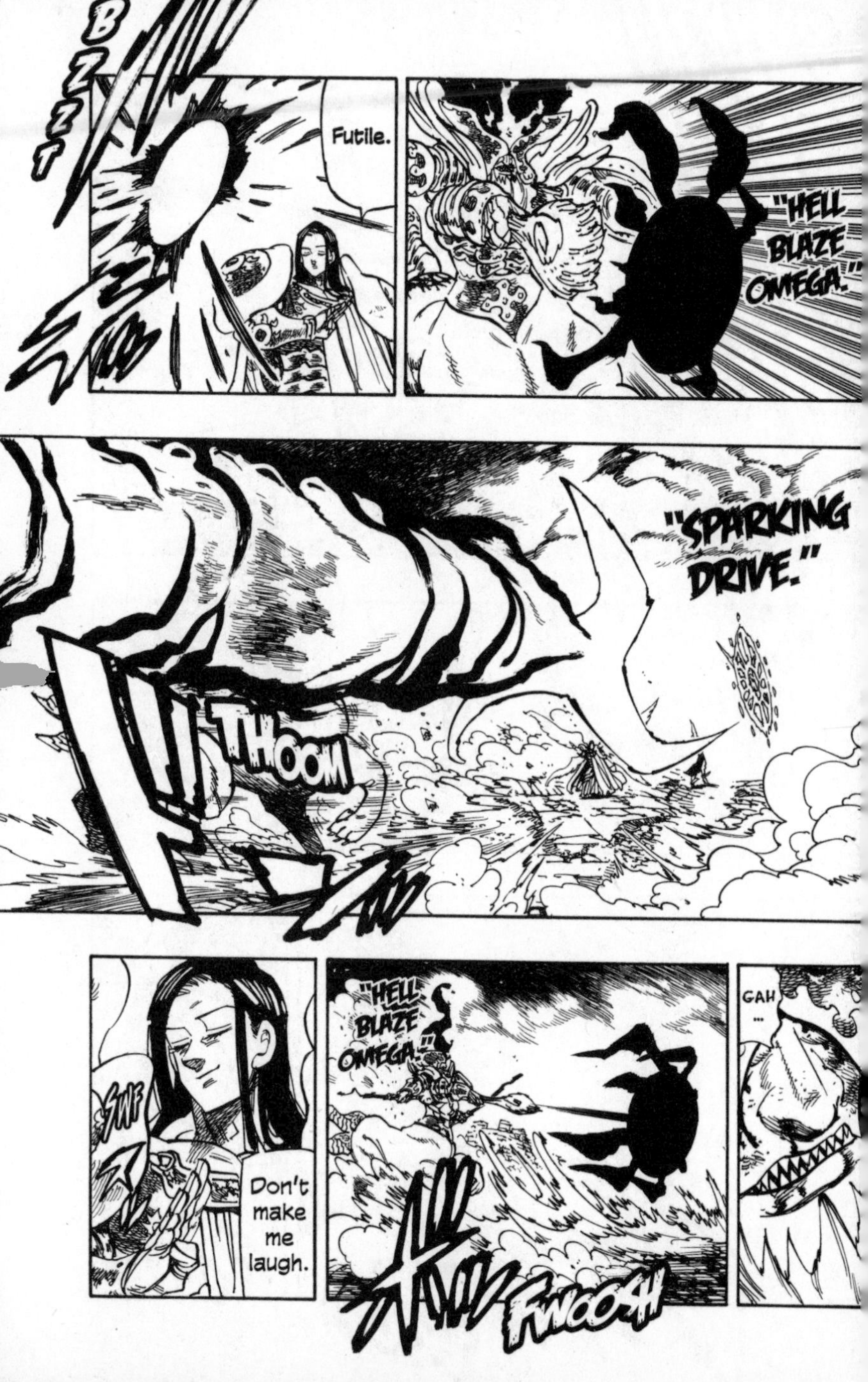
"HELL BLAZE OMEGA."
Futile.
BZZZT
"SPARKING DRIVE."
THOOM
GAH...
"HELL BLAZE OMEGA!!"
FWOOSH
SWF
Don't make me laugh.

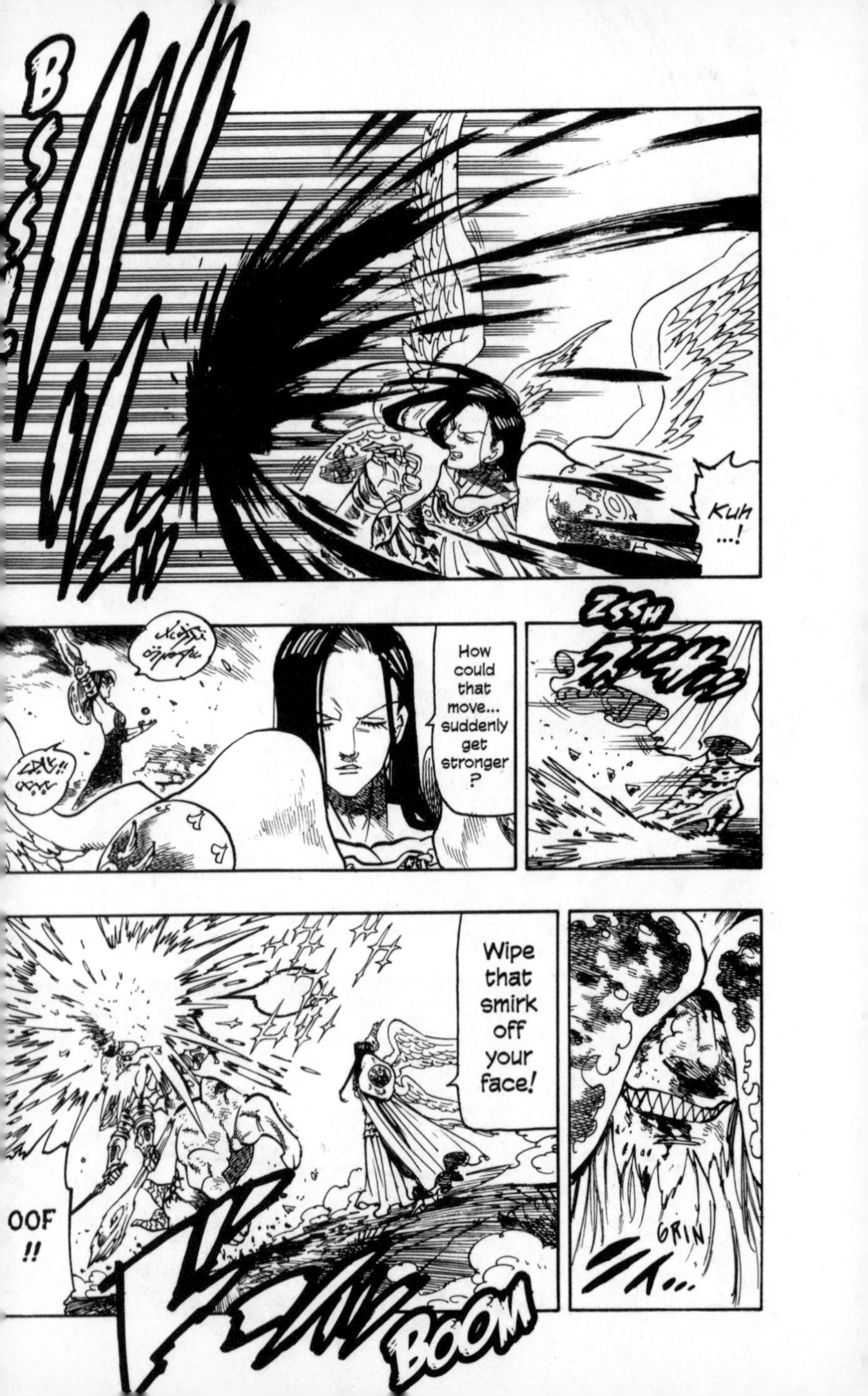
Kuh ...!
ZSSH
How could that move... suddenly get stronger ?
GRIN
Wipe that smirk off your face!
OOF !!
BOOM

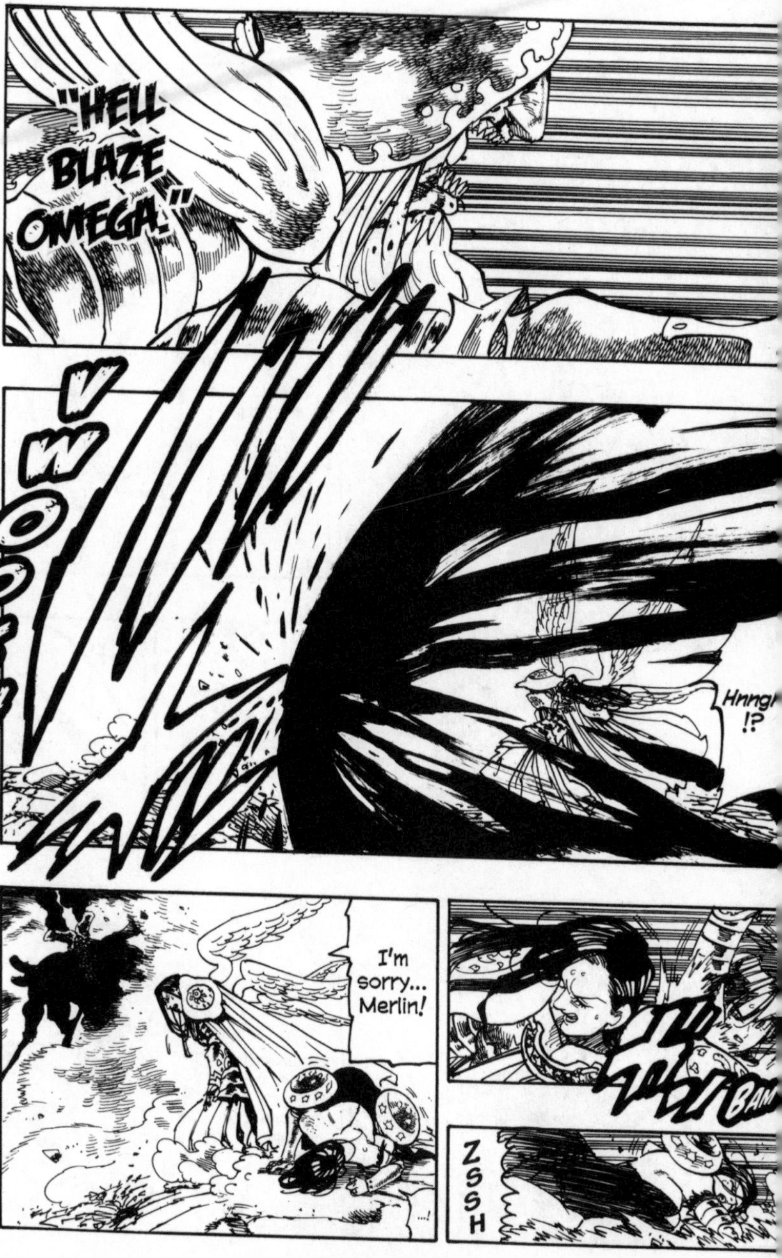
"HELL BLAZE OMEGA!"
VWOOOOSH
Hnng
!?
BAM
ZSSH
I'm sorry... Merlin!
...!

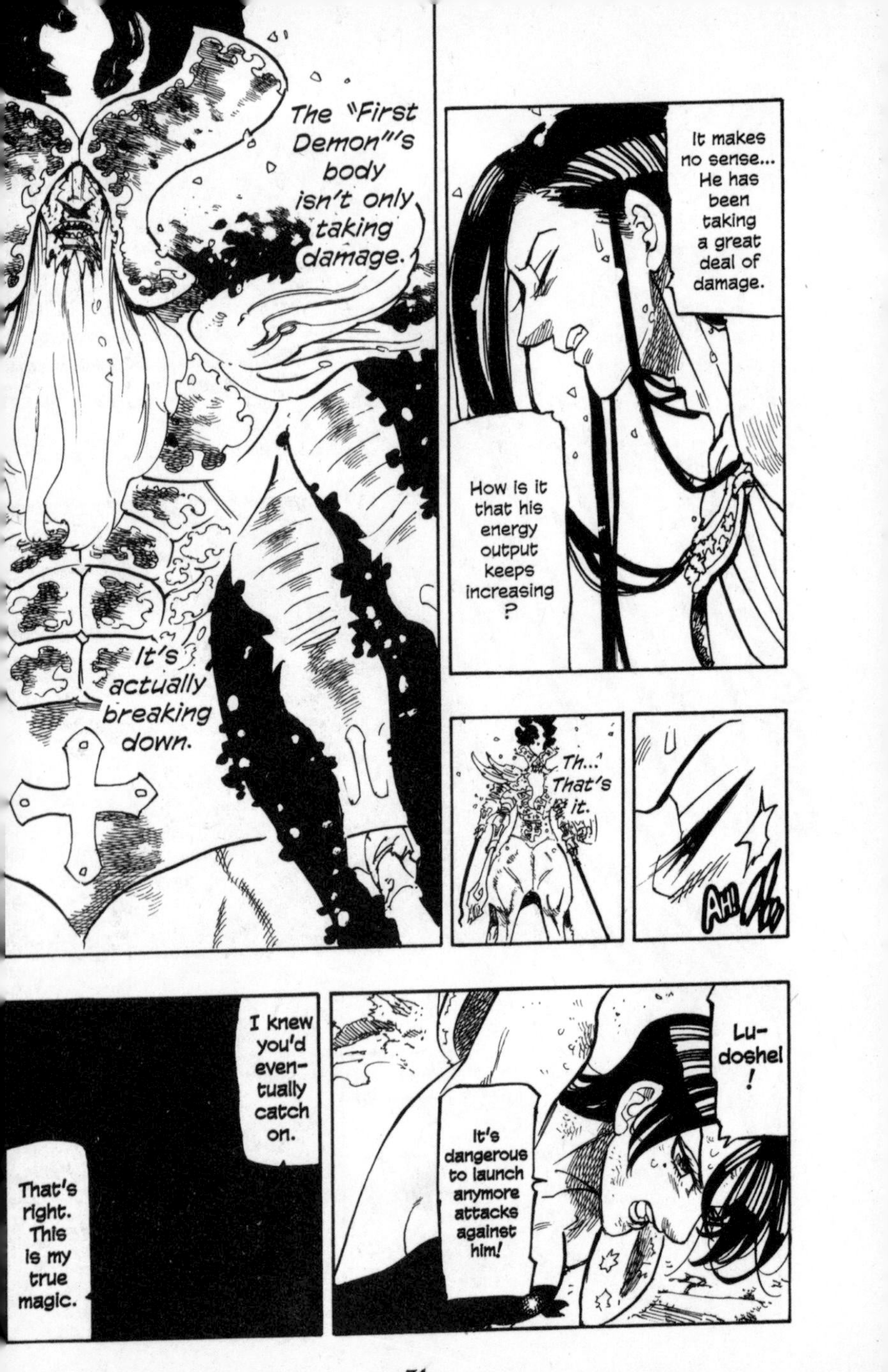
It makes no sense... He has been taking a great deal of damage.
How is it that his energy output keeps increasing?
AH!
Th... That's it.
The "First Demon"'s body isn't only taking damage.
It's actually breaking down.
Ludoshel!
It's dangerous to launch anymore attacks against him!
I knew you'd eventually catch on.
That's right. This is my true magic.

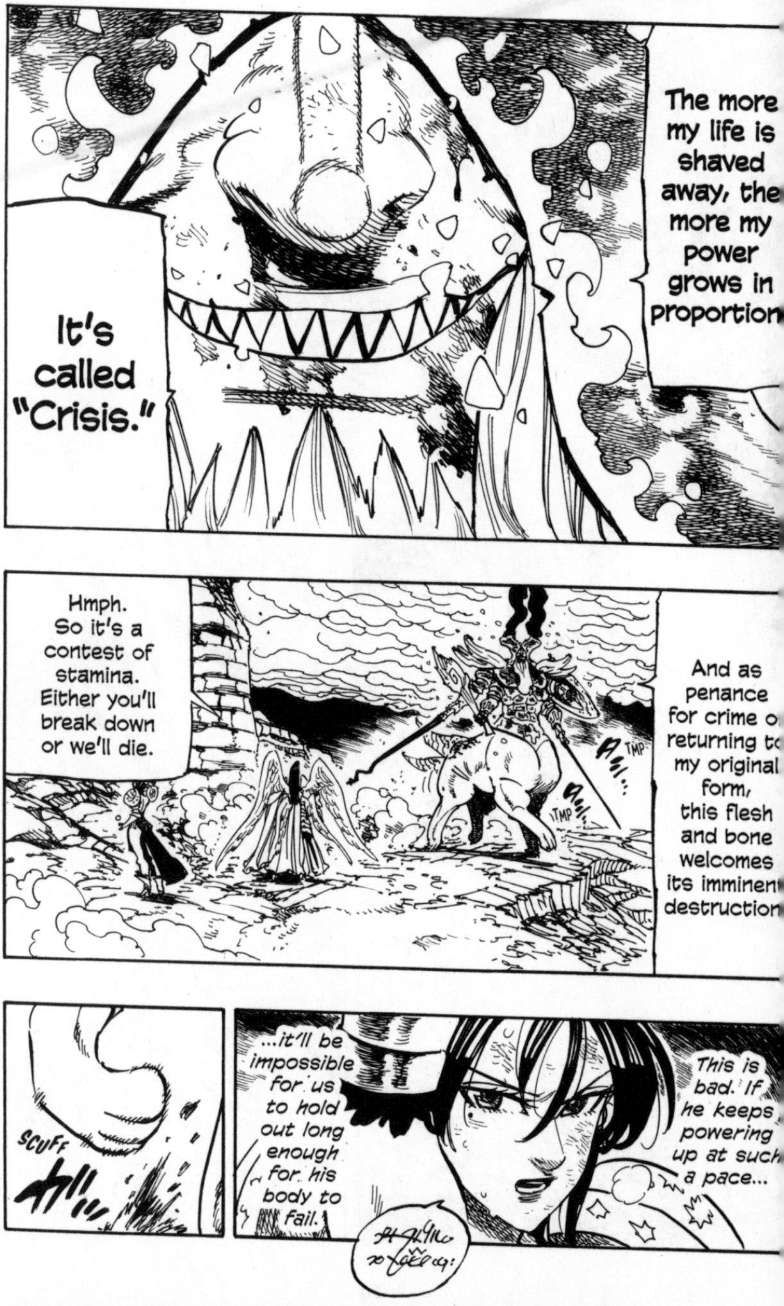
The more my life is shaved away, the more my power grows in proportion
It's called "Crisis."
And as penance for crime o returning t my original form, this flesh and bone welcomes its imminen destruction
TMP
TMP
Hmph. So it's a contest of stamina. Either you'll break down or we'll die.
This is bad. If he keeps powering up at such a pace...
...it'll be impossible for us to hold out long enough for his body to fail.
SCUFF

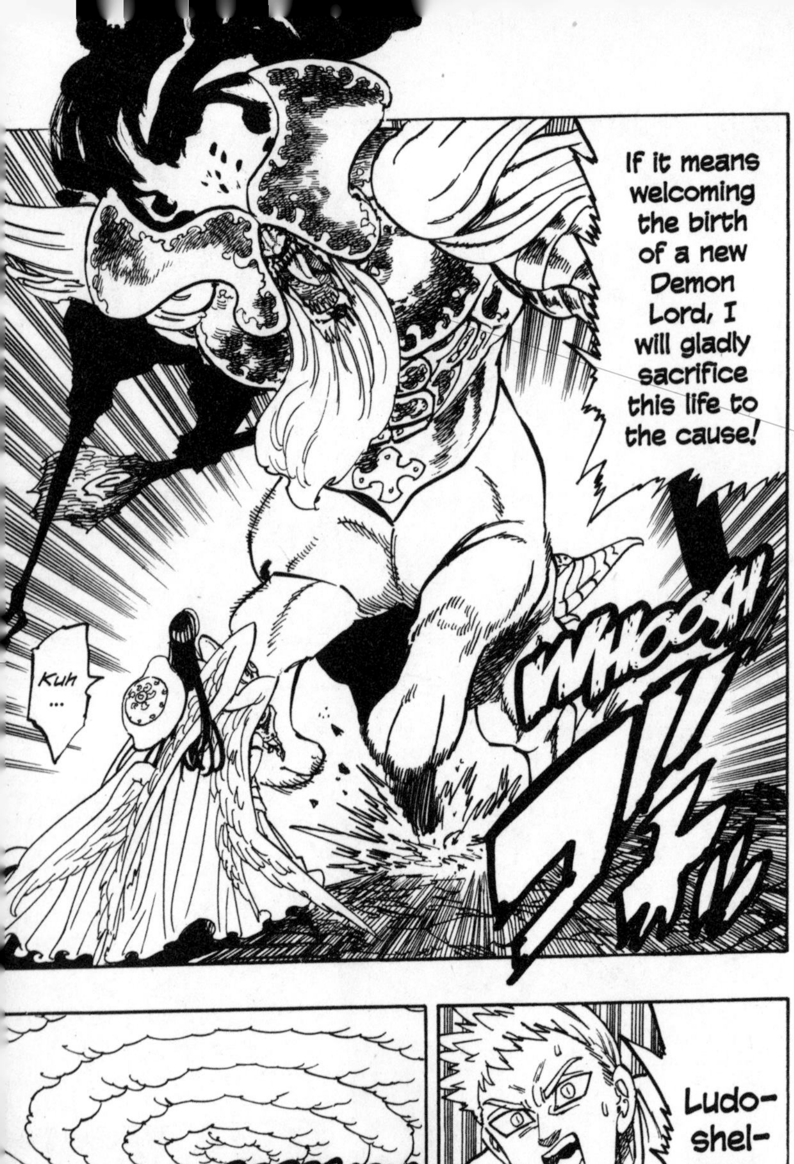
If it means welcoming the birth of a new Demon Lord, I will gladly sacrifice this life to the cause!
Kuh ...
WHOOSH
Ludo-shel-sama-aaa!!
RRRRUMBLE

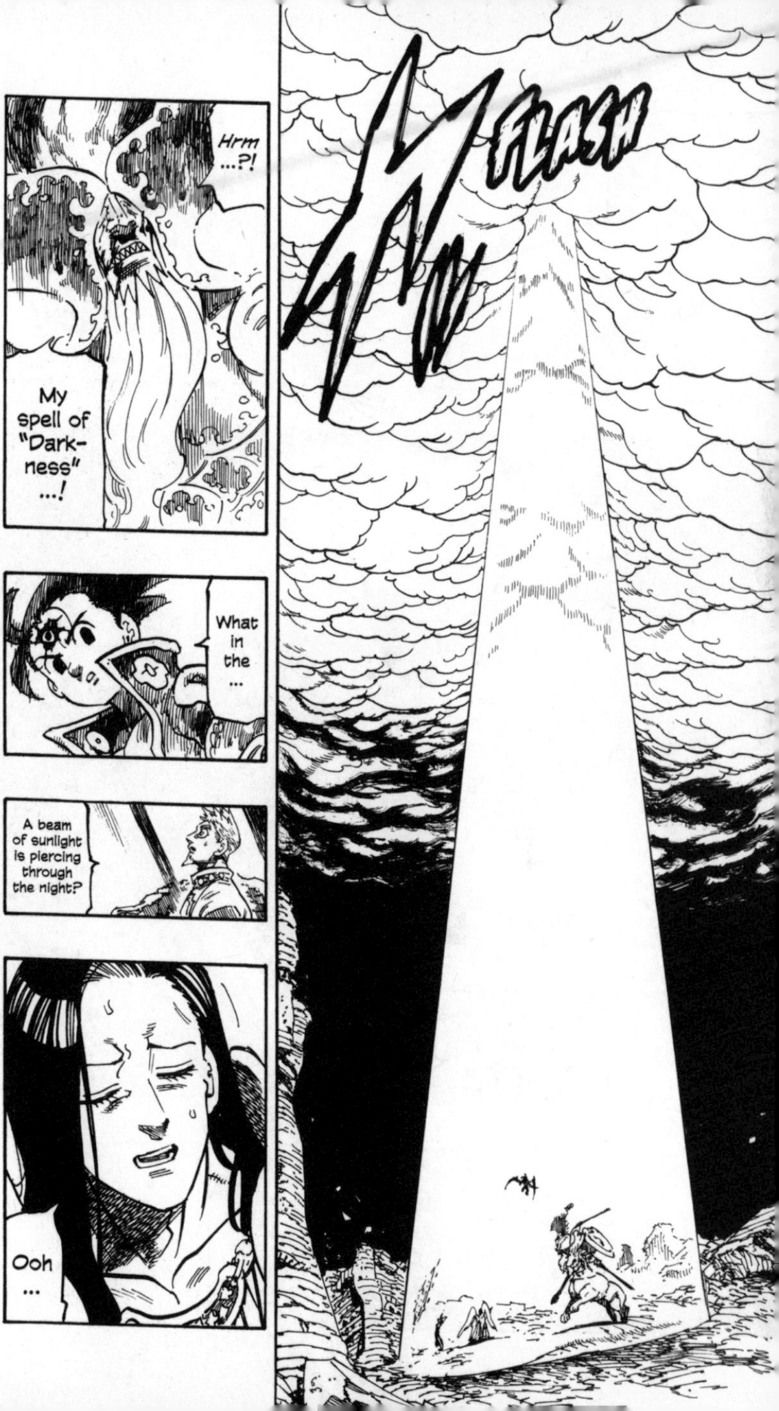
FLASH
Hrm ...?!
My spell of "Darkness" ...!
What in the ...
A beam of sunlight is piercing through the night?
Ooh ...

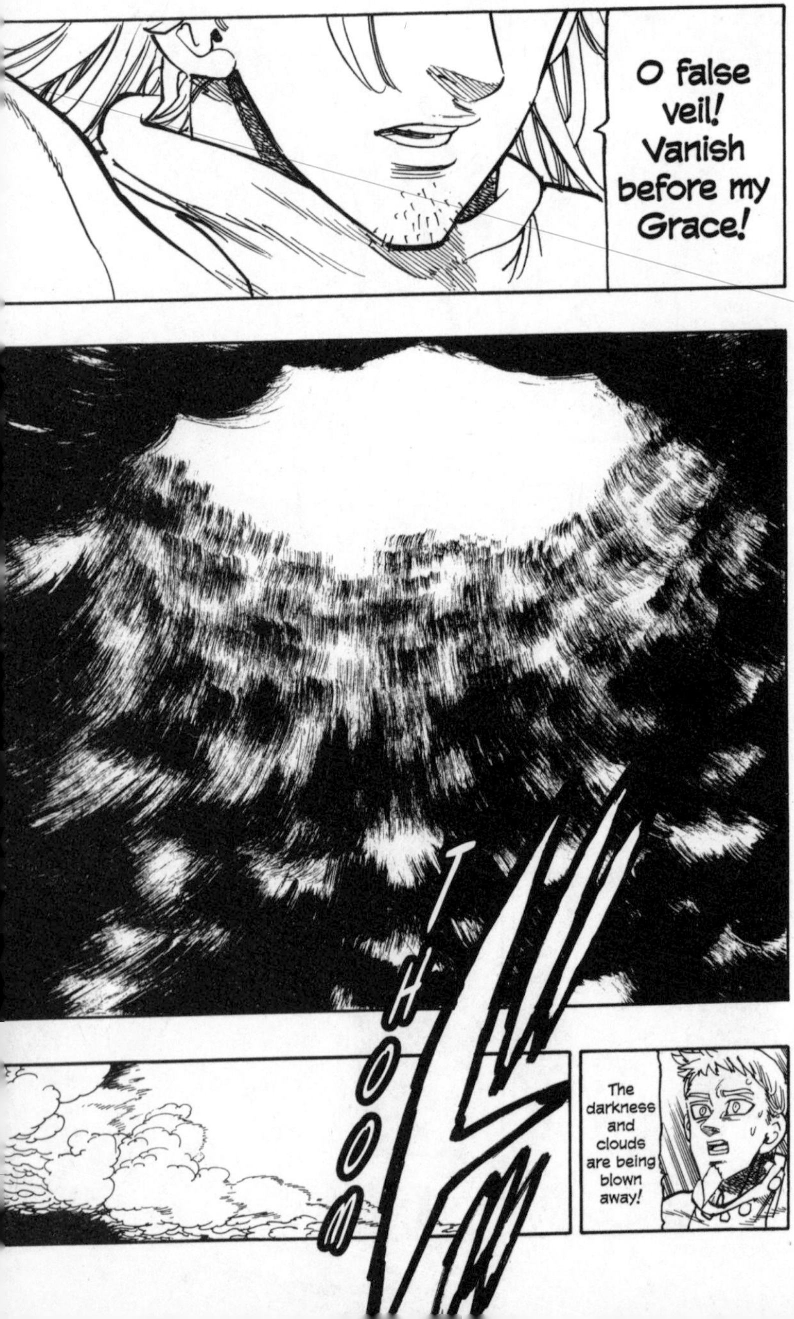
O false veil! Vanish before my Grace!
THOOM
The darkness and clouds are being blown away!

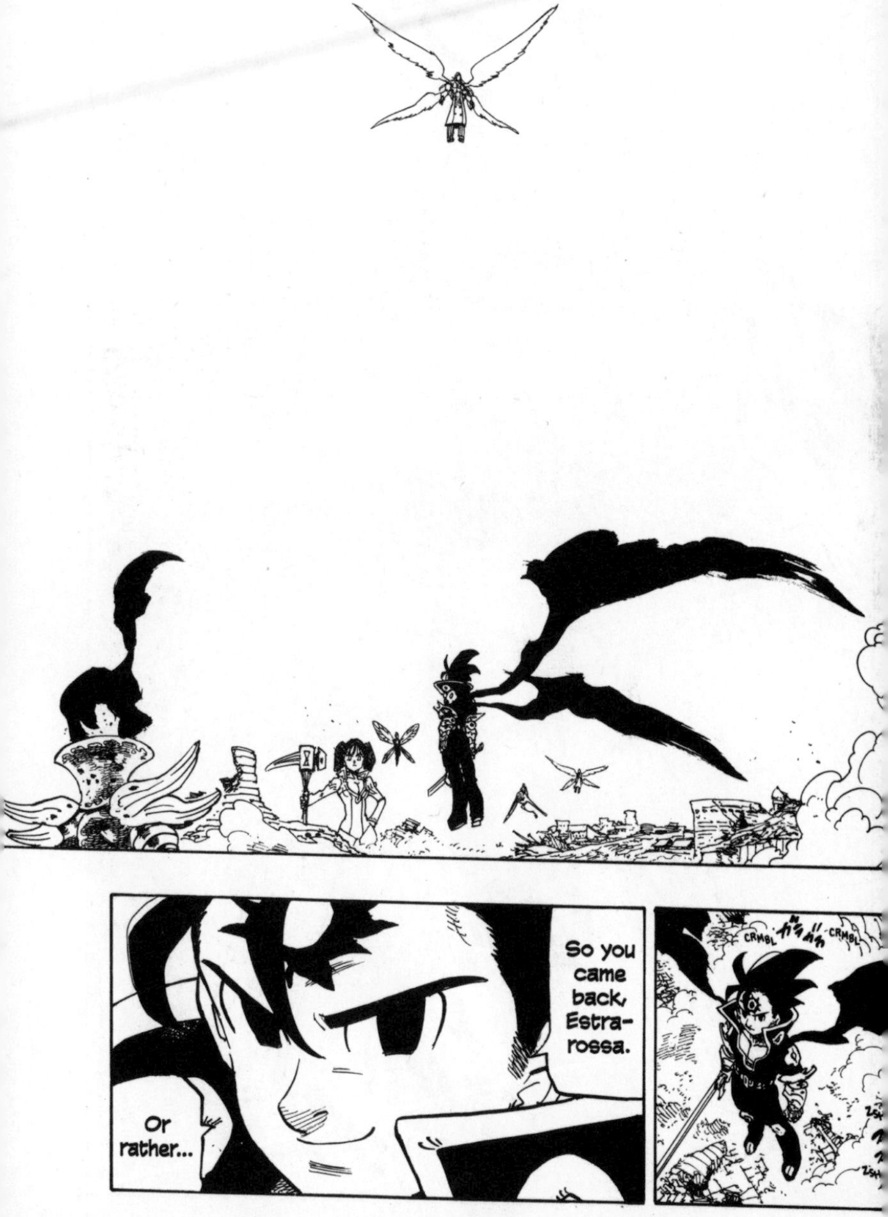
CRMBL
CRMBL
So you came back, Estra-rossa.
Or rather...

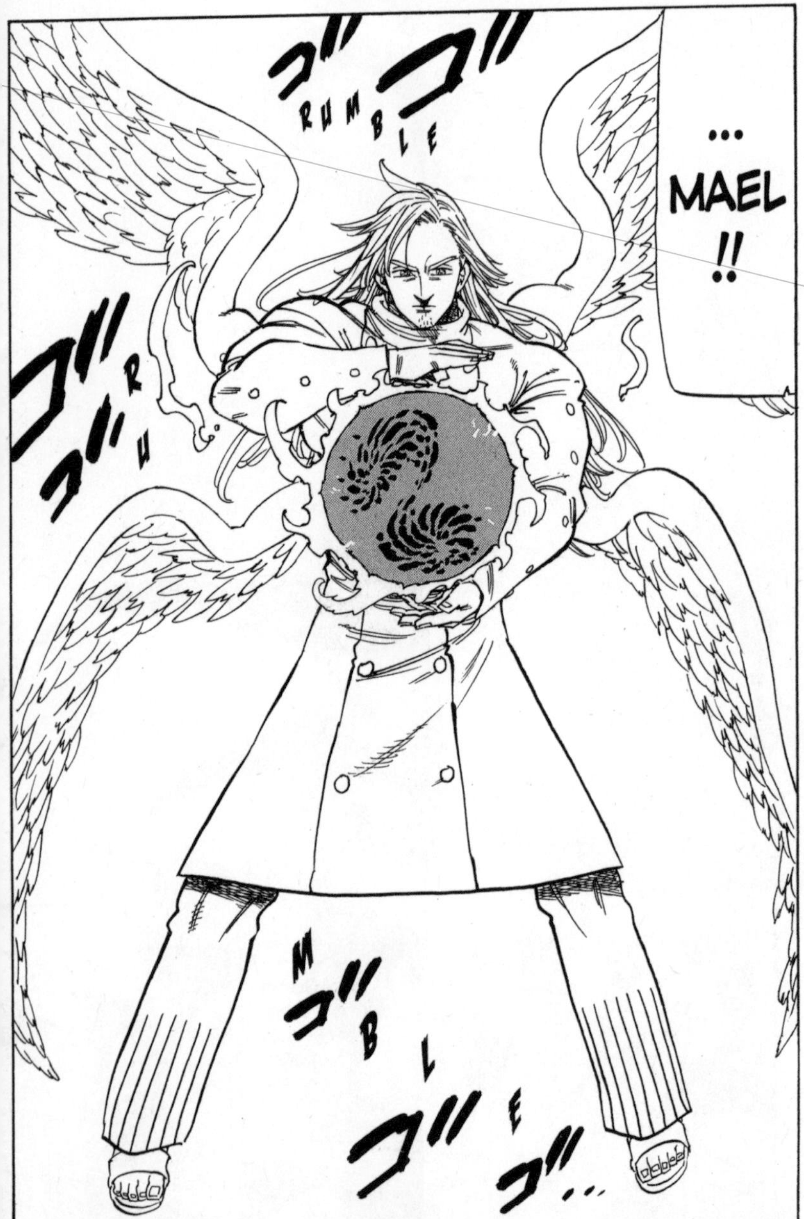
... MAEL !!
RUMBLE
RU
MBLE
ゴゴゴゴゴゴ...

Chapter 298 - Mael vs. Zeldris

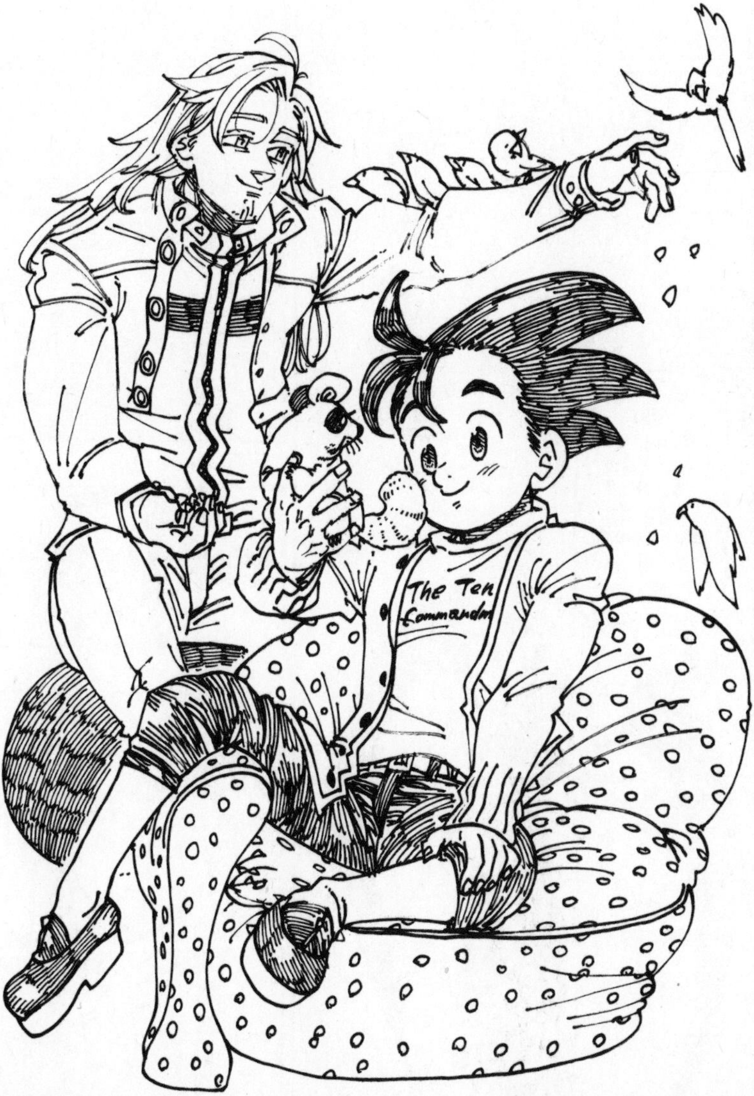
The Ten
Commandm

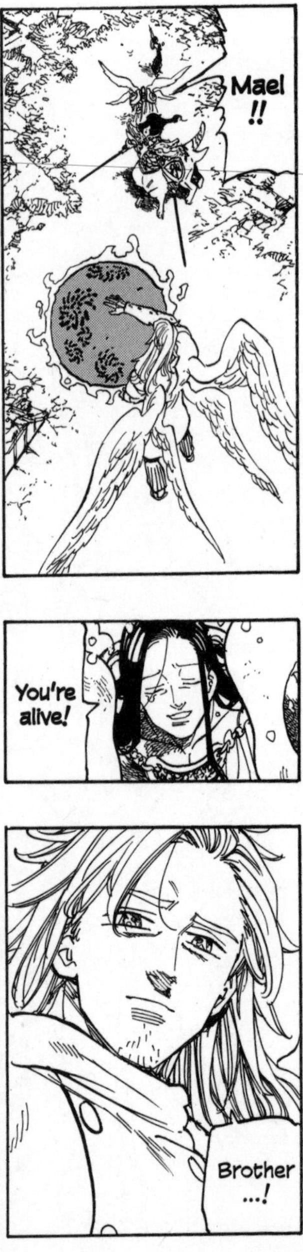
Mael !!
You're alive!
Brother ...!

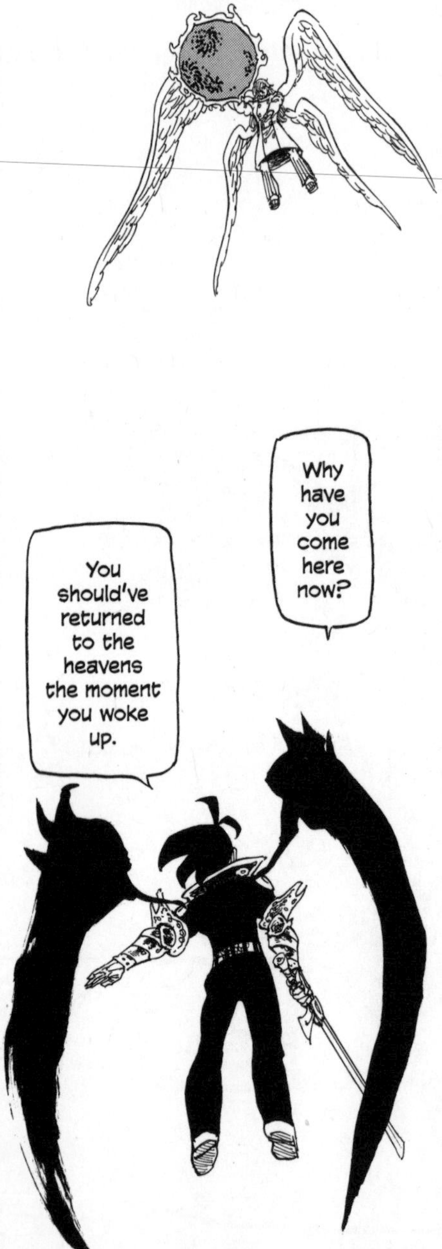
Why have you come here now?
You should've returned to the heavens the moment you woke up.

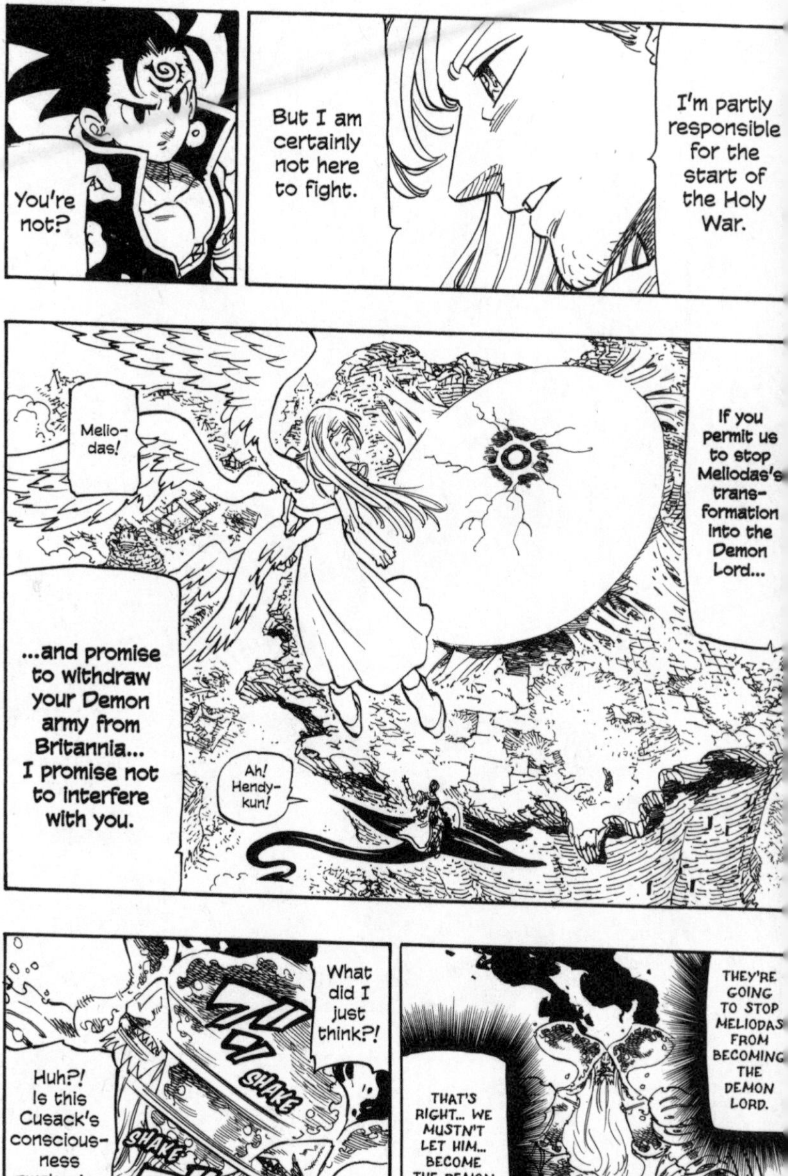
I'm partly responsible for the start of the Holy War.
But I am certainly not here to fight.
You're not?
If you permit us to stop Meliodas's transformation into the Demon Lord...
Melio-das!
...and promise to withdraw your Demon army from Britannia... I promise not to interfere with you.
Ah! Hendy-kun!
THEY'RE GOING TO STOP MELIODAS FROM BECOMING THE DEMON LORD.
THAT'S RIGHT... WE MUSTN'T LET HIM... BECOME THE DEMON LORD.
What did I just think?!
SHAKE
Huh?! Is this Cusack's conscious-ness awakening?!
SHAKE

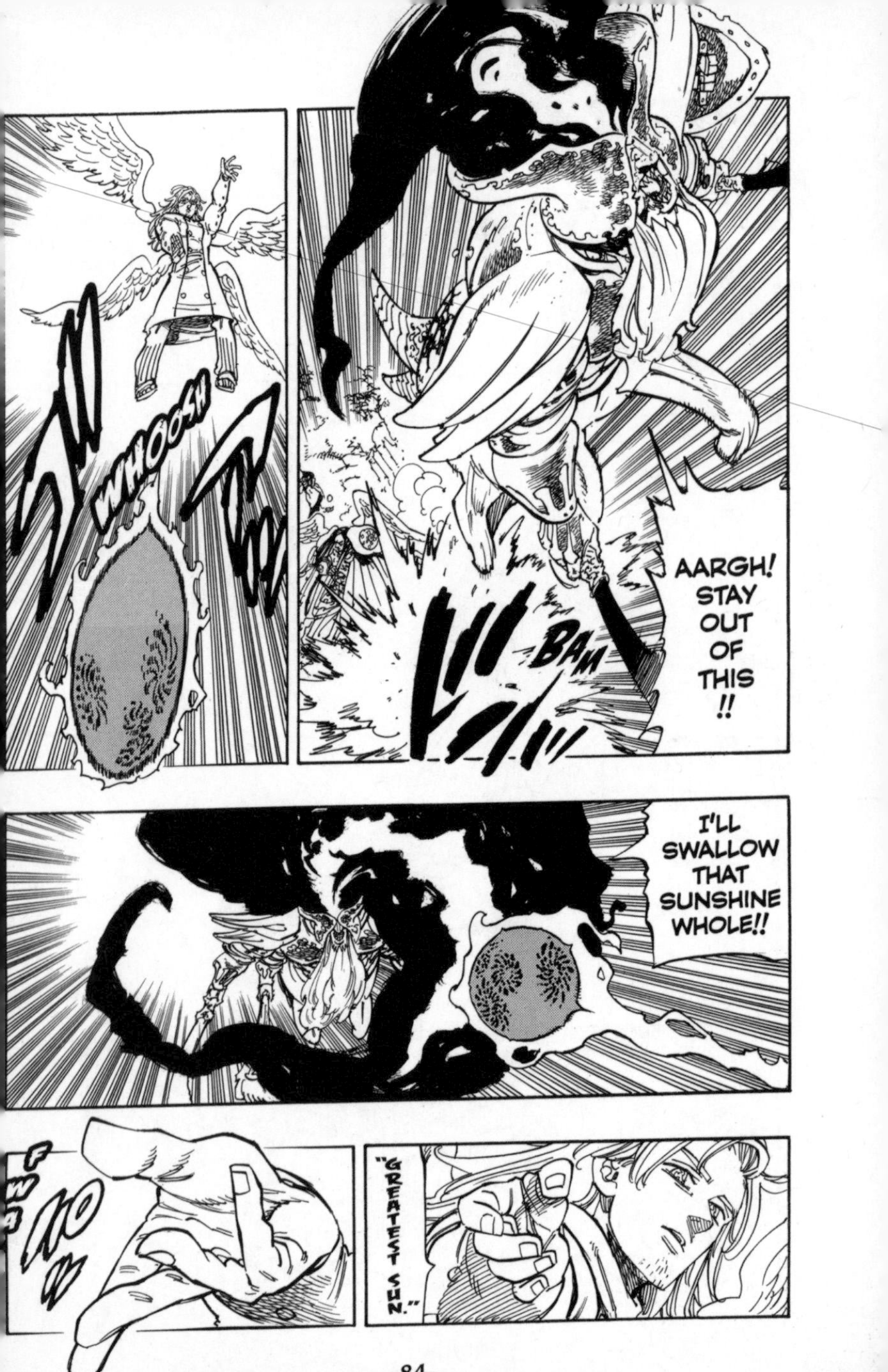
AARGH! STAY OUT OF THIS!!
BAM
WHOOSH
I'LL SWALLOW THAT SUNSHINE WHOLE!!
"GREATEST SUN."
FWA

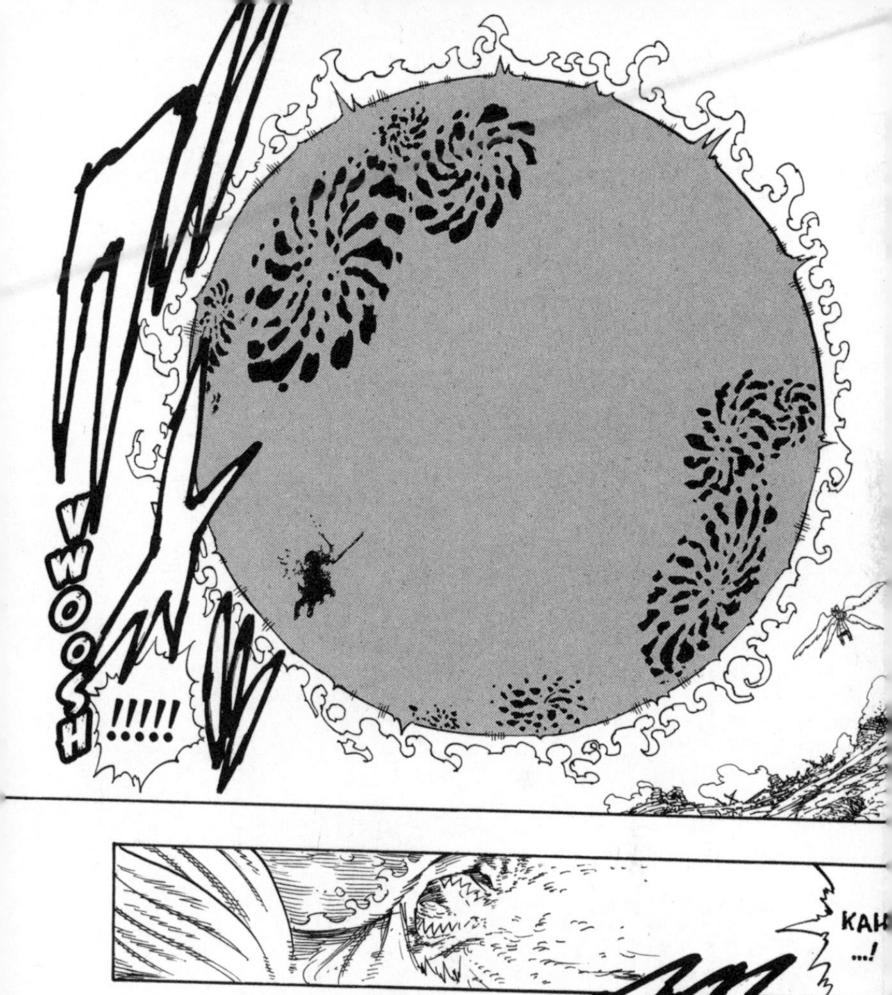
VWOOSH!!!!!
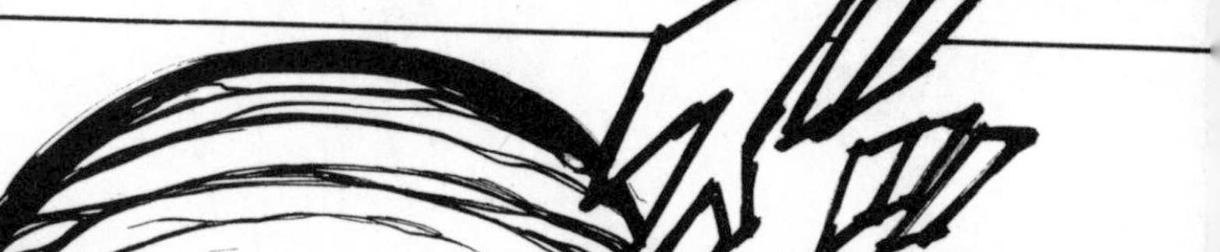
KAH ...!
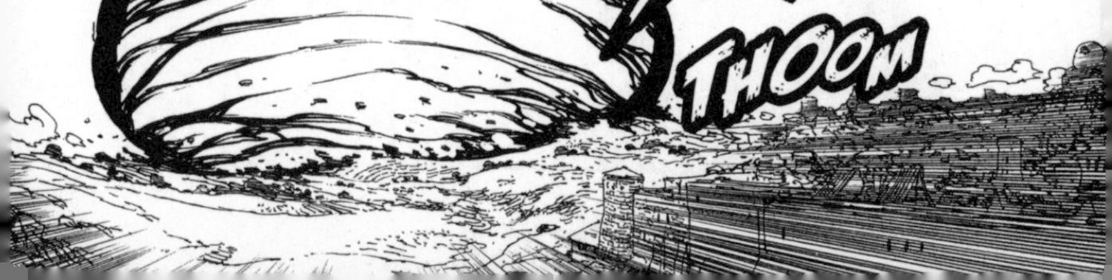
THOOM

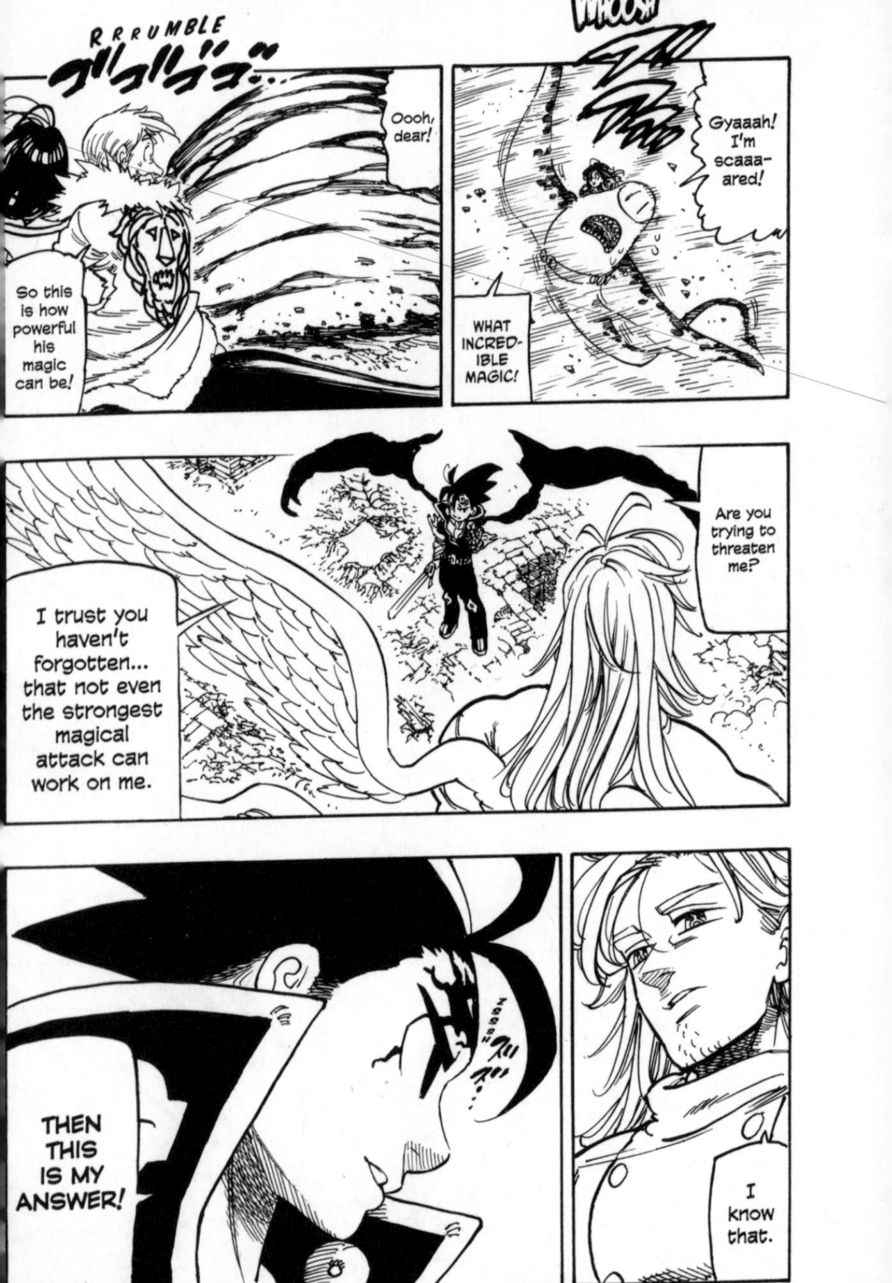
WHOOSH
Gyaaah! I'm scaaa-ared!
WHAT INCRED-IBLE MAGIC!
RRRUMBLE
Oooh, dear!
So this is how powerful his magic can be!
Are you trying to threaten me?
I trust you haven't forgotten... that not even the strongest magical attack can work on me.
I know that.
THEN THIS IS MY ANSWER!

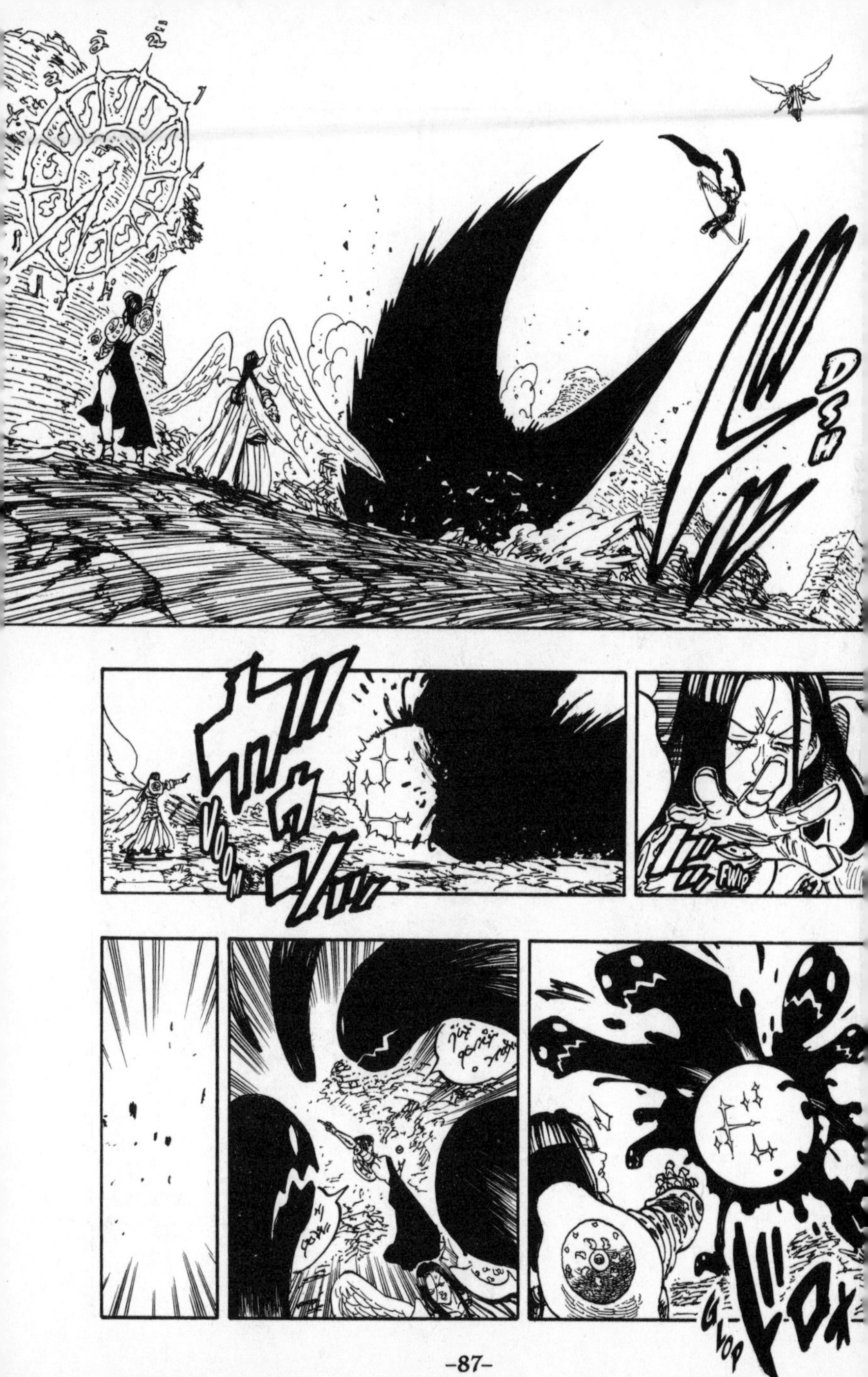

VOOM
FWIP

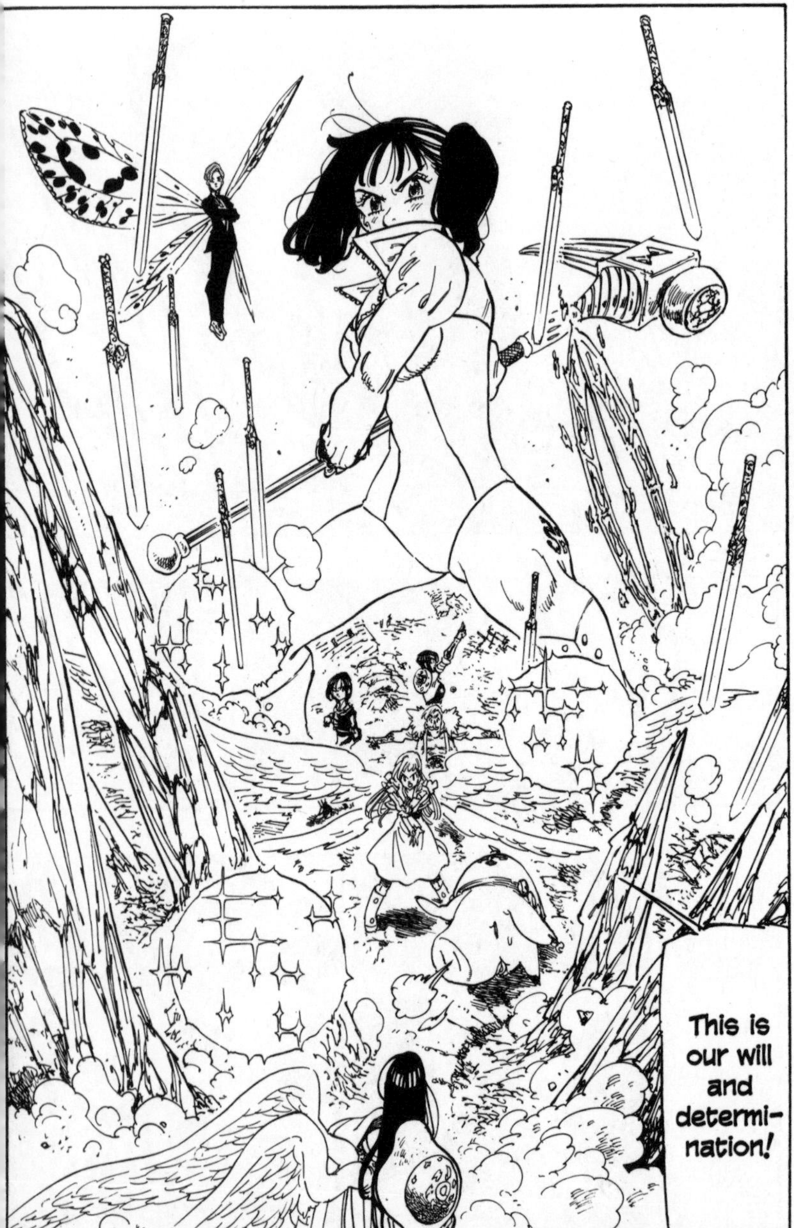
This is our will and determi-nation!

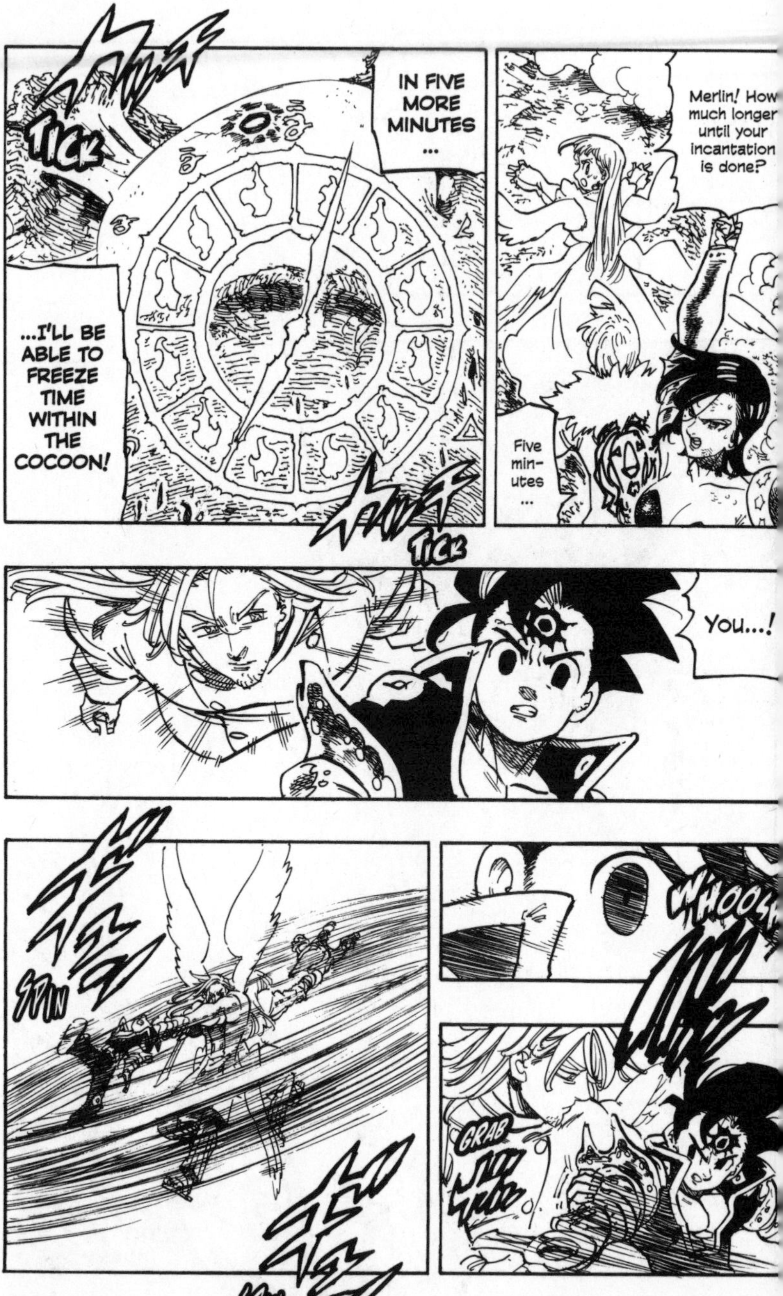
Merlin! How much longer until your incantation is done?
Five minutes ...
IN FIVE MORE MINUTES ...
TICK
...I'LL BE ABLE TO FREEZE TIME WITHIN THE COCOON!
TICK
You...!
WHOO
GRAB
SPIN
SPIN

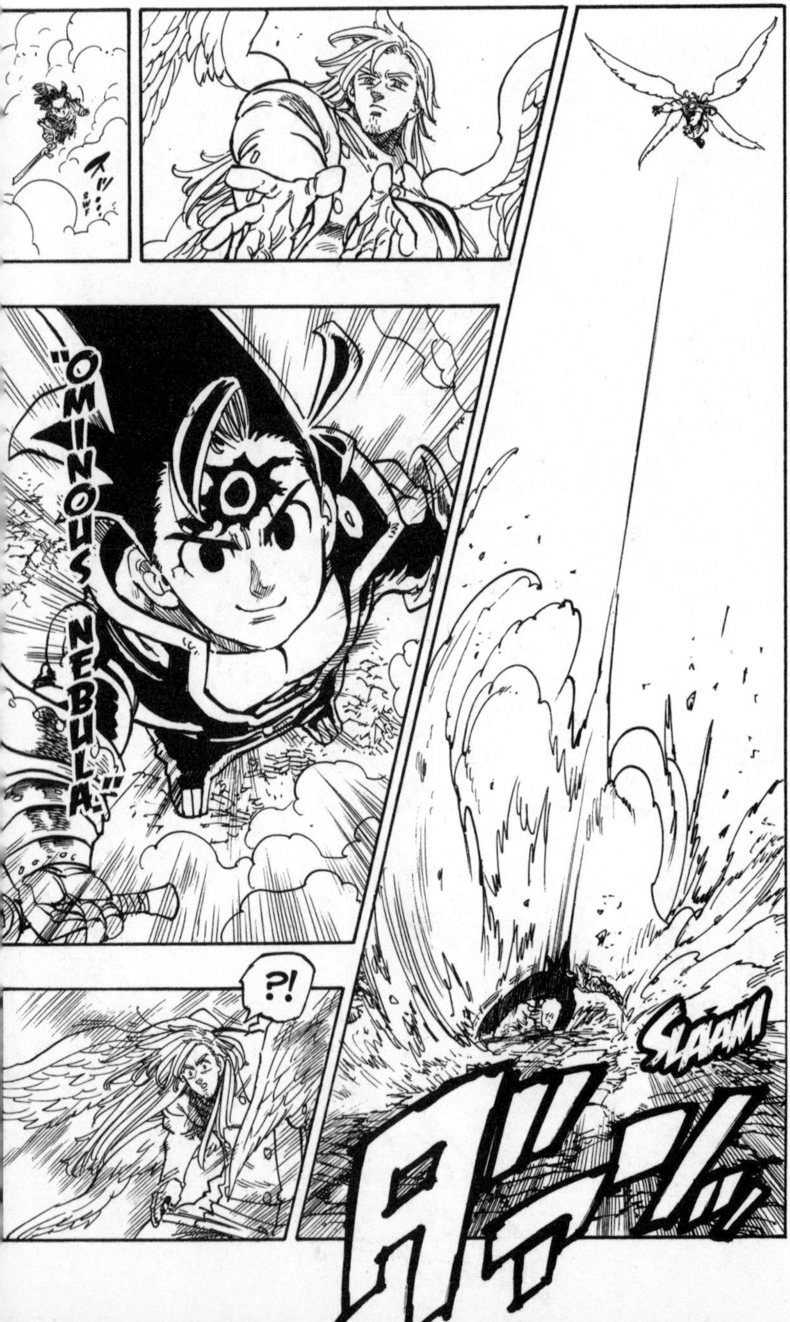
SLAAM
ダン!!
スッ…
SWF
"OMINOUS NEBULA."
?!

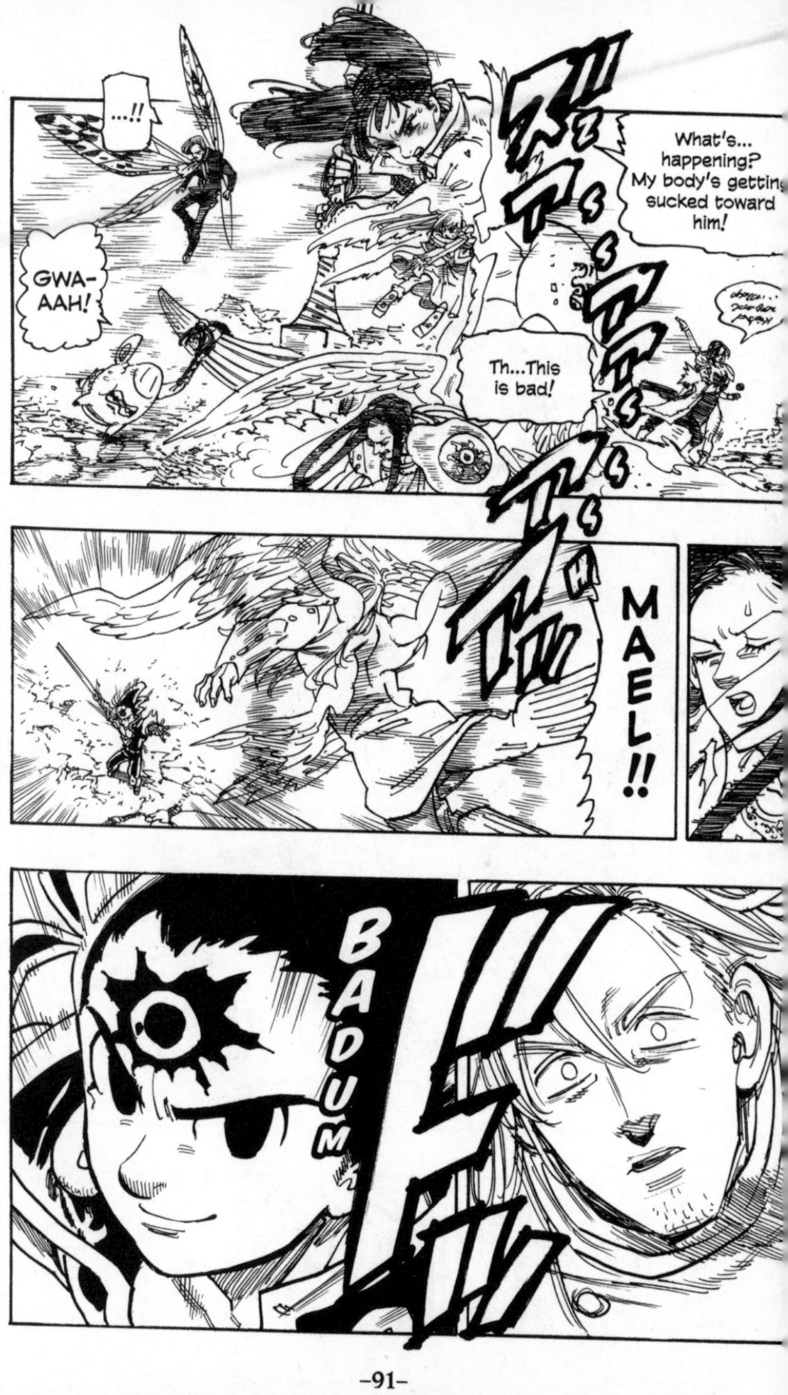
What's... happening? My body's getting sucked toward him!
Th...This is bad!
...!!
GWA-AAH!
MAEL!!
BADUM

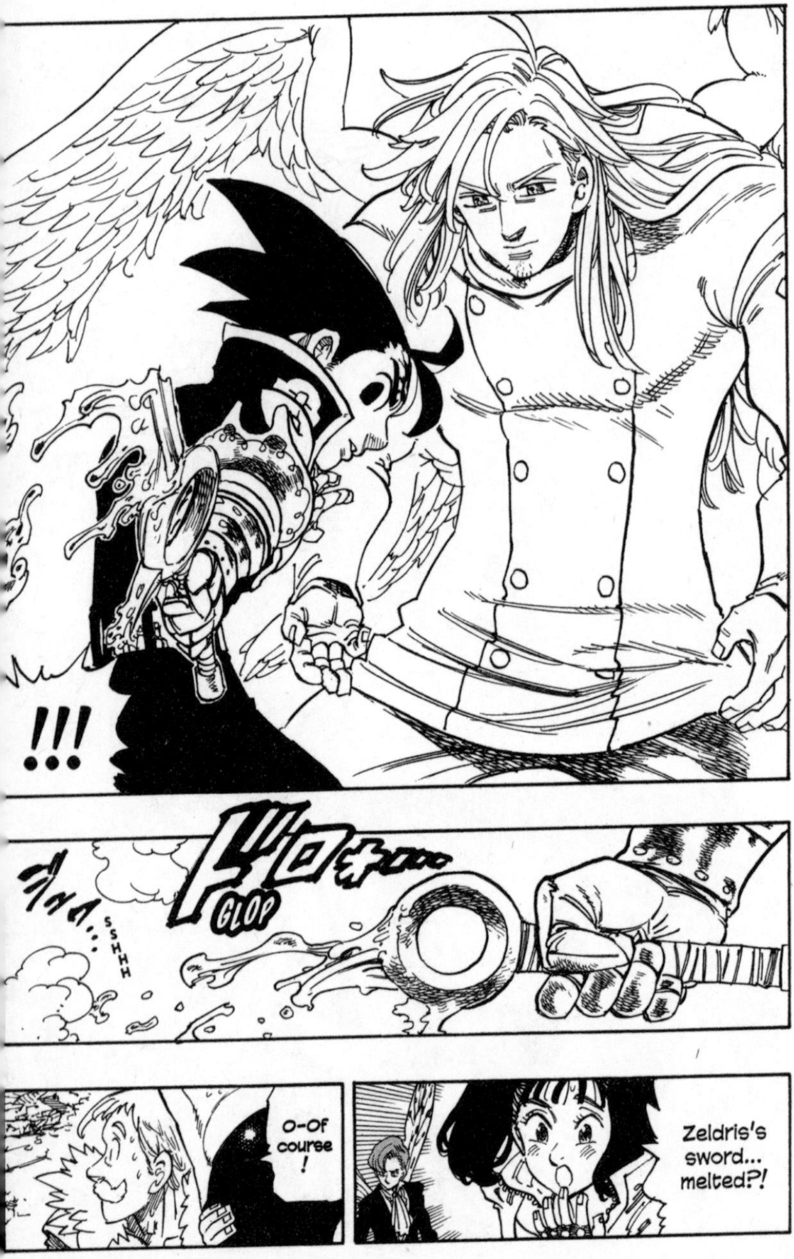
!!!
GLOP
SSHHH
Zeldris's sword... melted?!
O-Of course!

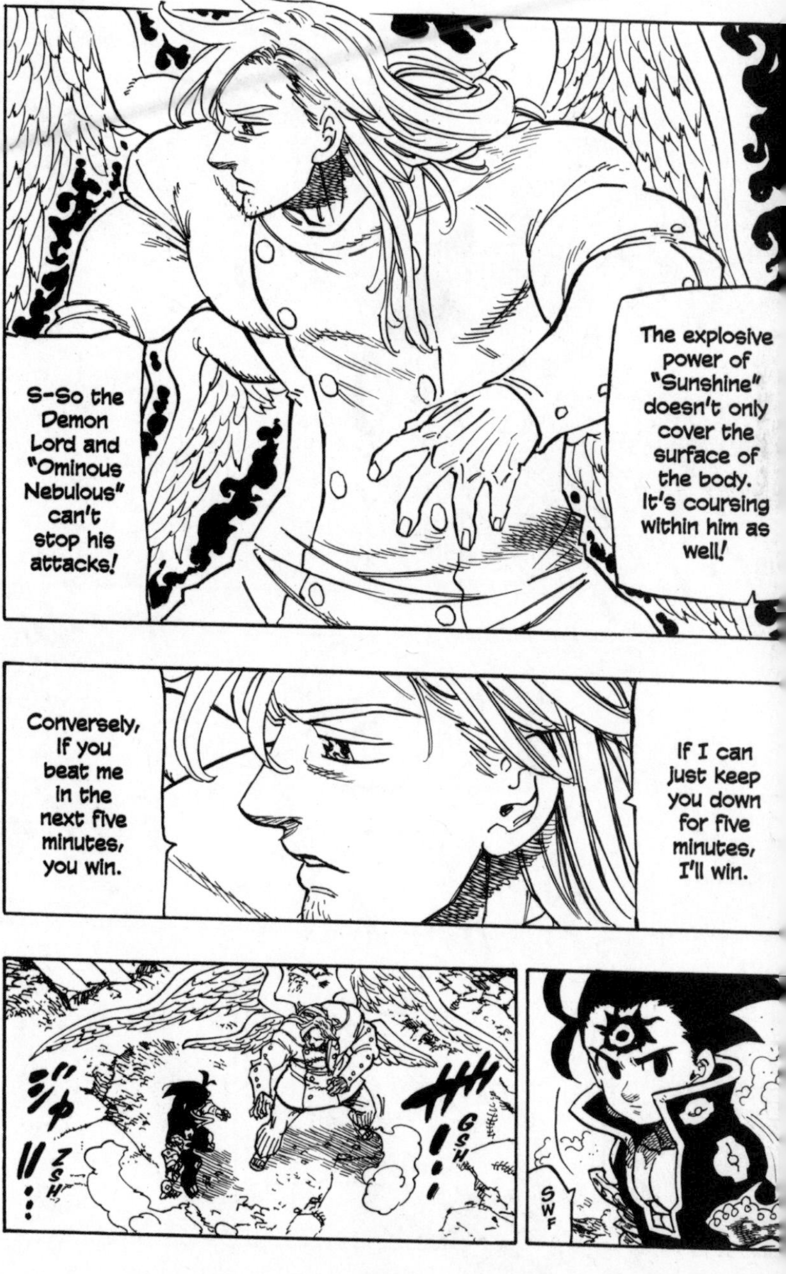
The explosive power of "Sunshine" doesn't only cover the surface of the body. It's coursing within him as well!
S-So the Demon Lord and "Ominous Nebulous" can't stop his attacks!
If I can just keep you down for five minutes, I'll win.
Conversely, if you beat me in the next five minutes, you win.
SWF
GSH
ZSH

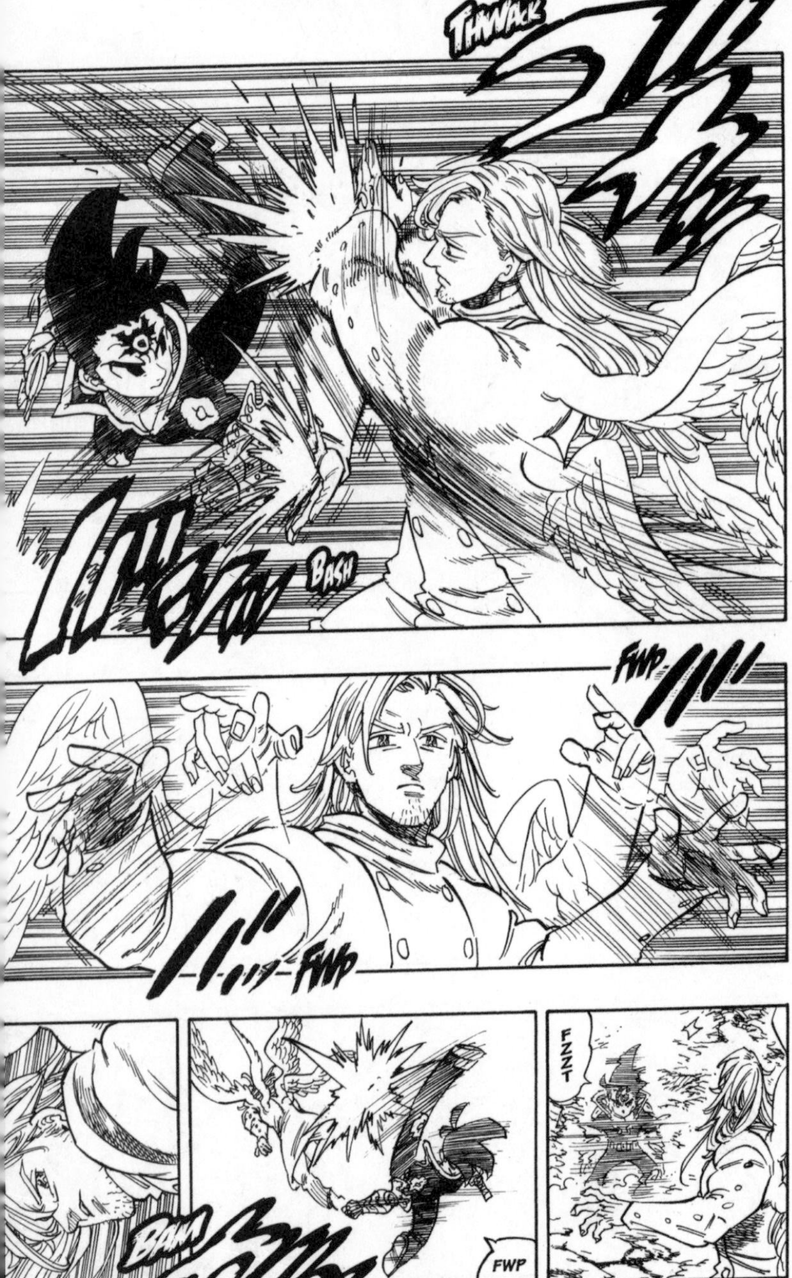
THWACK
BASH
FWP
FWP
FZZT
FWP
BAM

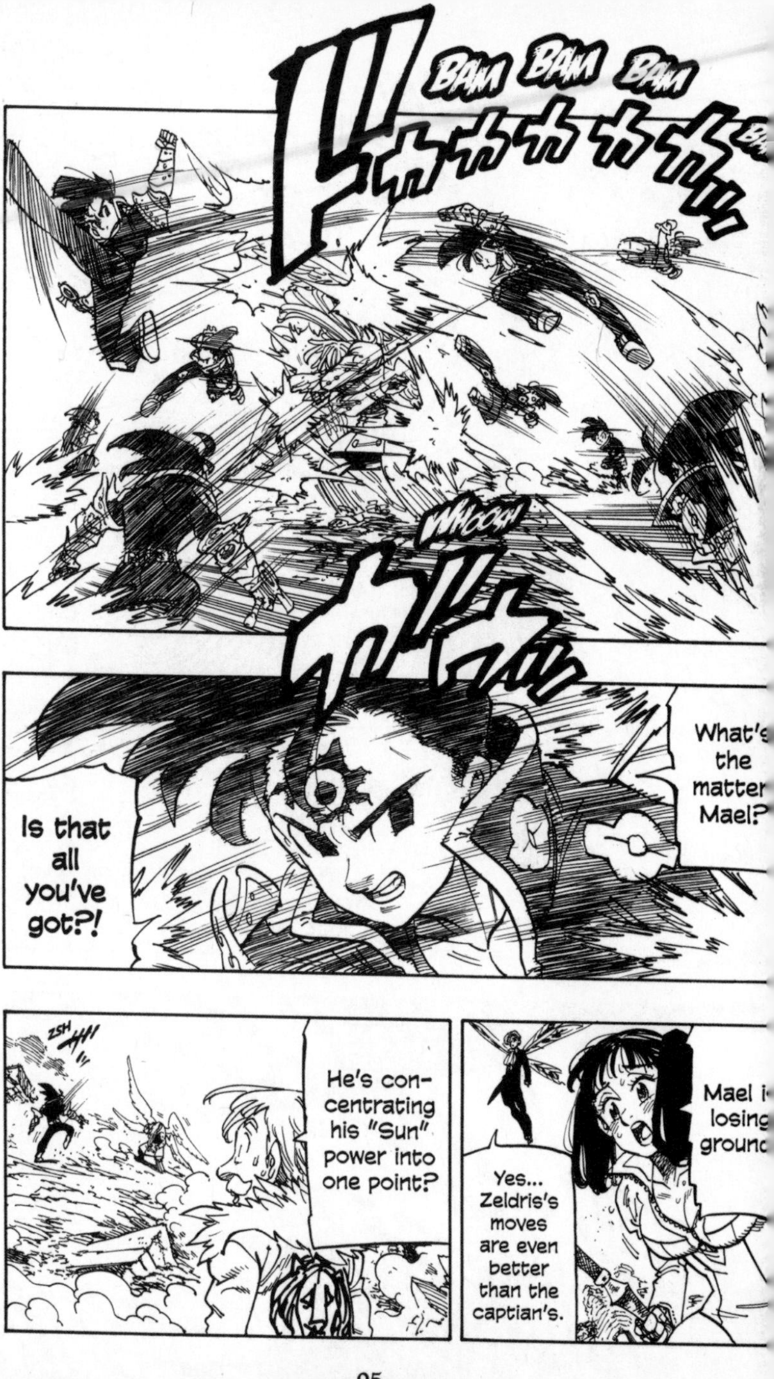
BAM BAM BAM
WHOOSH
What's the matter Mael?
Is that all you've got?!
Mael i losing ground
Yes... Zeldris's moves are even better than the captian's.
He's con-centrating his "Sun" power into one point?
ZSH

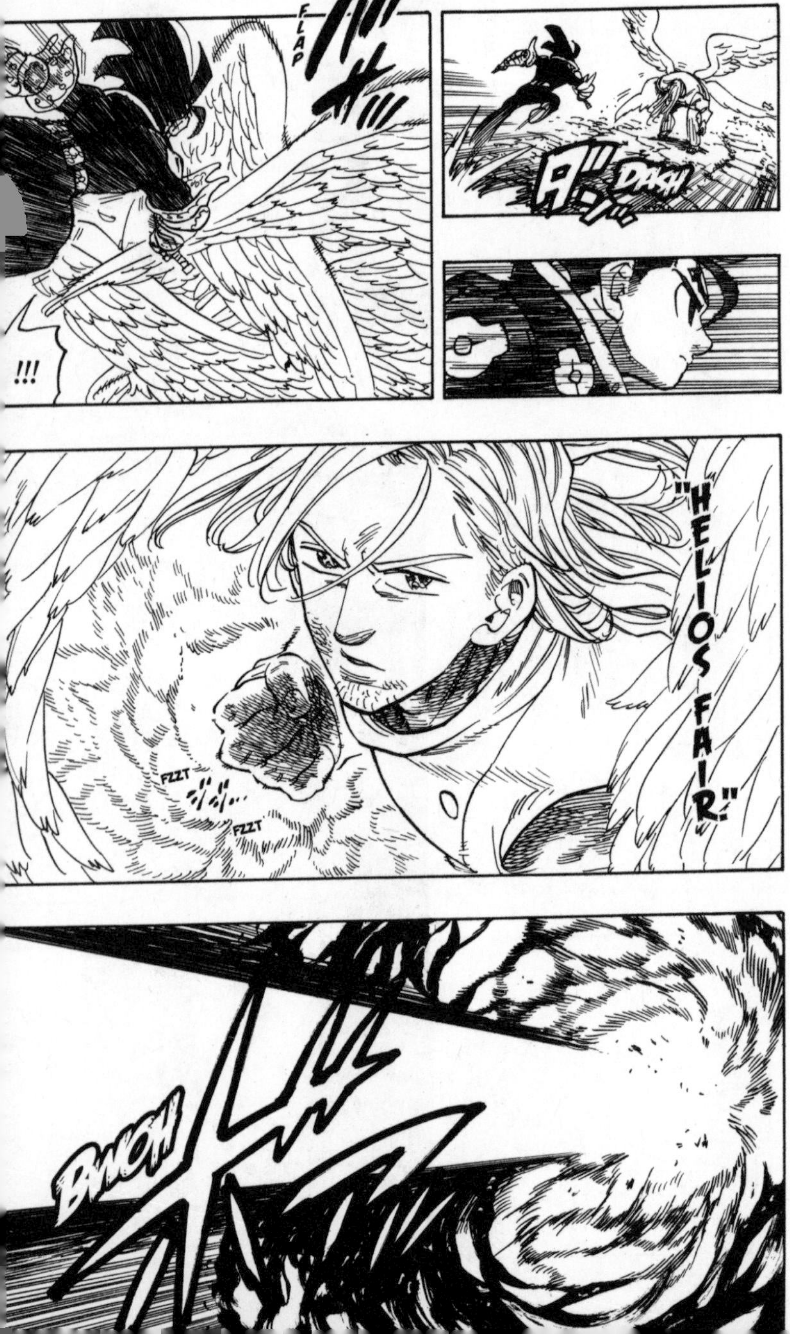
DASH
FLAP
!!!
"HELIOS FAIR"
FZZT
FZZT
BWOH

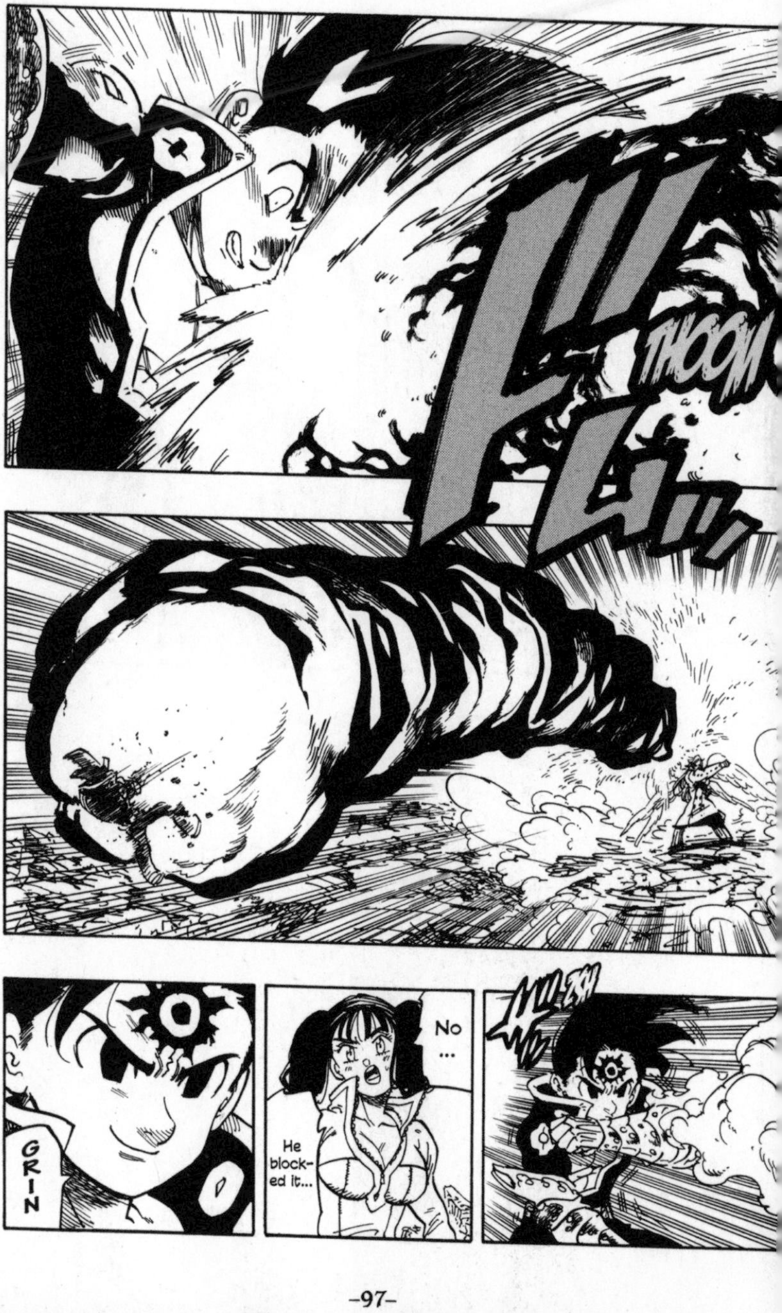
THOOM
No ...
He blocked it...
GRIN

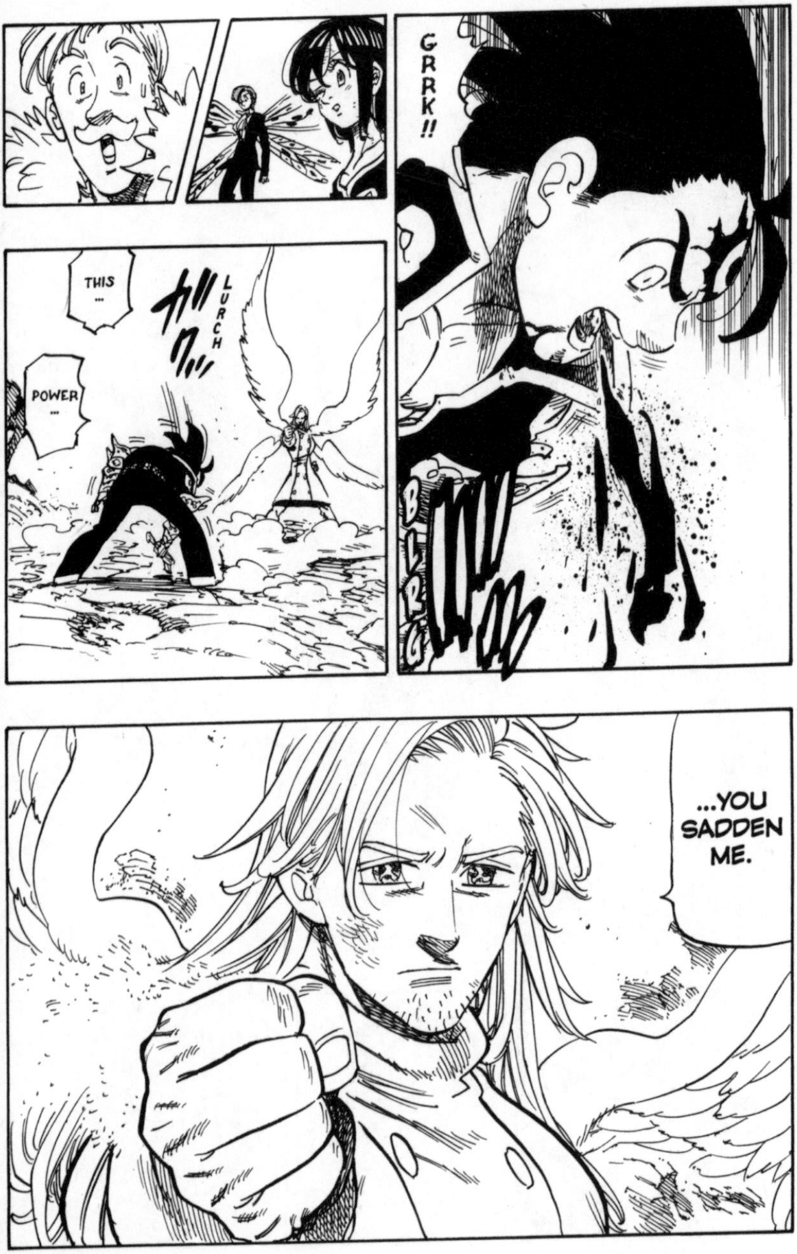
GRRK!!
BLRG
THIS ...
POWER ...
LURCH
...YOU SADDEN ME.

Chapter 299 - Everyone Freezes

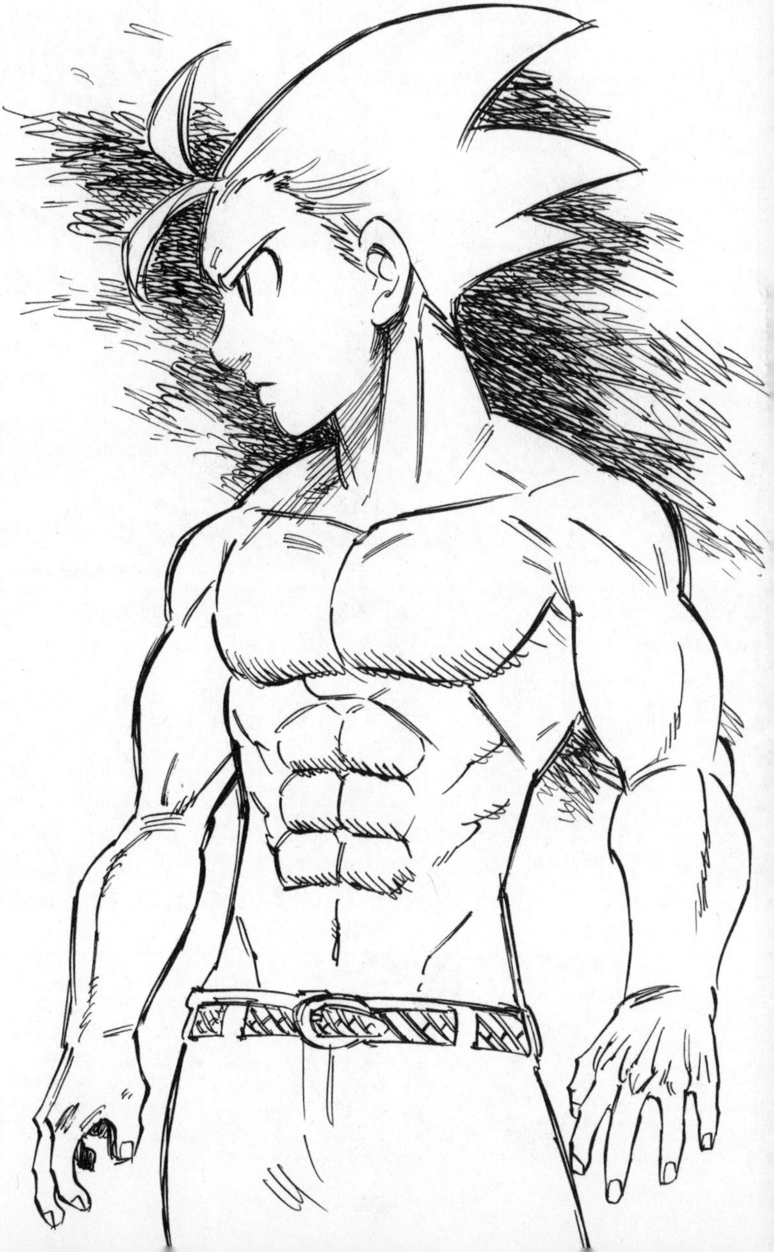

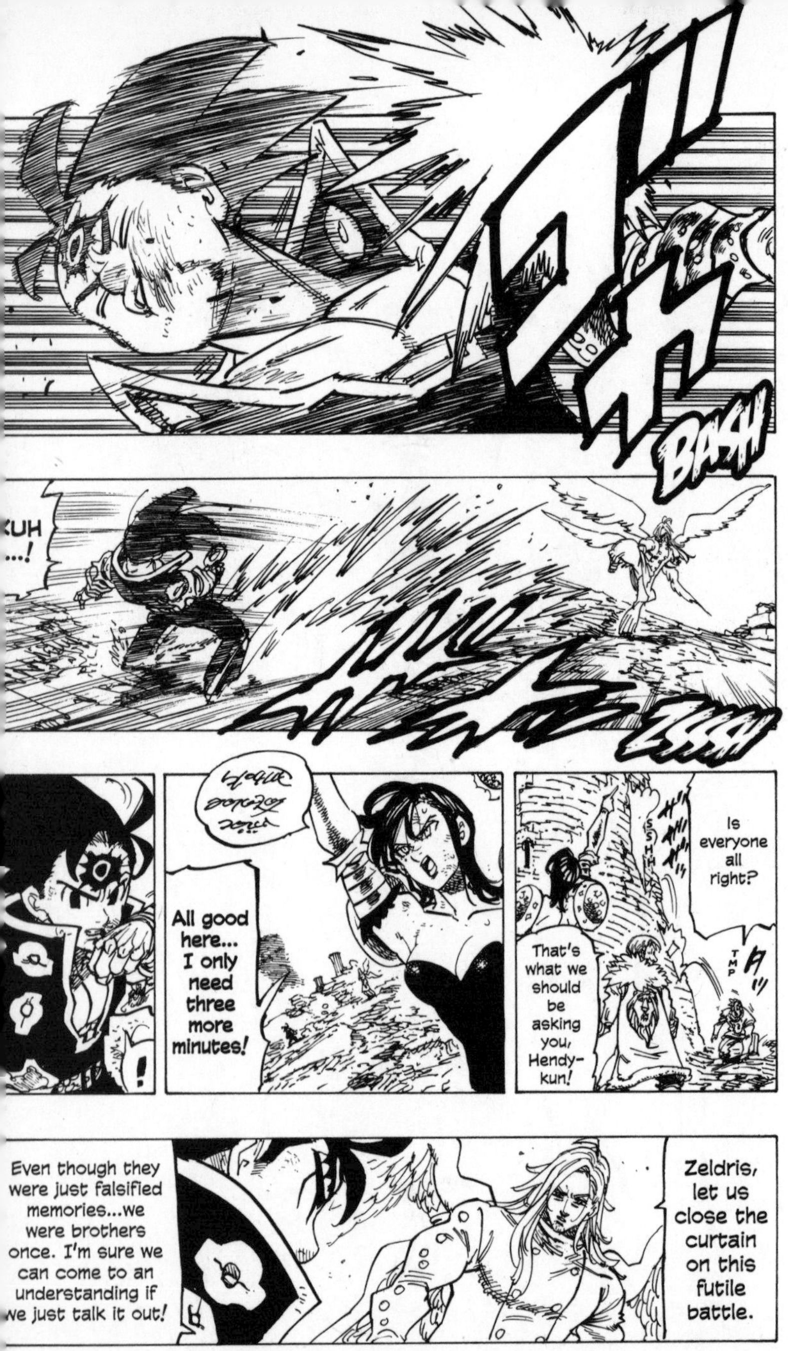

BASH
KUH ...!
ZSSH
Is everyone all right?
SSHH
TMP
That's what we should be asking you, Hendy-kun!
All good here... I only need three more minutes!
!
Zeldris, let us close the curtain on this futile battle.
Even though they were just falsified memories...we were brothers once. I'm sure we can come to an understanding if we just talk it out!

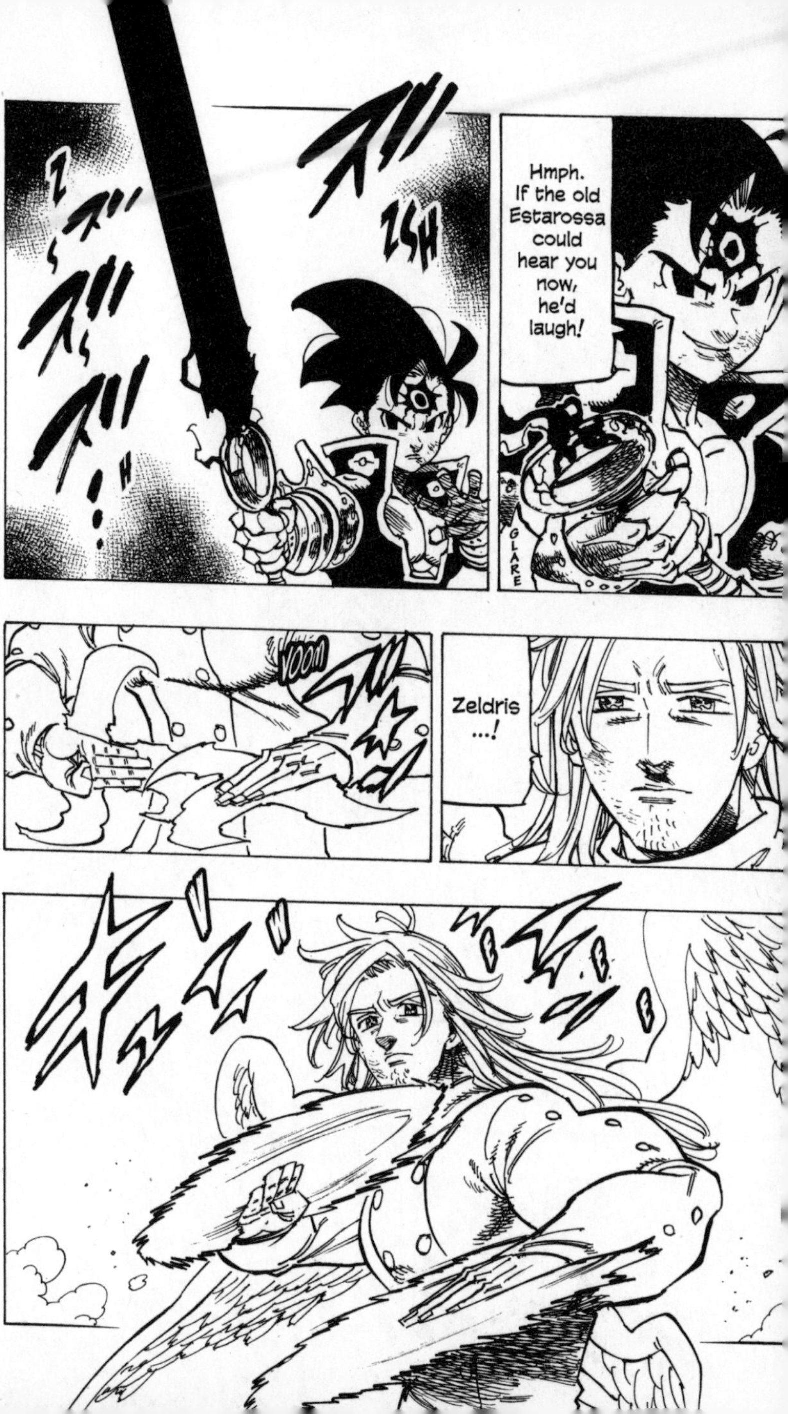
Hmph. If the old Estarossa could hear you now, he'd laugh!
GLARE
ZSH
Zeldris ...!
VOOM

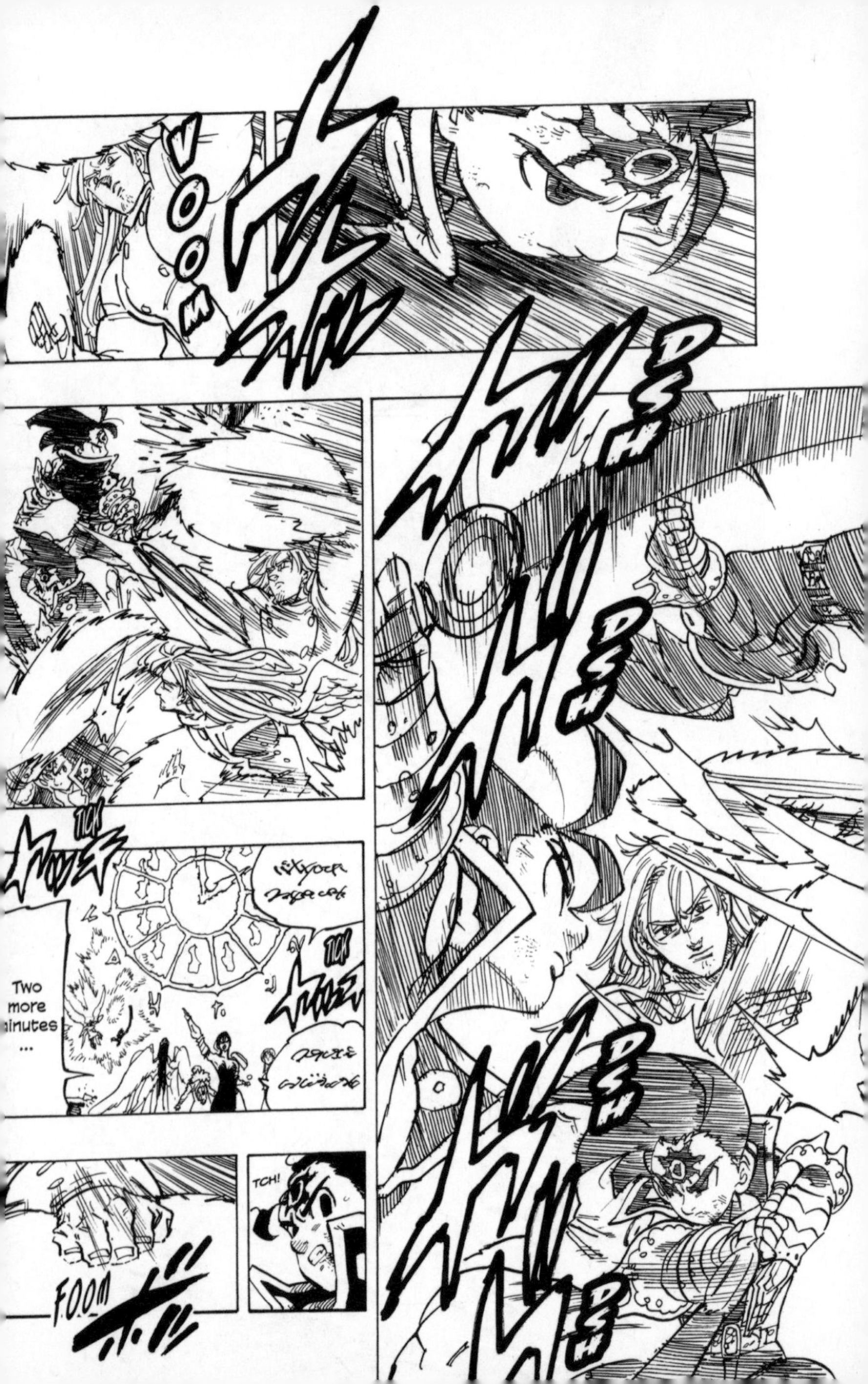
VOOOM
DSH
DSH
DSH
DSH
TCH
TCH
Two more minutes ...
TCH!
F.O.O.M

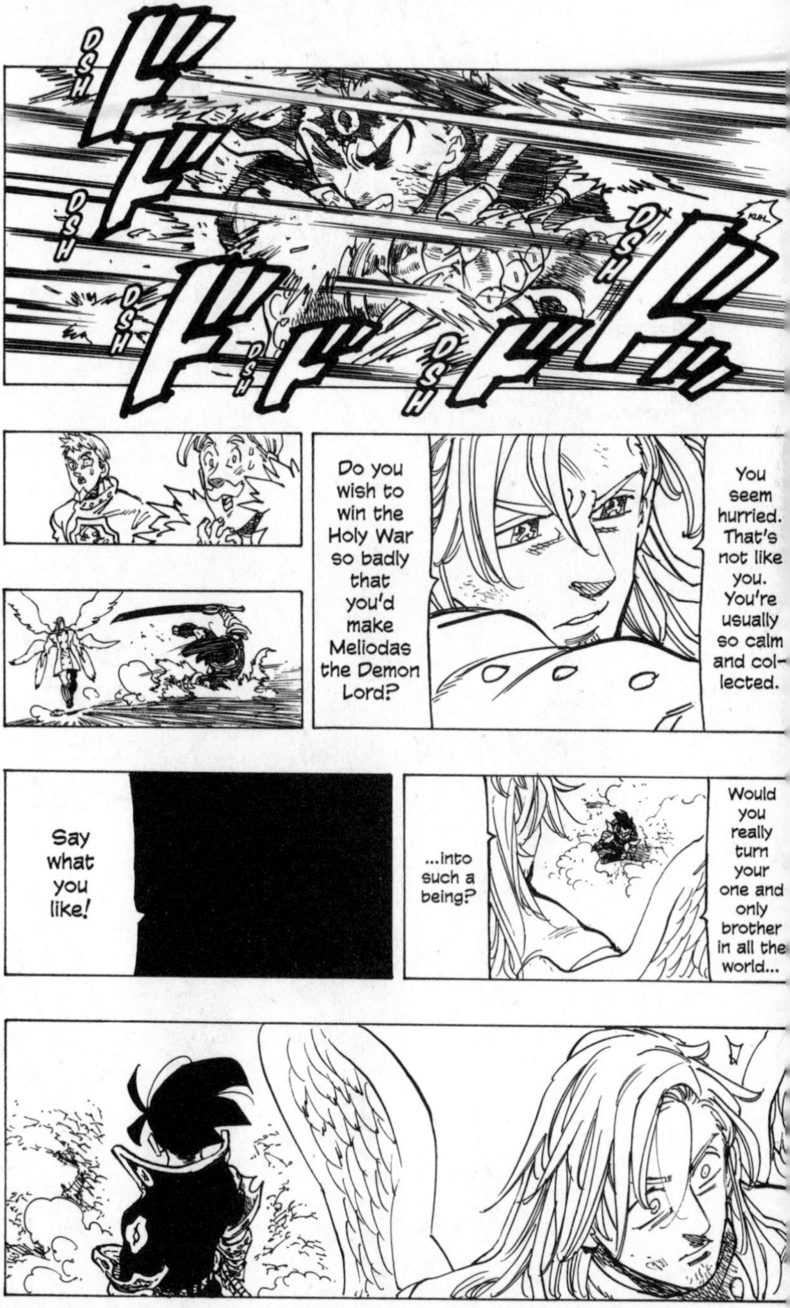
DSH
DSH
DSH
DSH
DSH
DSH
DSH
You seem hurried. That's not like you. You're usually so calm and collected.
Do you wish to win the Holy War so badly that you'd make Meliodas the Demon Lord?
Would you really turn your one and only brother in all the world...
...into such a being?
Say what you like!

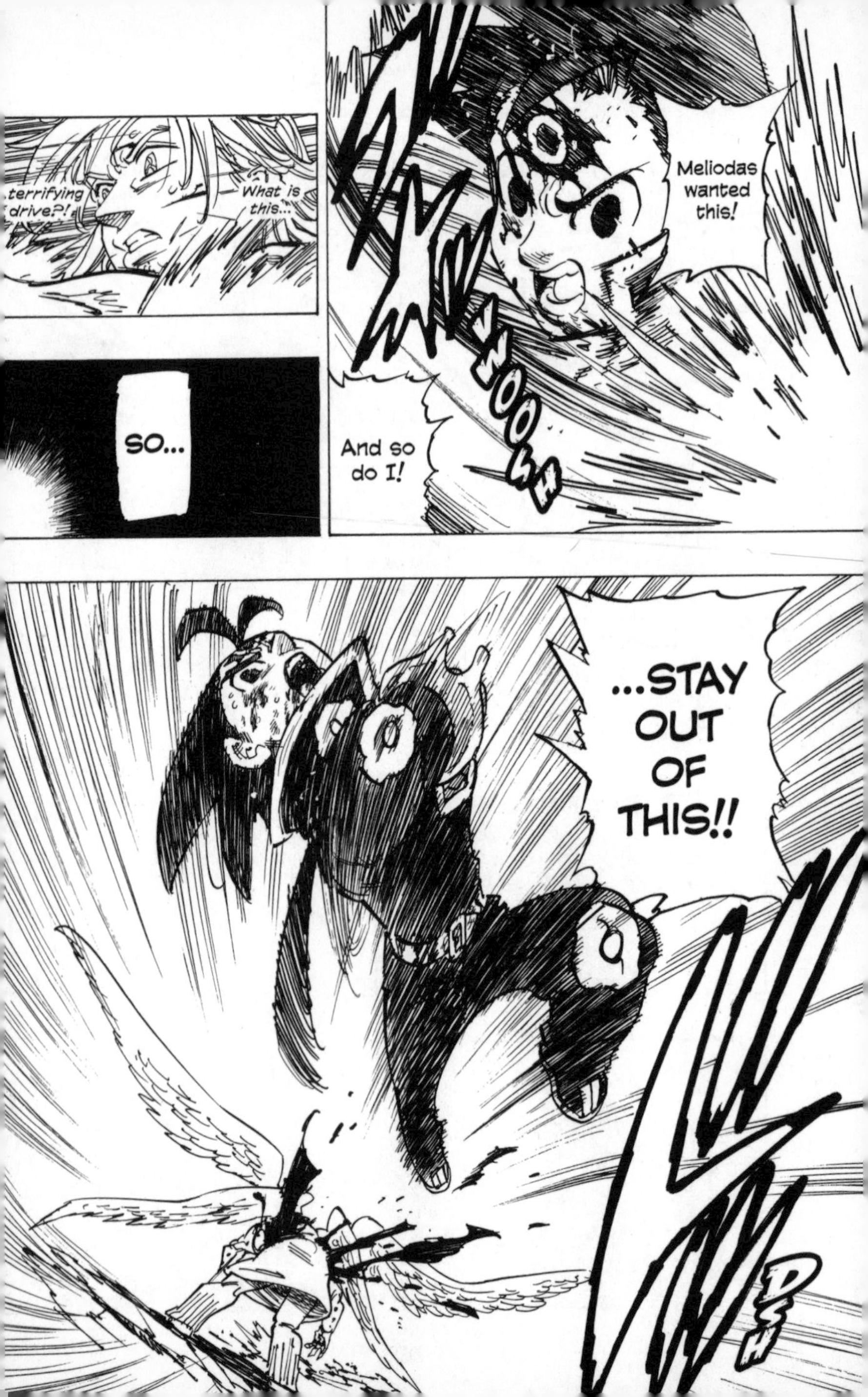
Meliodas wanted this!
And so do I!
What is this...
.terrifying drive?!
SO...
...STAY OUT OF THIS!!
DSH

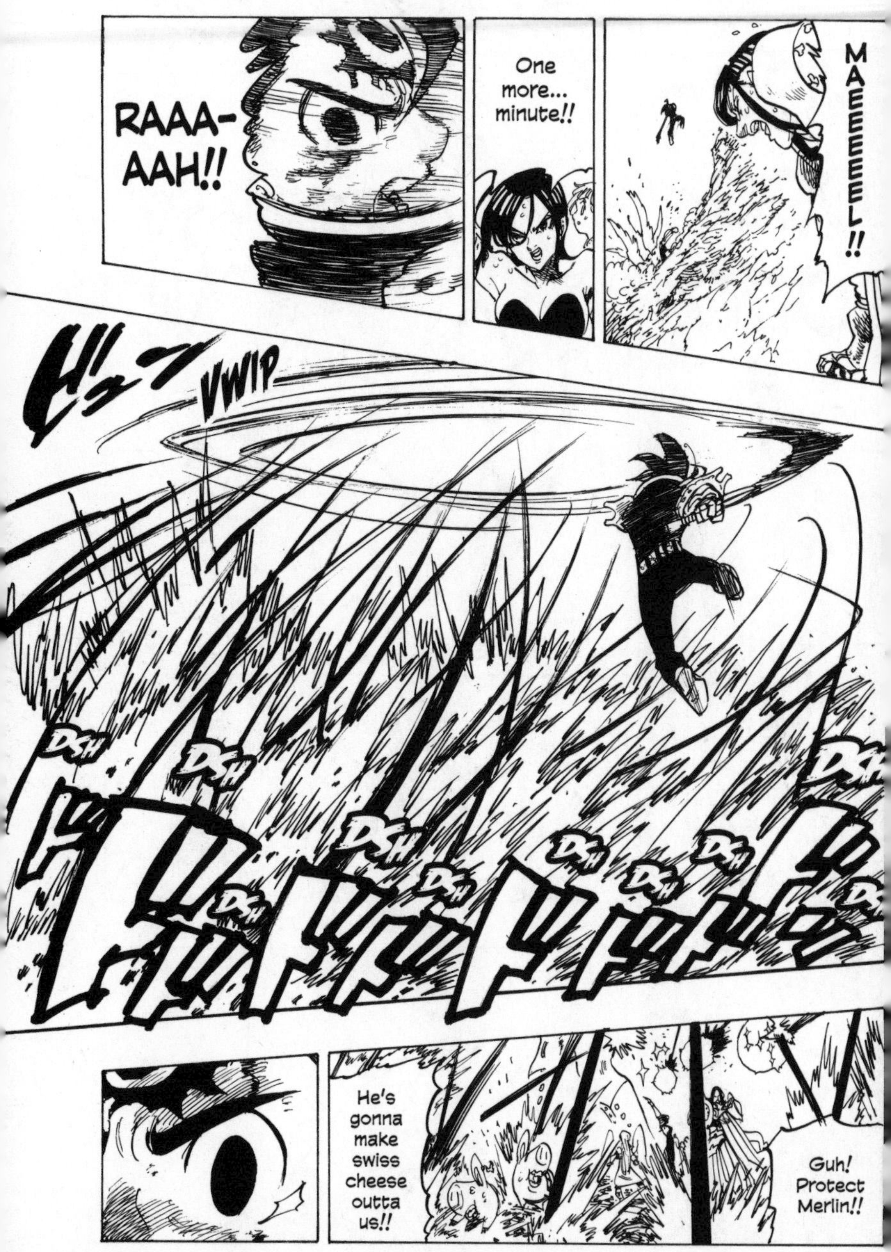
MAEEEEEL!!
One more... minute!!
RAAA-AAH!!
VWIP
DSH
DSH
DSH
DSH
DSH
DSH
DSH
DSH
DSH
DSH
Guh! Protect Merlin!!
He's gonna make swiss cheese outta us!!

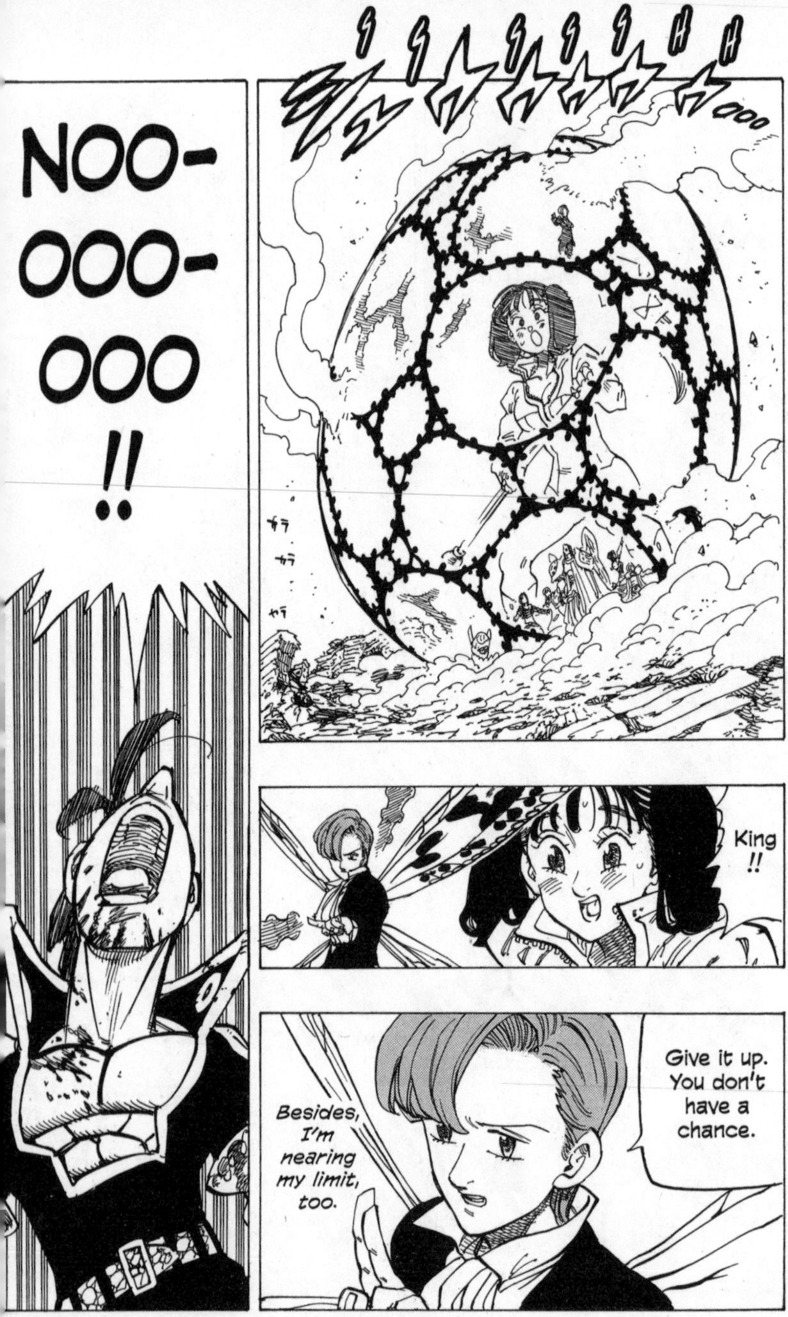
SSSSSHHooo
カラ
カラ
カラ
King!!
Give it up. You don't have a chance.
Besides, I'm nearing my limit, too.
NOO-OOO-OOO!!

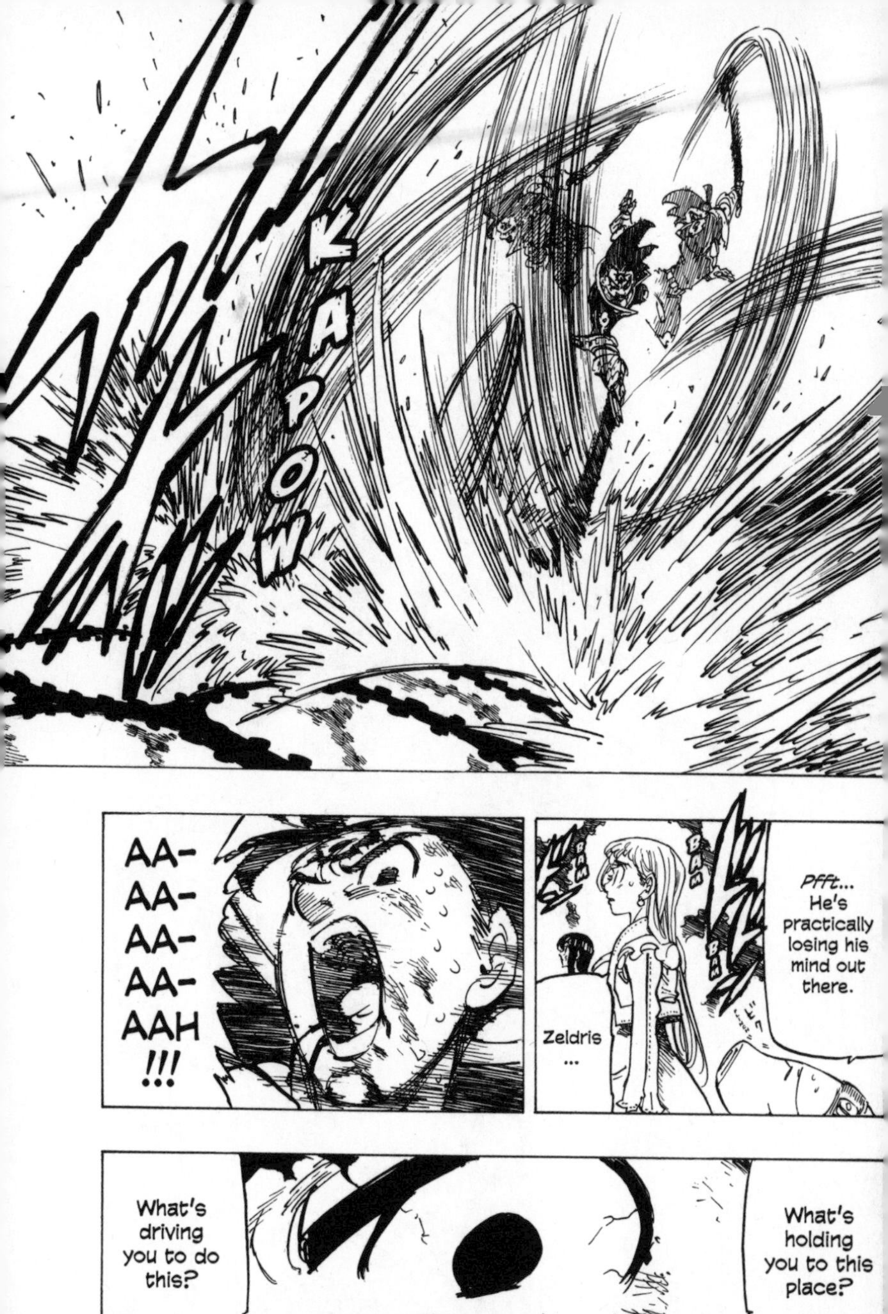
KAPOW
BAM
BAM
BAM
Pfft... He's practically losing his mind out there.
Zeldris...
AA-AA-AA-AA-AAH!!!
What's holding you to this place?
What's driving you to do this?

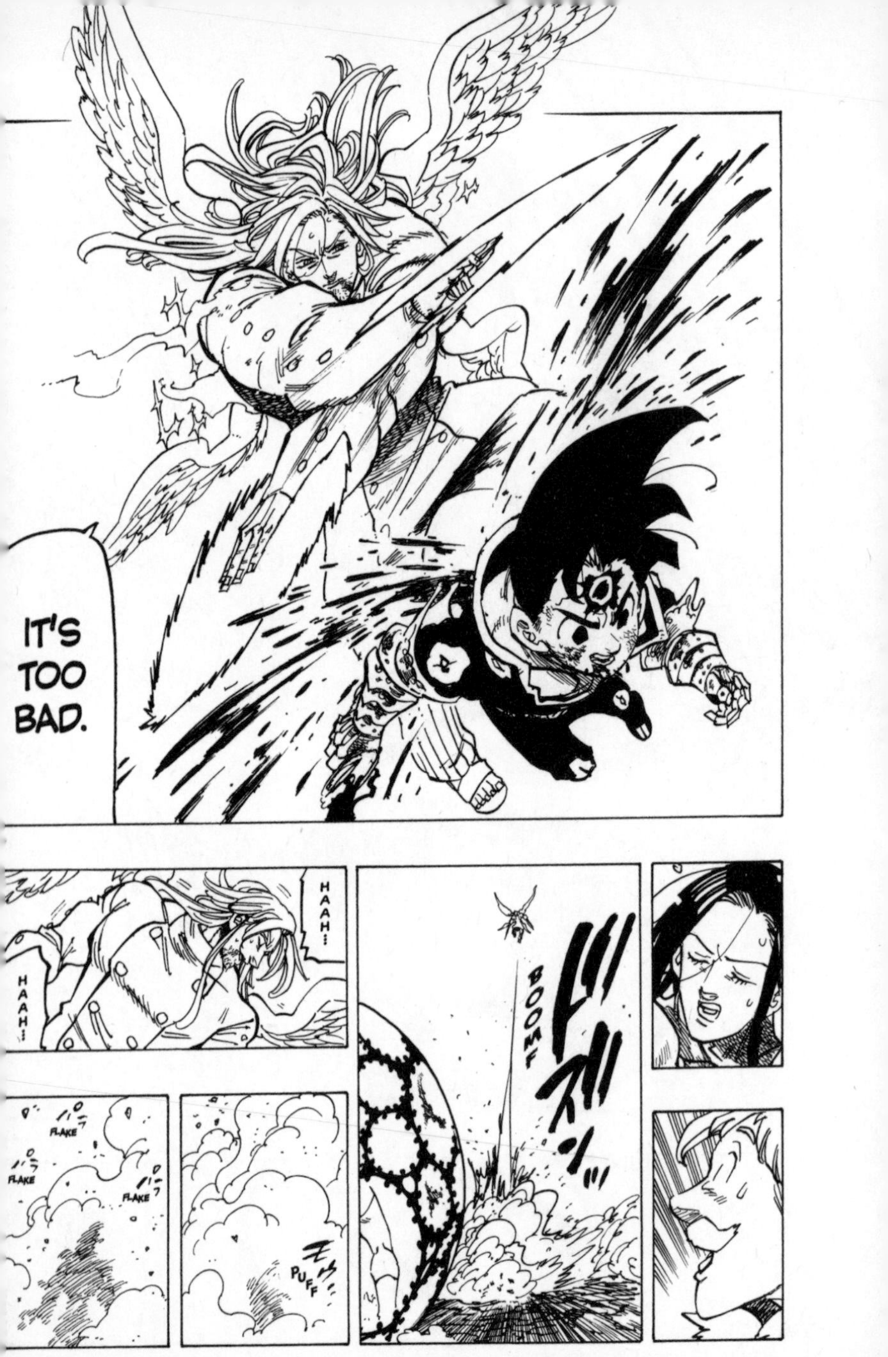
IT'S TOO BAD.
BOOMF
HAAH...
HAAH...
PUFF
FLAKE
FLAKE
FLAKE

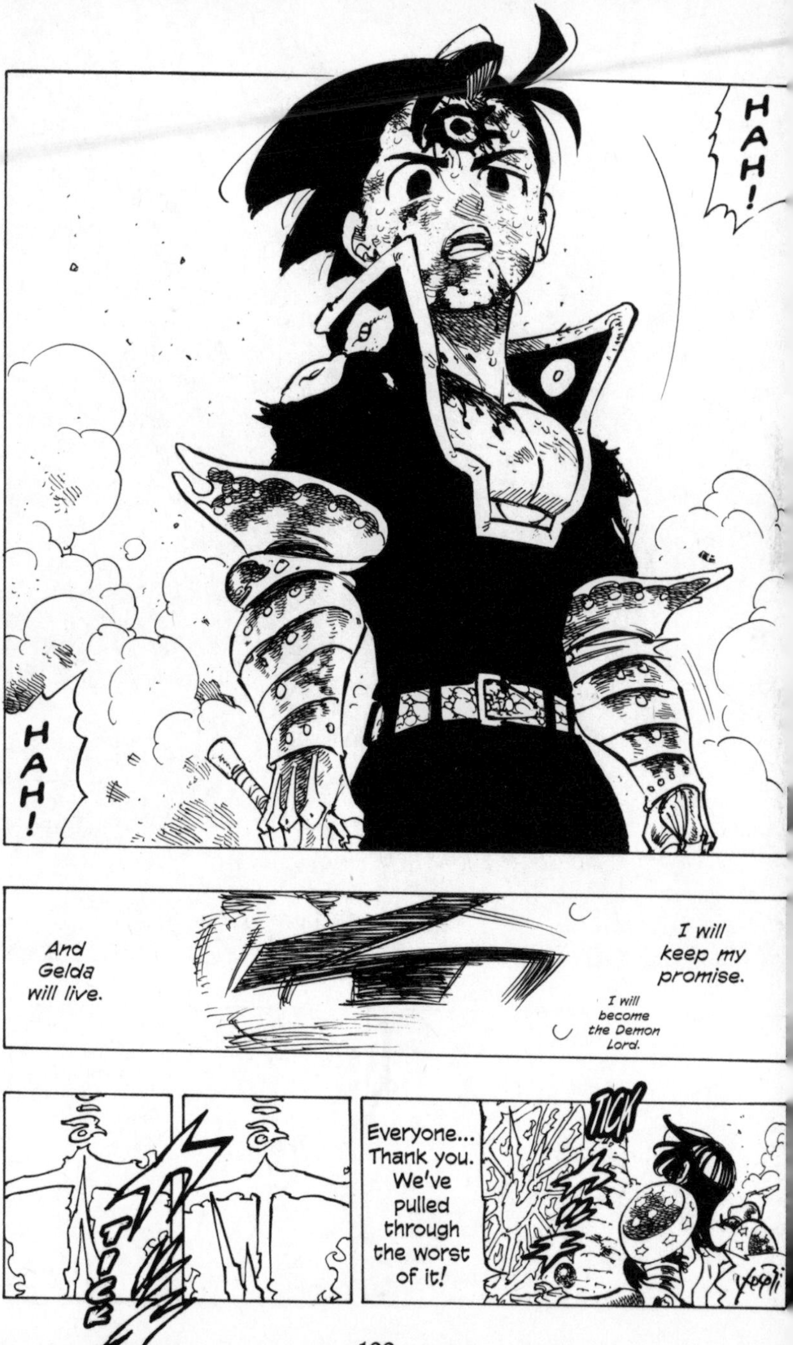
HAH!
HAH!
I will keep my promise.
I will become the Demon Lord.
And Gelda will live.
TICK
Everyone... Thank you. We've pulled through the worst of it!
TICK
TICK

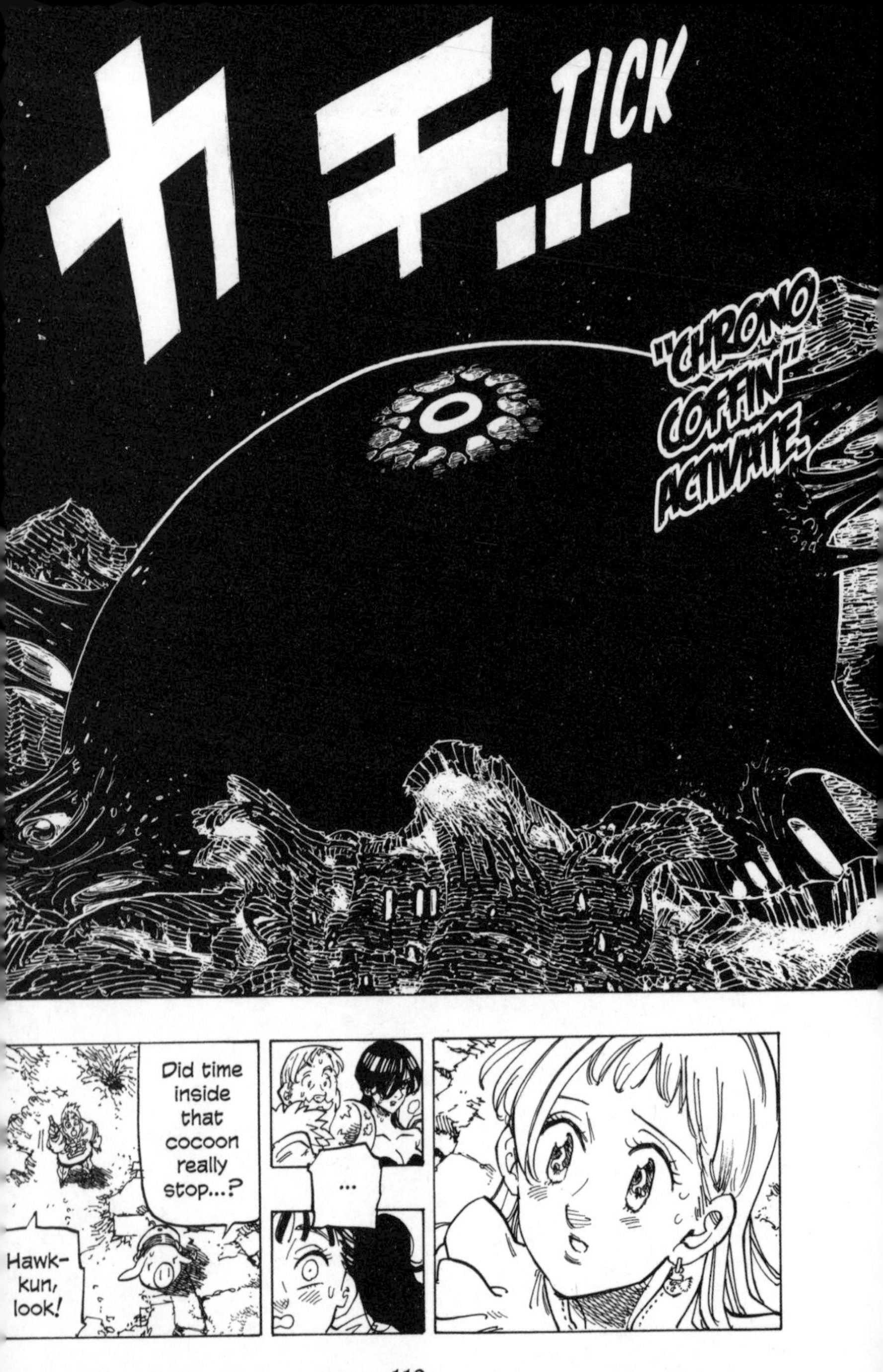

カチ...
TICK
"CHRONO COFFIN" ACTIVATE.
...
Did time inside that cocoon really stop...?
Hawk-kun, look!

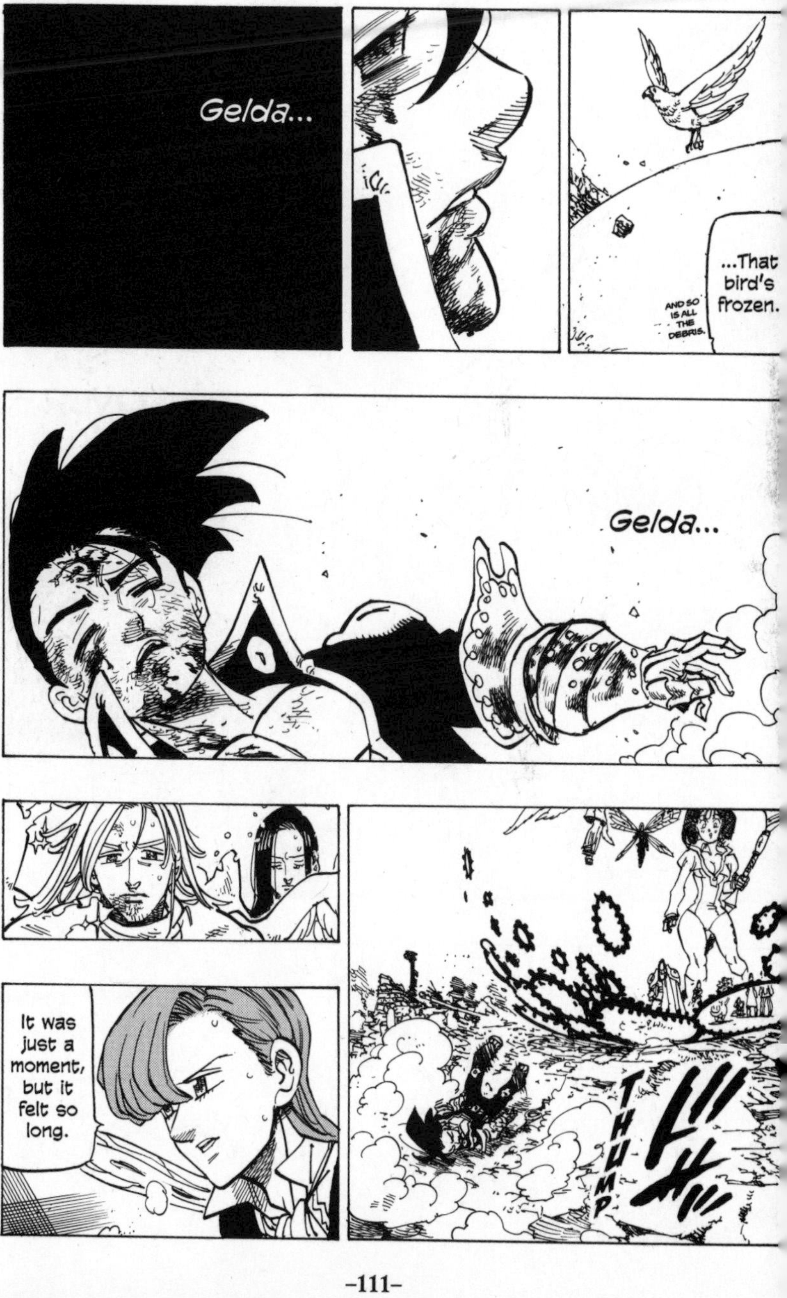
...That bird's frozen.
AND SO IS ALL THE DEBRIS.
Gelda...
Gelda...
THUMP
It was just a moment, but it felt so long.

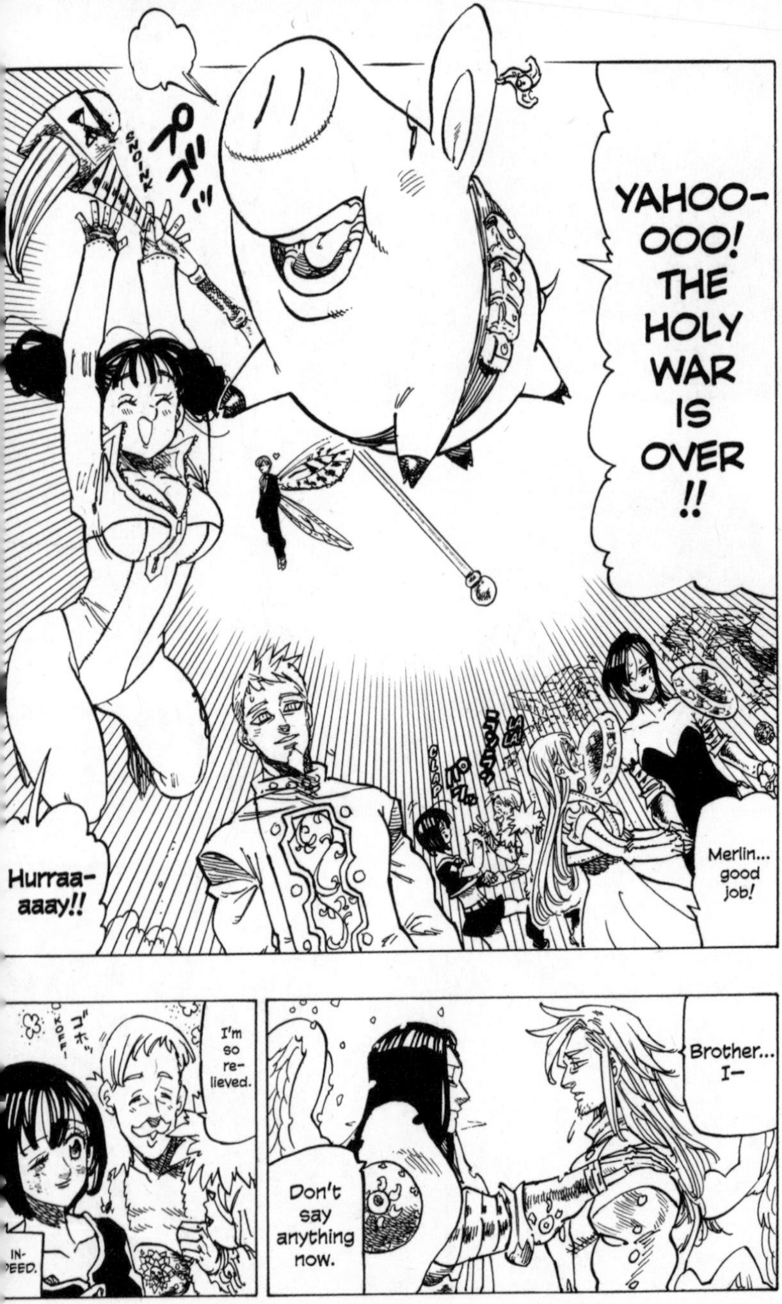
YAHOO-OOO! THE HOLY WAR IS OVER!!
SNOINK
LA LA!
CLAP
Merlin... good job!
Hurraa-aaay!!
Brother... I-
Don't say anything now.
KOFF!
I'm so re-lieved.
IN-DEED.

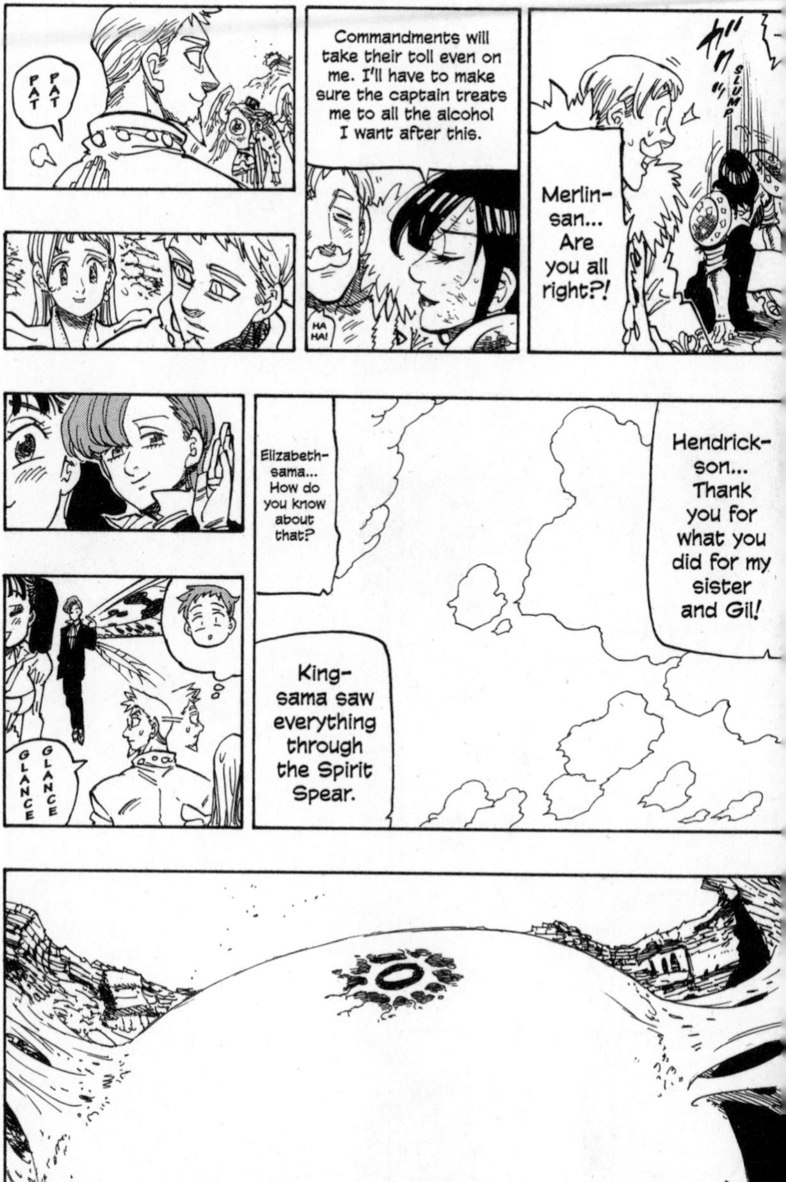
SLUMP
Merlin-san... Are you all right?!
Commandments will take their toll even on me. I'll have to make sure the captain treats me to all the alcohol I want after this.
HA HA!
PAT PAT
Hendrickson... Thank you for what you did for my sister and Gil!
Elizabeth-sama... How do you know about that?
King-sama saw everything through the Spirit Spear.
GLANCE GLANCE

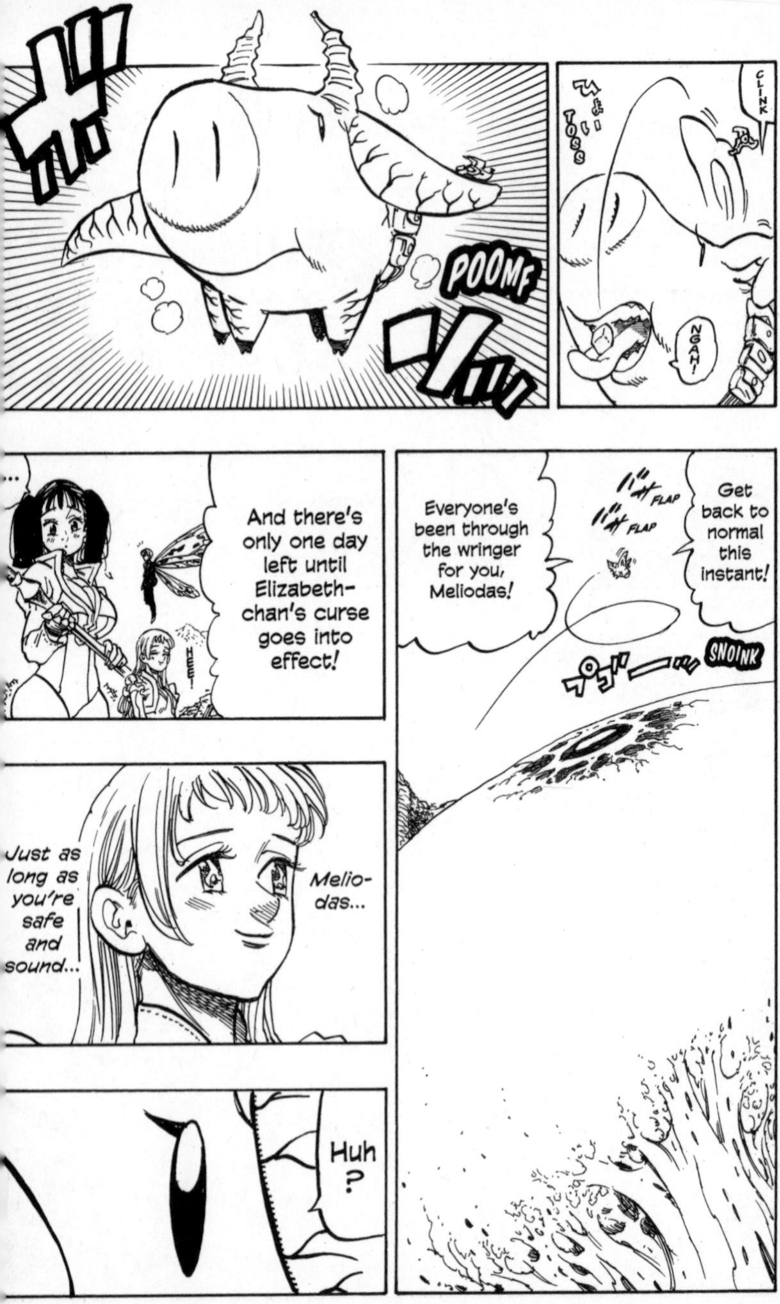
CLINK
TOSS
NGAH!
POOMF
Get back to normal this instant!
Everyone's been through the wringer for you, Meliodas!
FLAP
FLAP
SNOINK
And there's only one day left until Elizabeth-chan's curse goes into effect!
...
HEE!
Melio-das...
Just as long as you're safe and sound...
Huh?

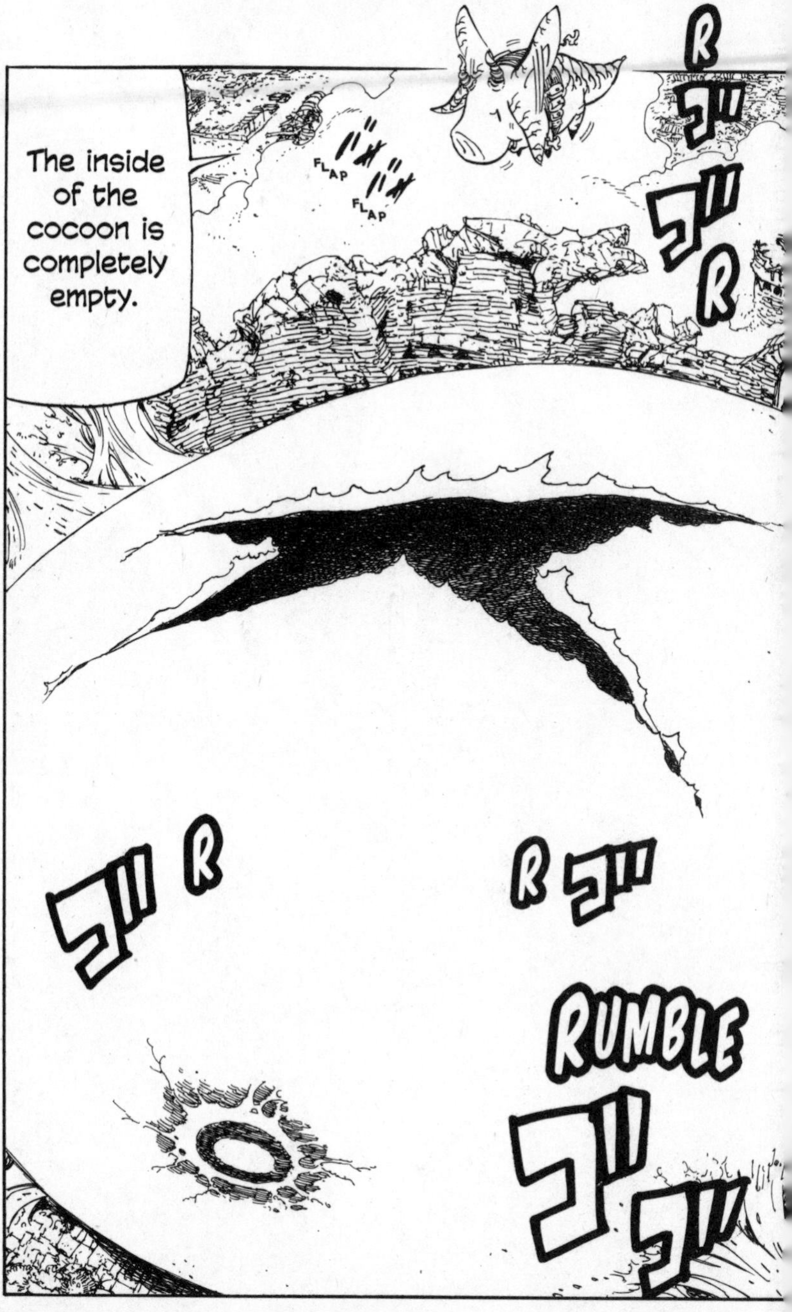

The inside of the cocoon is completely empty.
FLAP FLAP
RUMBLE

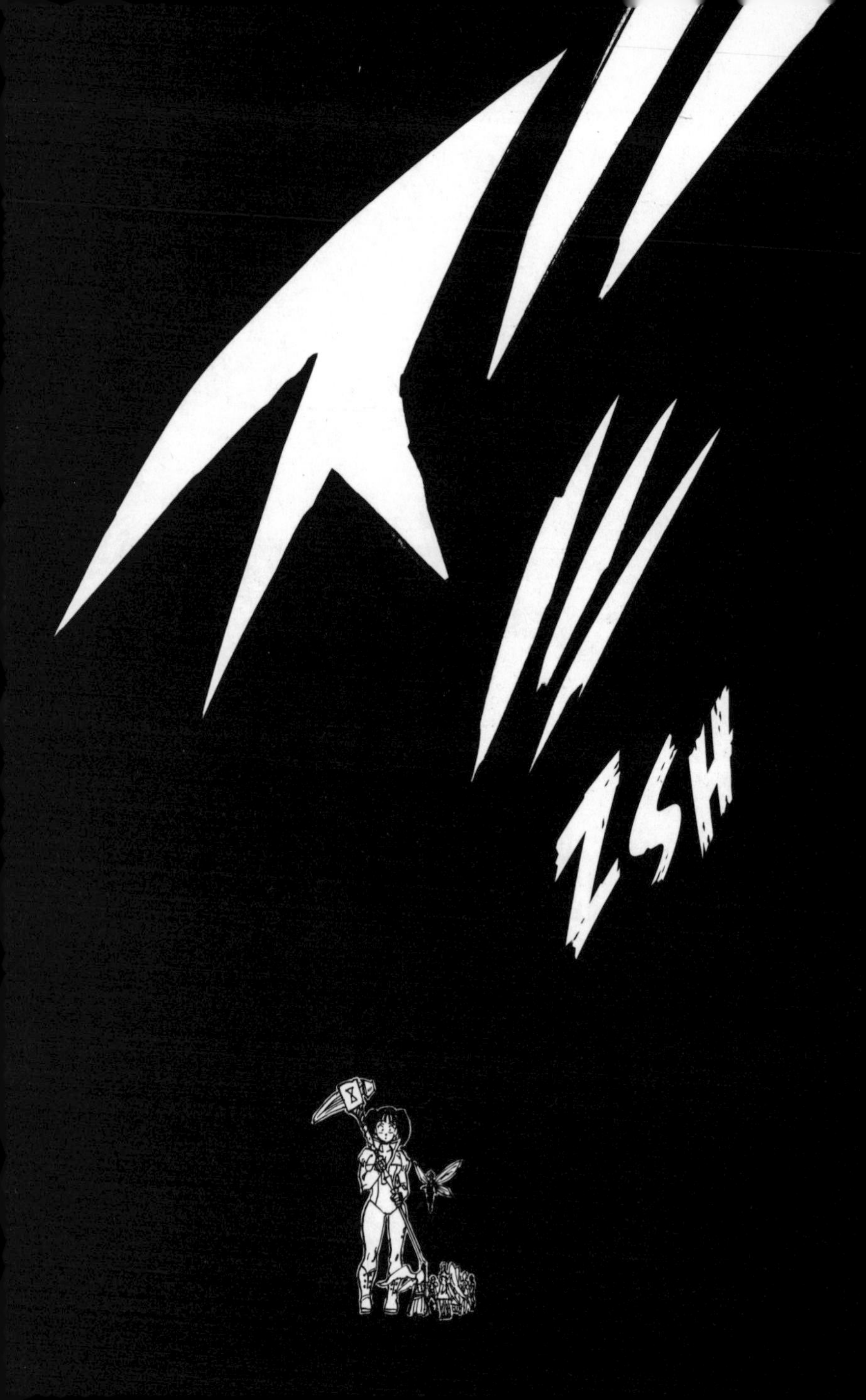
ZSH

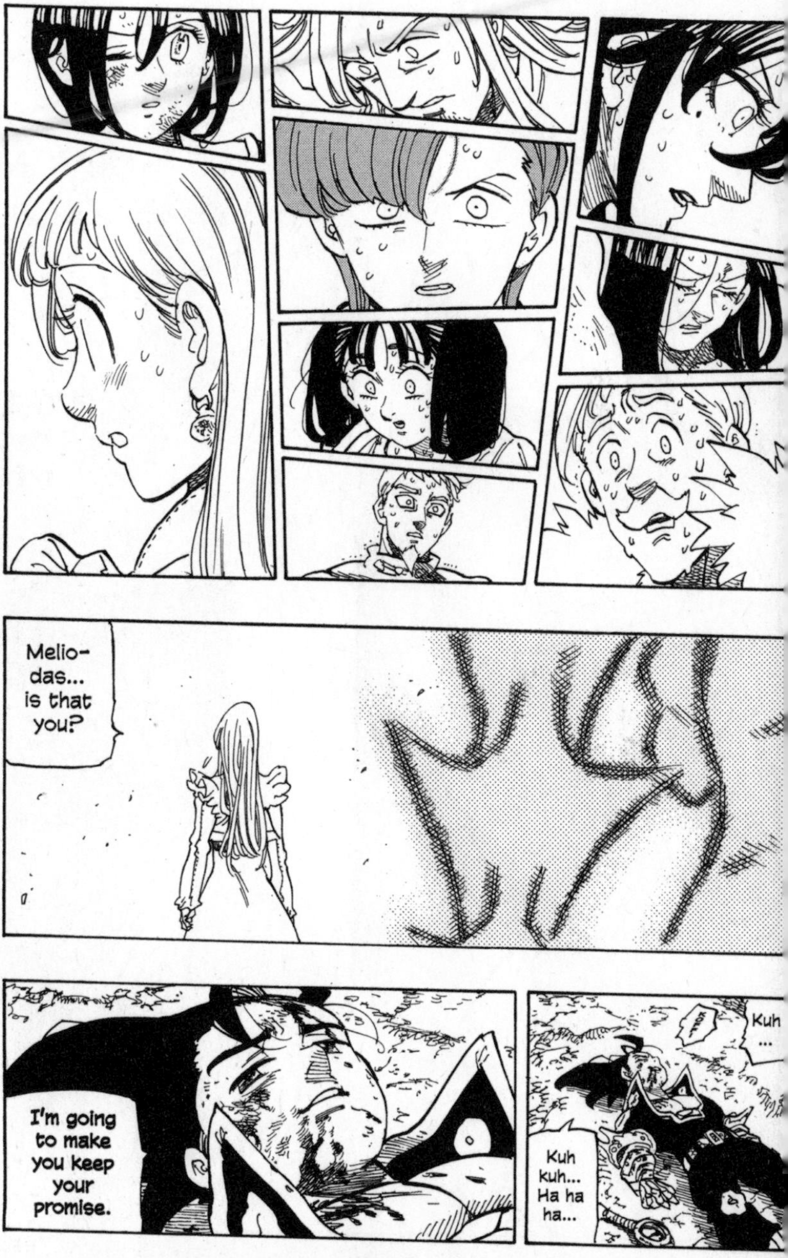
Melio-das... is that you?
Kuh ...
KOFF!
Kuh kuh... Ha ha ha...
I'm going to make you keep your promise.

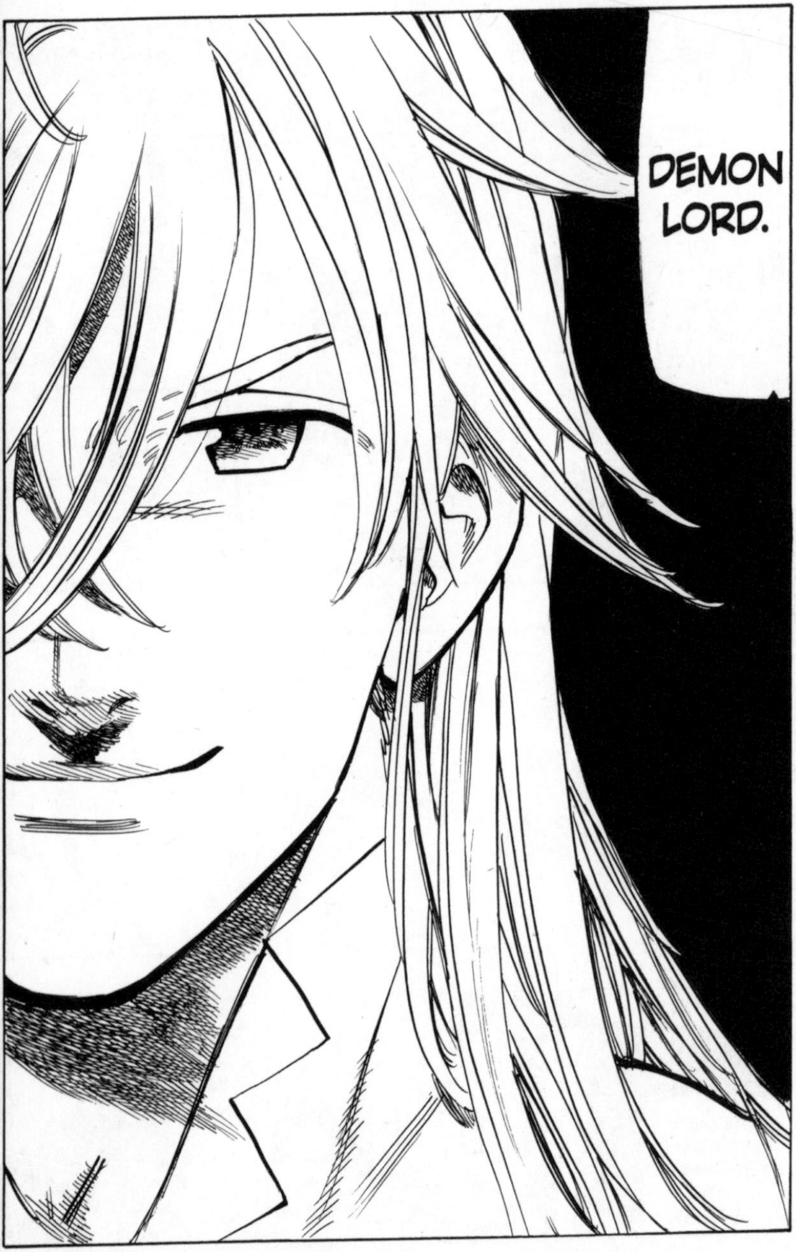
DEMON LORD.

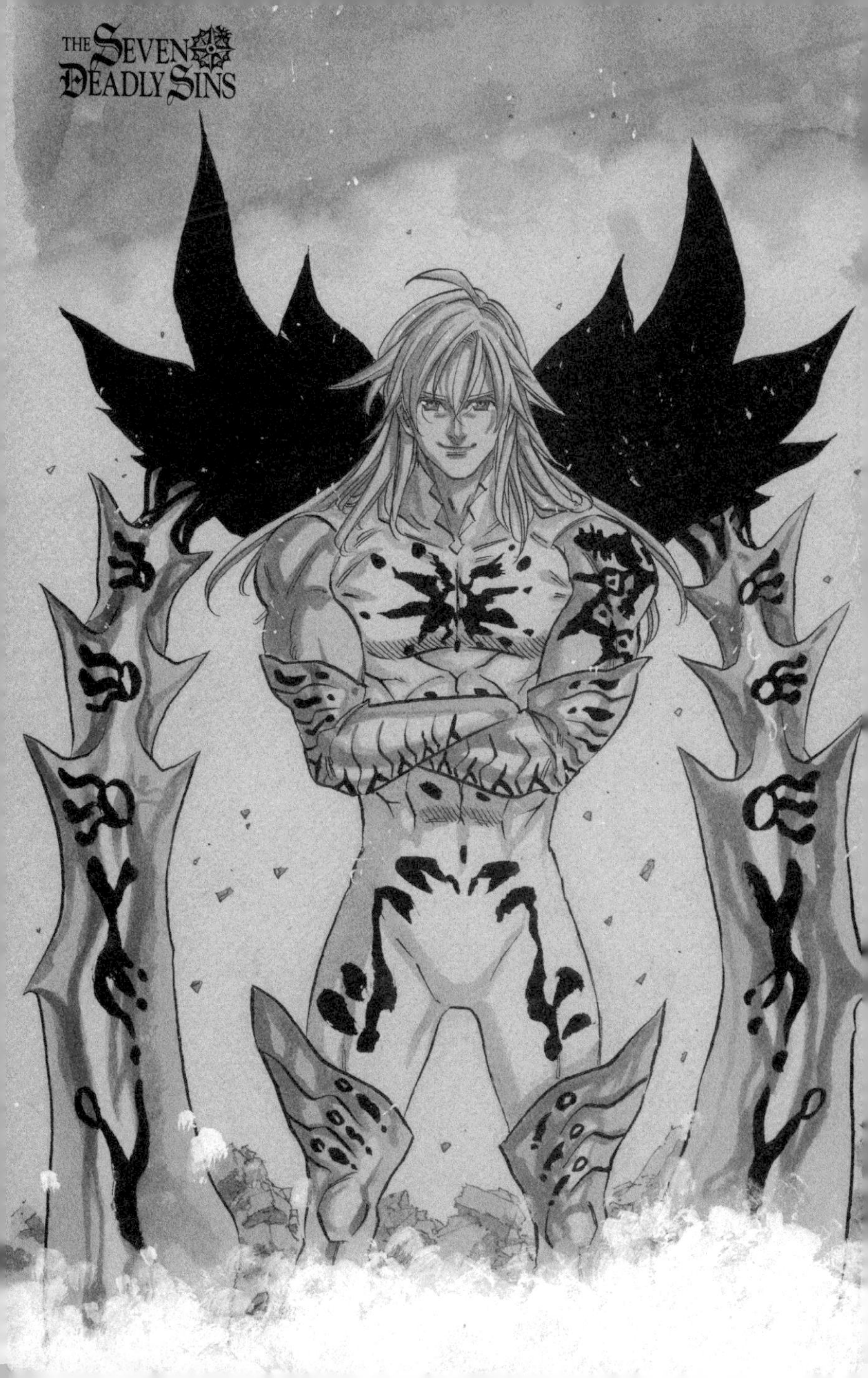
THE SEVEN DEADLY SINS

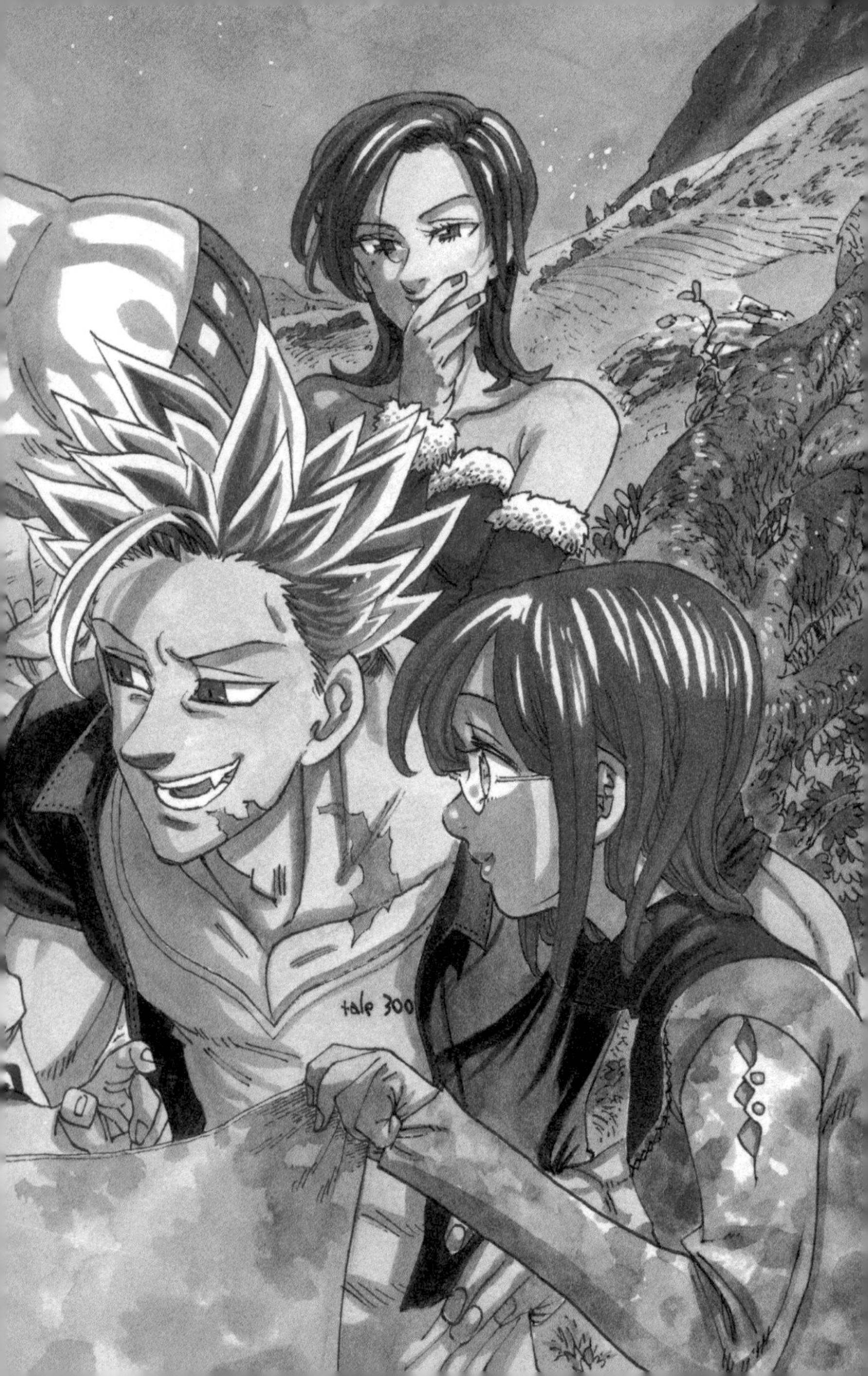
tale 300

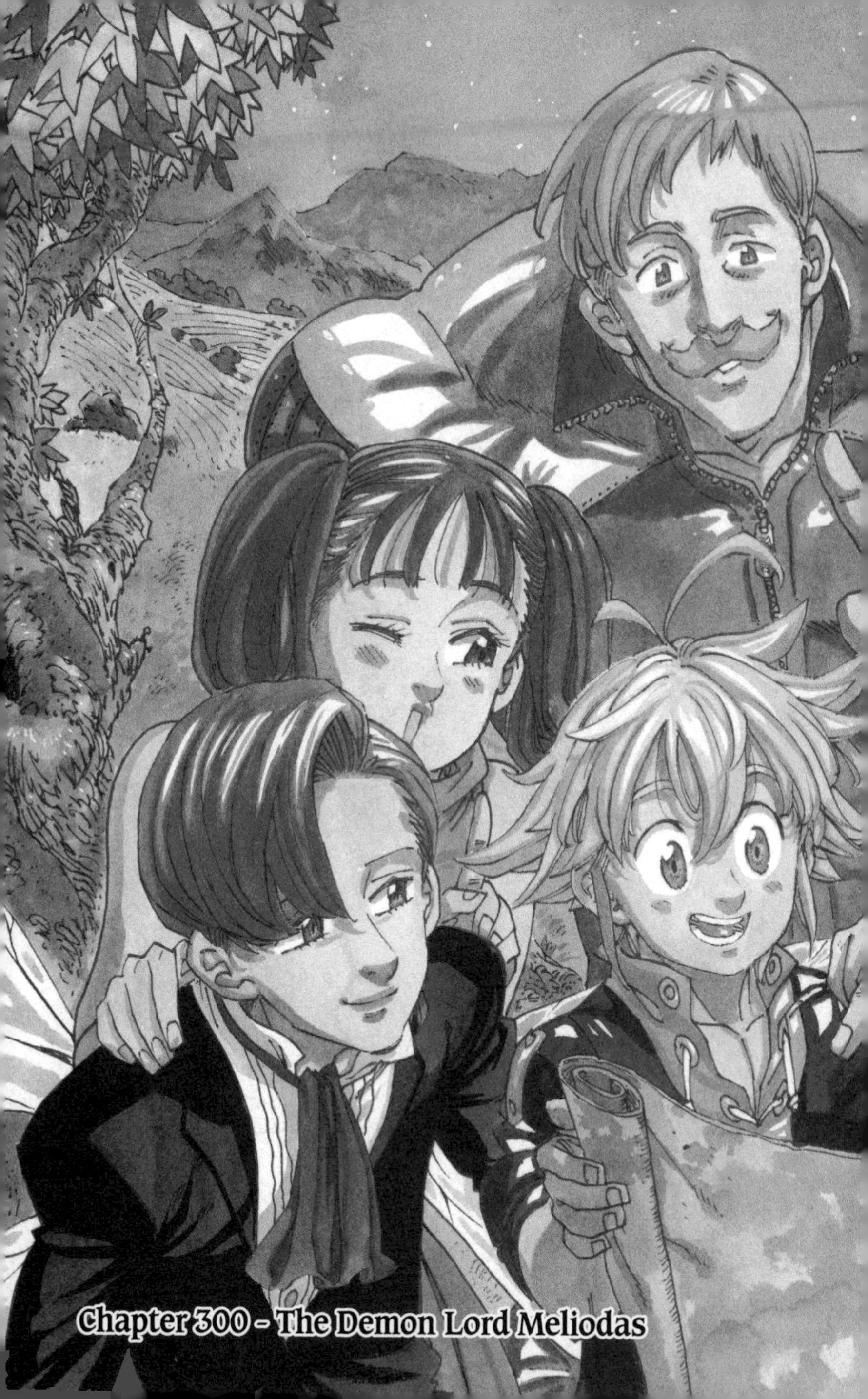

Chapter 300 - The Demon Lord Meliodas

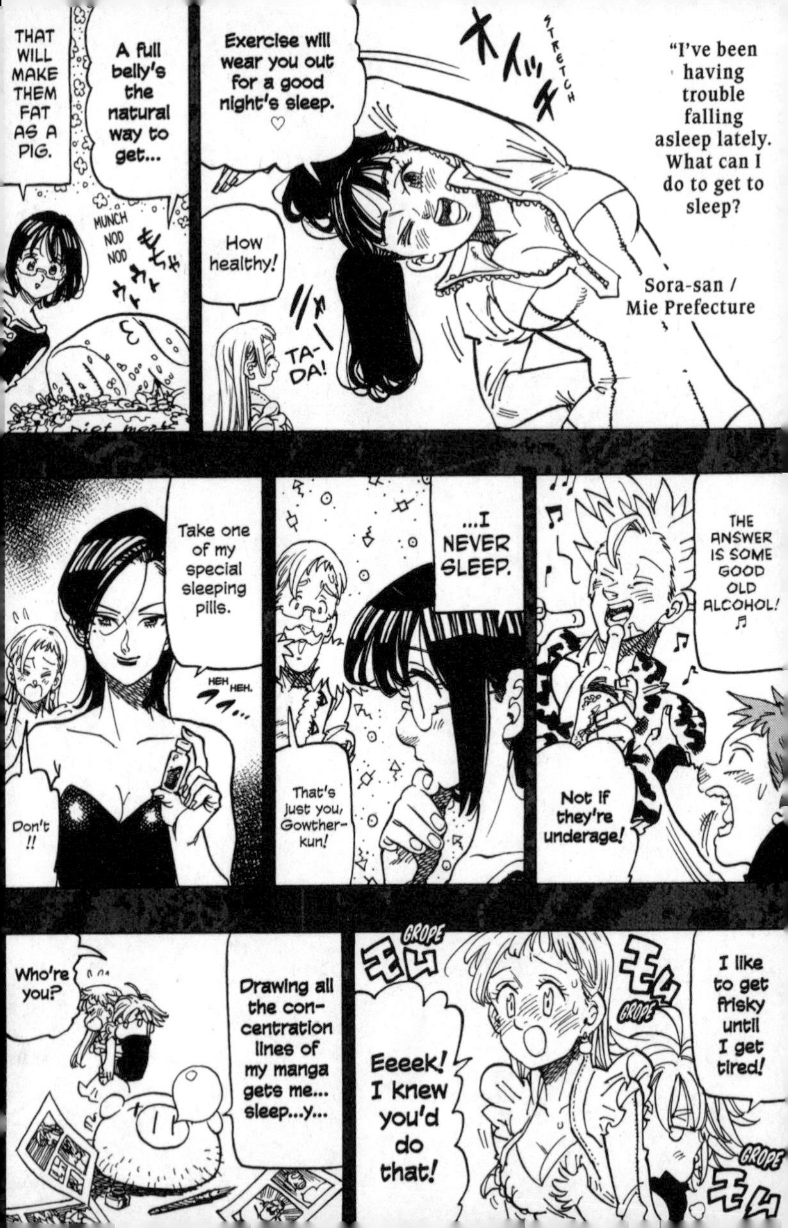
"I've been having trouble falling asleep lately. What can I do to get to sleep?
Sora-san / Mie Prefecture
STRETCH
Exercise will wear you out for a good night's sleep. ♡
How healthy!
TA-DA!
A full belly's the natural way to get...
THAT WILL MAKE THEM FAT AS A PIG.
MUNCH
NOD NOD
THE ANSWER IS SOME GOOD OLD ALCOHOL! ♬
Not if they're underage!
...I NEVER SLEEP.
That's just you, Gowther-kun!
Take one of my special sleeping pills.
HEH HEH.
Don't !!
I like to get frisky until I get tired!
GROPE
GROPE
GROPE
Eeeek! I knew you'd do that!
Drawing all the concentration lines of my manga gets me... sleep...y...
Who're you?

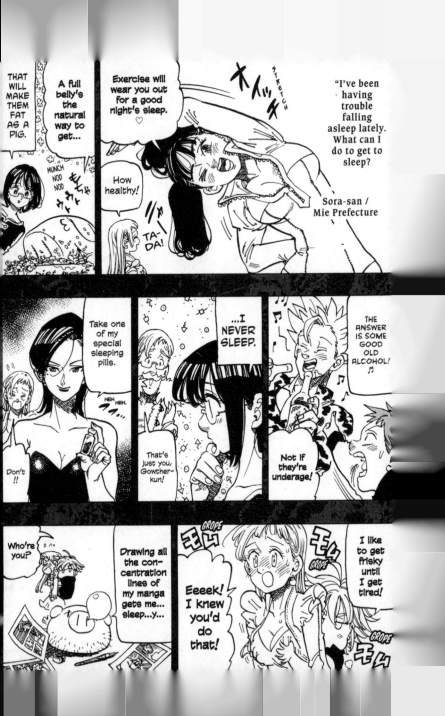

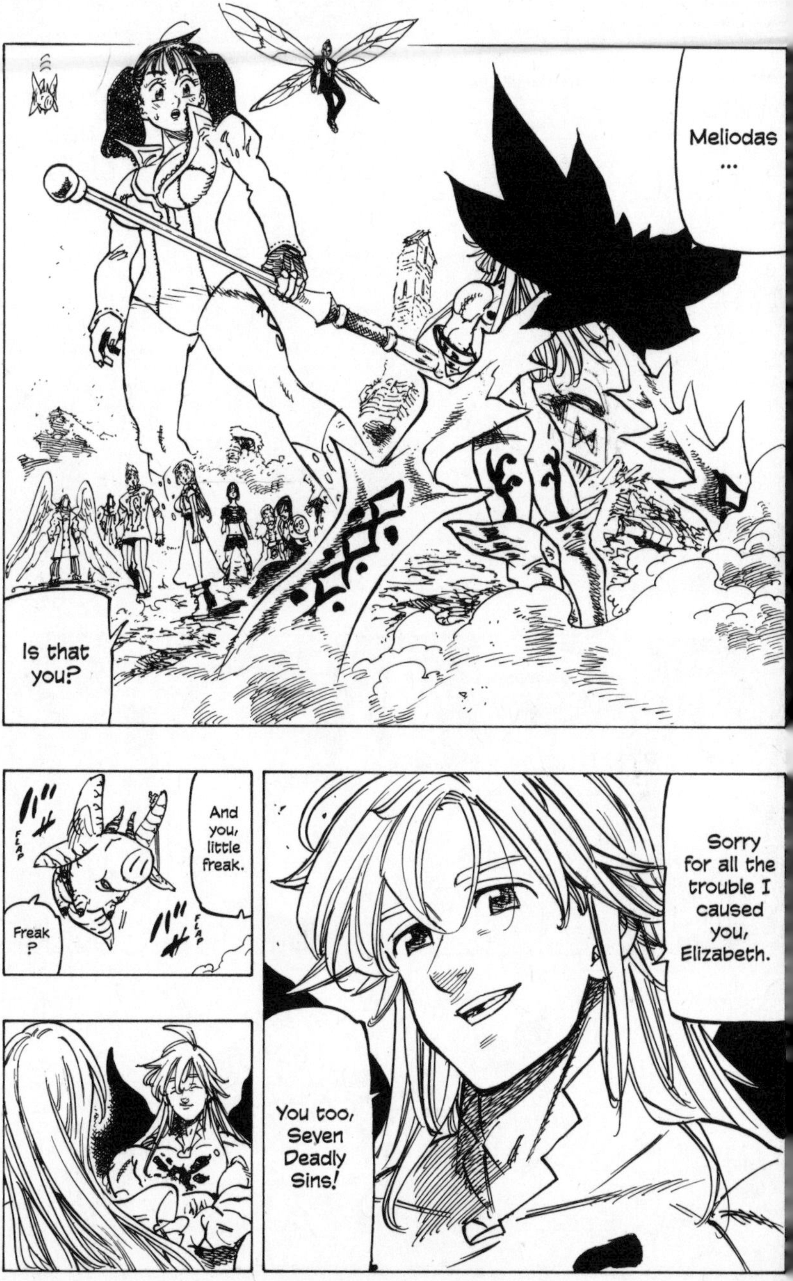
Meliodas ...
Is that you?
Sorry for all the trouble I caused you, Elizabeth.
You too, Seven Deadly Sins!
And you, little freak.
FLAP
FLAP
Freak?

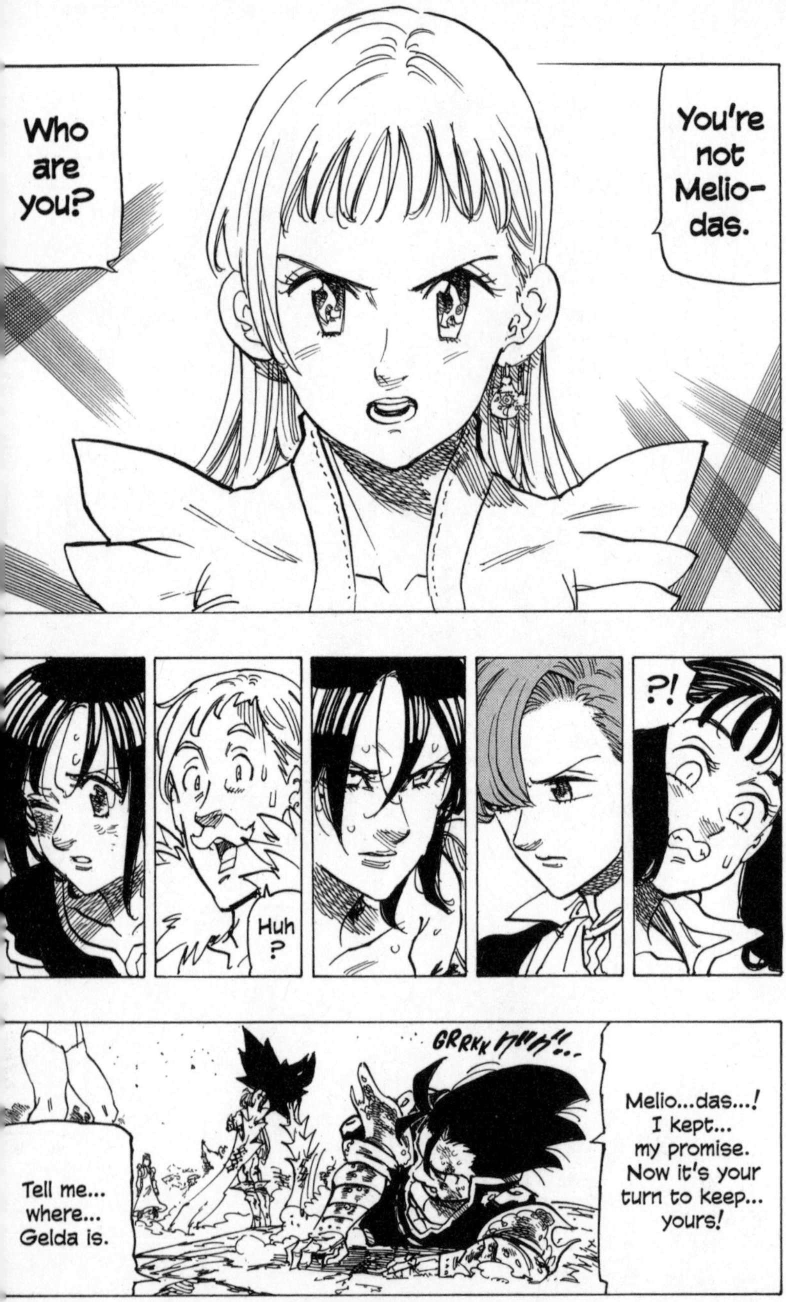
You're not Melio-das.
Who are you?
?!
Huh ?
Melio...das...! I kept... my promise. Now it's your turn to keep... yours!
GRRKK
Tell me... where... Gelda is.

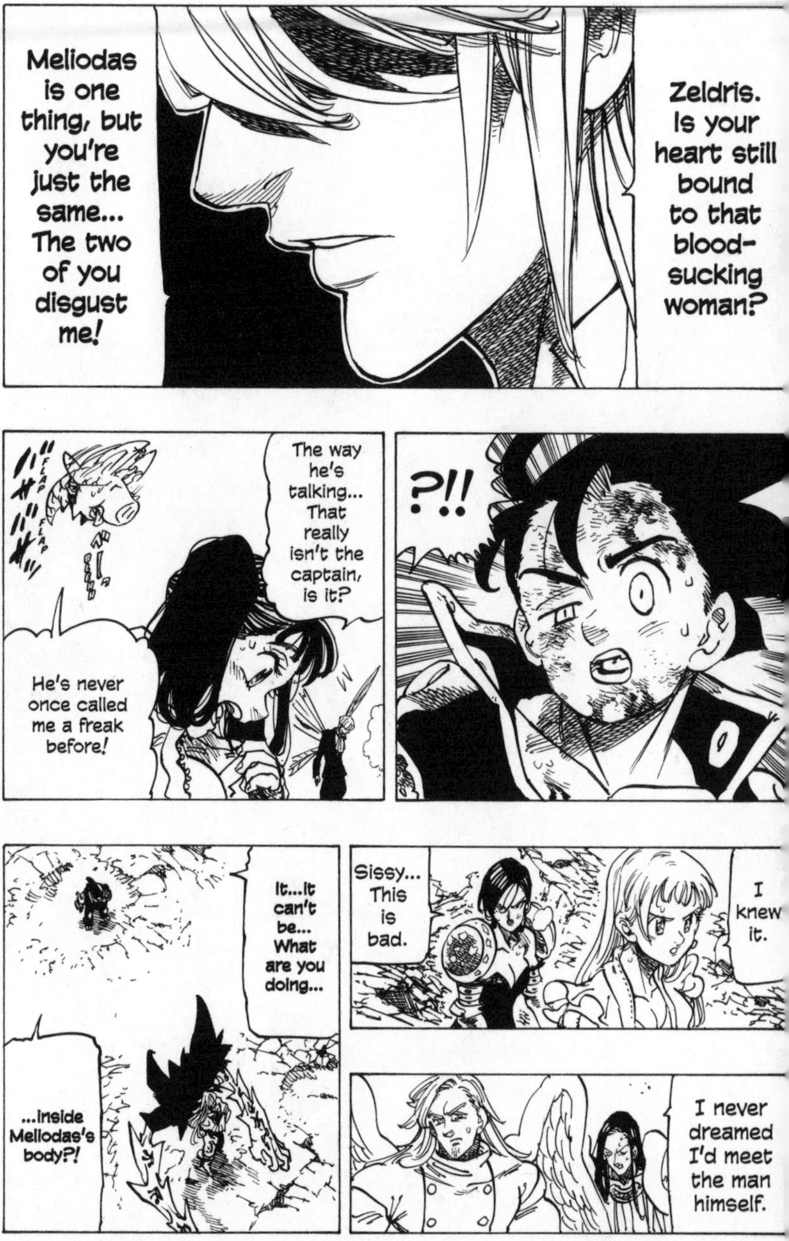
Zeldris. Is your heart still bound to that blood-sucking woman?
Meliodas is one thing, but you're just the same... The two of you disgust me!
?!!
The way he's talking... That really isn't the captain, is it?
He's never once called me a freak before!
I knew it.
Sissy... This is bad.
I never dreamed I'd meet the man himself.
It...it can't be... What are you doing...
...inside Meliodas's body?!

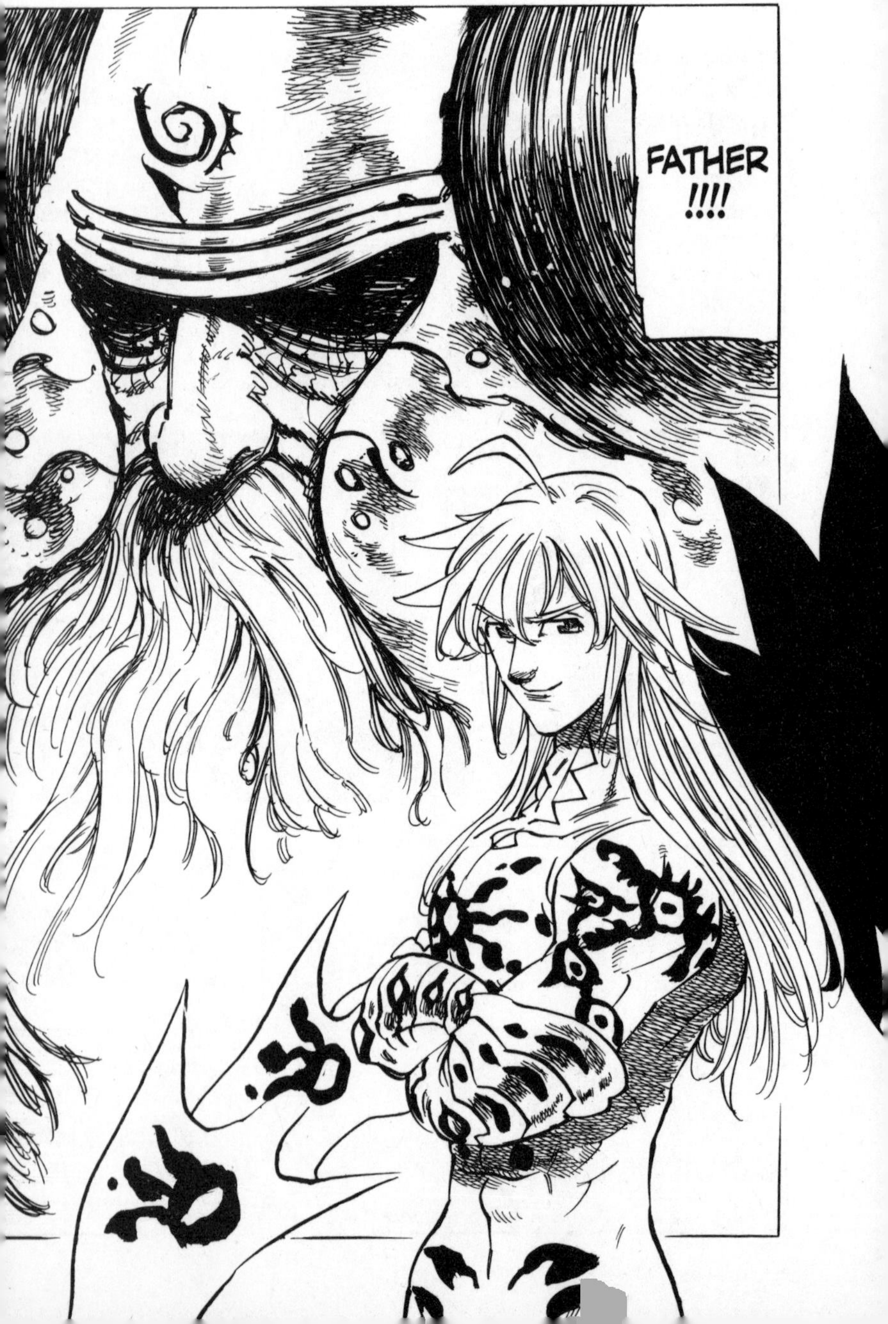
FATHER !!!!

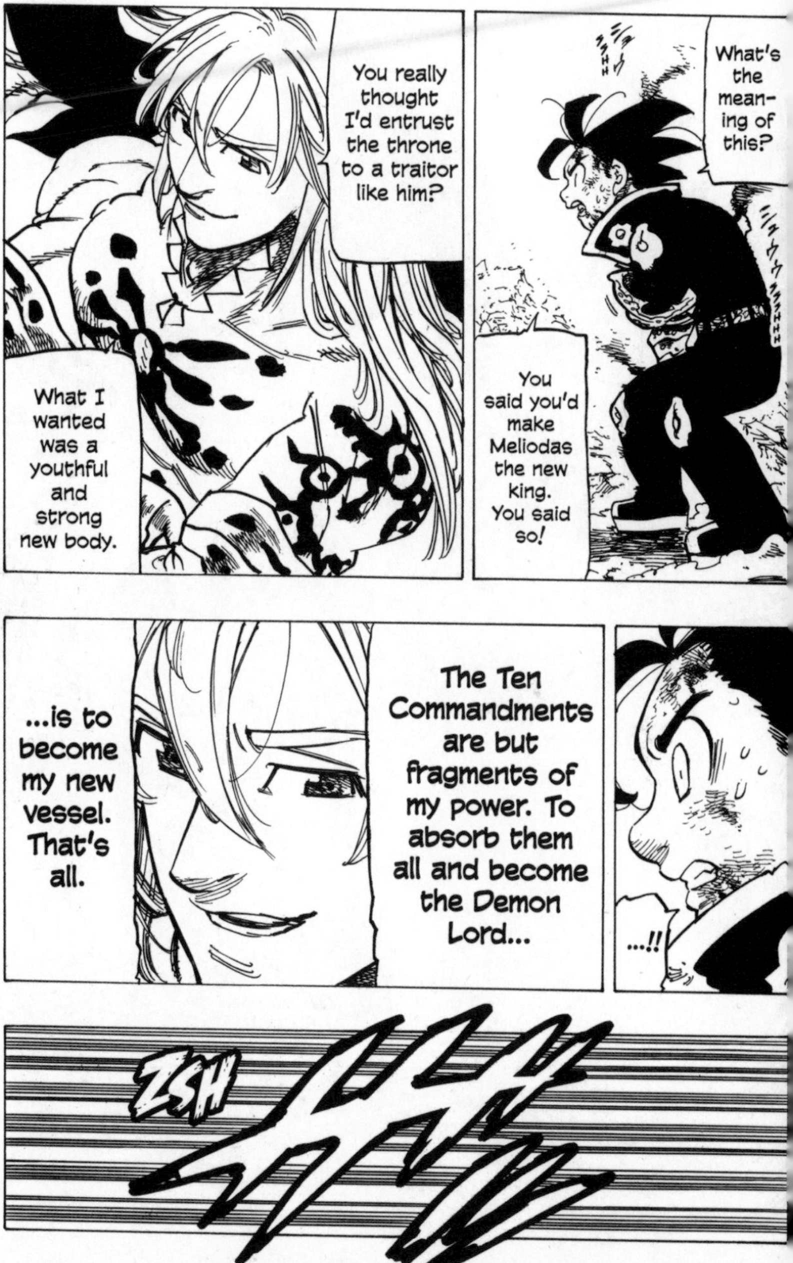
What's the meaning of this?
You said you'd make Meliodas the new king. You said so!
You really thought I'd entrust the throne to a traitor like him?
What I wanted was a youthful and strong new body.
...!!
The Ten Commandments are but fragments of my power. To absorb them all and become the Demon Lord...
...is to become my new vessel. That's all.
ZSH

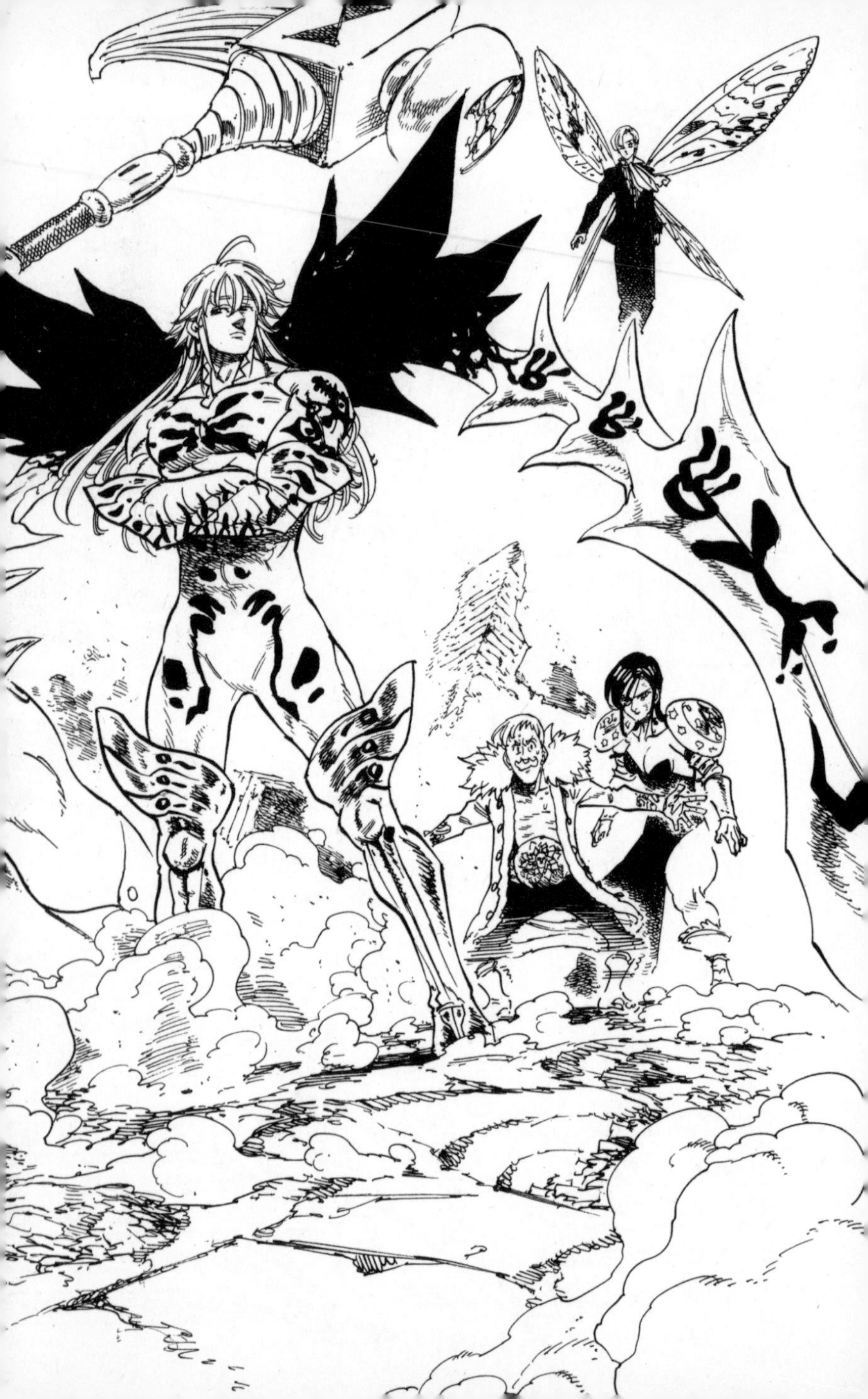

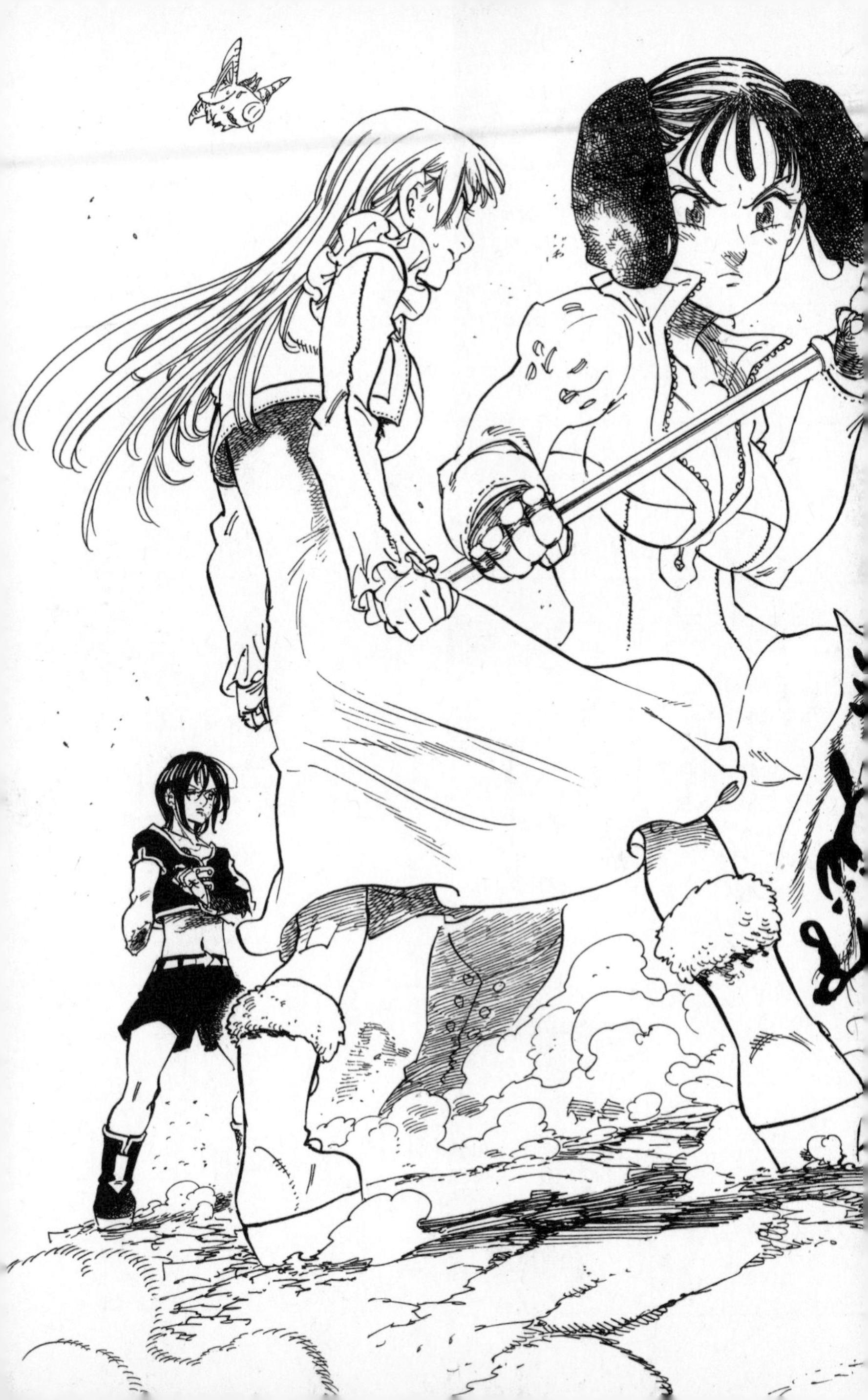

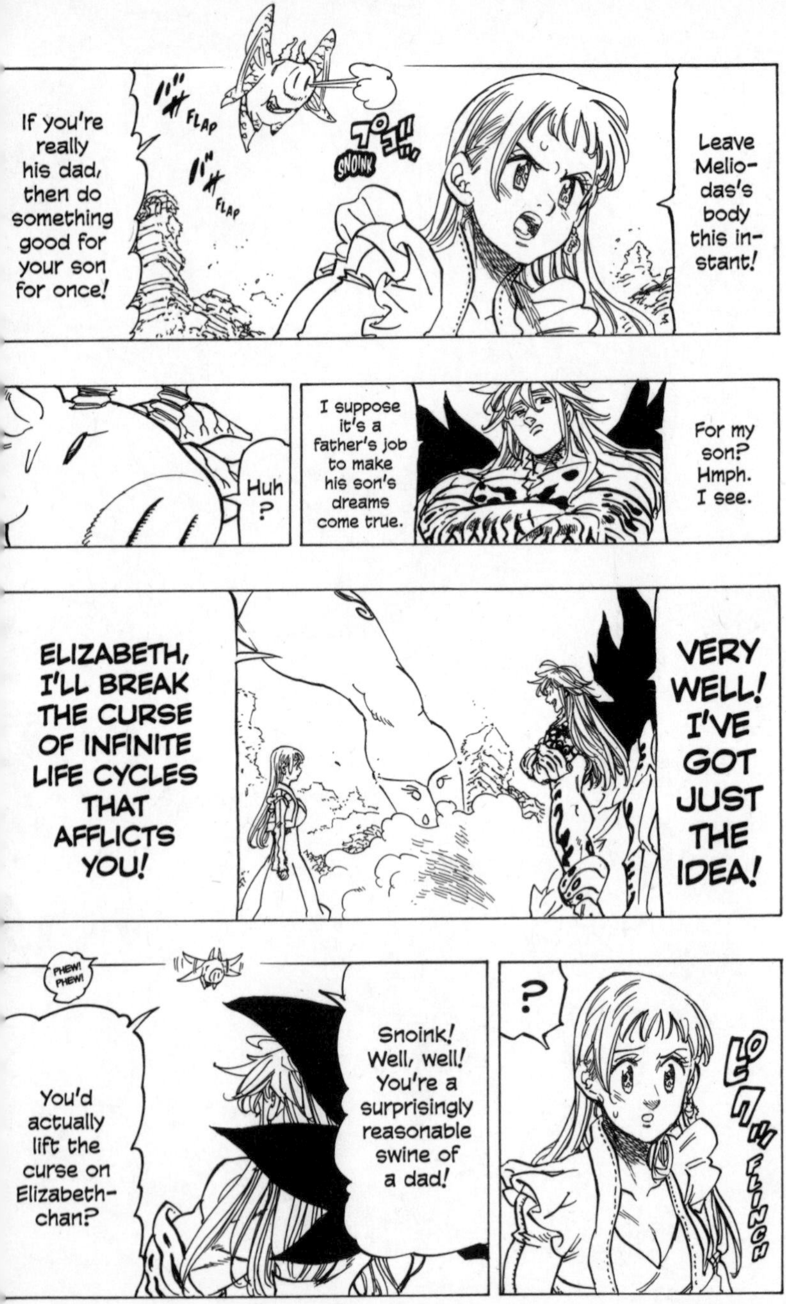
Leave Melio-das's body this in-stant!
If you're really his dad, then do something good for your son for once!
FLAP
FLAP
SNOINK
For my son? Hmph. I see.
I suppose it's a father's job to make his son's dreams come true.
Huh?
VERY WELL! I'VE GOT JUST THE IDEA!
ELIZABETH, I'LL BREAK THE CURSE OF INFINITE LIFE CYCLES THAT AFFLICTS YOU!
?
FLINCH
Snoink! Well, well! You're a surprisingly reasonable swine of a dad!
You'd actually lift the curse on Elizabeth-chan?
PHEW! PHEW!

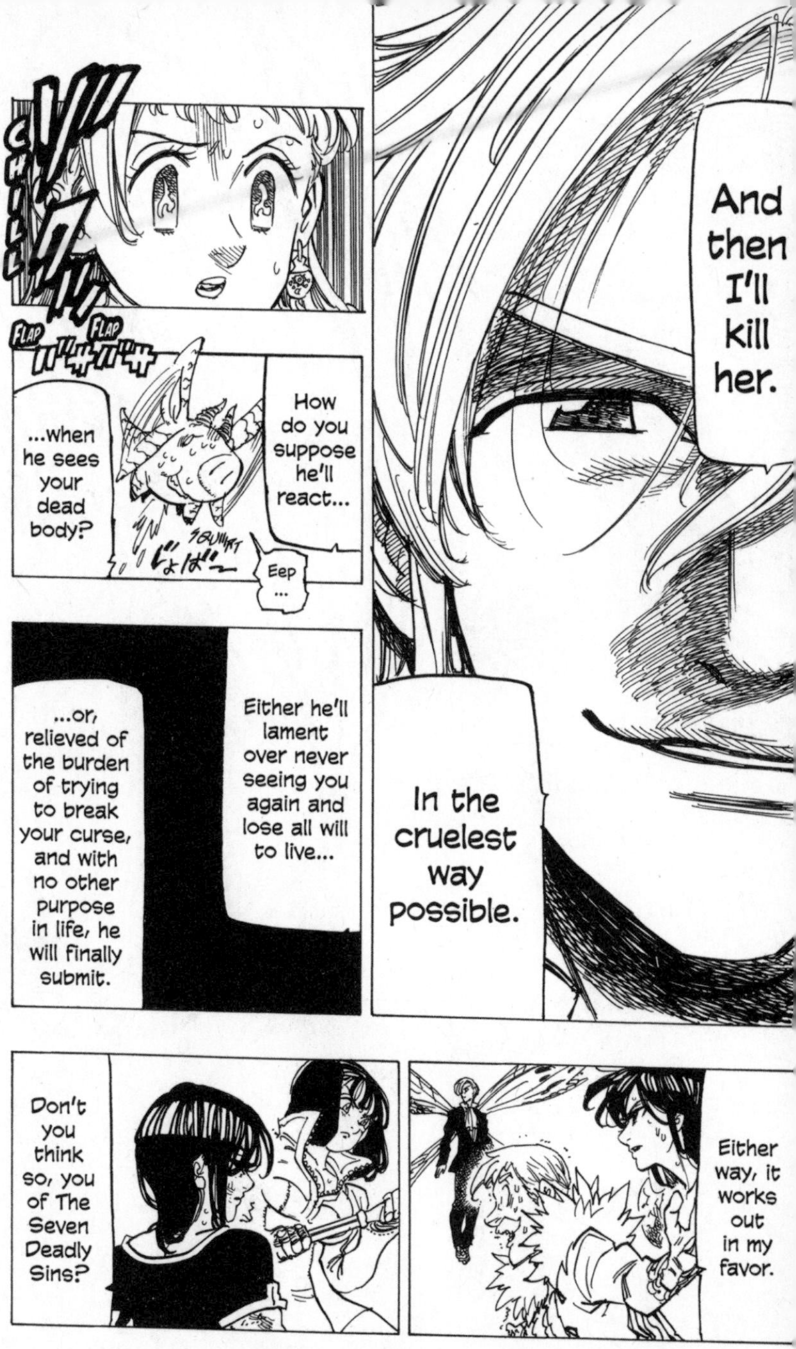
And then I'll kill her.
In the cruelest way possible.
CHILL
FLAP FLAP
How do you suppose he'll react...
...when he sees your dead body?
SQUIRT
Eep...
Either he'll lament over never seeing you again and lose all will to live...
...or, relieved of the burden of trying to break your curse, and with no other purpose in life, he will finally submit.
Either way, it works out in my favor.
Don't you think so, you of The Seven Deadly Sins?

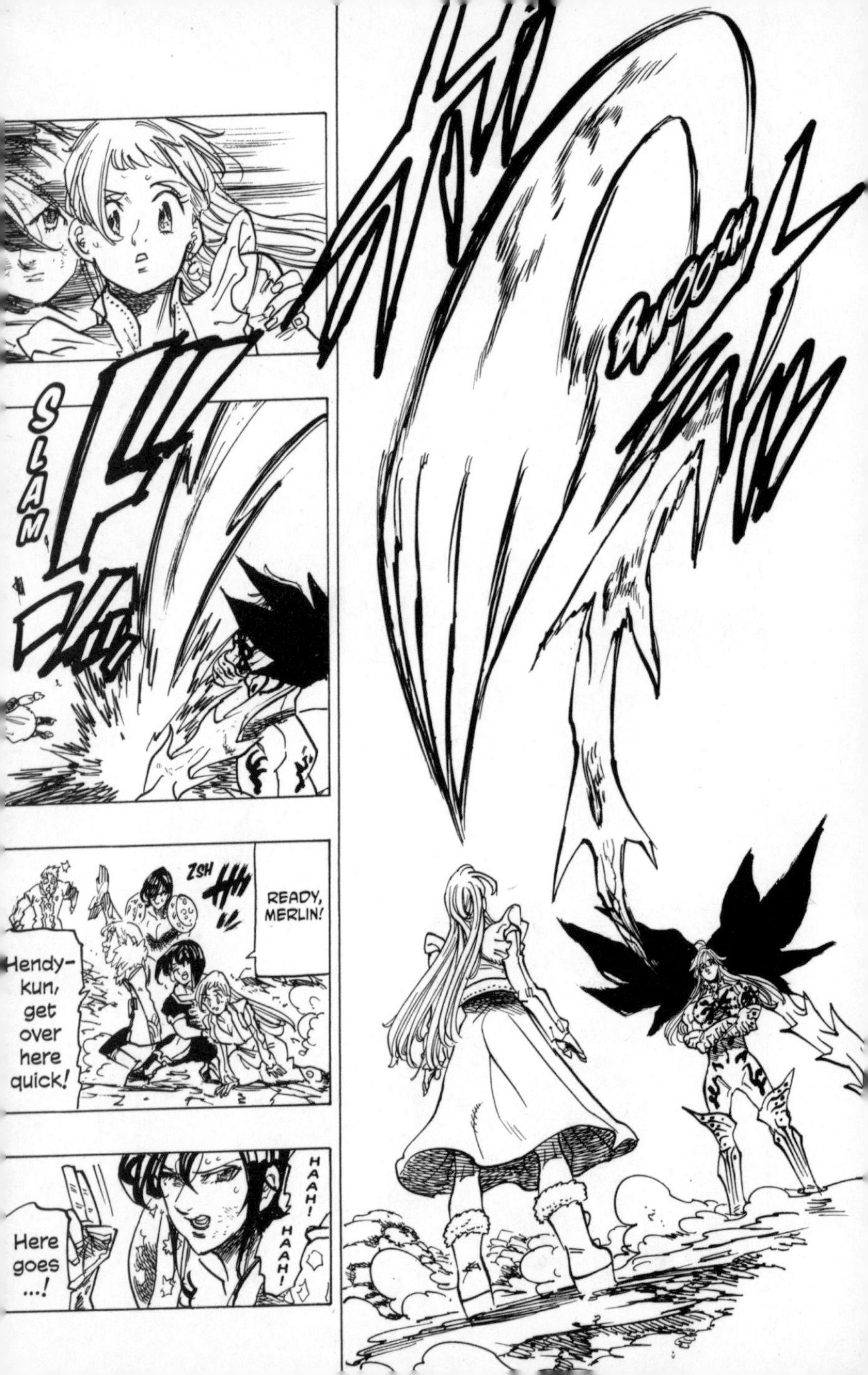
FWOOSH
SLAM
READY, MERLIN!
ZSH
Hendy-kun, get over here quick!
HAAH! HAAH!
Here goes ...!

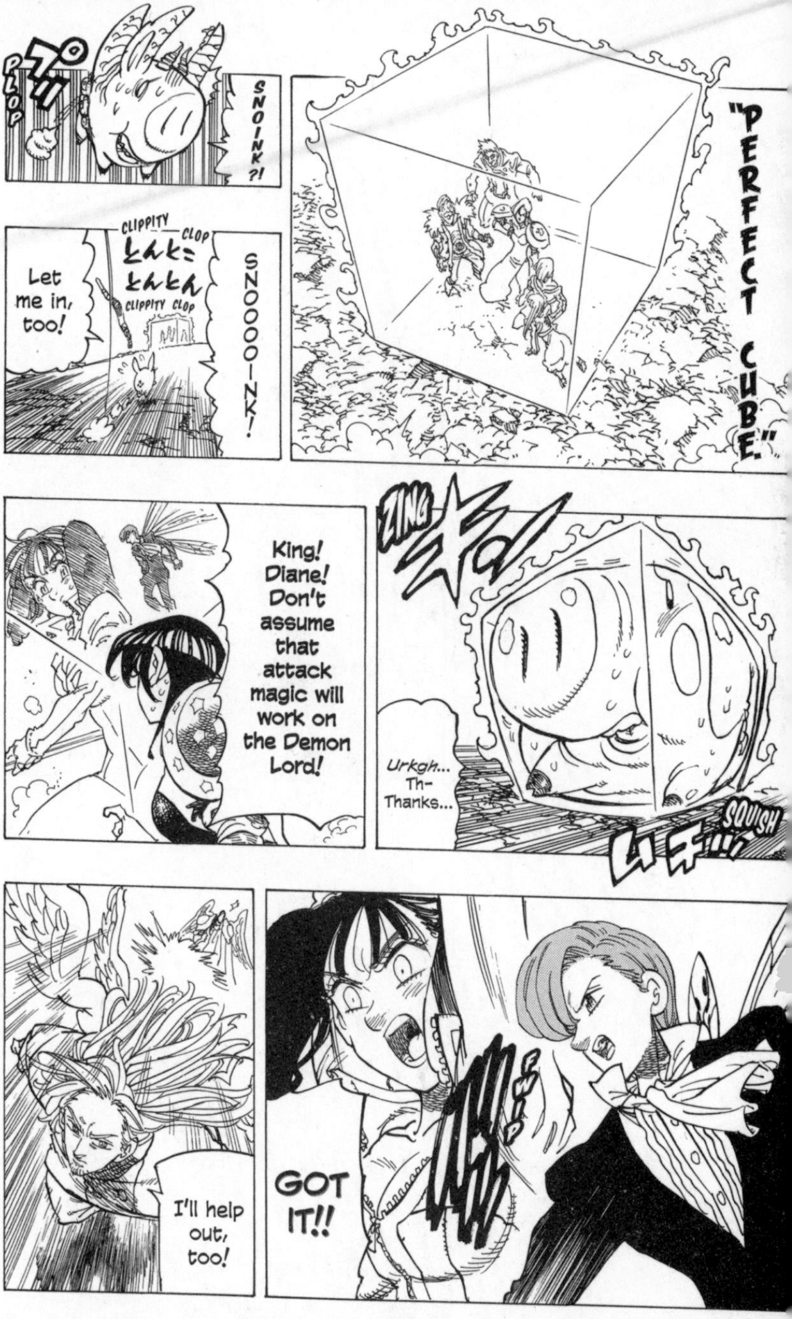

"PERFECT CUBE."
SNOINK?!
PLOP
CLIPPITY CLOP
とんとこ
とんとん
CLIPPITY CLOP
SNOOOOO-INK!
Let me in, too!
ZING
Urkgh... Th- Thanks...
SQUISH
King! Diane! Don't assume that attack magic will work on the Demon Lord!
FWIP
GOT IT!!
I'll help out, too!

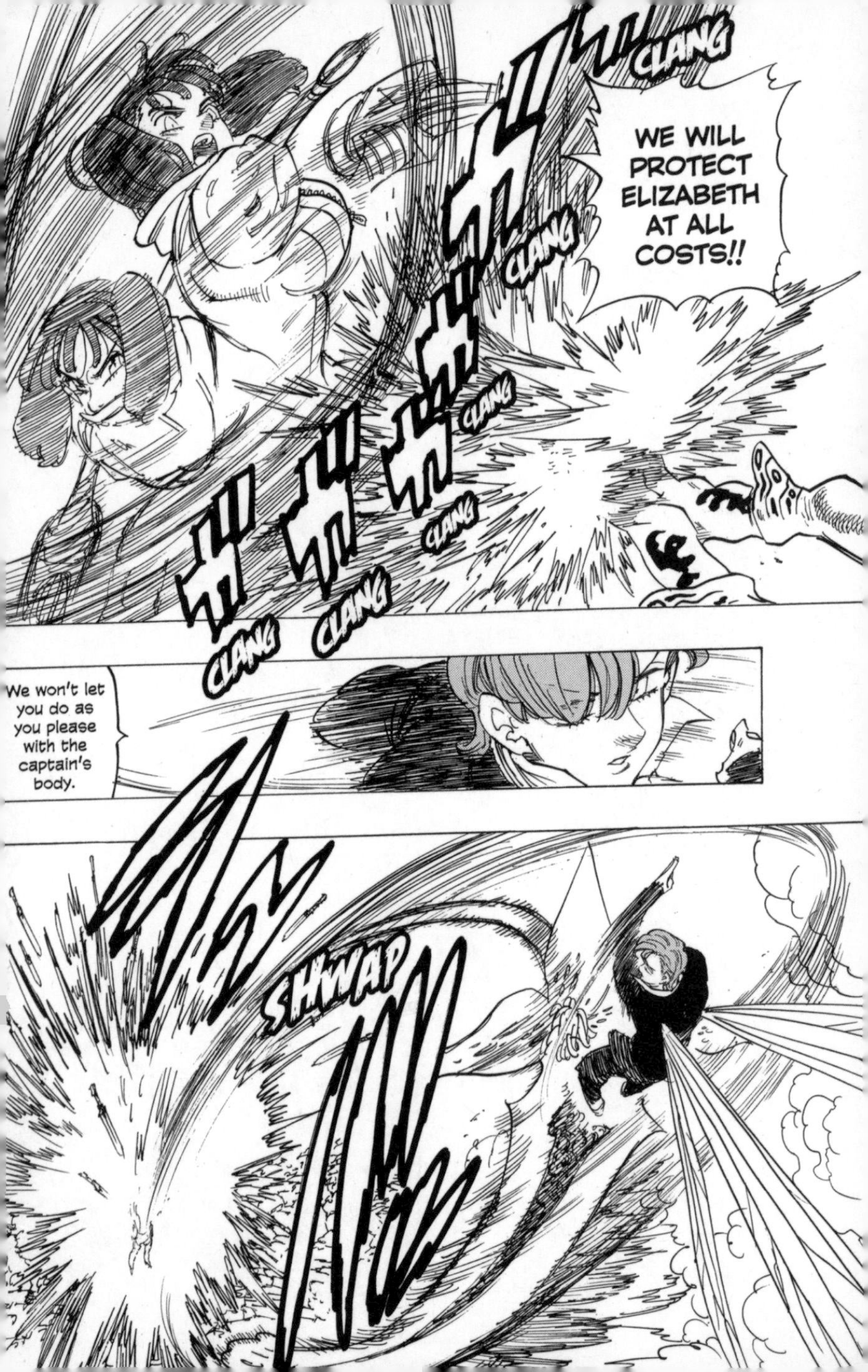
CLANG
WE WILL PROTECT ELIZABETH AT ALL COSTS!!
CLANG
CLANG
CLANG
CLANG
CLANG
CLANG
We won't let you do as you please with the captain's body.
SHWAP

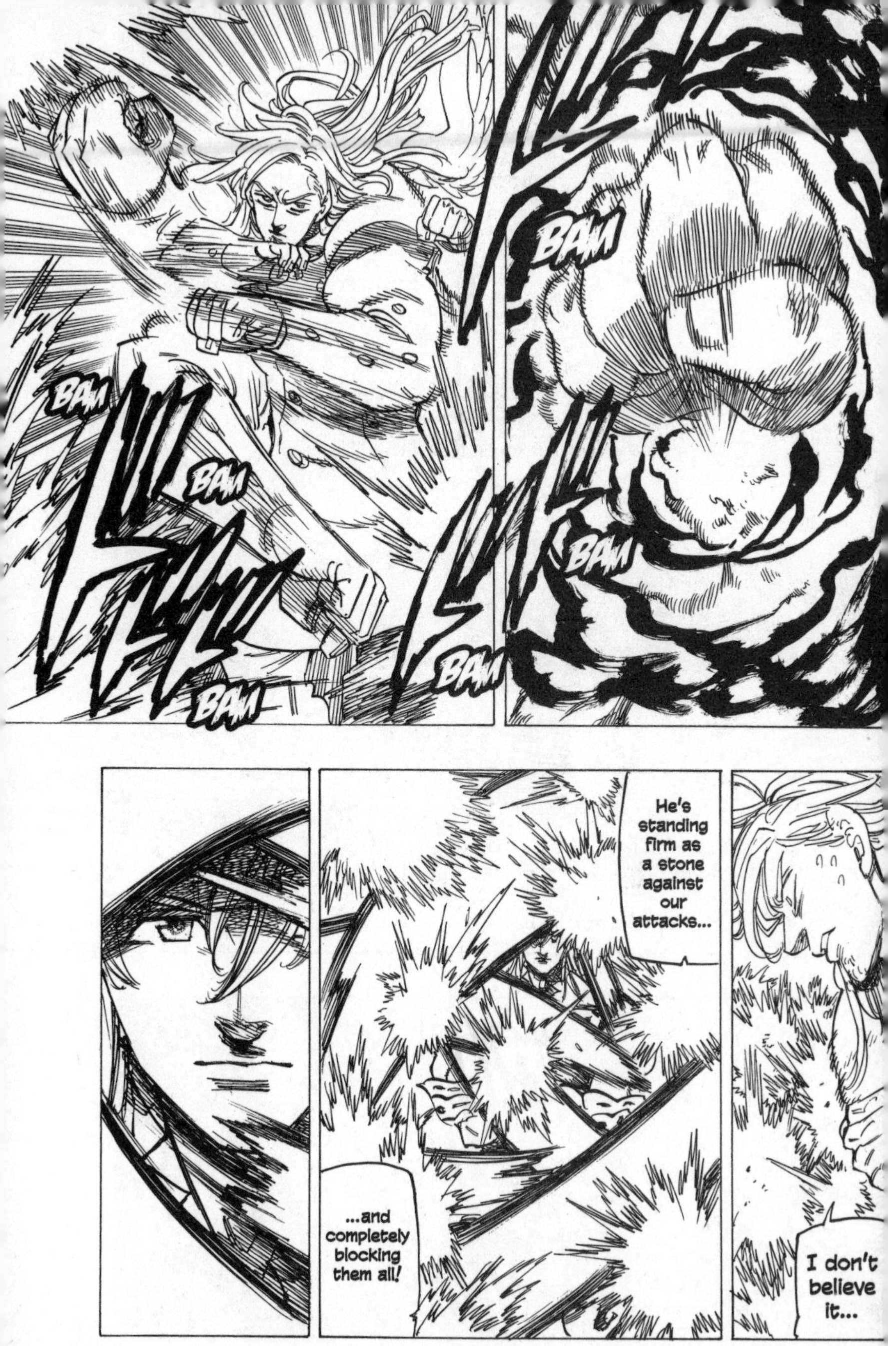

BAM
BAM
BAM
BAM
BAM
BAM
I don't believe it...
He's standing firm as a stone against our attacks...
...and completely blocking them all!

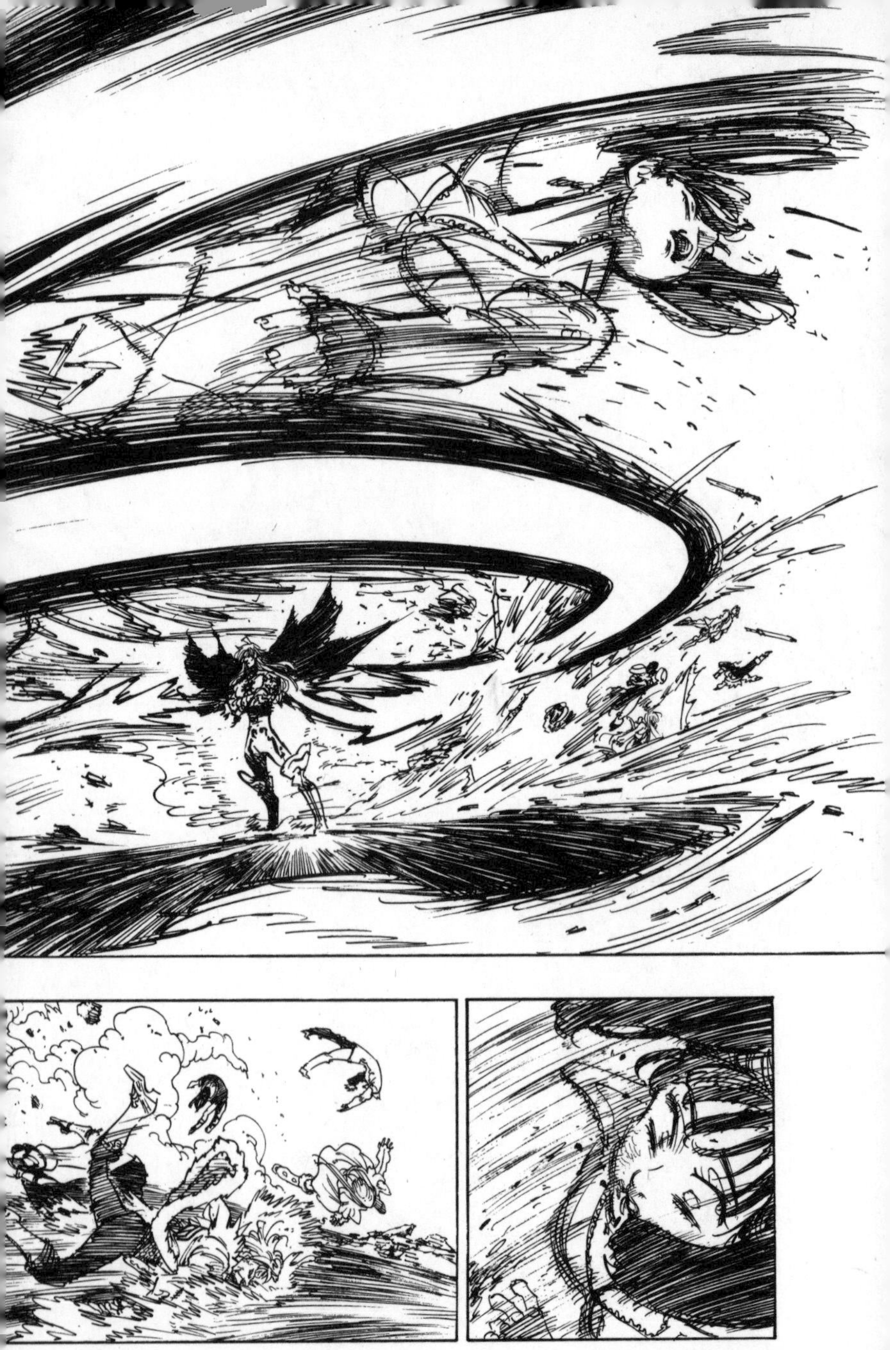

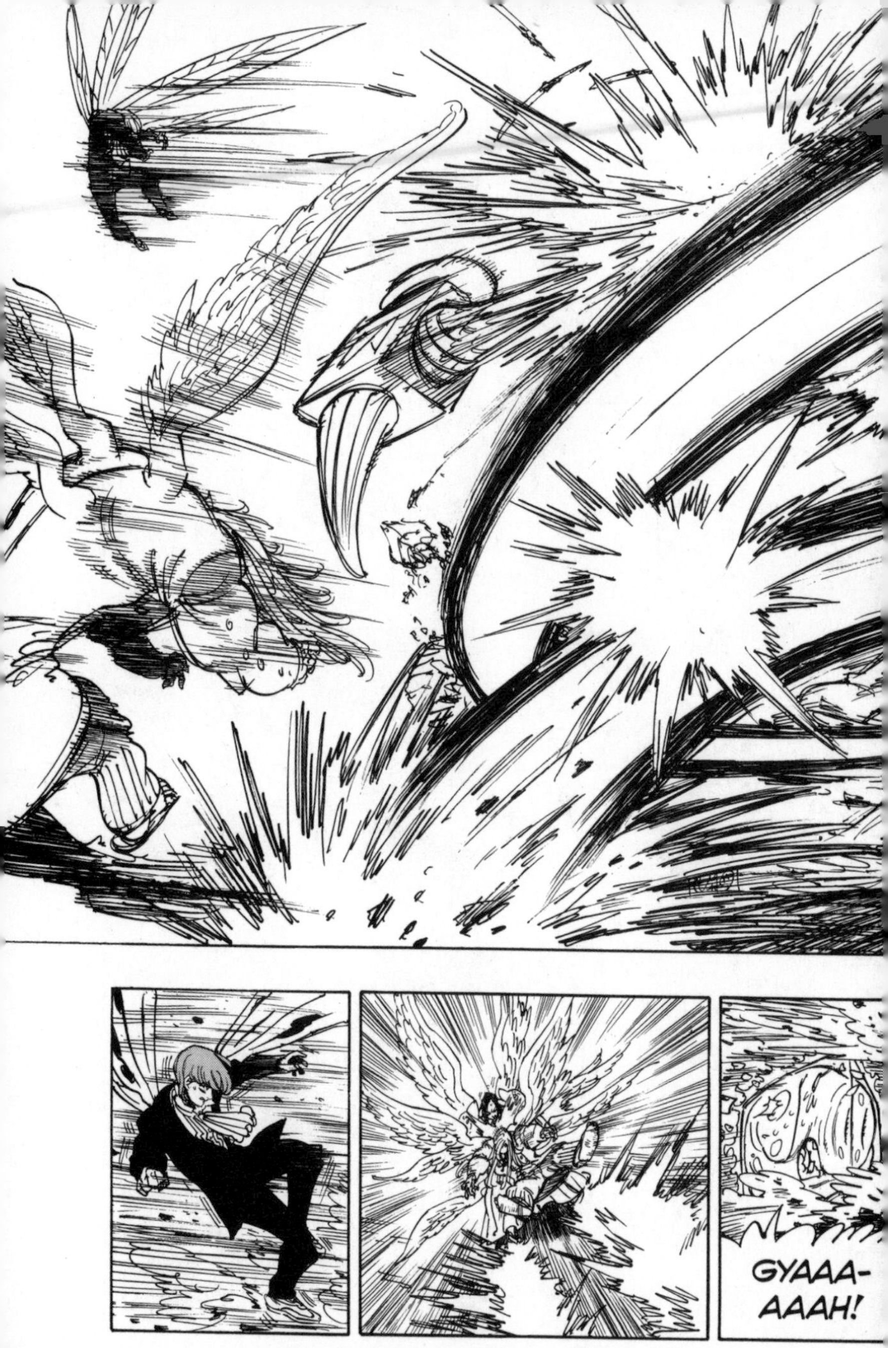
GYAAA-
AAAH!

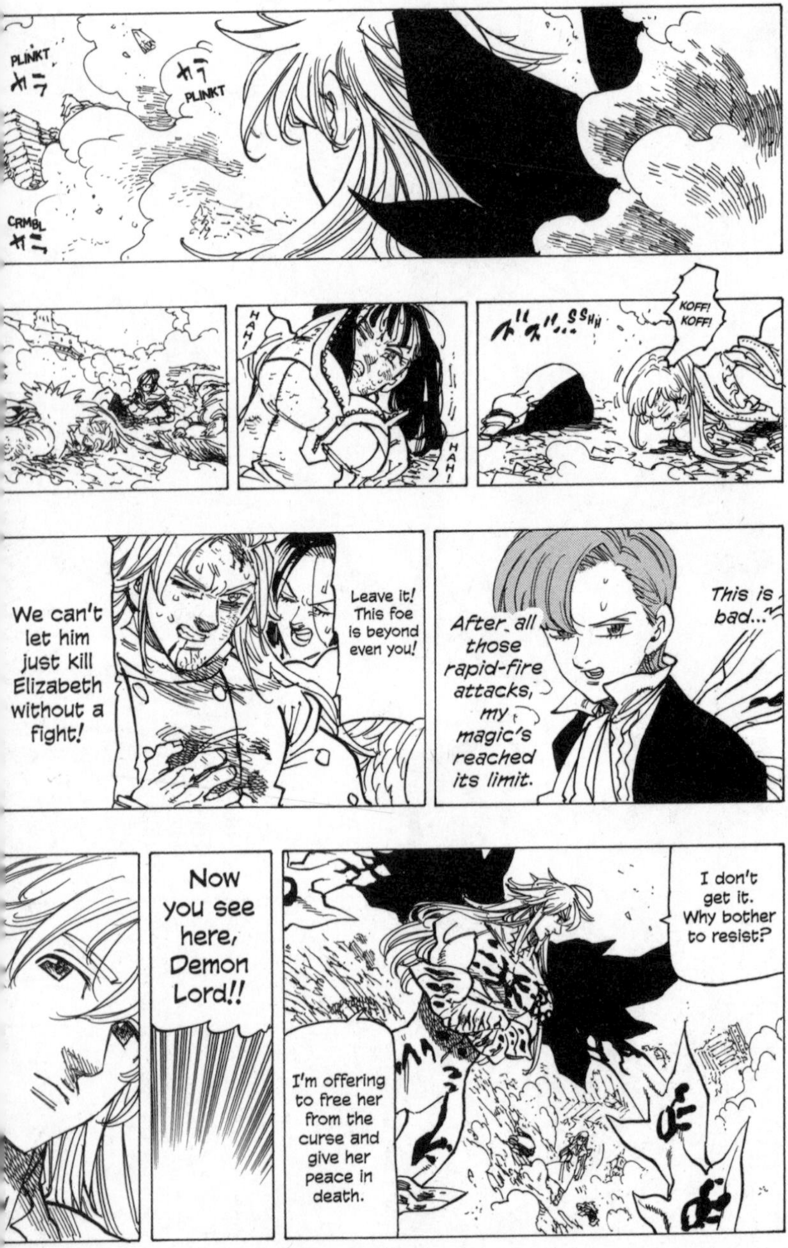
PLINKT
PLINKT
CRMBL
KOFF! KOFF!
SSHH
HAH!
HAH!
This is bad...
After all those rapid-fire attacks, my magic's reached its limit.
Leave it! This foe is beyond even you!
We can't let him just kill Elizabeth without a fight!
I don't get it. Why bother to resist?
I'm offering to free her from the curse and give her peace in death.
Now you see here, Demon Lord!!

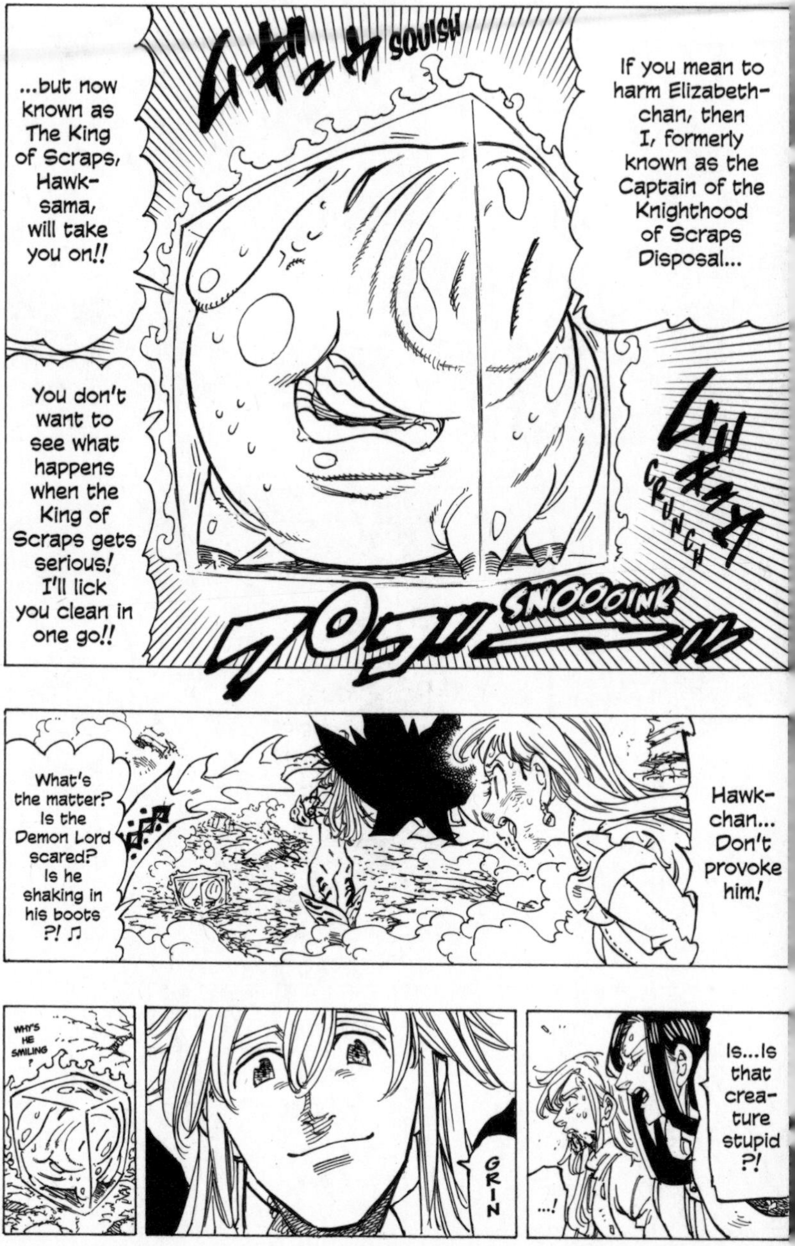
If you mean to harm Elizabeth-chan, then I, formerly known as the Captain of the Knighthood of Scraps Disposal...
SQUISH
...but now known as The King of Scraps, Hawk-sama, will take you on!!
CRUNCH
You don't want to see what happens when the King of Scraps gets serious! I'll lick you clean in one go!!
SNOOOINK
Hawk-chan... Don't provoke him!
What's the matter? Is the Demon Lord scared? Is he shaking in his boots?! ♫
Is...Is that creature stupid?!
...!
GRIN
WHY'S HE SMILING?

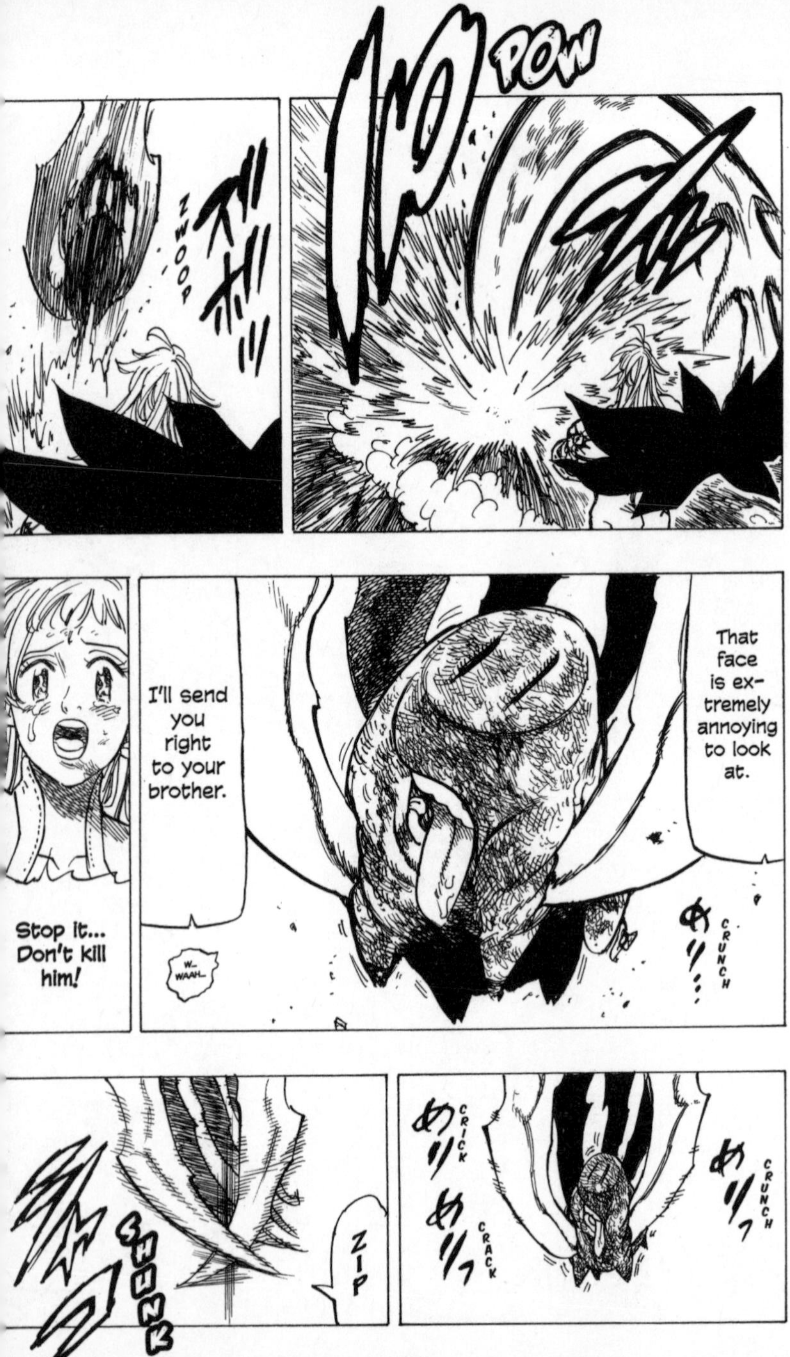
POW
ZWOOP
That face is extremely annoying to look at.
CRUNCH
I'll send you right to your brother.
W... WAAH...
Stop it... Don't kill him!
CRUNCH
CRICK
CRACK
ZIP
SHUNK

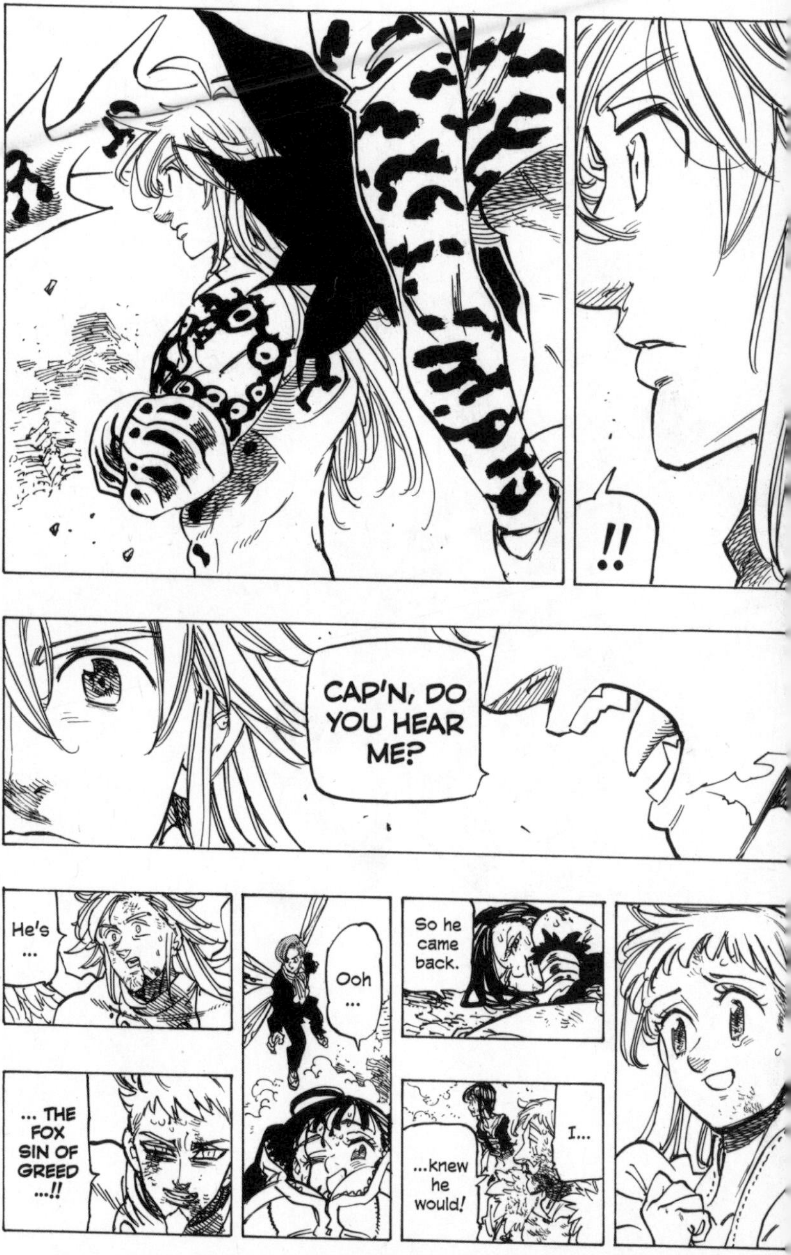
!!
CAP'N, DO YOU HEAR ME?
So he came back.
I...
...knew he would!
Ooh ...
He's ...
... THE FOX SIN OF GREED ...!!

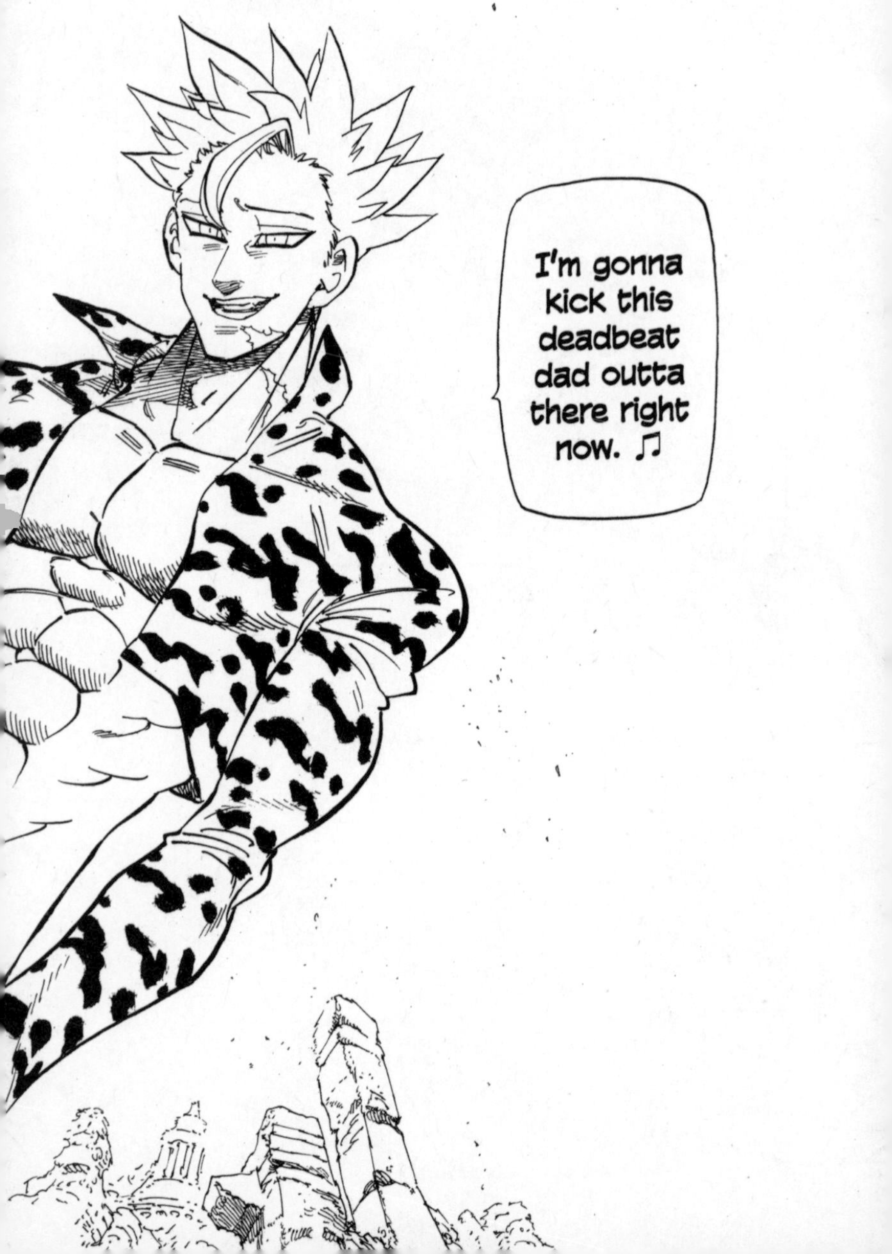
I'm gonna kick this deadbeat dad outta there right now. ♫

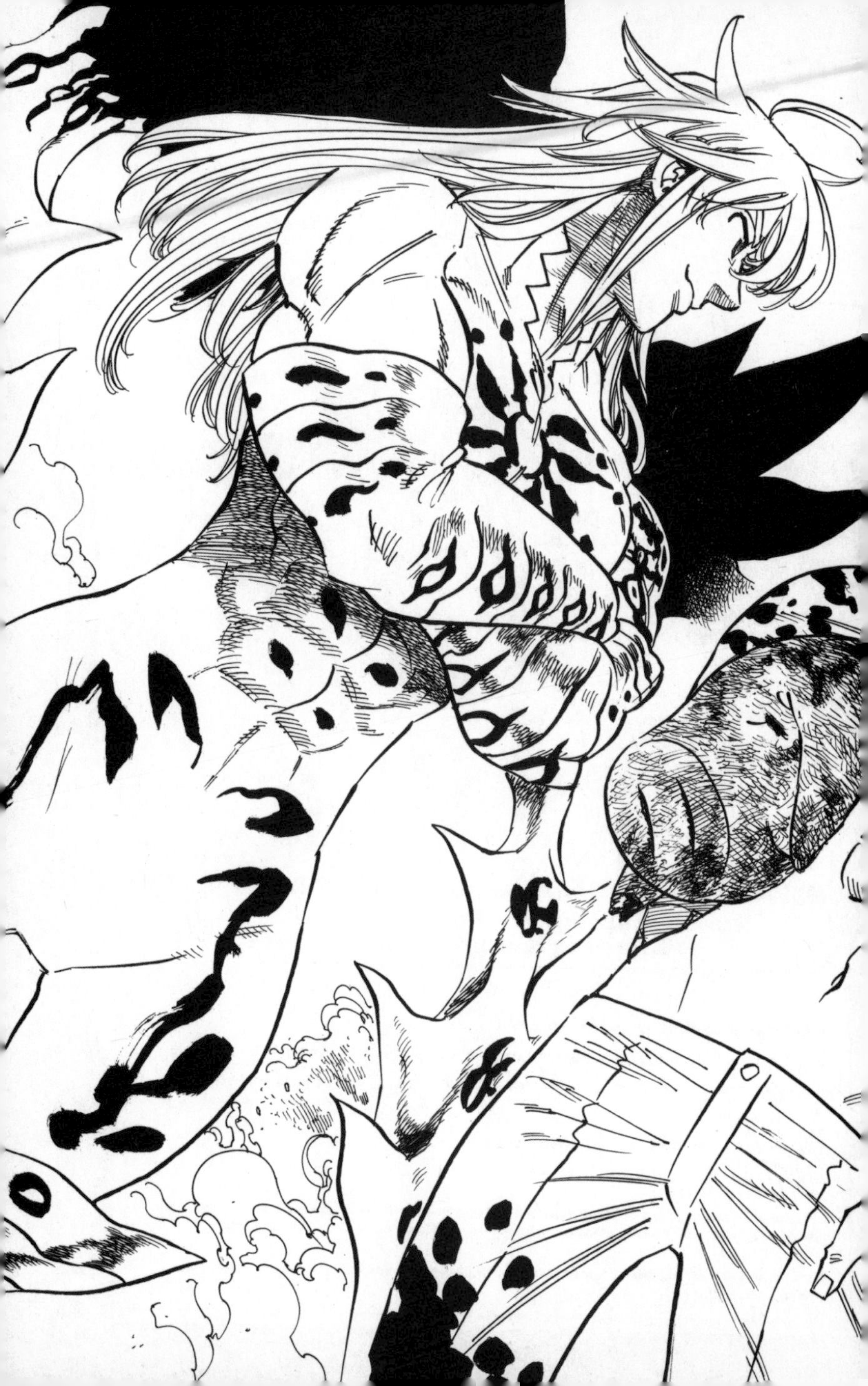

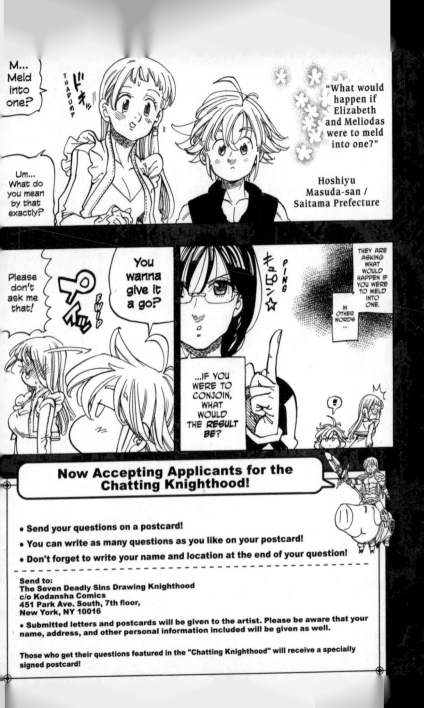

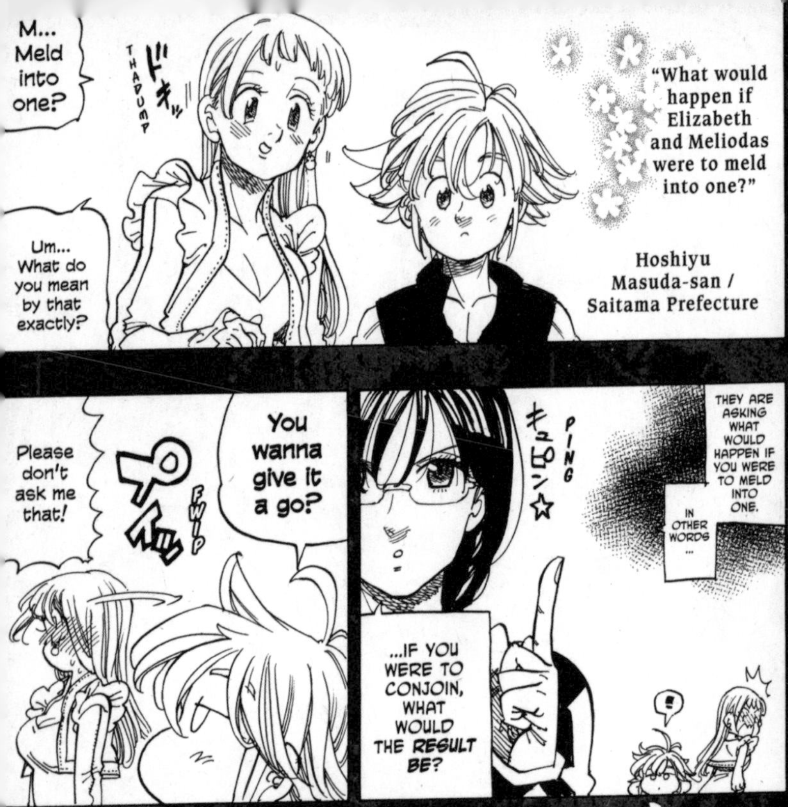
"What would happen if Elizabeth and Meliodas were to meld into one?"
Hoshiyu Masuda-san / Saitama Prefecture
THADUMP
M... Meld into one?
Um... What do you mean by that exactly?
THEY ARE ASKING WHAT WOULD HAPPEN IF YOU WERE TO MELD INTO ONE.
IN OTHER WORDS...
PING
...IF YOU WERE TO CONJOIN, WHAT WOULD THE RESULT BE?
You wanna give it a go?
FWIP
Please don't ask me that!

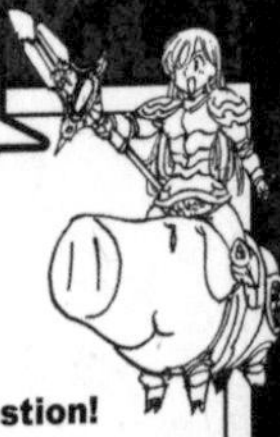

Now Accepting Applicants for the Chatting Knighthood!

- Send your questions on a postcard!
- You can write as many questions as you like on your postcard!
- Don't forget to write your name and location at the end of your question!

Send to:
The Seven Deadly Sins Drawing Knighthood
c/o Kodansha Comics
451 Park Ave. South, 7th floor,
New York, NY 10016

- Submitted letters and postcards will be given to the artist. Please be aware that your name, address, and other personal information included will be given as well.

Those who get their questions featured in the "Chatting Knighthood" will receive a specially signed postcard!

Chapter 301 - The One Who Stands Against a God

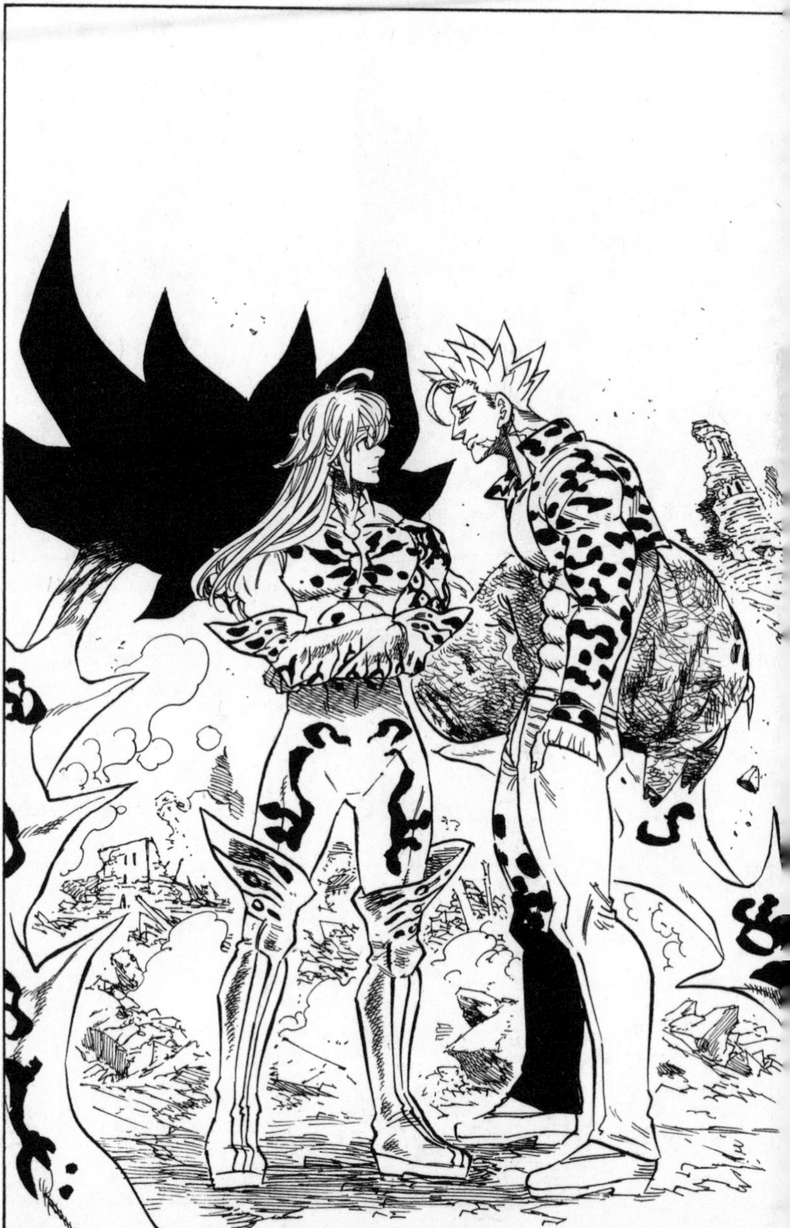

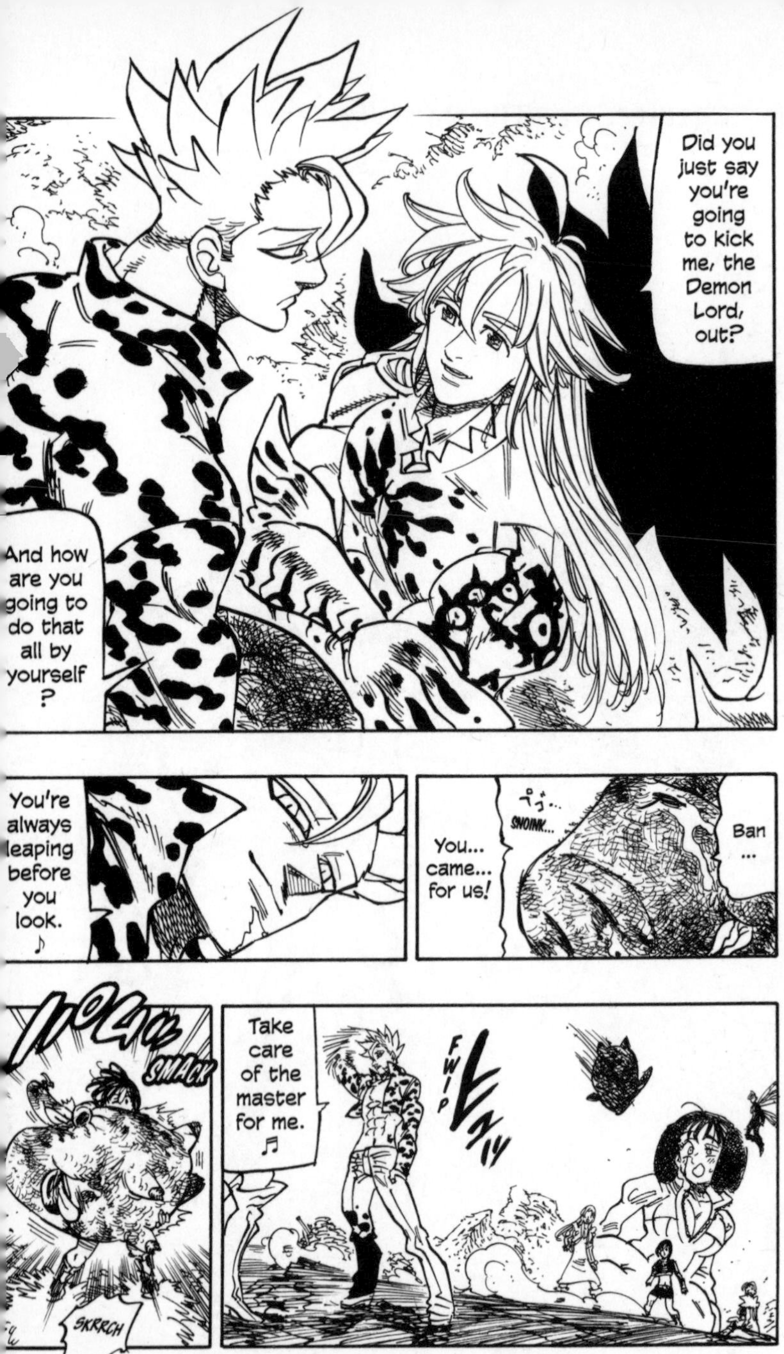
Did you just say you're going to kick me, the Demon Lord, out?
And how are you going to do that all by yourself?
Ban...
SNOINK...
You... came... for us!
You're always leaping before you look. ♪
FWIP
Take care of the master for me. ♬
SMACK
SKRRCH

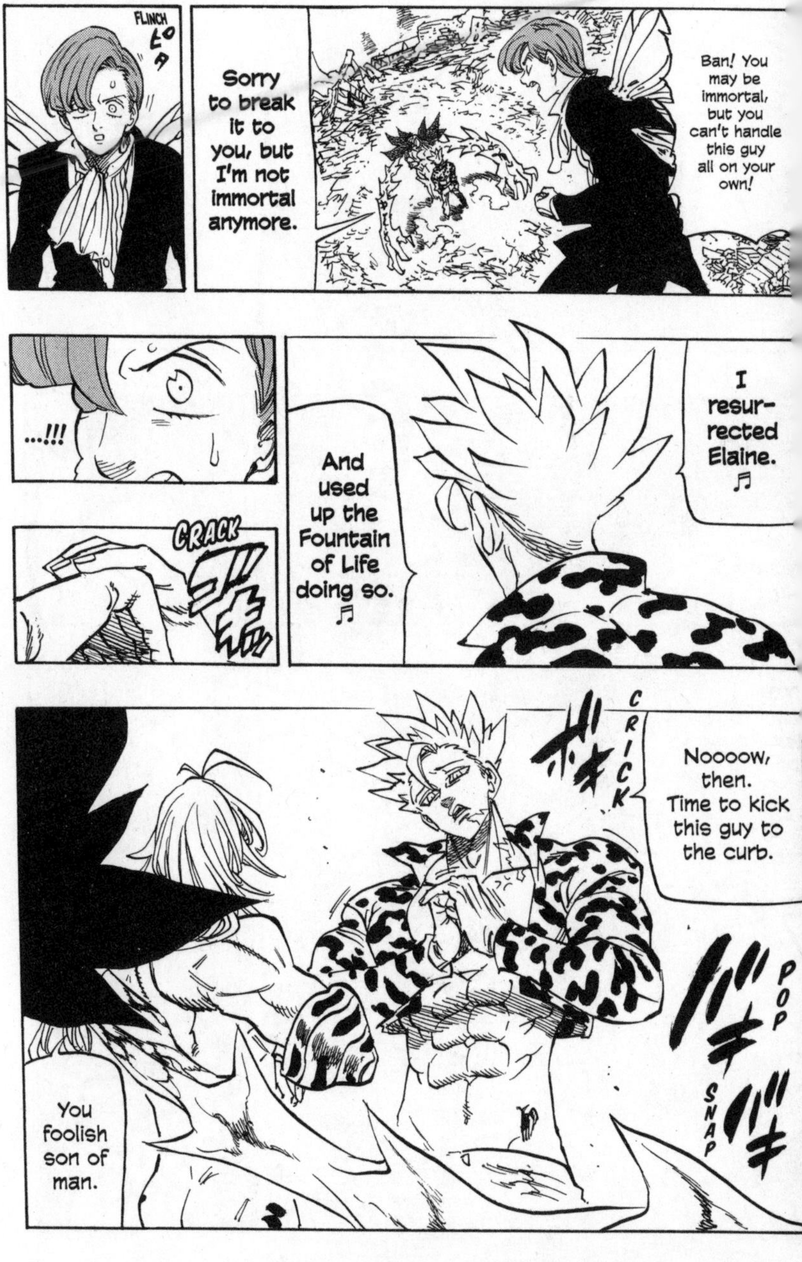
Ban! You may be immortal, but you can't handle this guy all on your own!
Sorry to break it to you, but I'm not immortal anymore.
FLINCH
I resurrected Elaine. ♫
And used up the Fountain of Life doing so. ♫
...!!!
CRACK
CRICK
Noooow, then. Time to kick this guy to the curb.
POP
SNAP
You foolish son of man.

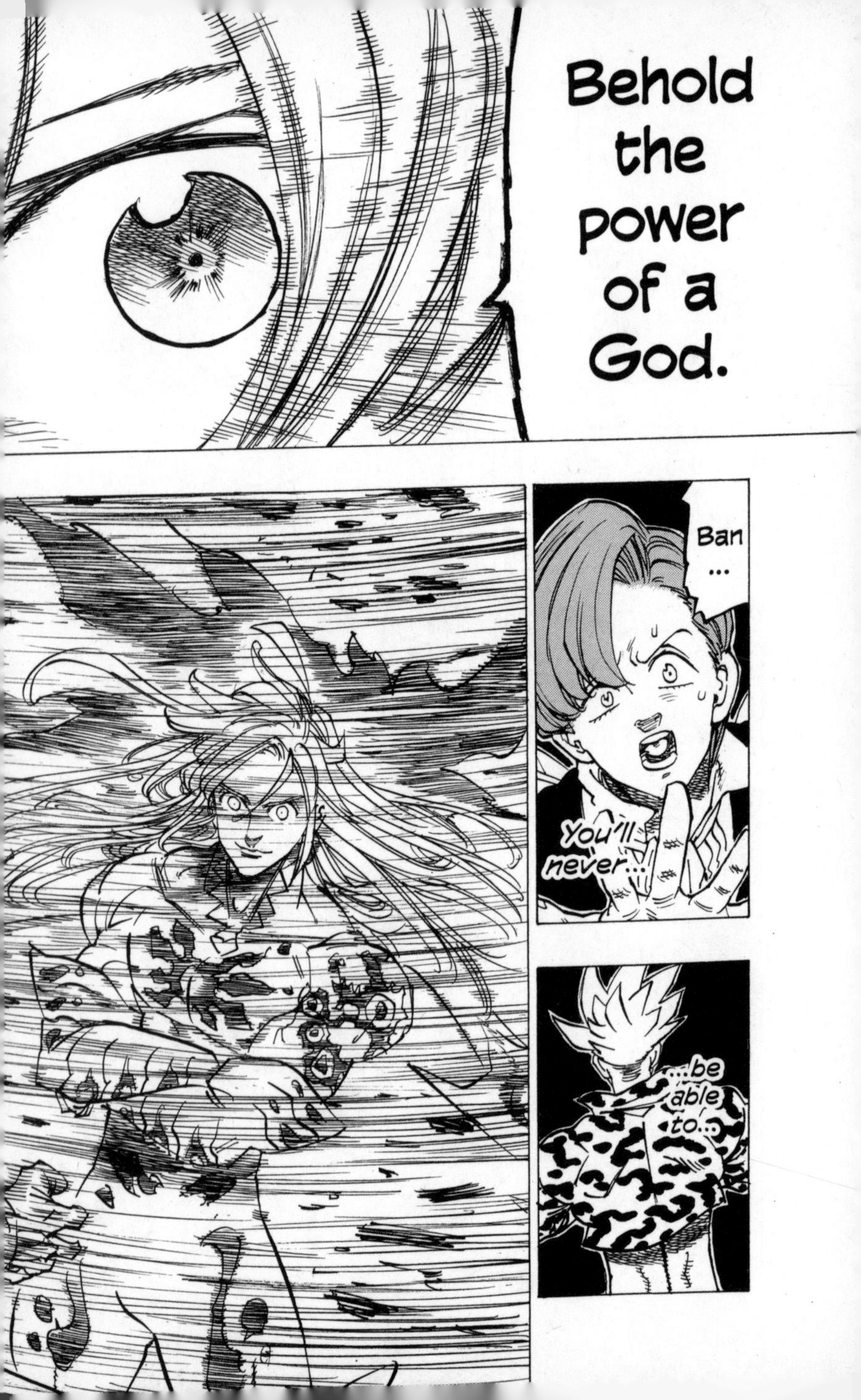
Behold the power of a God.
Ban ...
You'll never...
...be able to...

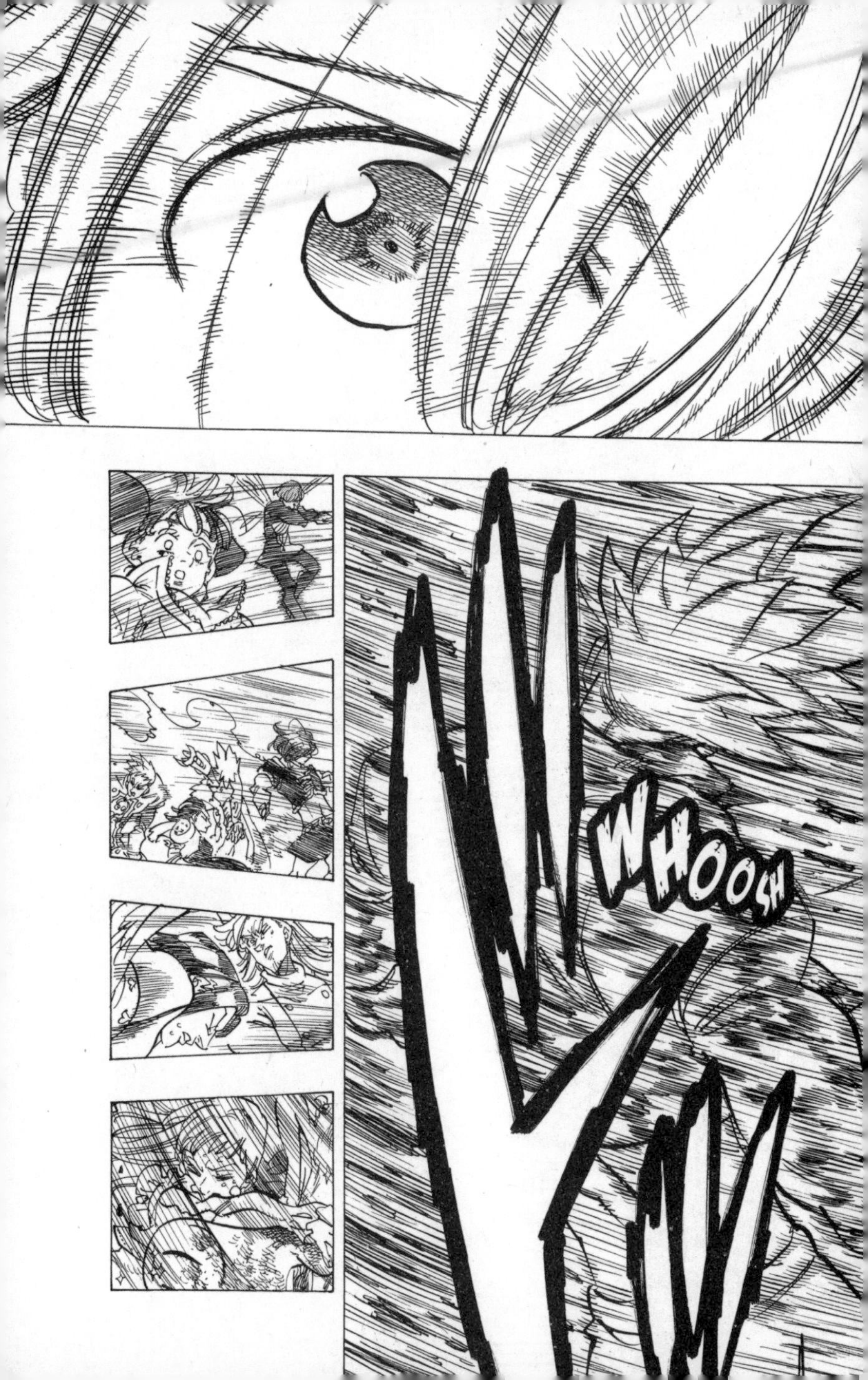
WHOOSH

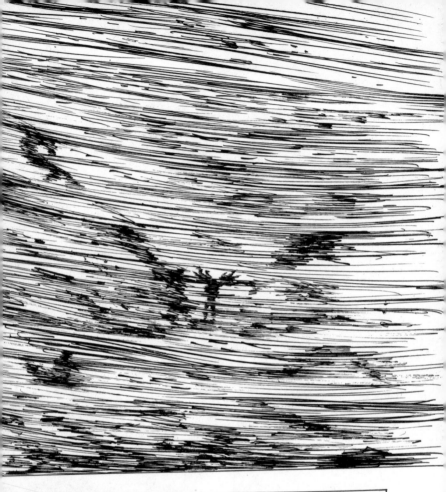

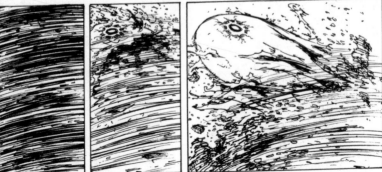

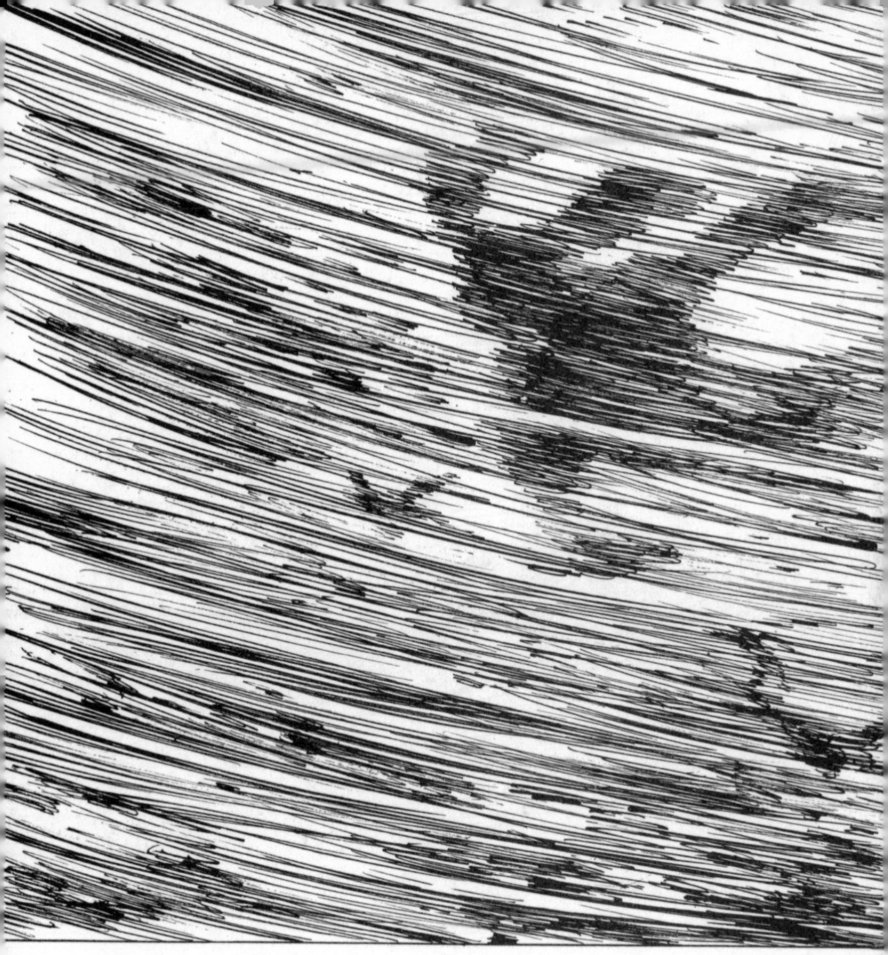

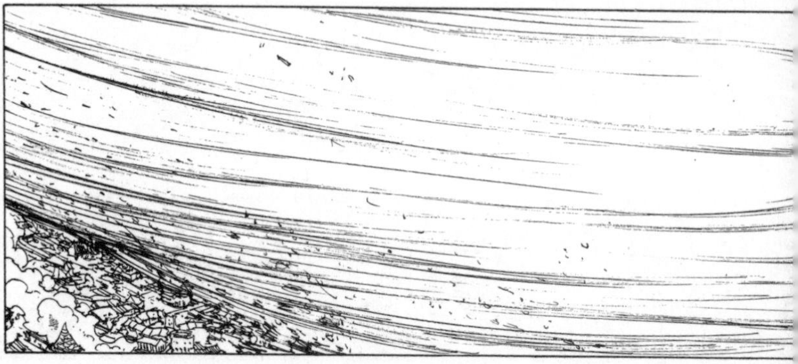

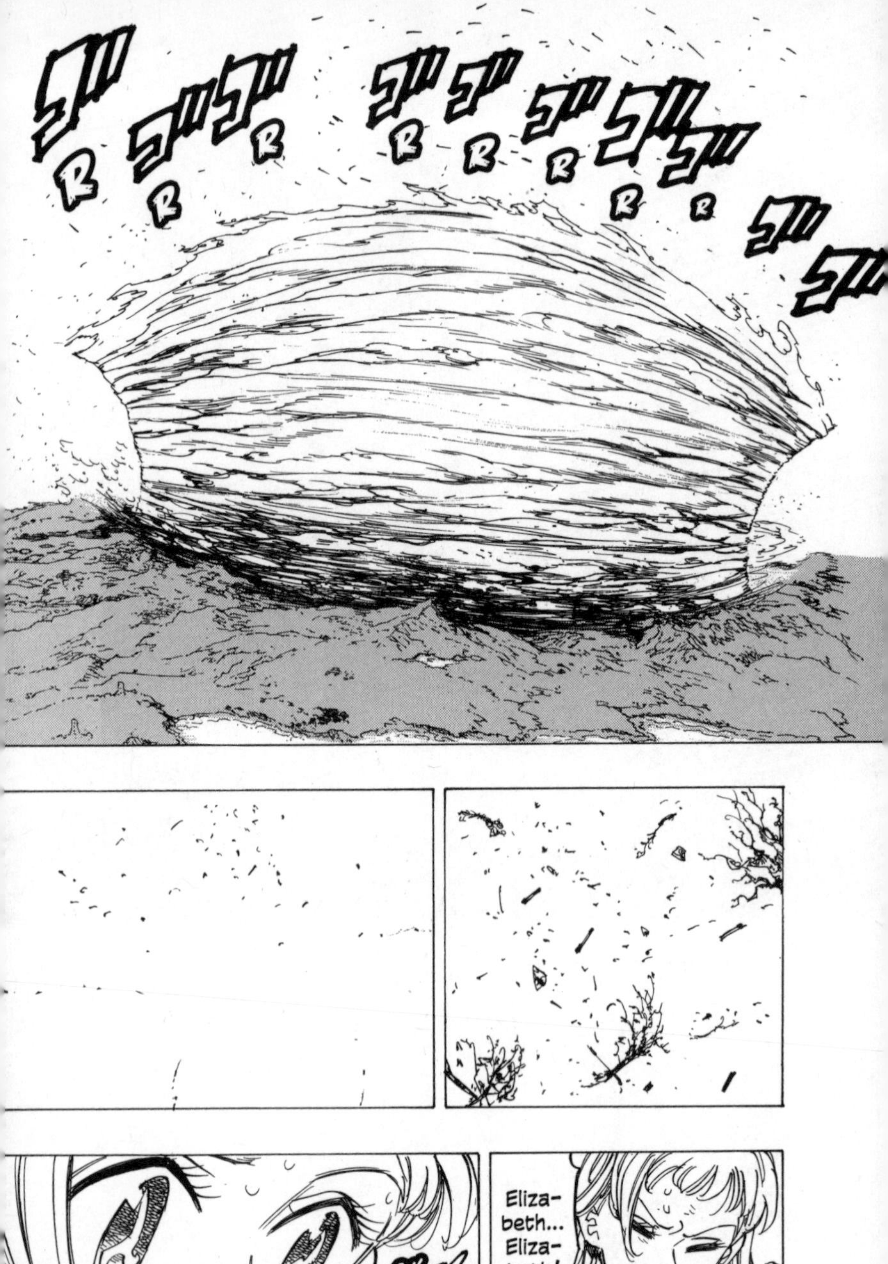
Eliza-beth... Eliza-beth!
AH!

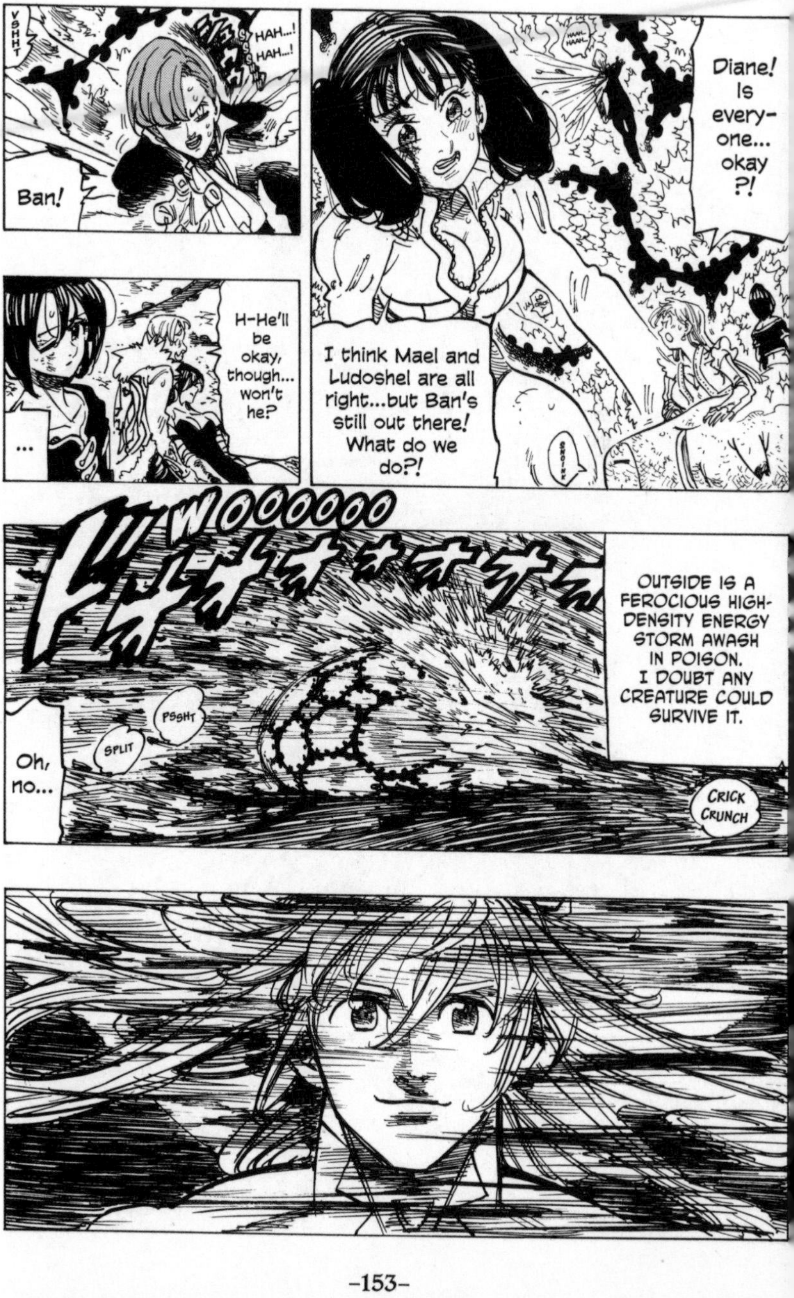
Diane! Is every-one... okay?!
I think Mael and Ludoshel are all right...but Ban's still out there! What do we do?!
HAH...! HAH...!
VSHHT
Ban!
H-He'll be okay, though... won't he?
...
WOOOOOO
OUTSIDE IS A FEROCIOUS HIGH-DENSITY ENERGY STORM AWASH IN POISON. I DOUBT ANY CREATURE COULD SURVIVE IT.
PSSHT
SPLIT
Oh, no...
CRICK CRUNCH

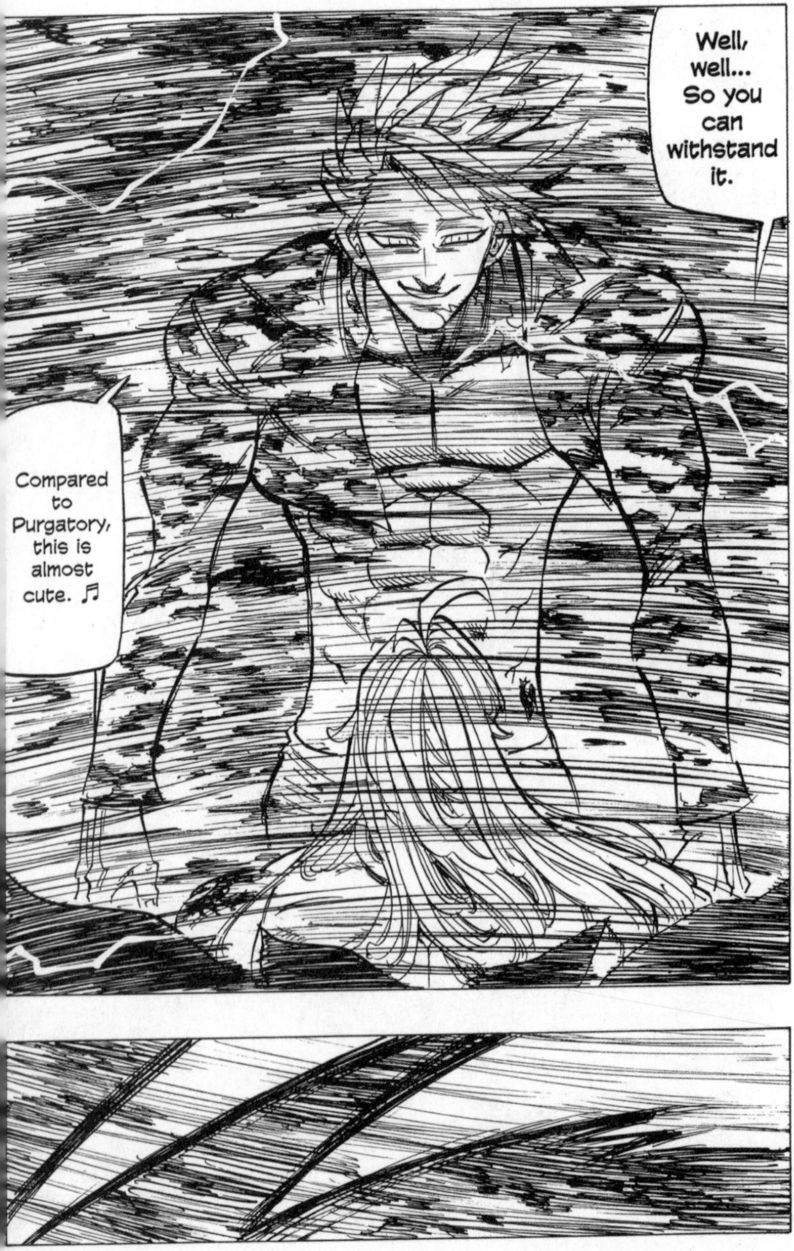
Well, well... So you can withstand it.
Compared to Purgatory, this is almost cute. ♫

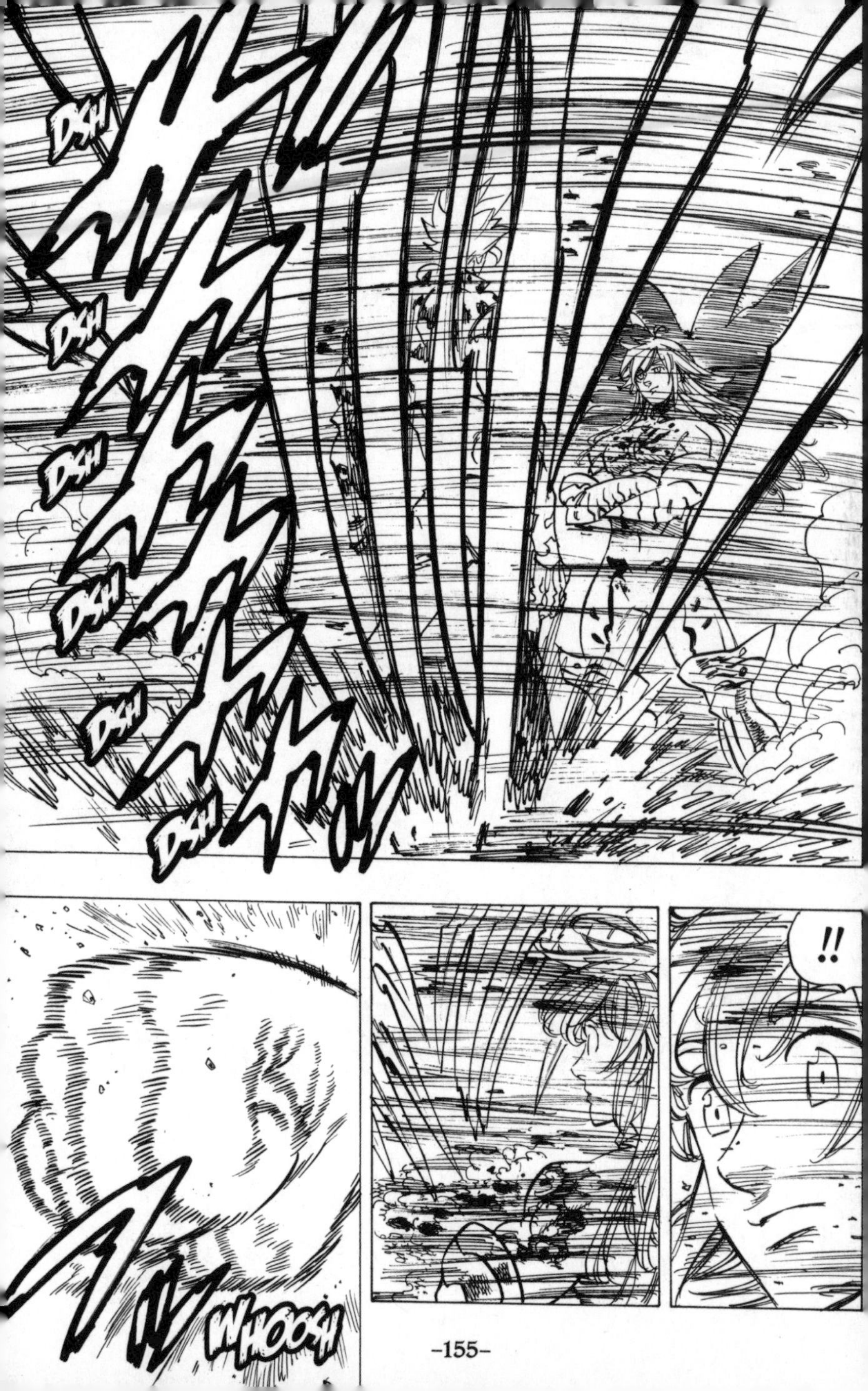
DSH
DSH
DSH
DSH
DSH
DSH
!!
WHOOSH

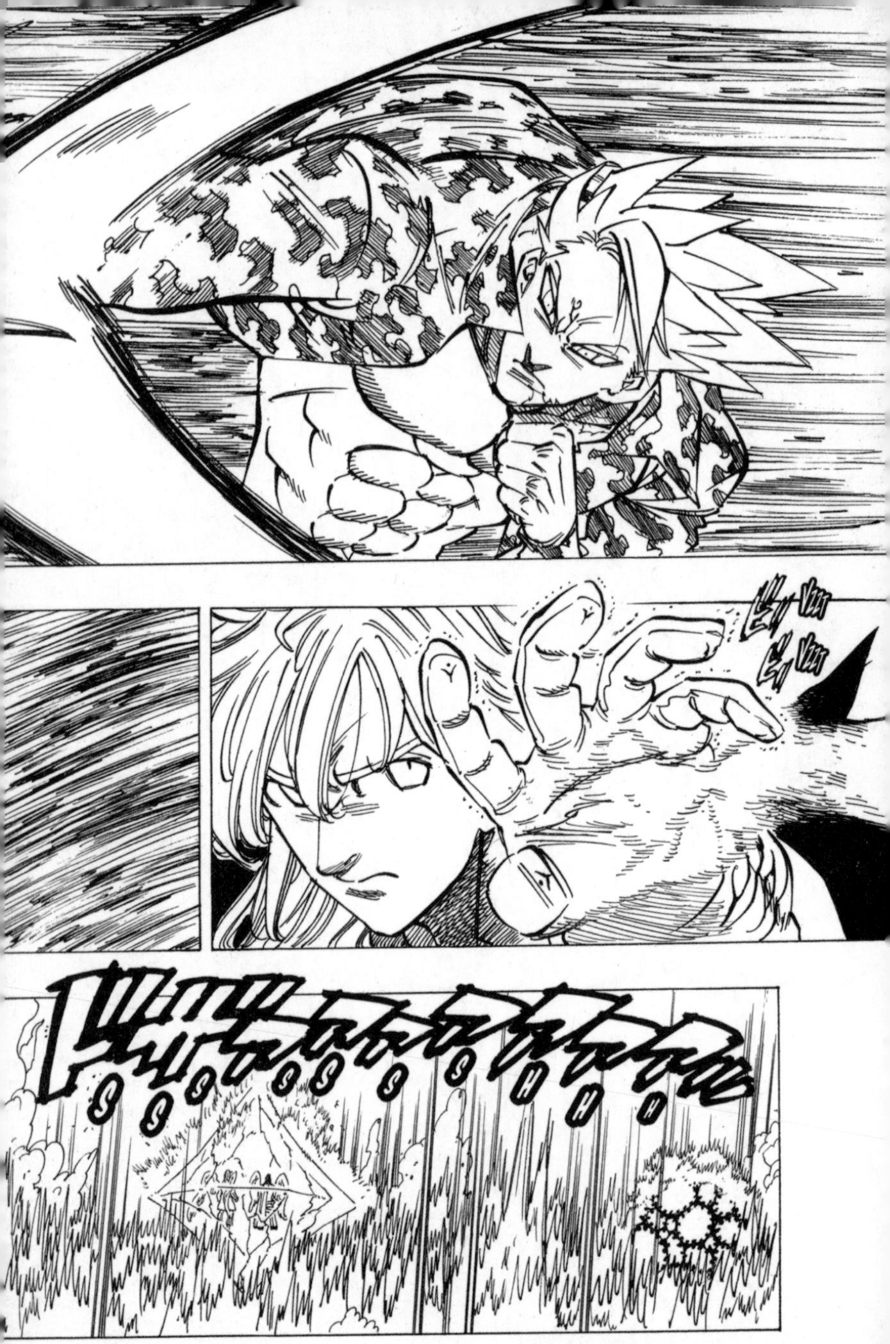
VZZT
VZZT
SSSSSSSHHH

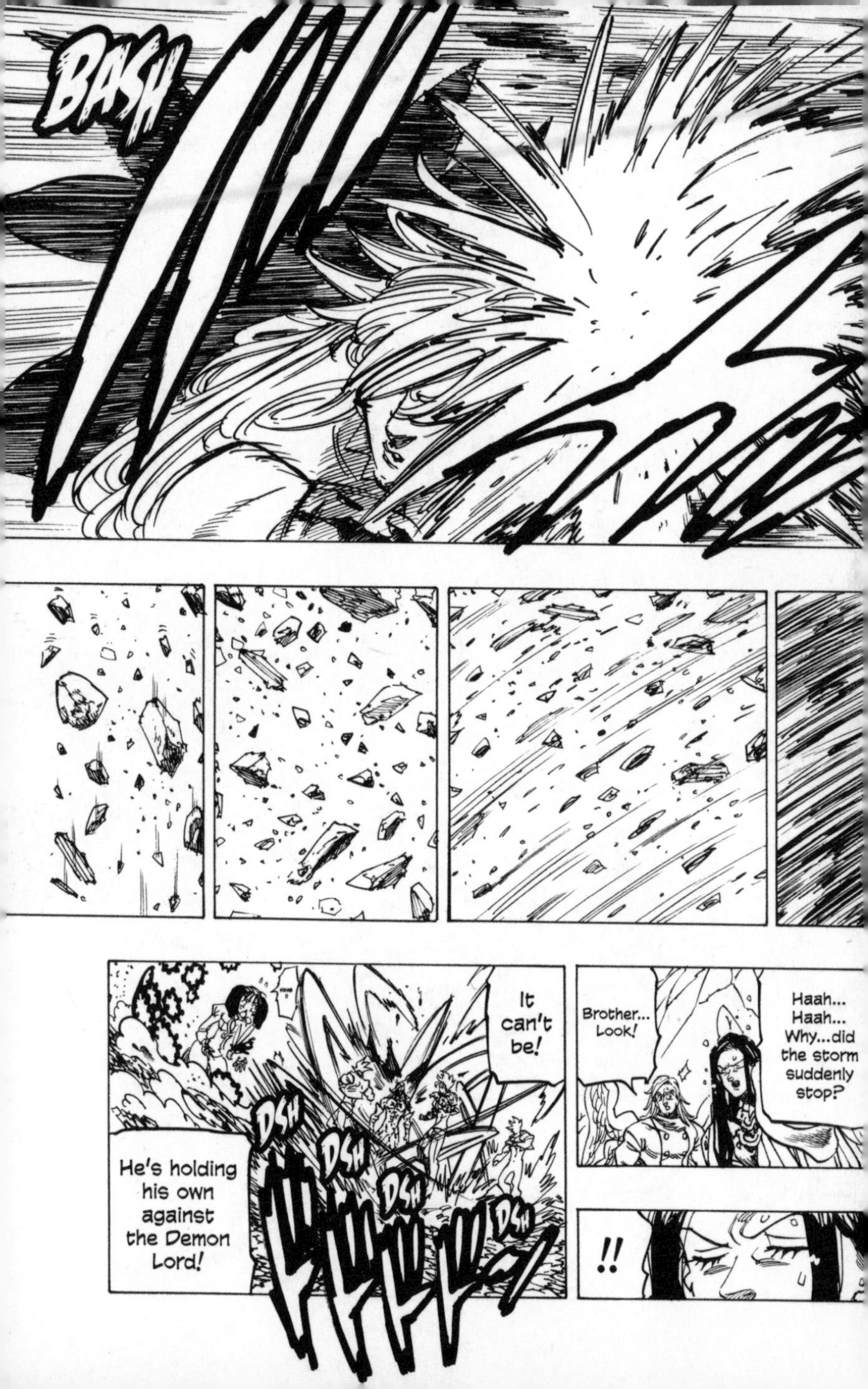
BASH
Haah... Haah... Why...did the storm suddenly stop?
Brother... Look!
!!
It can't be!
DSH
DSH
DSH
DSH
He's holding his own against the Demon Lord!

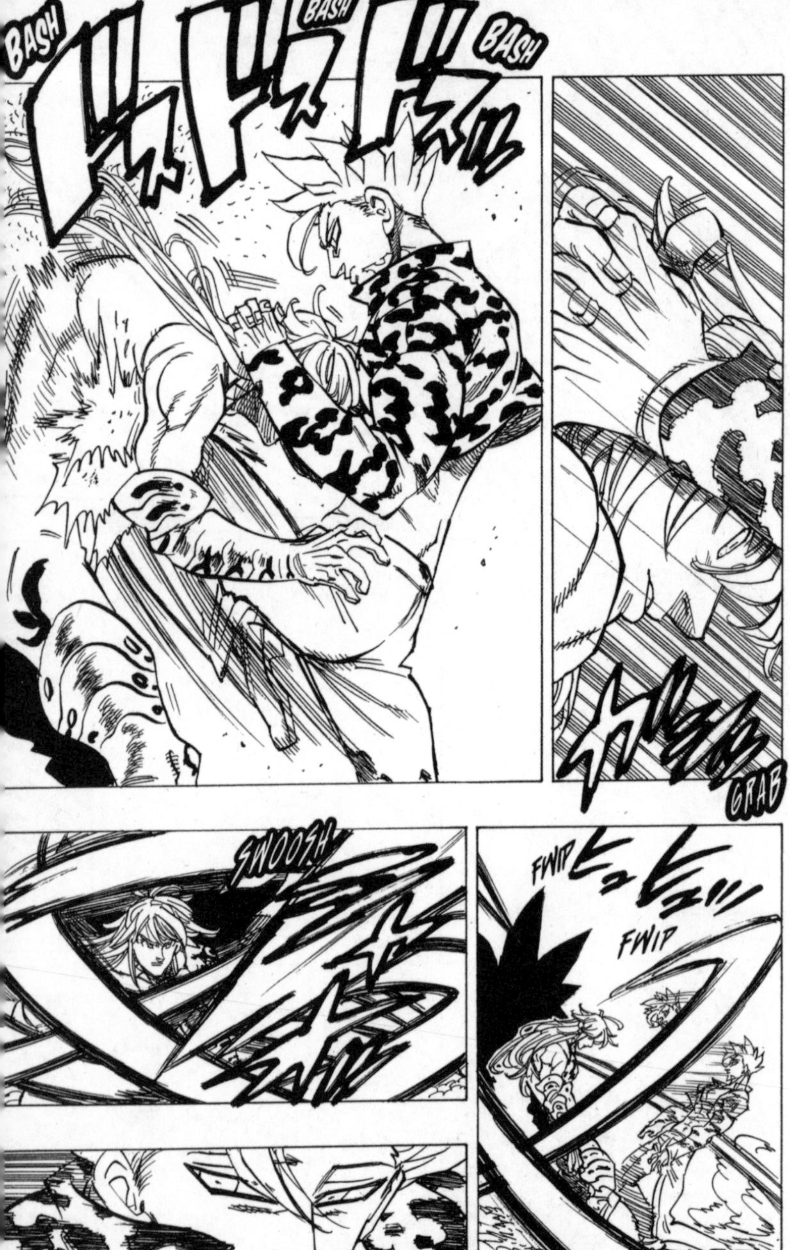
BASH
BASH
BASH
GRAB
FWIP
FWIP
SWOOSH

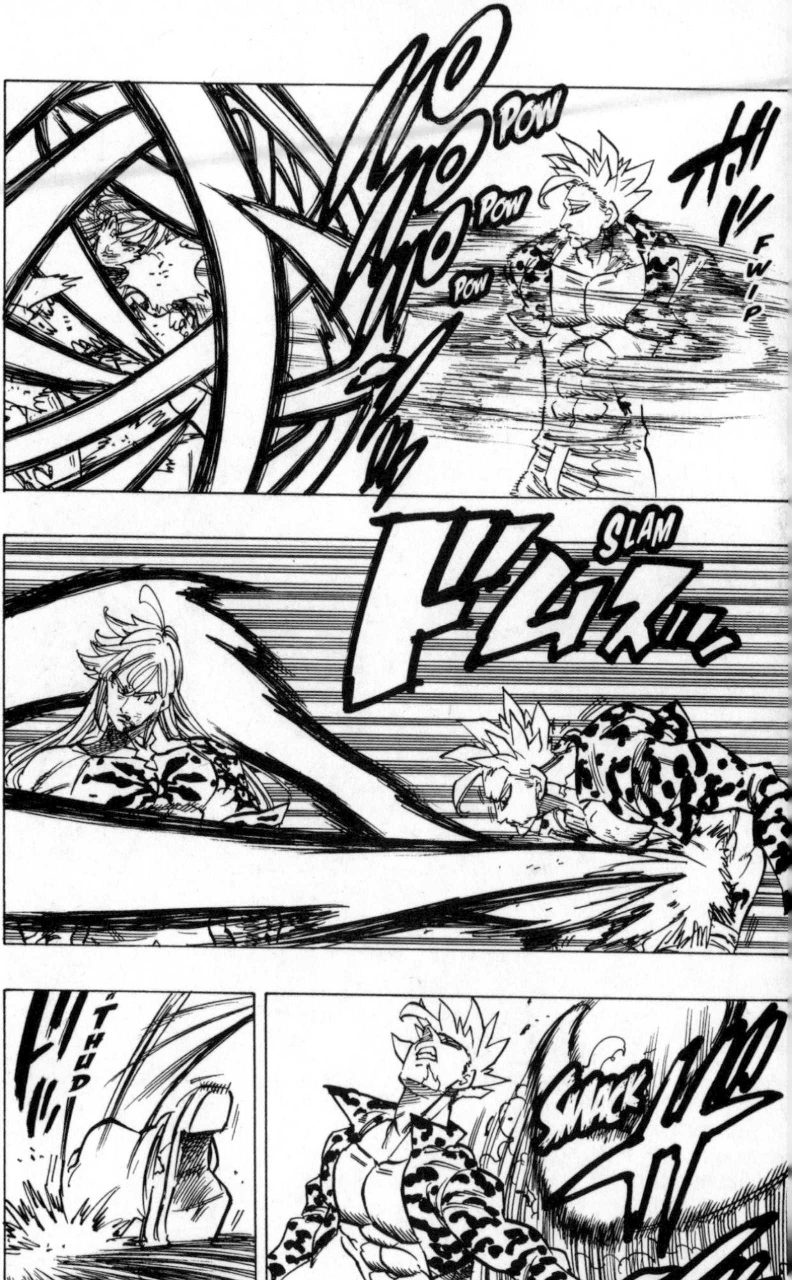
FWIP
POW
POW
POW
SLAM
SMACK
THUD

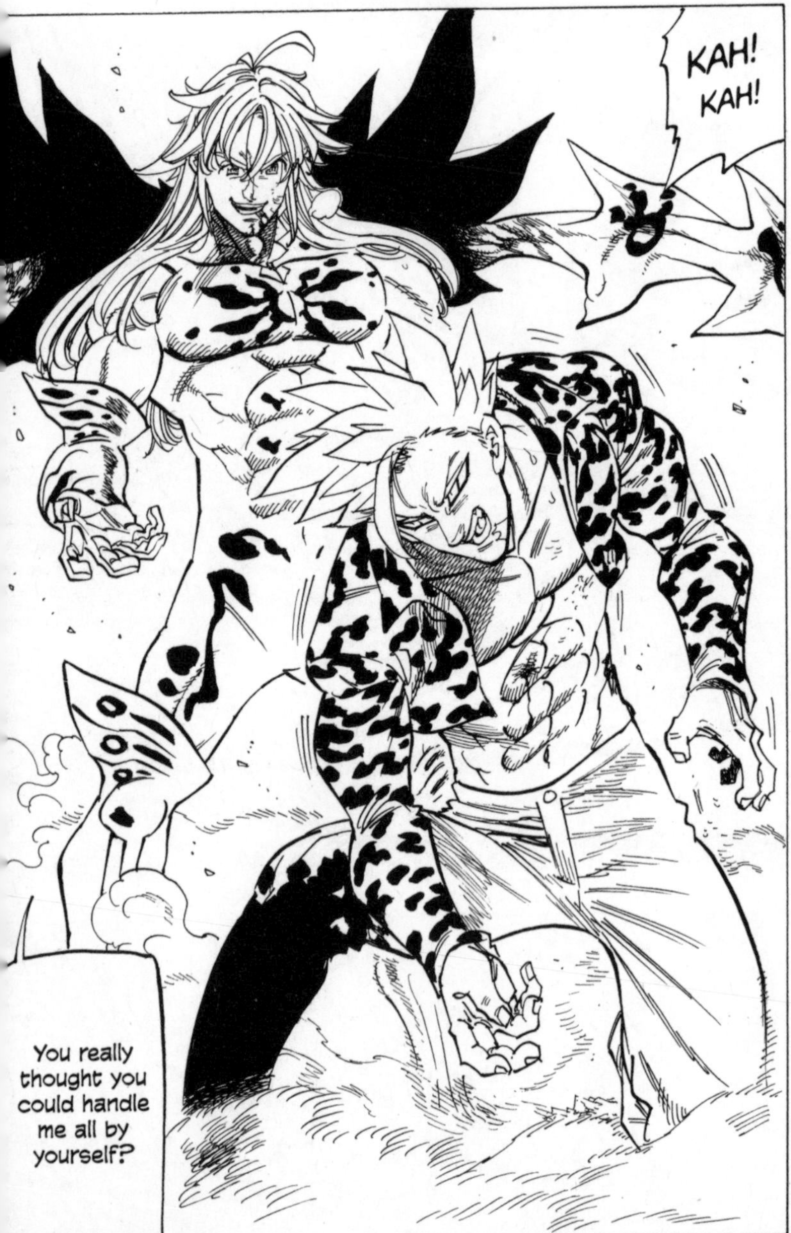
KAH! KAH!
You really thought you could handle me all by yourself?

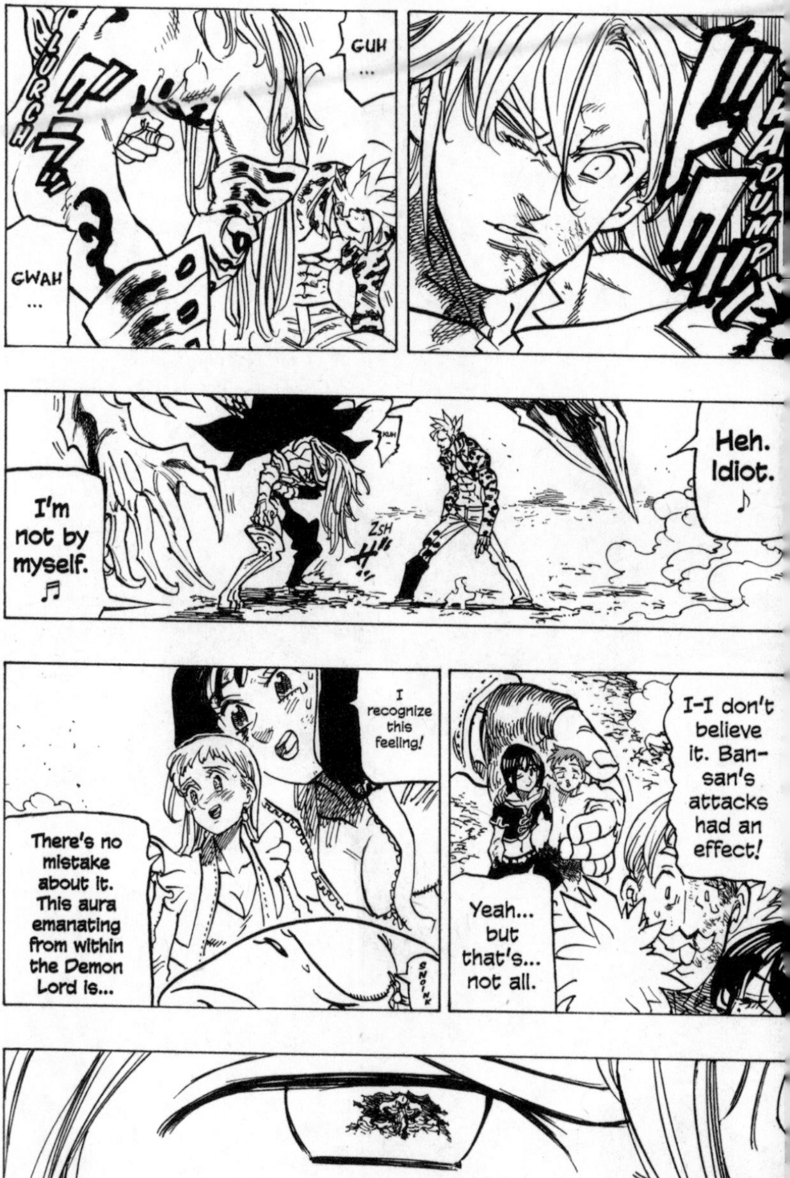
HADUMP
GUH ...
LURCH
GWAH ...
Heh. Idiot. ♪
KUH –
ZSH
I'm not by myself. ♬
I-I don't believe it. Ban-san's attacks had an effect!
Yeah... but that's... not all.
I recognize this feeling!
There's no mistake about it. This aura emanating from within the Demon Lord is...
SNOINK

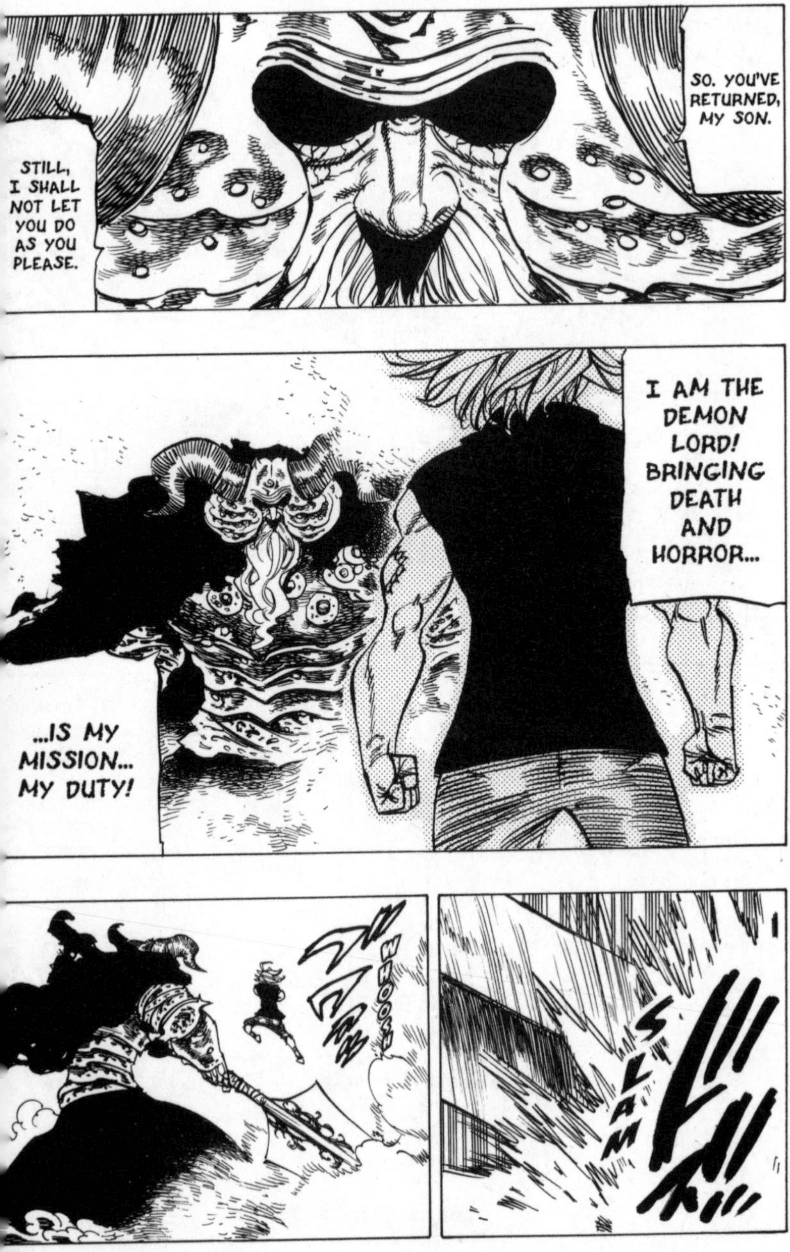
SO. YOU'VE RETURNED, MY SON.
STILL, I SHALL NOT LET YOU DO AS YOU PLEASE.
I AM THE DEMON LORD! BRINGING DEATH AND HORROR...
...IS MY MISSION... MY DUTY!
SLAM
WHOOSH

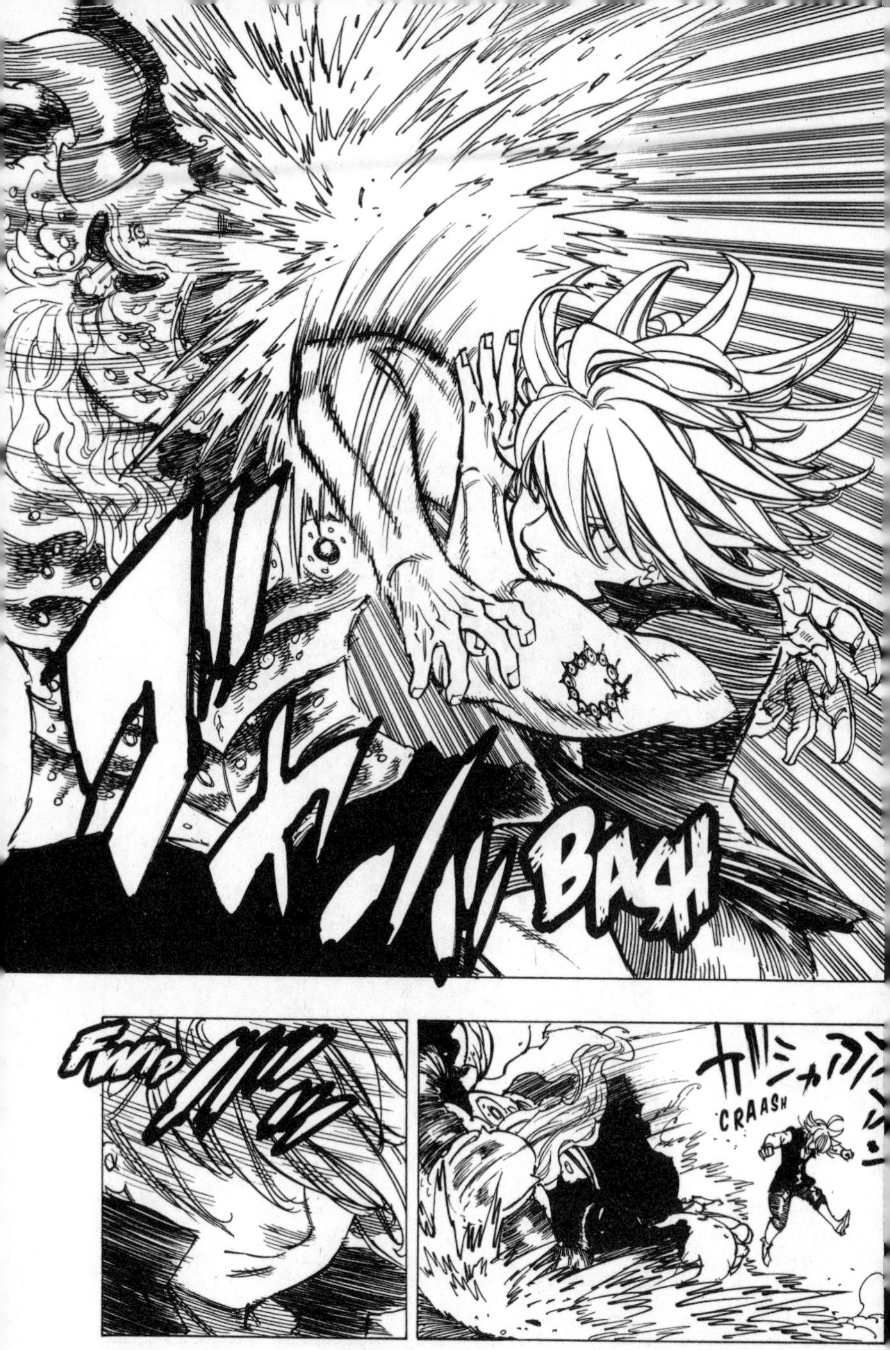
BASH
CRAASH
FWIP

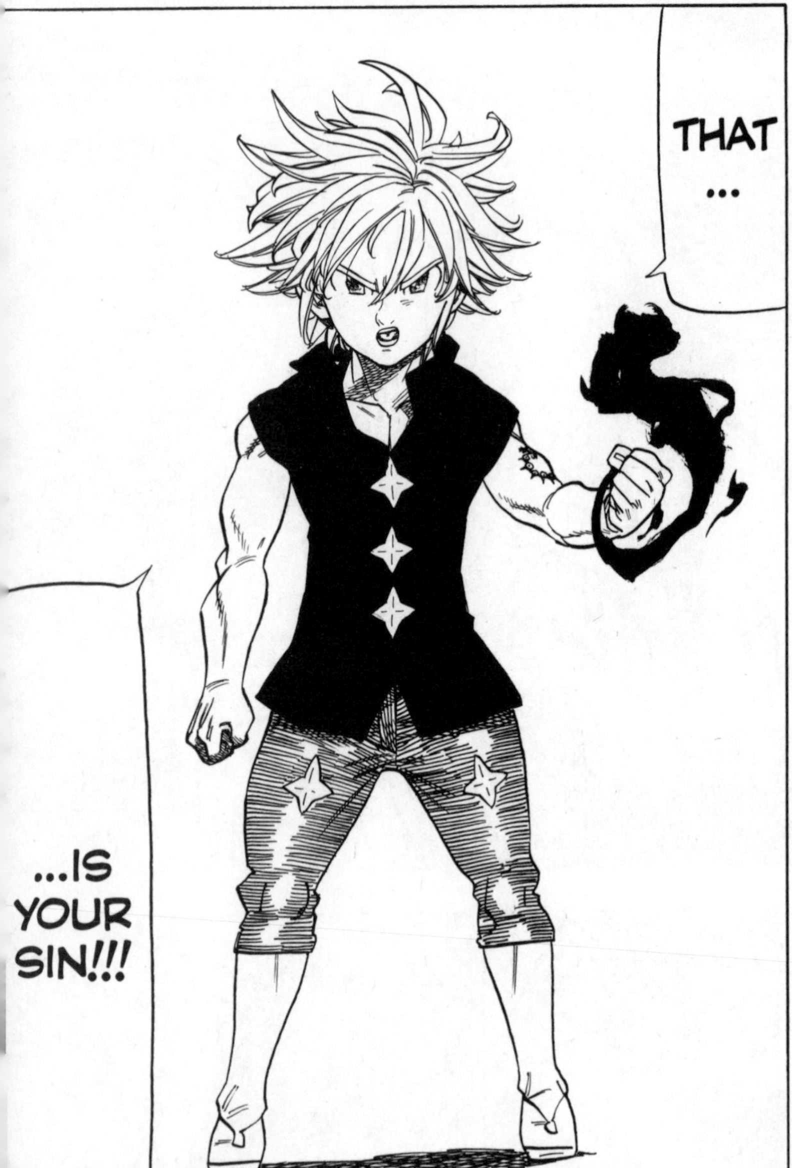
THAT ...
...IS YOUR SIN!!!

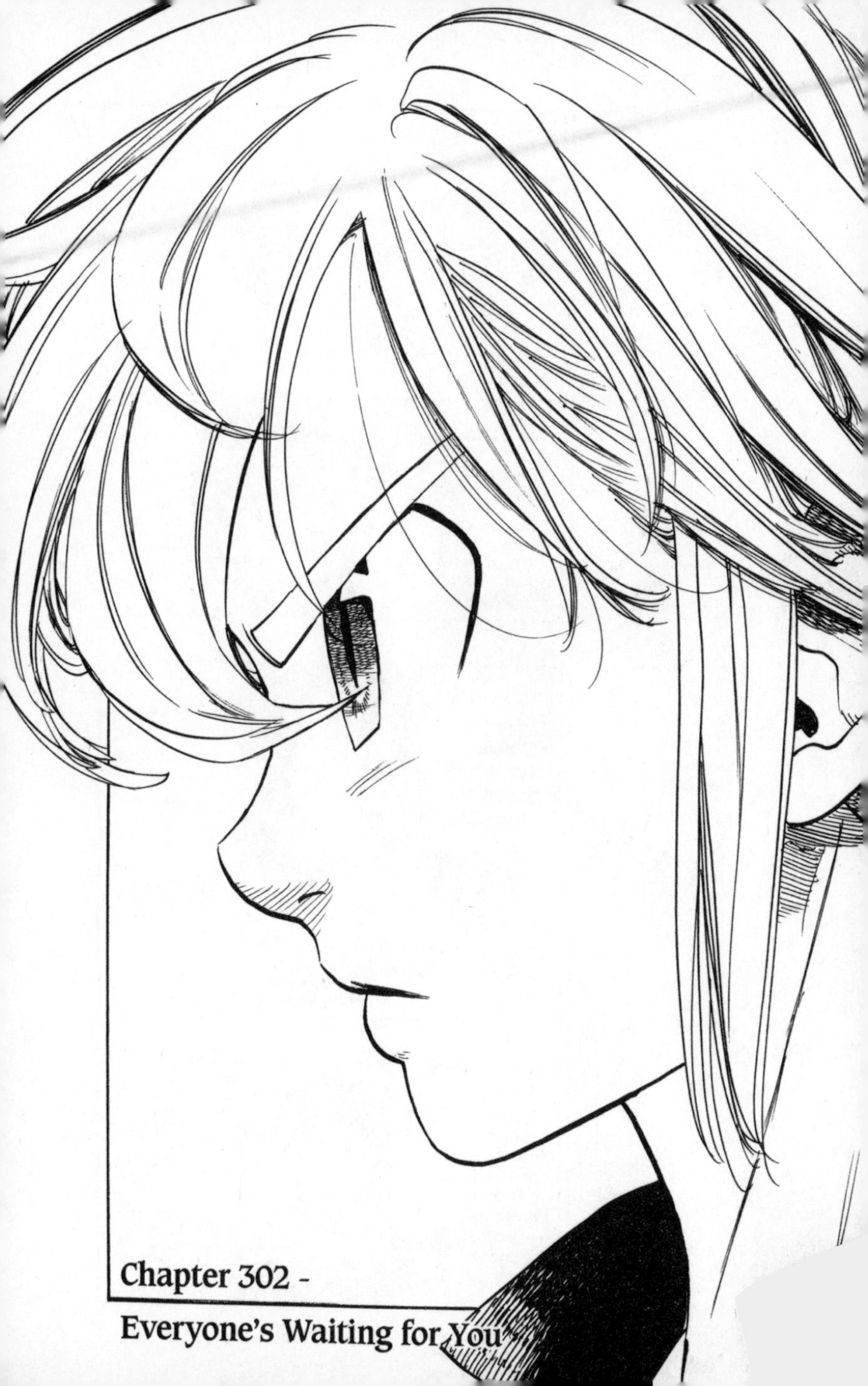

Chapter 302 - Everyone's Waiting for You

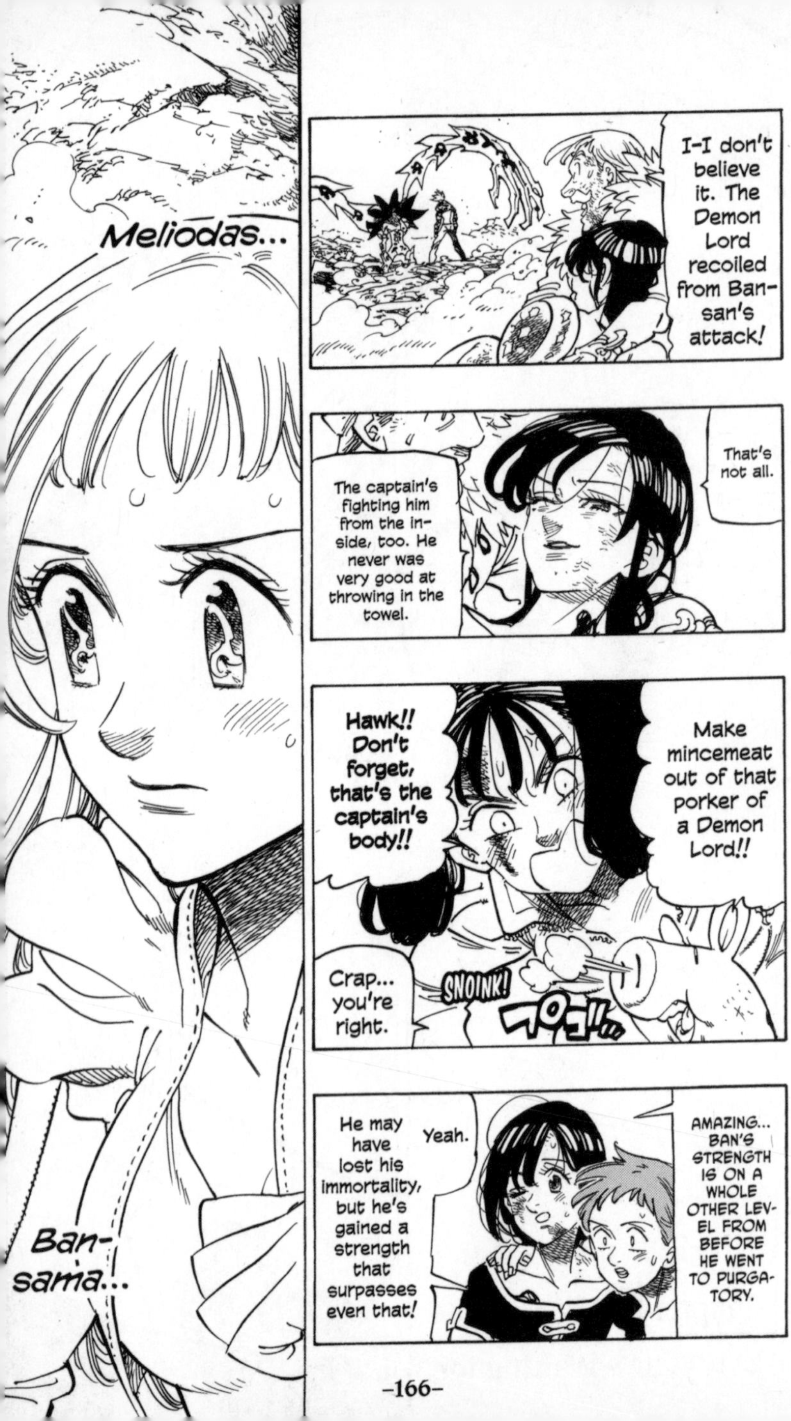
I-I don't believe it. The Demon Lord recoiled from Ban-san's attack!
That's not all.
The captain's fighting him from the inside, too. He never was very good at throwing in the towel.
Make mincemeat out of that porker of a Demon Lord!!
Hawk!! Don't forget, that's the captain's body!!
SNOINK!
Crap... you're right.
AMAZING... BAN'S STRENGTH IS ON A WHOLE OTHER LEVEL FROM BEFORE HE WENT TO PURGATORY.
Yeah.
He may have lost his immortality, but he's gained a strength that surpasses even that!
Meliodas...
Ban-sama...

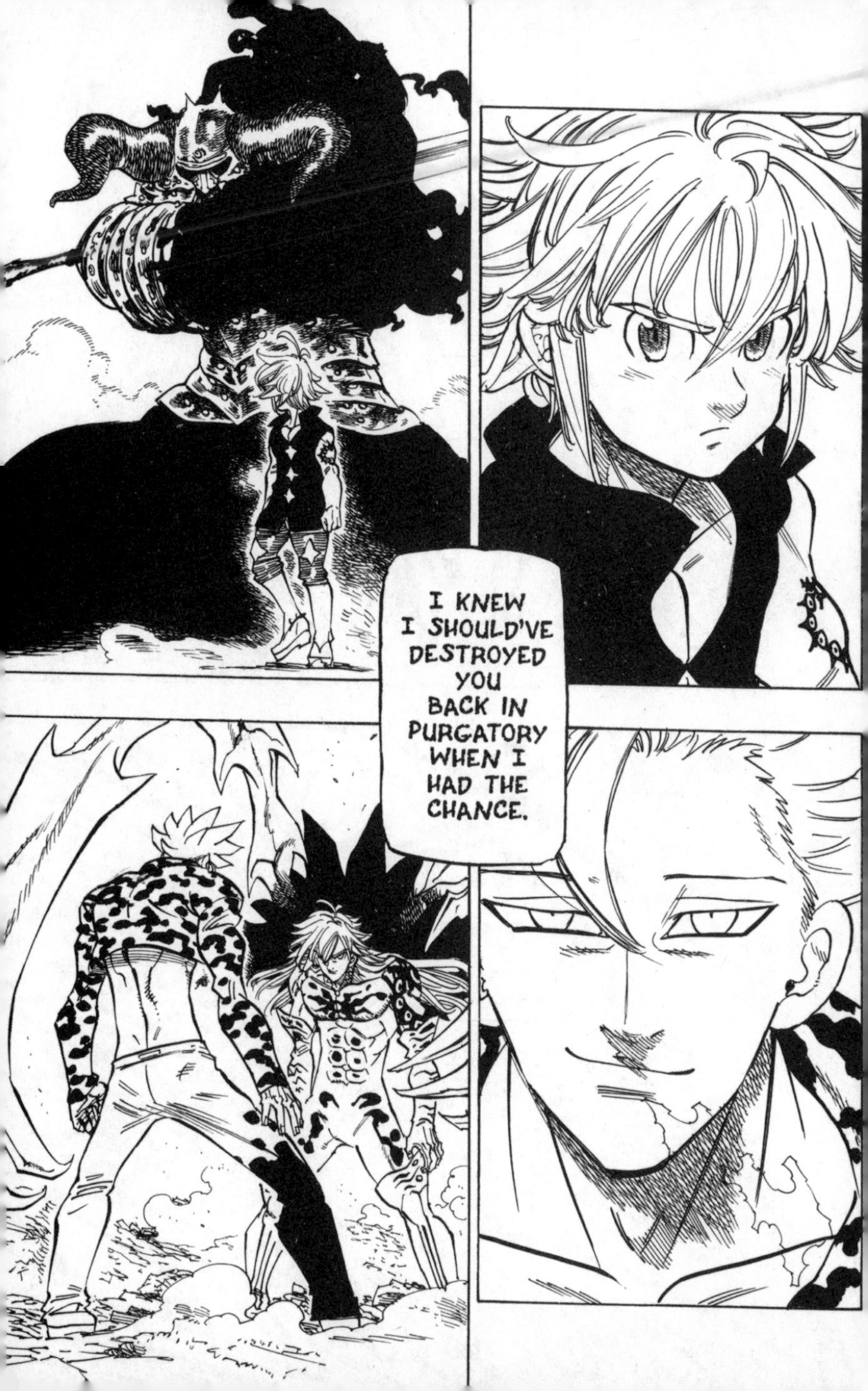
I KNEW I SHOULD'VE DESTROYED YOU BACK IN PURGATORY WHEN I HAD THE CHANCE.

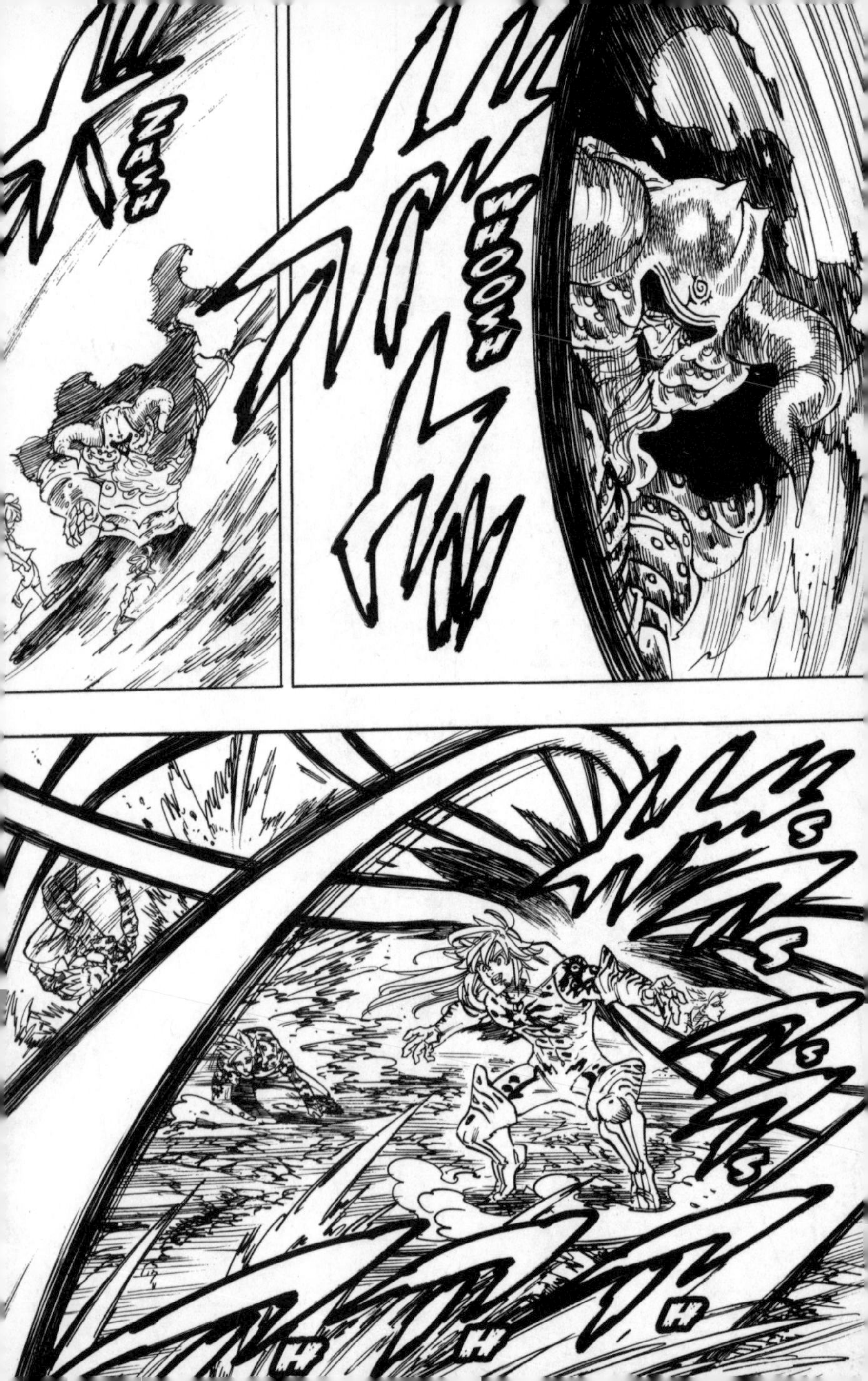
WHOOSH
ZASH

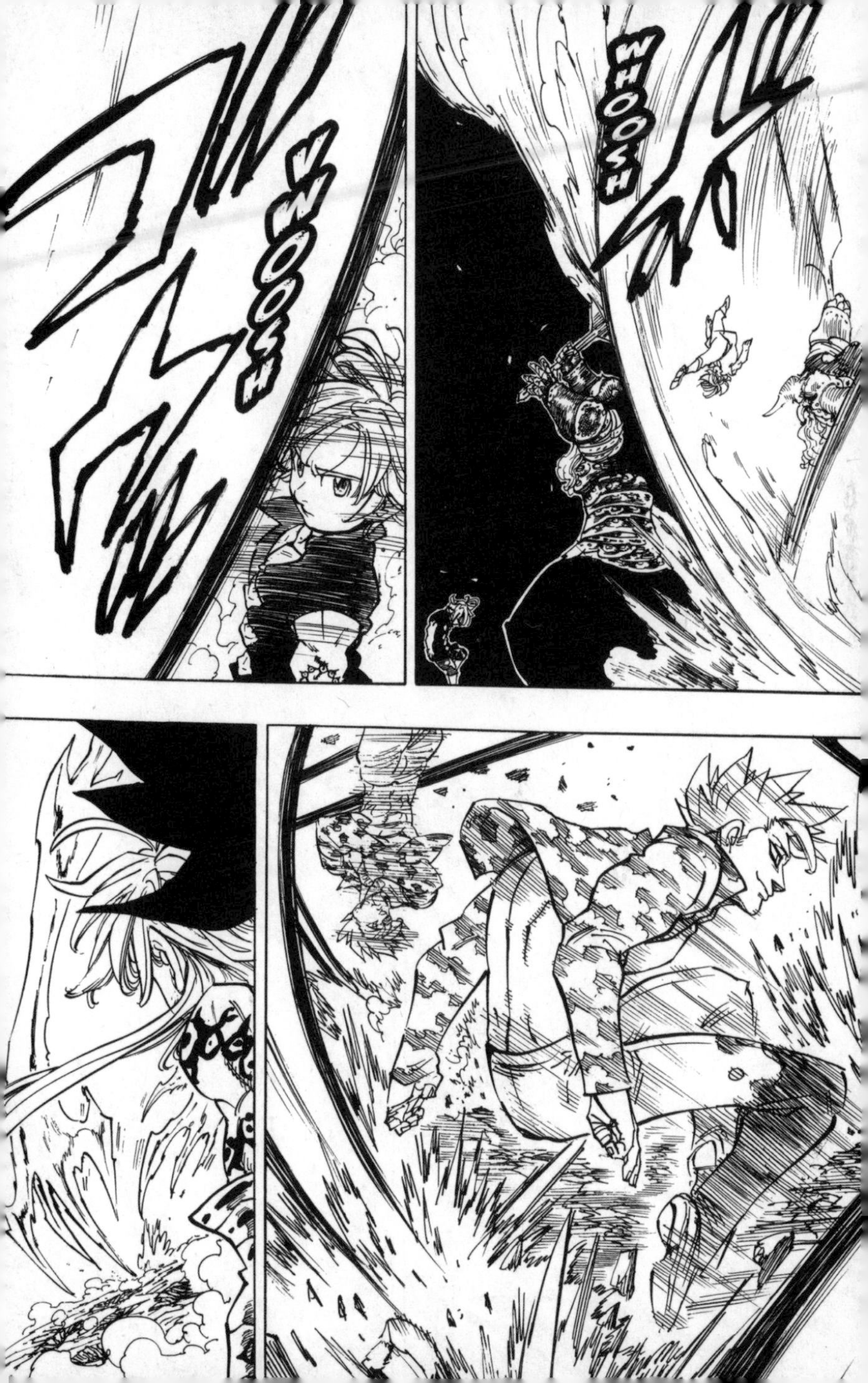
WHOOSH
WHOOSH

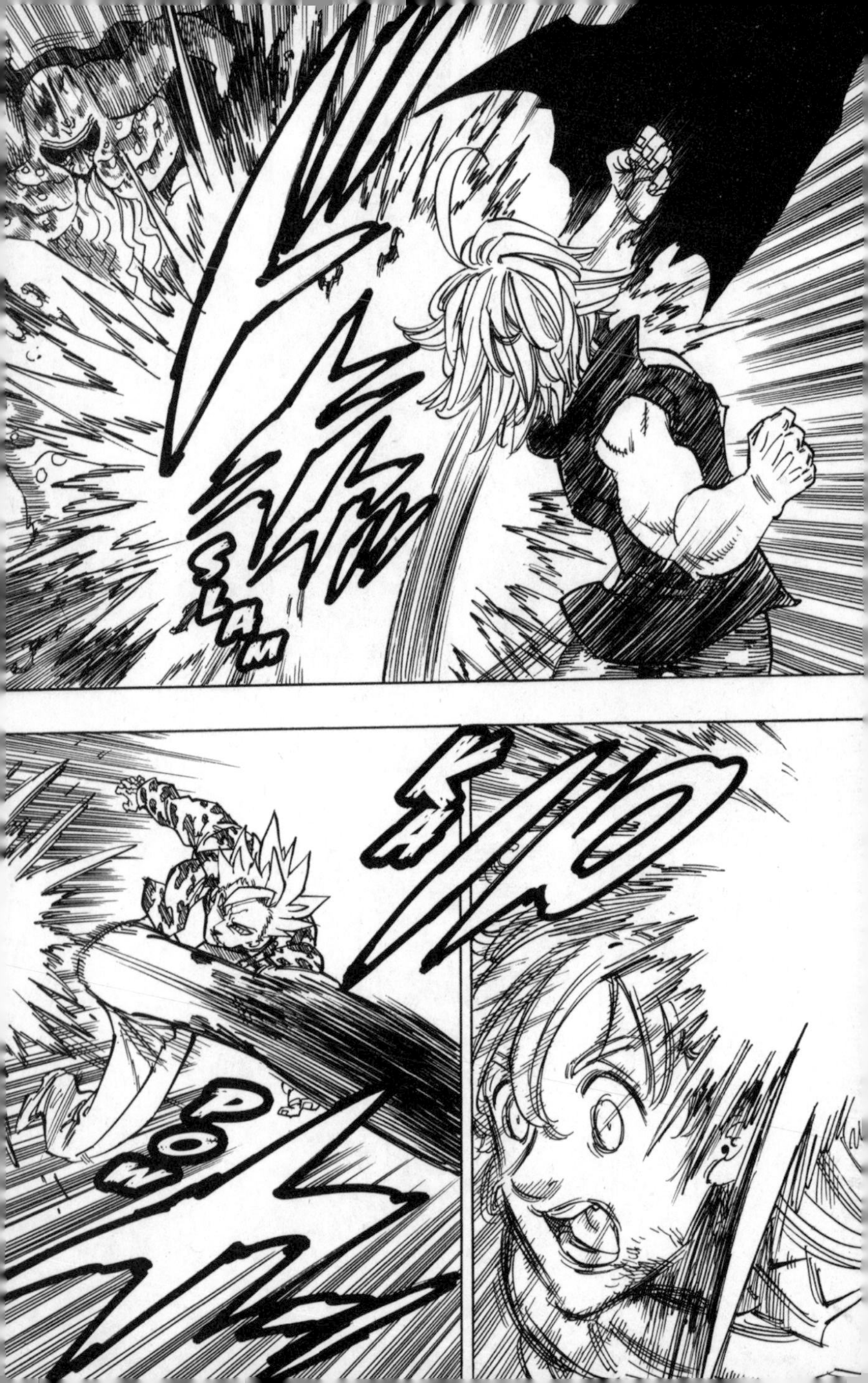
SLAM
POW

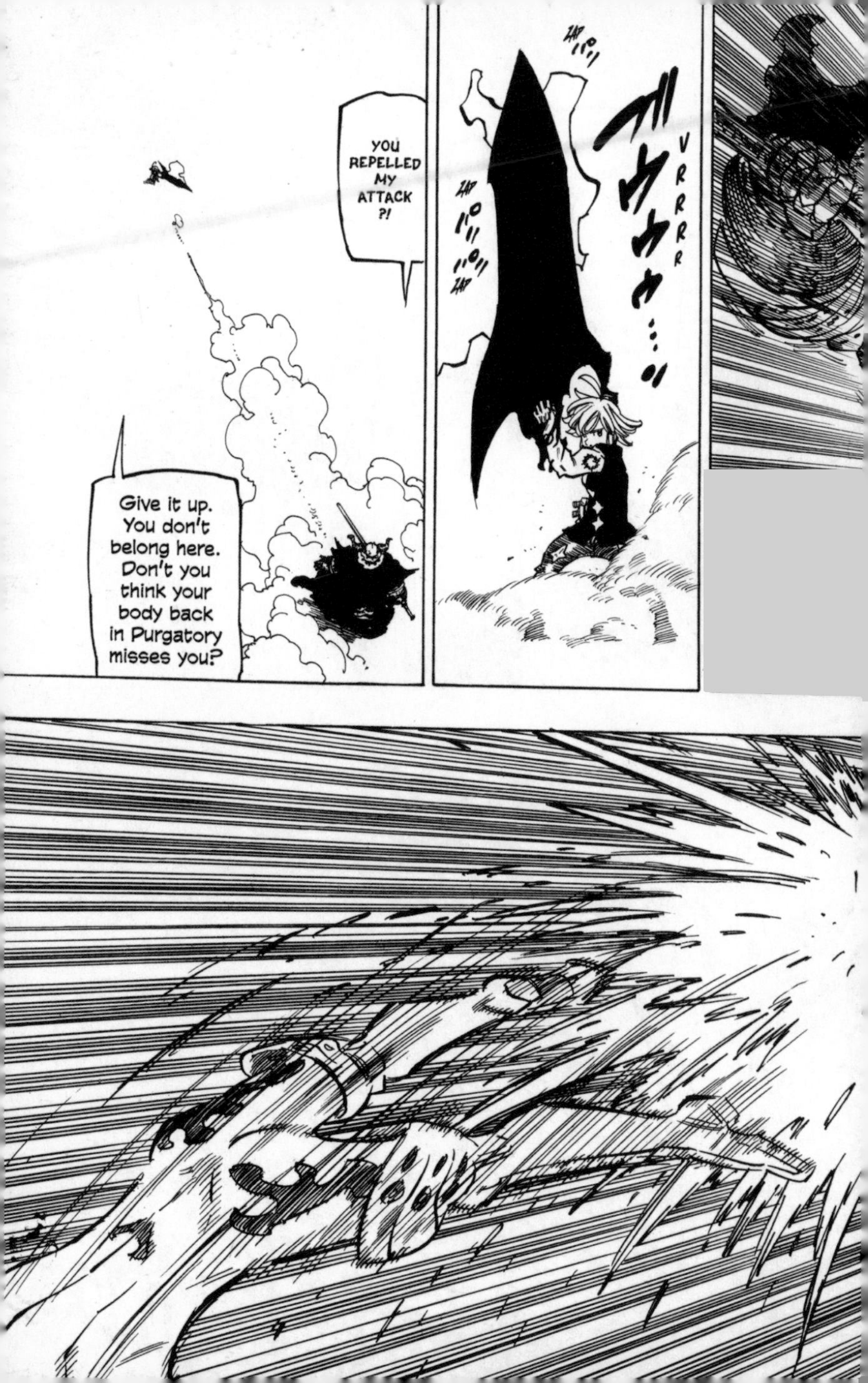
ZAP
VRRRR
ZAP
ZAP
YOU REPELLED MY ATTACK ?!
Give it up. You don't belong here. Don't you think your body back in Purgatory misses you?

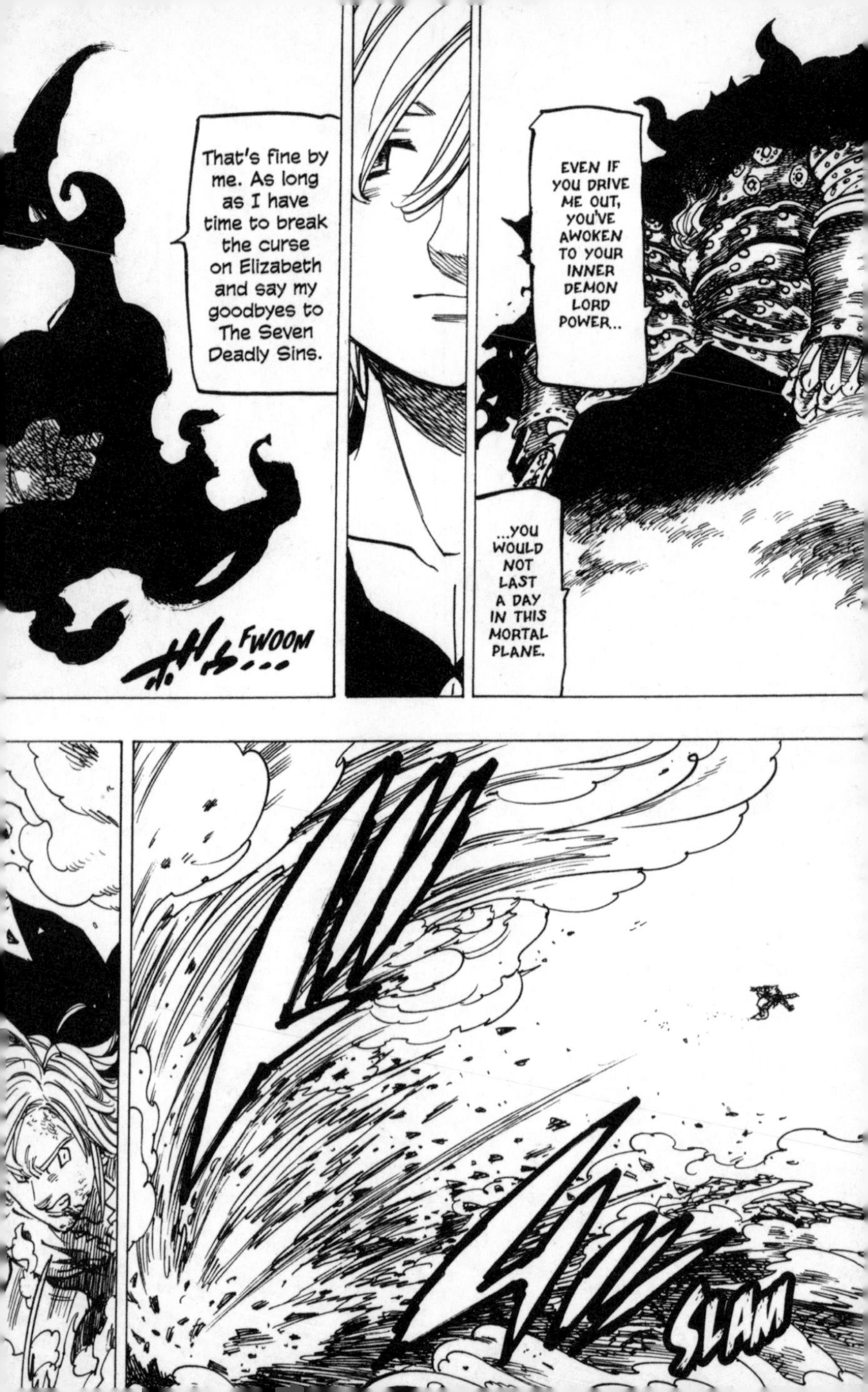
EVEN IF YOU DRIVE ME OUT, YOU'VE AWOKEN TO YOUR INNER DEMON LORD POWER..
...YOU WOULD NOT LAST A DAY IN THIS MORTAL PLANE.
That's fine by me. As long as I have time to break the curse on Elizabeth and say my goodbyes to The Seven Deadly Sins.
FWOOM...
SLAM

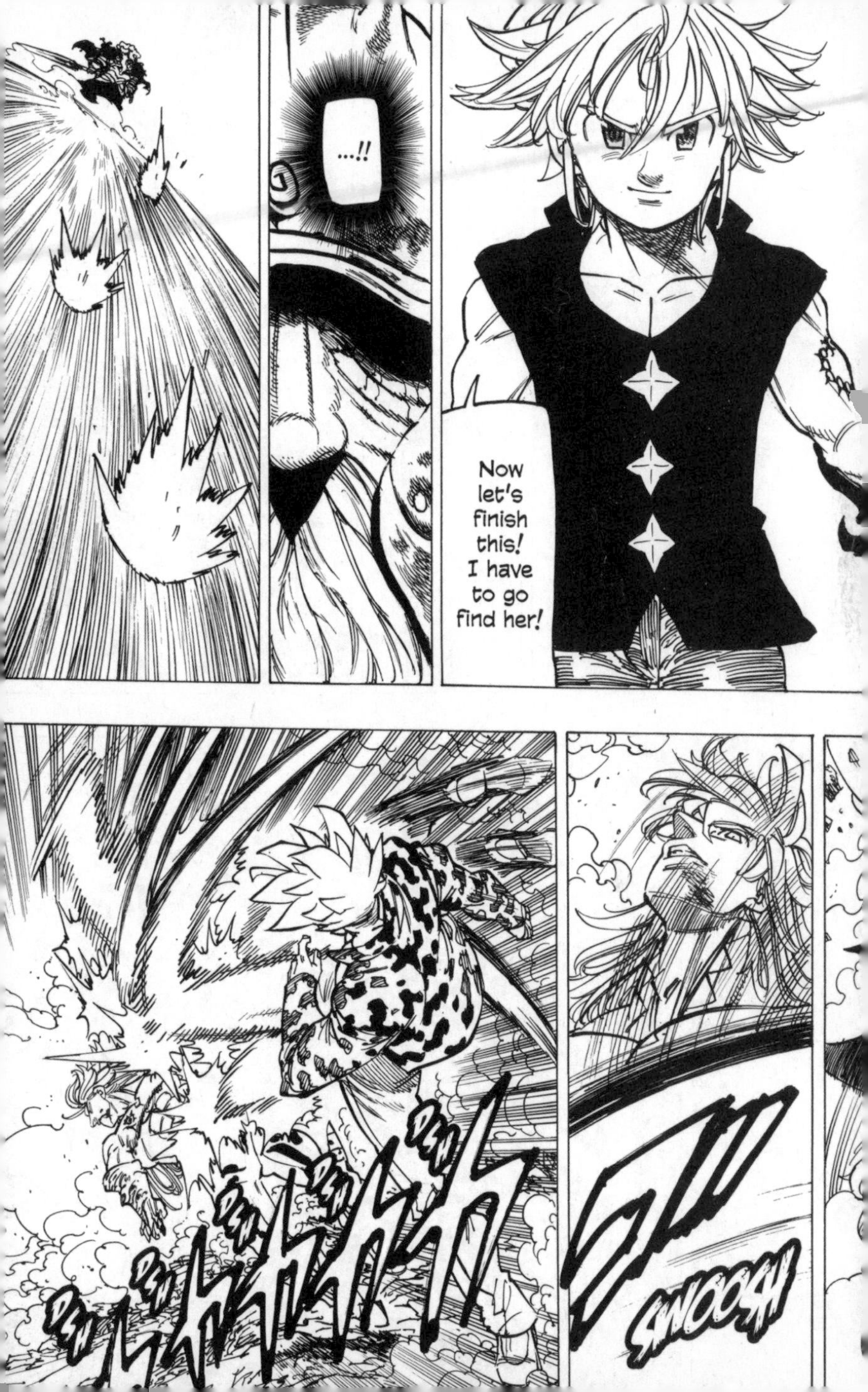
Now let's finish this! I have to go find her!
...!!
SWOOSH
DEH
DEH
DEH
DEH
DEH
DEH

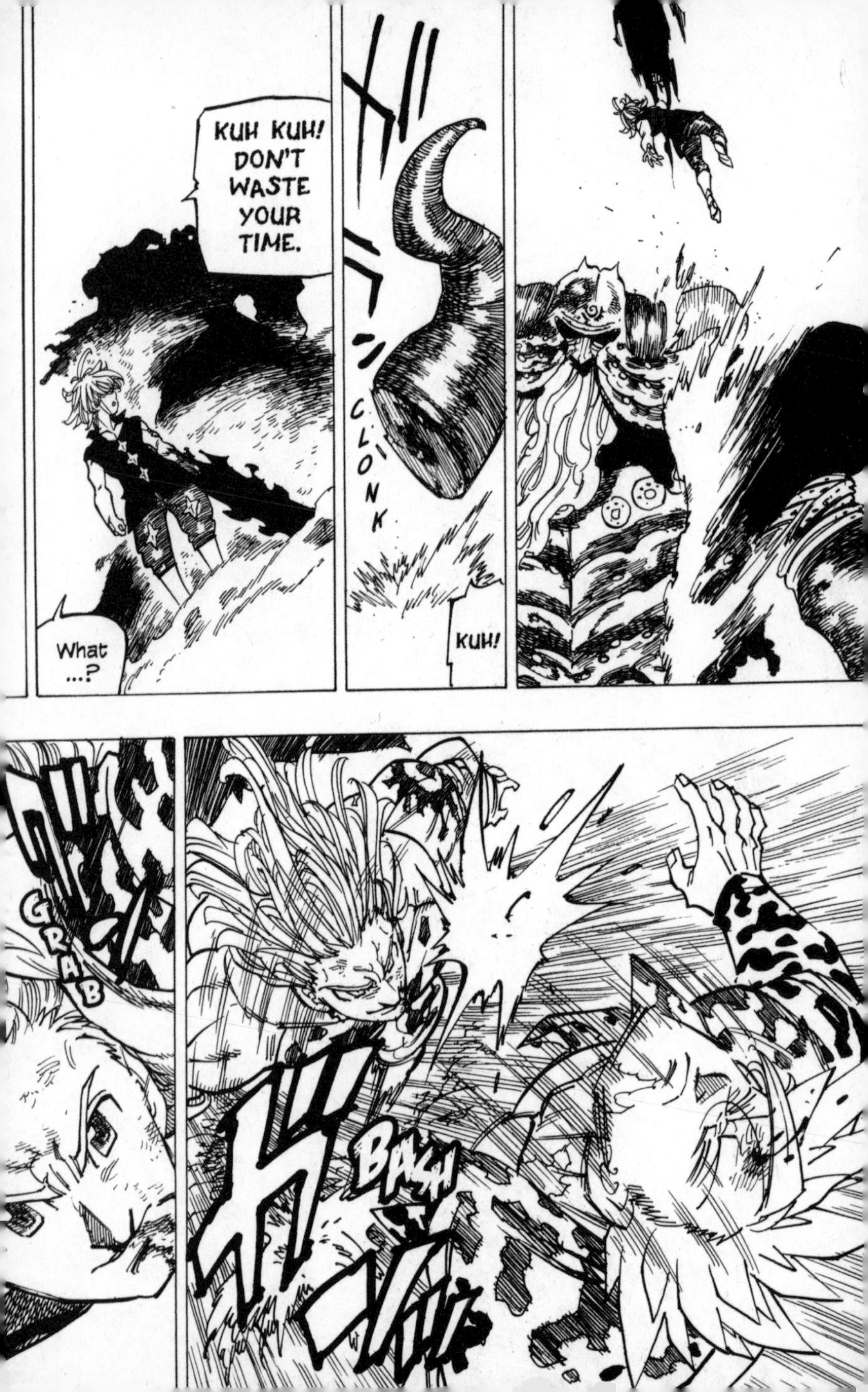
CLONK
KUH!
KUH KUH! DON'T WASTE YOUR TIME.
What ...?
BASH
GRAB

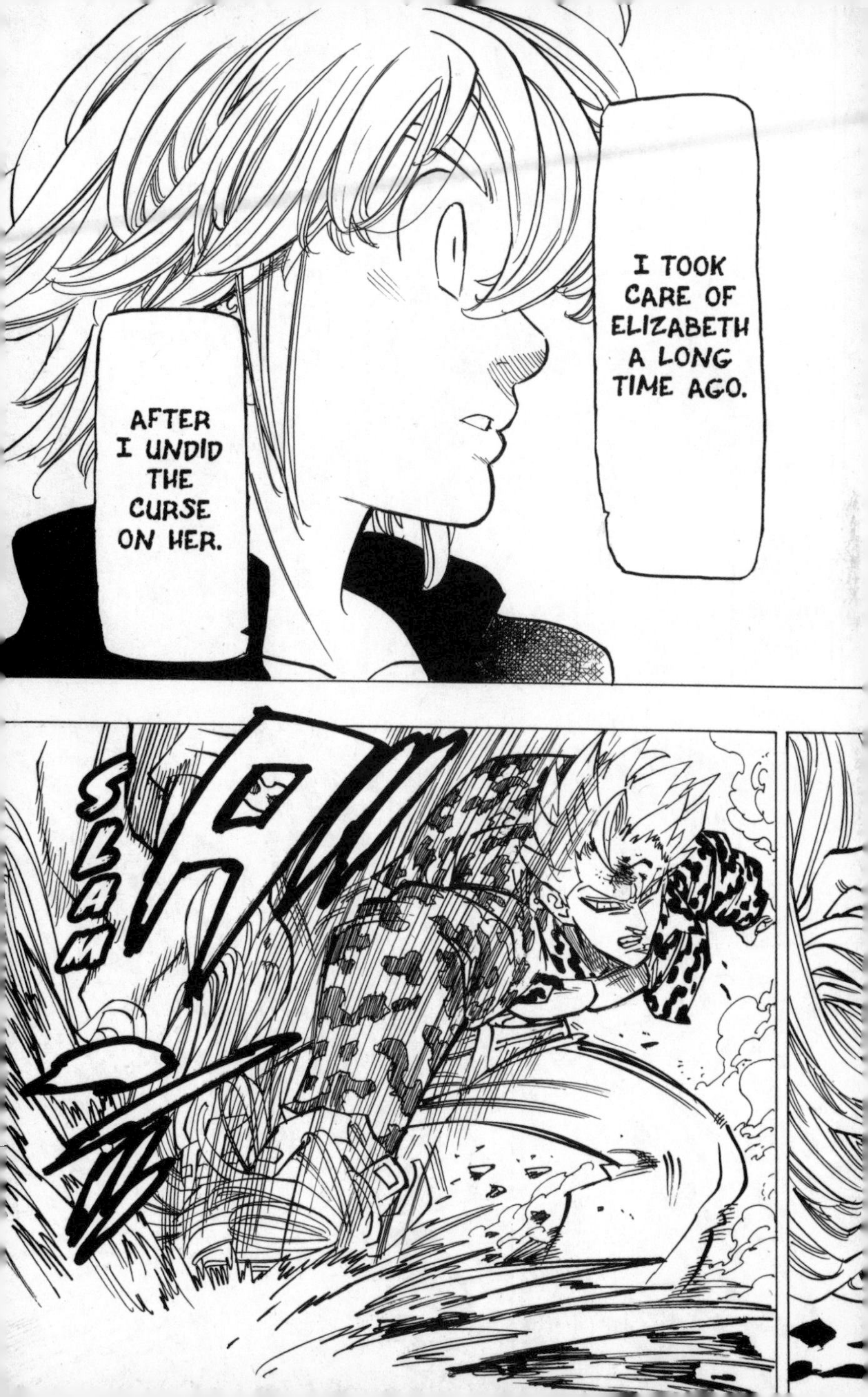
I TOOK CARE OF ELIZABETH A LONG TIME AGO.
AFTER I UNDID THE CURSE ON HER.
SLAM

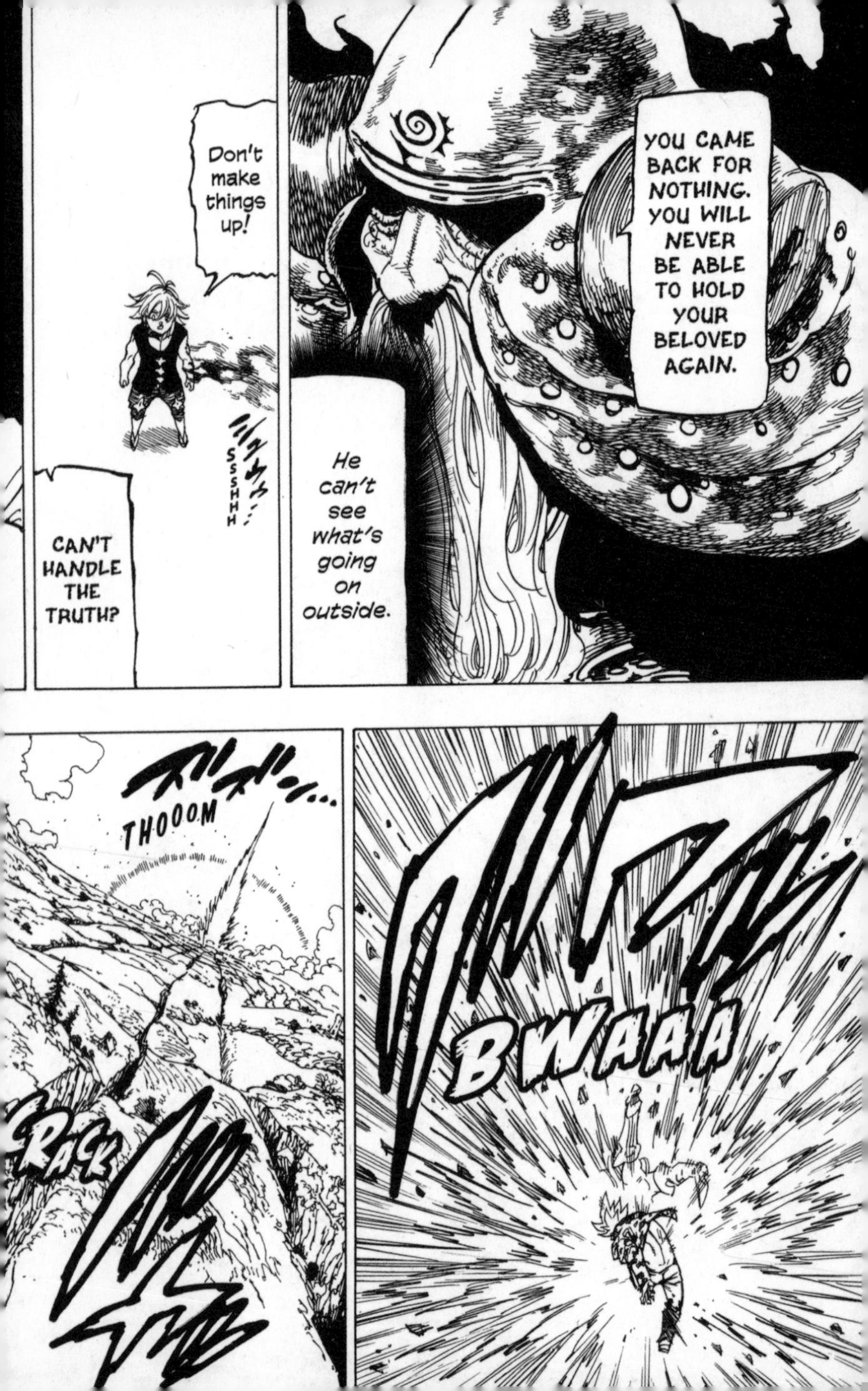
YOU CAME BACK FOR NOTHING. YOU WILL NEVER BE ABLE TO HOLD YOUR BELOVED AGAIN.
He can't see what's going on outside.
Don't make things up!
SSSHHH
CAN'T HANDLE THE TRUTH?
BWAAA
THOOOM
CRACK

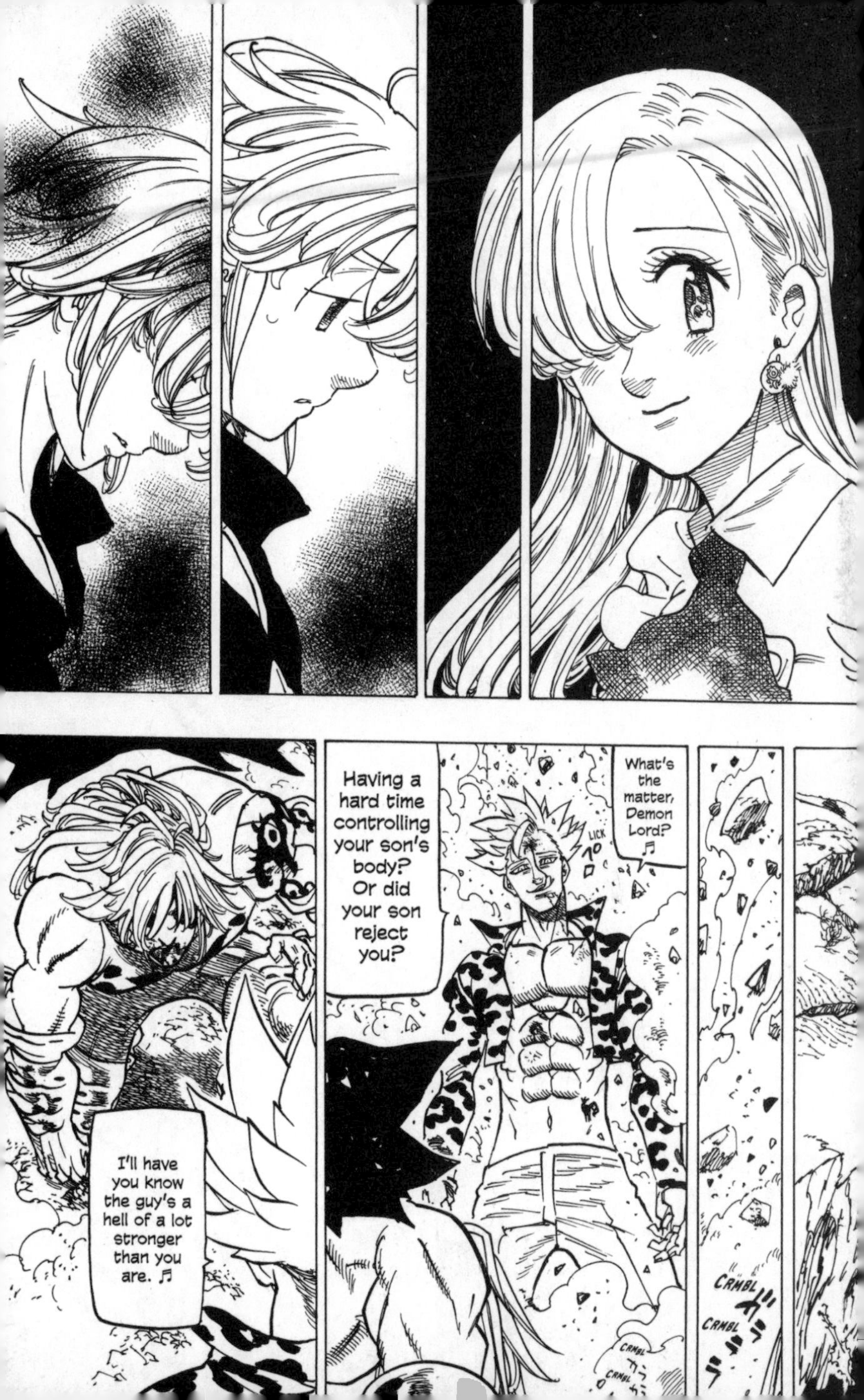
CRMBL
CRMBL
What's the matter, Demon Lord? ♪
LICK
Having a hard time controlling your son's body? Or did your son reject you?
CRMBL
CRMBL
I'll have you know the guy's a hell of a lot stronger than you are. ♬

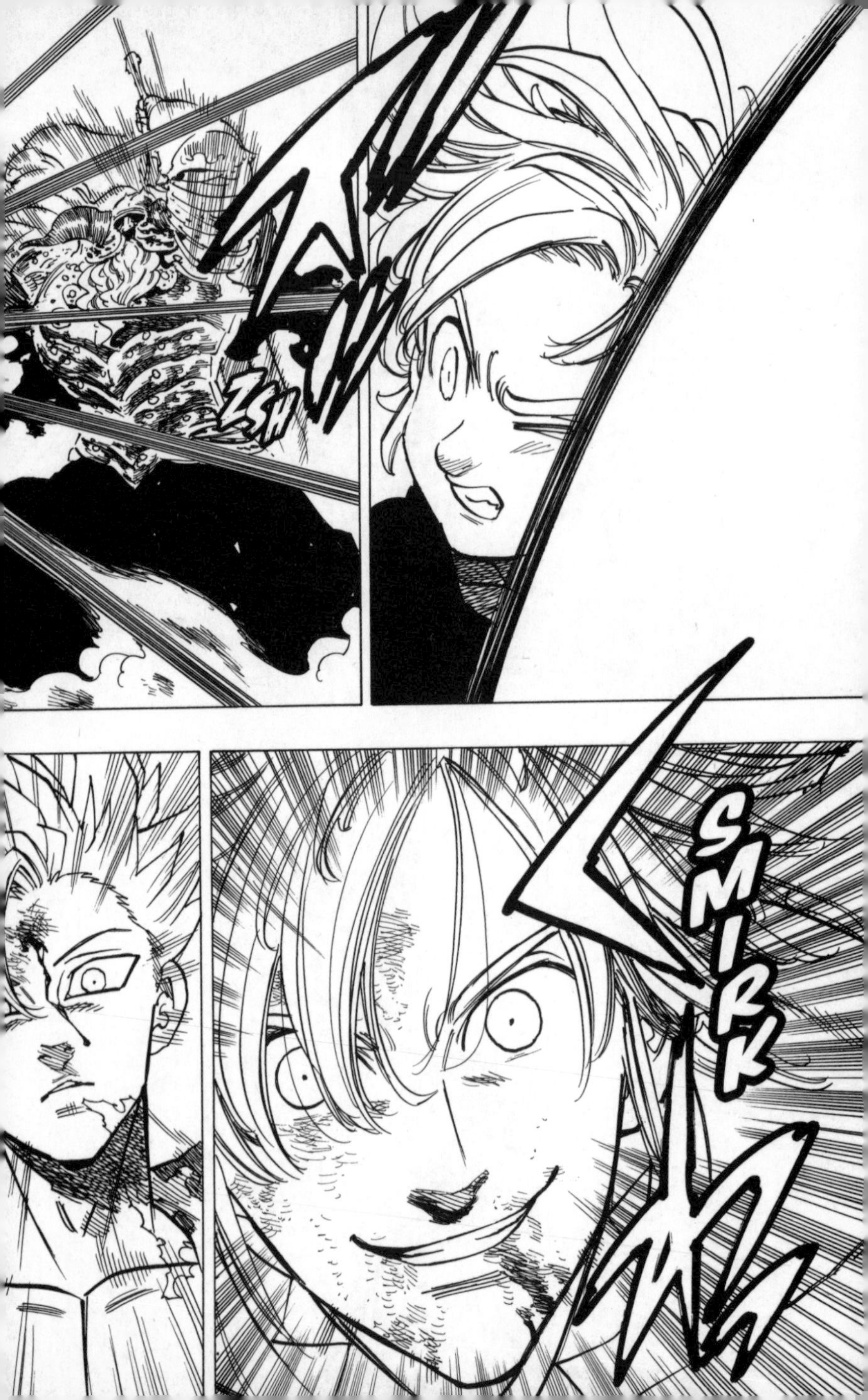
ZSH
SMIRK

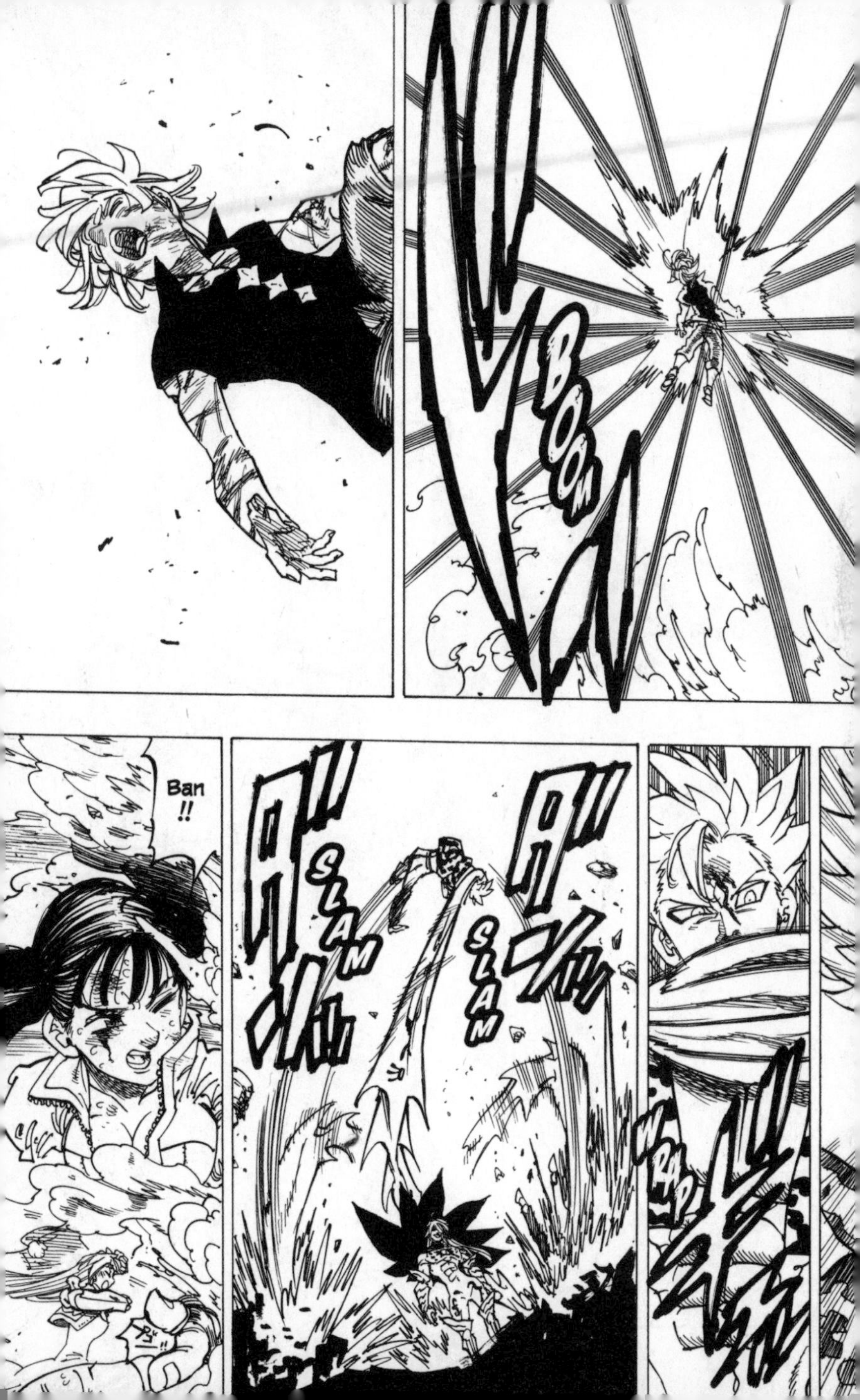
BOOM
WRAP
SLAM
SLAM
Ban !!

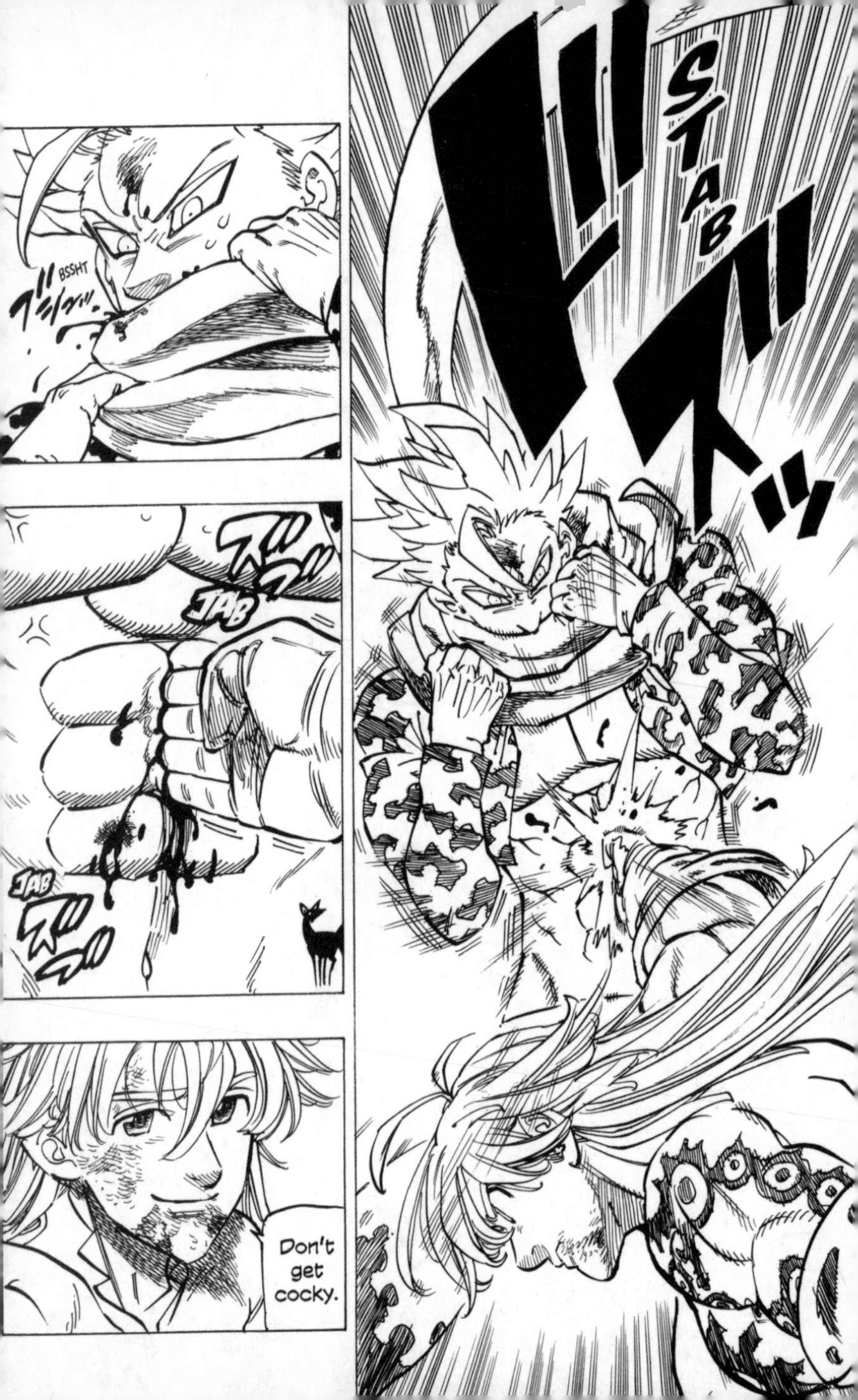
STAB
BSSHT
JAB
JAB
Don't get cocky.

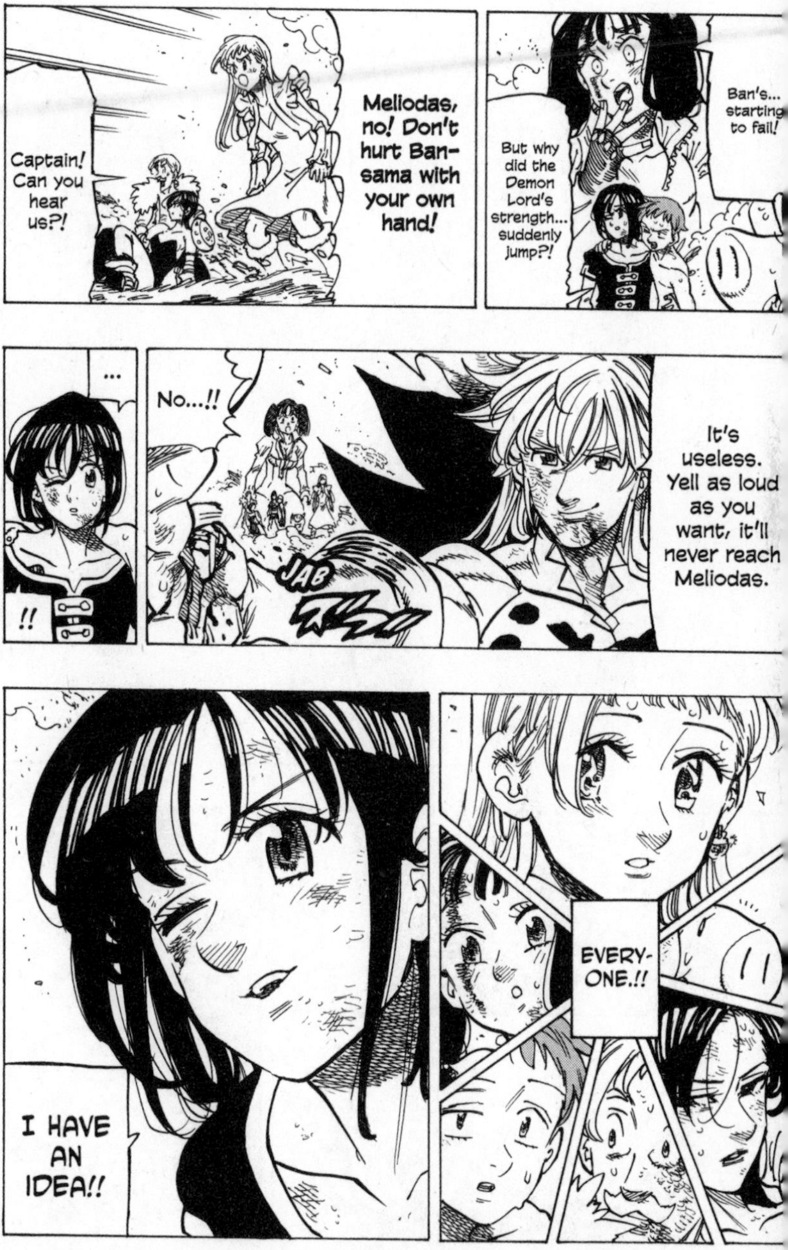
Ban's... starting to fail!
But why did the Demon Lord's strength... suddenly jump?!
Meliodas, no! Don't hurt Ban-sama with your own hand!
Captain! Can you hear us?!
It's useless. Yell as loud as you want, it'll never reach Meliodas.
JAB
No...!!
...
!!
EVERY-ONE.!!!
I HAVE AN IDEA!!

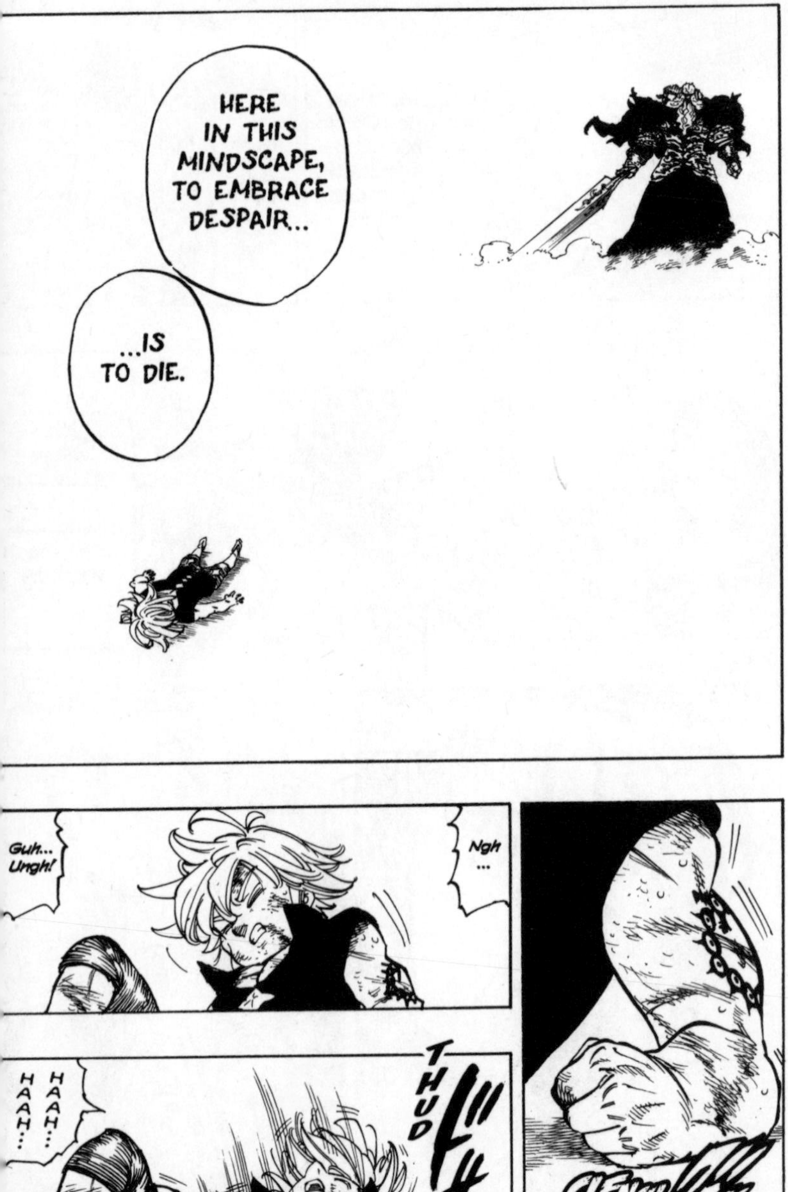
HERE IN THIS MINDSCAPE, TO EMBRACE DESPAIR...
...IS TO DIE.
CLENCH
Ngh ...
Guh... Ungh!
THUD
HAAAH...
HAAAH...

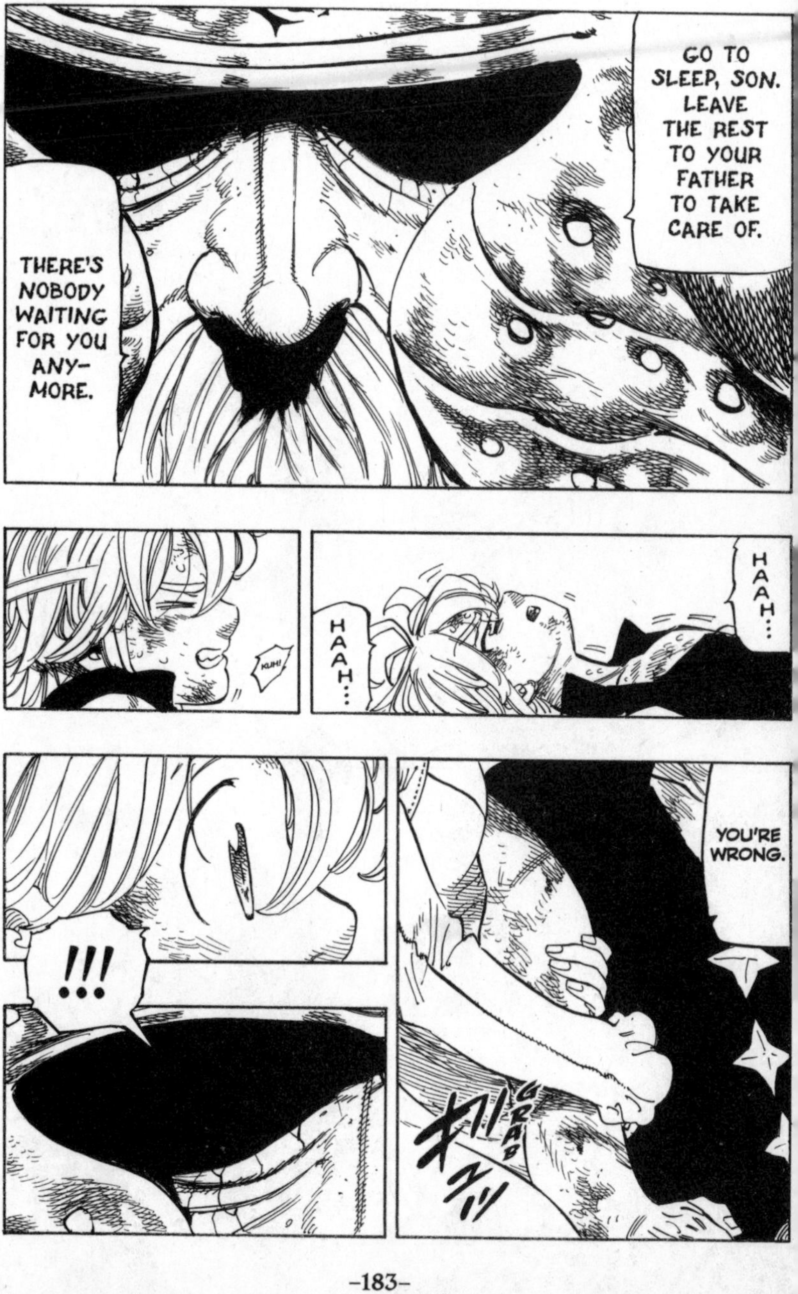
GO TO SLEEP, SON. LEAVE THE REST TO YOUR FATHER TO TAKE CARE OF.
THERE'S NOBODY WAITING FOR YOU ANY-MORE.
HAAH...
HAAH...
KUH!
YOU'RE WRONG.
GRAB
!!!

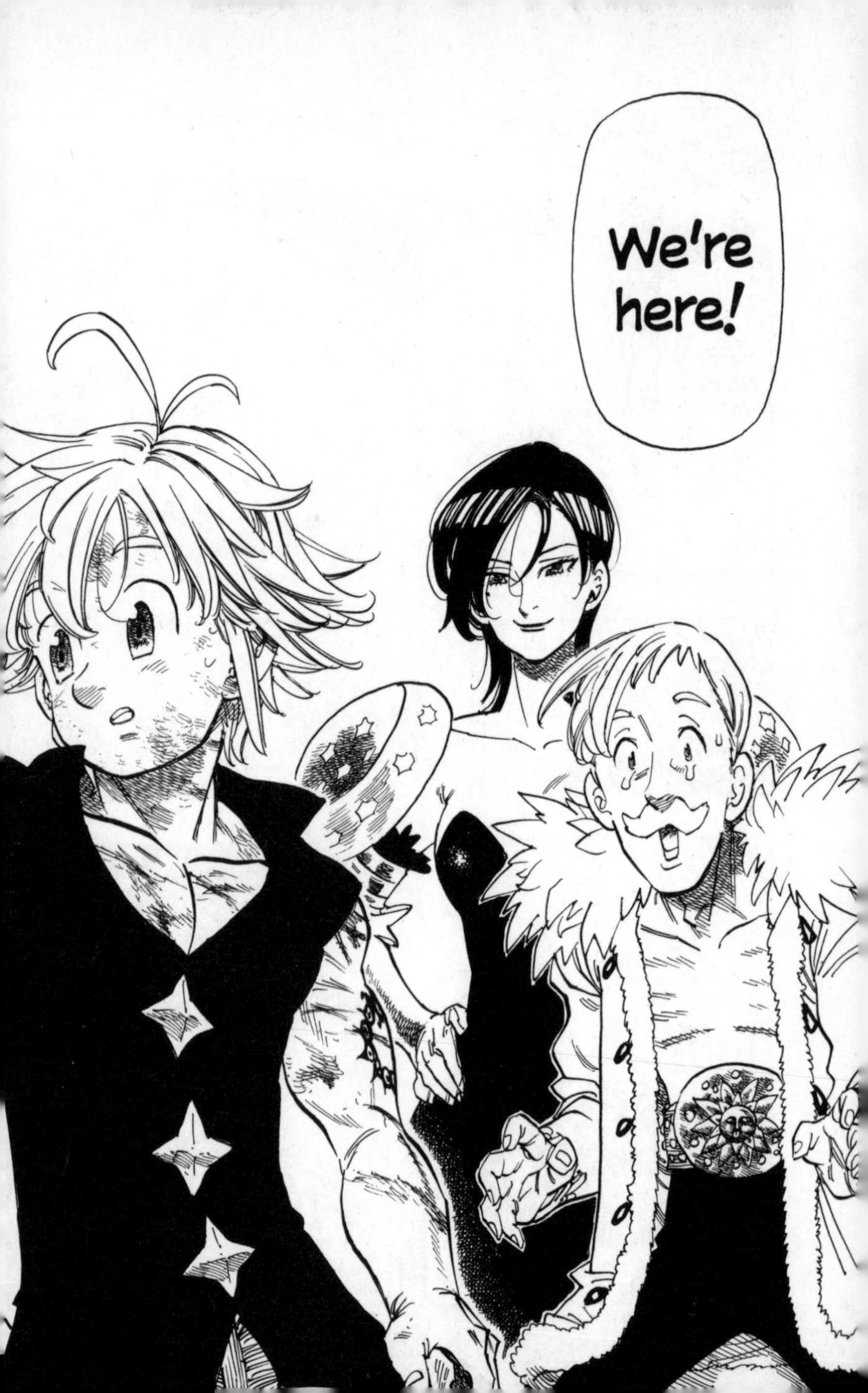
We're here!

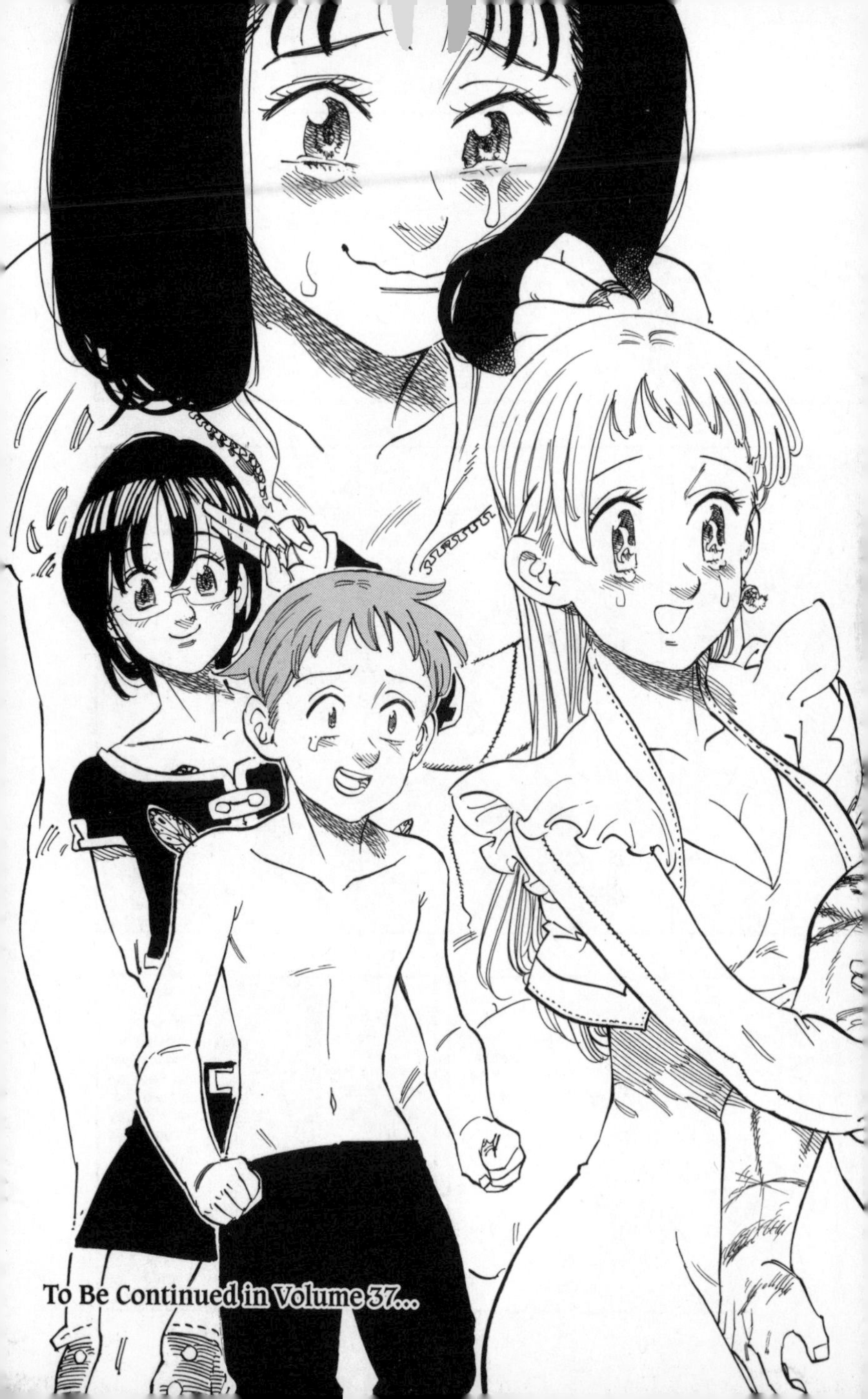
To Be Continued in Volume 37...

Bonus Story - Little Sisters

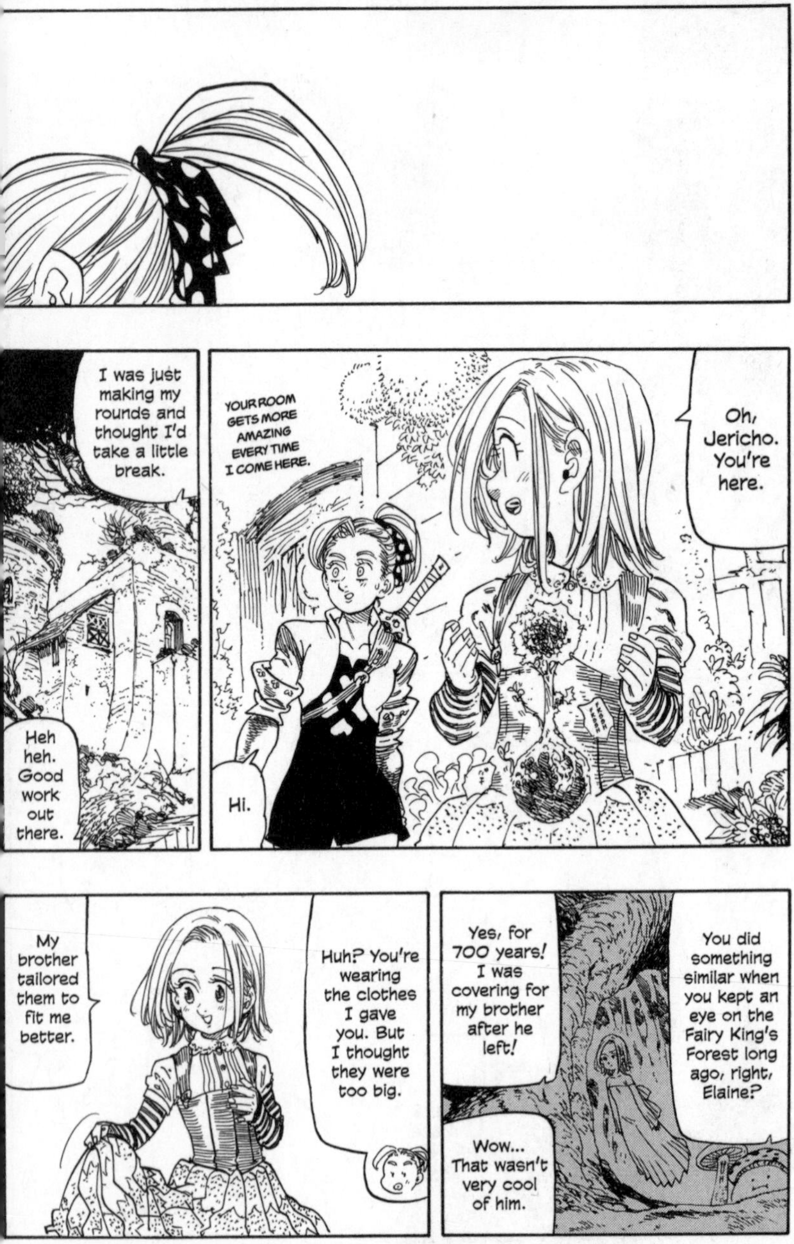
Oh, Jericho. You're here.
YOUR ROOM GETS MORE AMAZING EVERY TIME I COME HERE.
Hi.
I was just making my rounds and thought I'd take a little break.
Heh heh. Good work out there.
You did something similar when you kept an eye on the Fairy King's Forest long ago, right, Elaine?
Yes, for 700 years! I was covering for my brother after he left!
Wow... That wasn't very cool of him.
Huh? You're wearing the clothes I gave you. But I thought they were too big.
My brother tailored them to fit me better.

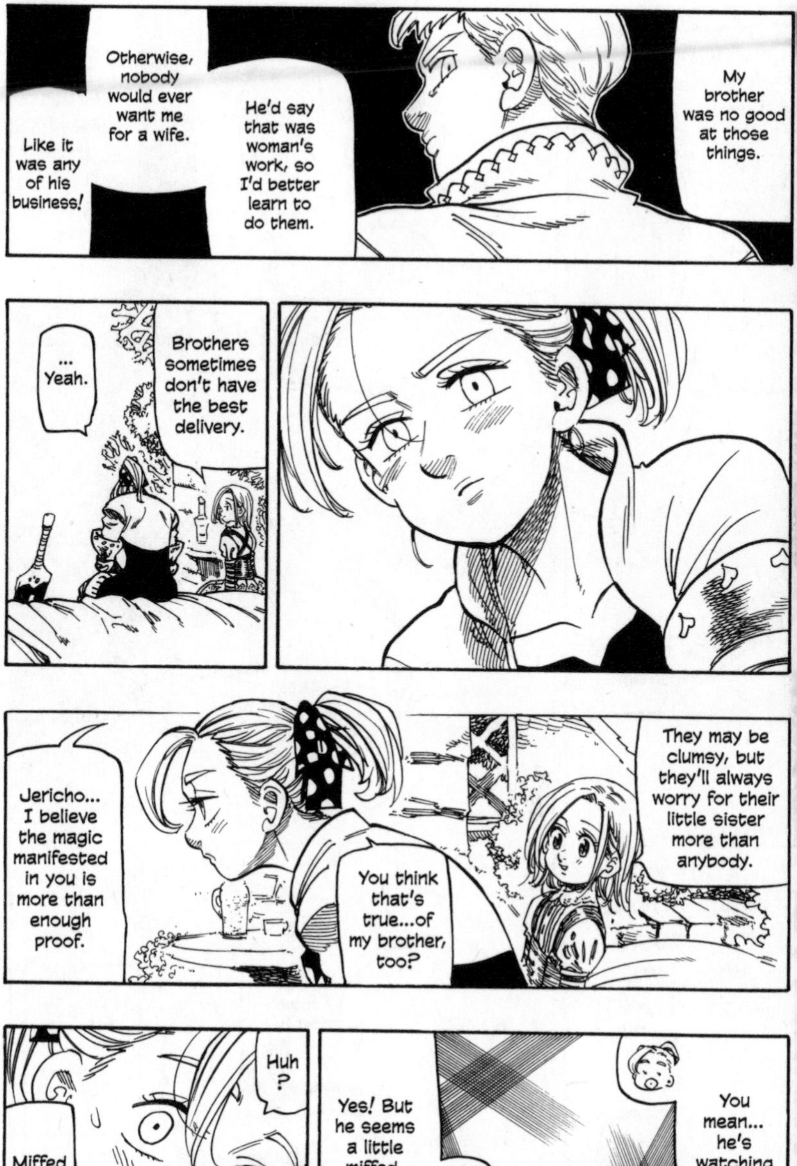
My brother was no good at those things.
He'd say that was woman's work, so I'd better learn to do them.
Otherwise, nobody would ever want me for a wife.
Like it was any of his business!
Brothers sometimes don't have the best delivery.
... Yeah.
They may be clumsy, but they'll always worry for their little sister more than anybody.
You think that's true...of my brother, too?
Jericho... I believe the magic manifested in you is more than enough proof.
You mean... he's watching over me?
Yes! But he seems a little miffed.
Huh?
Miffed?

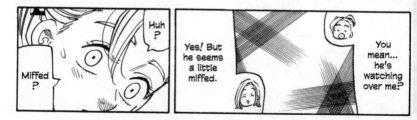

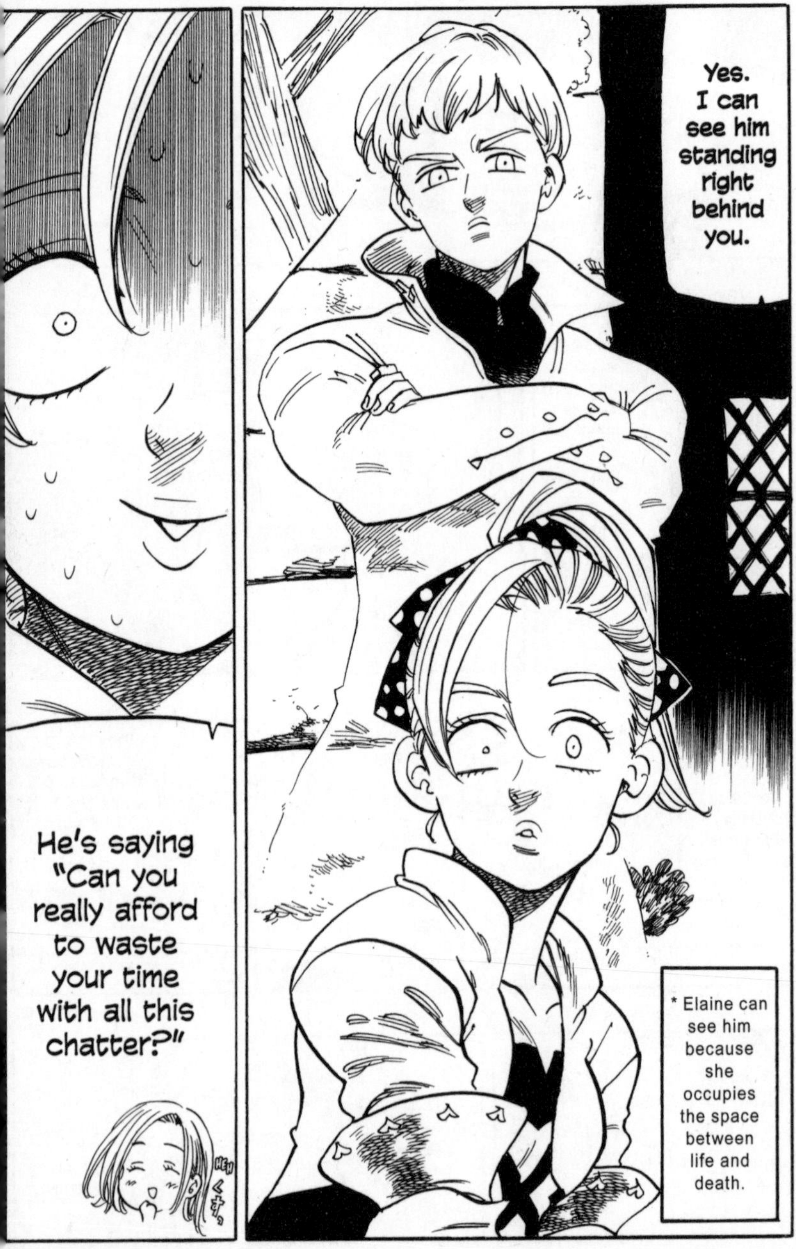
Yes. I can see him standing right behind you.
* Elaine can see him because she occupies the space between life and death.
He's saying "Can you really afford to waste your time with all this chatter?"
HEH

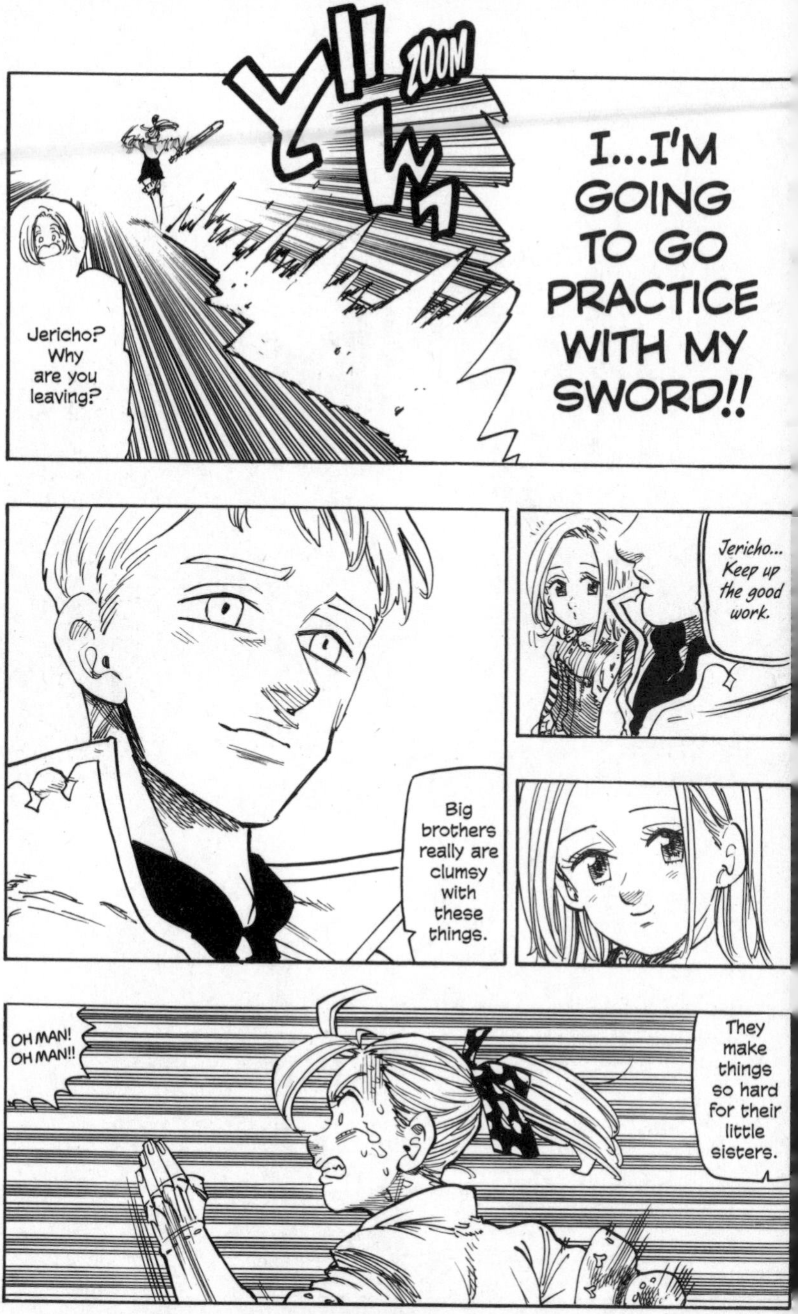
ZOOM
I...I'M GOING TO GO PRACTICE WITH MY SWORD!!
Jericho? Why are you leaving?
Jericho... Keep up the good work.
Big brothers really are clumsy with these things.
They make things so hard for their little sisters.
OH MAN! OH MAN!!

The End

DELUXE EDITION

BATTLE ANGEL ALITA

After more than a decade out of print, the original cyberpunk action classic returns in glorious 400-page hardcover deluxe editions, featuring an all-new translation, color pages, and new cover designs!

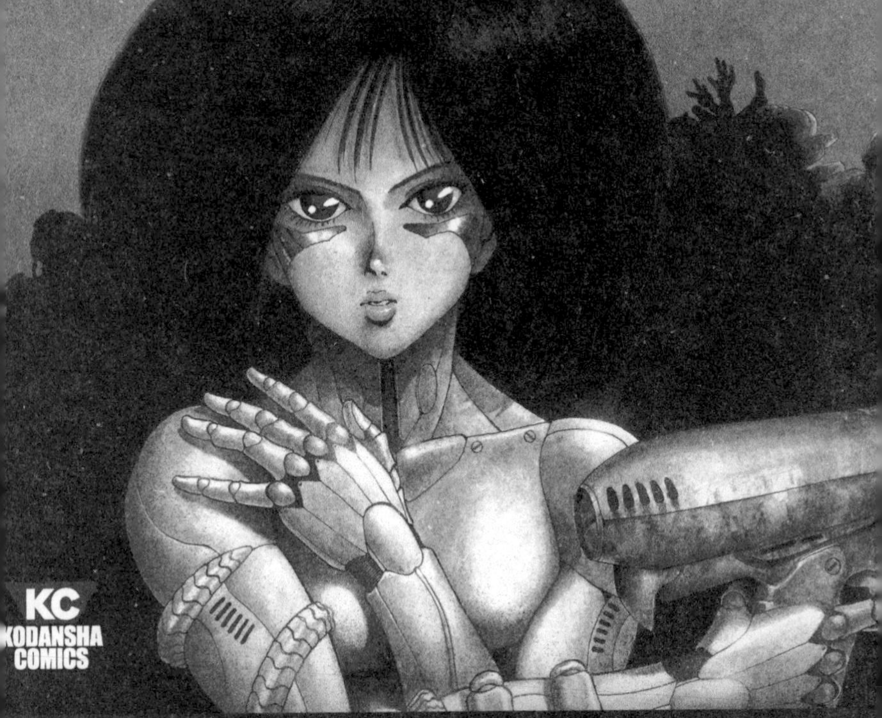
KC
KODANSHA COMICS

Far beneath the shimmering space-city of Zalem lie the trash-heaps of The Scrapyard... Here, cyber-doctor and bounty hunter Daisuke Ido finds the head and torso of an amnesiac cyborg girl. He names her Alita and vows to fill her life with beauty, but in a moment of desperation, a fragment of Alita's mysterious past awakens in her. She discovers that she possesses uncanny prowess in the legendary martial art known as panzerkunst. With her newfound skills, Alita decides to become a hunter-warrior - tracking down and taking out those who prey on the weak. But can she hold onto her humanity in the dark and gritty world of The Scrapyard?

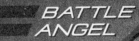

‹ KAMOME ›
SHIRAHAMA

Witch Hat Atelier

A magical manga adventure for fans of Disney and Studio Ghibli!

Witch Hat Atelier © Kamome Shirahama/Kodansha

The magical adventure that took Japan by storm is finally here, from acclaimed DC and Marvel cover artist Kamome Shirahama!

In a world where everyone takes wonders like magic spells and dragons for granted, Coco is a girl with a simple dream: She wants to be a witch. But everybody knows magicians are born, not made, and Coco was not born with a gift for magic. Resigned to her un-magical life, Coco is about to give up on her dream to become a witch...until the day she meets Qifrey, a mysterious, traveling magician. After secretly seeing Qifrey perform magic in a way she's never seen before, Coco soon learns what everybody "knows" might not be the truth, and discovers that her magical dream may not be as far away as it may seem...

A Kodansha Comics Trade Paperback Original
The Seven Deadly Sins 36 copyright © 2019 Nakaba Suzuki
English translation copyright © 2020 Nakaba Suzuki

Published in the United States by Kodansha Comics, an imprint of Kodansha USA Publishing, LLC, New York.

Publication rights for this English edition arranged through
Kodansha Ltd., Tokyo.

First published in Japan in 2019 by **Kodansha Ltd., Tokyo.**

ISBN 978-1-63236-874-4

Printed in the United States of America.

www.kodanshacomics.com

9 8 7 6 5 4 3 2 1

Translation: **Christine Dashiell**
Lettering: **James Dashiell**
Kodansha Comics edition cover design by **Phil Balsman**

Publisher: Kiichiro Sugawara
Managing editor: Maya Rosewood
Vice president of marketing & publicity: Naho Yamada

Director of publishing services: Ben Applegate
Associate director of operations: Stephen Pakula
Publishing services managing editor: Noelle Webster
Assistant production manager: Emi Lotto